Lecture Notes in Computer Science   **10487**

Commenced Publication in 1973
Founding and Former Series Editors:
Gerhard Goos, Juris Hartmanis, and Jan van Leeuwen

Editorial Board

More information about this series at http://www.springer.com/series/7408

José Proença · Markus Lumpe (Eds.)

Formal Aspects of Component Software

14th International Conference, FACS 2017
Braga, Portugal, October 10–13, 2017
Proceedings

 Springer

Editors
José Proença
University of Minho
Braga
Portugal

Markus Lumpe
Swinburne University of Technology
Hawthorn, VIC
Australia

ISSN 0302-9743   ISSN 1611-3349 (electronic)
Lecture Notes in Computer Science
ISBN 978-3-319-68033-0   ISBN 978-3-319-68034-7   (eBook)
DOI 10.1007/978-3-319-68034-7

Library of Congress Control Number: 2017953419

LNCS Sublibrary: SL2 – Programming and Software Engineering

Printed on acid-free paper

This Springer imprint is published by Springer Nature
The registered company is Springer International Publishing AG
The registered company address is: Gewerbestrasse 11, 6330 Cham, Switzerland

Preface

This volume contains the papers presented at the 14th International Conference on Formal Aspects of Component Software (FACS 2017), held in Braga, Portugal, during October 10–13, 2017.

The objective of FACS is to bring together practitioners and researchers in the areas of component software and formal methods in order to promote a deeper understanding of how formal methods can or should be used to make component-based software development succeed. The component-based software development approach has emerged as a promising paradigm to transport sound production and engineering principles into software engineering and to cope with the ever-increasing complexity of present-day software solutions. However, many conceptual and technological issues remain in component-based software development theory and practice that pose challenging research questions. Moreover, the advent of cloud computing, cyber-physical systems, and of the Internet of Things has brought to the fore new dimensions. These include quality of service, reconfiguration, and robustness to withstand inevitable faults, which require established concepts to be revisited and new ones to be developed in order to meet the opportunities offered by these architectures.

We received 26 submissions from 20 countries, out of which the Program Committee selected 14 papers. All submitted papers were reviewed by at least three referees. The conference proceedings were made available at the conference date, including the final versions of the papers that took into account the comments received by the reviewers. The authors of a selected subset of accepted papers were invited to submit extended versions of their papers to appear in a special issue of Elsevier's *Science of Computer Programming* journal.

We would like to express our gratitude to all the researchers who submitted their work to the symposium, to the Steering Committee members who provided precious guidelines and support, to all colleagues who served on the Program Committee, as well as the external reviewers, who helped us to prepare a high-quality conference program. Particular thanks to the invited speakers, David Costa from NewMotion in Amsterdam and Catuscia Palamidessi from Inria in Saclay, for their efforts and dedication to present their research and to share their perspective on formal methods for component software at the conference. We are extremely grateful for the help in managing all practical arrangements by the local organizers at the University of Minho, and in particular to Catarina Fernandes and Paula Rodrigues. We also thank the Engineering School of the University of Minho, INESC TEC, FCT, and Elsevier for their sponsorship.

October 2017

José Proença
Markus Lumpe

Organization

Program Chairs

José Proença   INESC TEC and Universidade do Minho, Portugal
Markus Lumpe   Swinburne University of Technology, Australia

Steering Committee

Farhad Arbab	CWI and Leiden University, The Netherlands
Luís Barbosa	INESC TEC and Universidade do Minho, Portugal
Christiano Braga	Universidade Federal Fluminense, Brazil
Carlos Canal	University of Málaga, Spain
José Luiz Fiadeiro	Royal Holloway, University of London, UK
Ramtin Khosravi	University of Tehran, Iran
Olga Kouchnarenko	Université Bourgogne Franche-Comté, France
Zhiming Liu	Southwest University, China
Markus Lumpe	Swinburne University of Technology, Australia
Eric Madelaine	Inria, France
Peter Csaba Ölveczky	University of Oslo, Norway
Bernhard Schätz	TU München, Germany

Program Committee

Farhad Arbab	CWI and Leiden University, The Netherlands
Paolo Arcaini	Charles University, Czech Republic
Kyungmin Bae	Carnegie Mellon University, USA
Luís Barbosa	INESC TEC and Universidade do Minho, Portugal
Simon Bliudze	EPFL, Switzerland
Christiano Braga	Universidade Federal Fluminense, Brazil
Roberto Bruni	University of Pisa, Italy
Carlos Canal	University of Málaga, Spain
Dave Clarke	Uppsala University, Sweden
Javier Cámara Moreno	Carnegie Mellon University, USA
Frank De-Boer	CWI, The Netherlands
José Luiz Fiadeiro	Royal Holloway, University of London, UK
Rolf Hennicker	Ludwig-Maximilians-Universität München, Germany
Einar Broch Johnsen	University of Oslo, Norway
Sung-Shik T.Q. Jongmans	Open University of the Netherlands, The Netherlands and Imperial College London, UK
Natallia Kokash	LIACS, The Netherlands
Olga Kouchnarenko	Université Bourgogne Franche-Comté, France
Ivan Lanese	University of Bologna, Italy and Inria, France

Zhiming Liu	Southwest University, China
Alberto Lluch Lafuente	Technical University of Denmark, Denmark
Markus Lumpe	Swinburne University of Technology, Australia
Eric Madelaine	Inria, France
Mieke Massink	CNR-ISTI, Italy
Hernan Melgratti	Universidad de Buenos Aires, Argentina
Corina Pasareanu	CMU/NASA Ames Research Center, USA
José Proença	INESC TEC and Universidade do Minho, Portugal
Eric Rutten	Inria, France
Gwen Salaün	University of Grenoble Alpes, France
Francesco Santini	Università di Perugia, Italy
Marjan Sirjani	Malardalen University, Sweden and Reykjavik University, Iceland
Meng Sun	Peking University, China
Heike Wehrheim	University of Paderborn, Germany
Peter Csaba Ölveczky	University of Oslo, Norway

Organizing Committee

Luís Barbosa	INESC TEC and University of Minho, Portugal
Catarina Fernandes	University of Minho, Portugal
Markus Lumpe	Swinburne University of Technology, Australia
José Proença	INESC TEC and University of Minho, Portugal
Paula Rodrigues	INESC TEC, Portugal

Additional Reviewers

Abd Alrahman, Yehia
Bauer, Bernhard
Delaval, Gwenaël
Helvensteijn, Michiel
Jafari, Ali
Jakobs, Marie-Christine
Khamespanah, Ehsan

Li, Yi
Majster-Cederbaum, Mila
Rabbi, Fazle
Sabouri, Hamideh
Serwe, Wendelin
Wang, Shuling
Zhang, Miaomiao

Contents

Component-Based Modeling in Mediator

Yi Li and Meng Sun[(✉)]

LMAM and Department of Informatics, School of Mathematical Sciences,
Peking University, Beijing, China
liyi_math@pku.edu.cn, sunmeng@math.pku.edu.cn

Abstract. In this paper we propose a new language *Mediator* to formalize component-based system models. Mediator supports a two-step modeling approach. *Automata*, encapsulated with an interface of ports, are the basic behavior units. *Systems* declare components or connectors through automata, and glue them together. With the help of Mediator, components and systems can be modeled separately and precisely. Through various examples, we show that this language can be used in practical scenarios.

Keywords: Component-based modeling · Coordination · Formal method

1 Introduction

Component-based software engineering has been prospering for decades. Through proper encapsulations and clearly declared interfaces, *components* can be reused by different applications without knowledge of their implementation details.

Currently, there are various tool supporting component-based modeling. NI LabVIEW [14], MATLAB Simulink [8] and Ptolomy [10] provide powerful modeling platforms and a large number of built-in component libraries to support commonly-used platforms. However, due to the complexity of models, such tools mainly focus on synthesis and simulation, instead of formal verification. There is also a set of formal tools that prefer simple but verifiable model, e.g. Esterel SCADE [2] and rCOS [12]. SCADE, based on a synchronous data flow language LUSTRE, is equipped with a powerful tool-chain and widely used in development of embedded systems. rCOS, on the other hand, is a refinement calculus on object-oriented designs.

Existing work [15] has shown that, formal verification based on existing industrial tools is hard to realize due to the complexity and non-open architecture of these tools. Unfortunately, unfamiliarity of formal specifications is still the main obstacle hampering programmers from using formal tools. For example, even in the most famous formal modeling tools with perfect graphical user interfaces (like PRISM [11] and UPPAAL [3]), sufficient knowledge about automata theory is necessary to properly encode the models.

The channel-based coordination language Reo [4] provides a solution where advantages of both formal languages and graphical representations can be integrated in a natural way. As an exogenous coordination language, Reo doesn't

© Springer International Publishing AG 2017
J. Proença and M. Lumpe (Eds.): FACS 2017, LNCS 10487, pp. 1–19, 2017.
DOI: 10.1007/978-3-319-68034-7_1

care about the implementation details of components. Instead, it takes *connectors* as the first-class citizens. Connectors are organized and encapsulated through a compositional approach to capture complex interaction and communication behavior among components.

In this paper we introduce a new modeling language *Mediator*. Mediator is a hierarchical modeling language that provides proper formalism for both high-level *system* layouts and low-level *automata*-based behavior units. A rich-featured type system describes complex data structures and powerful automata in a formal way. Both components and connectors can be declared through automata to compose a system. Moreover, automata and systems are encapsulated with *a set of input or output ports* (which we call an *interface*) and *a set of template parameters* so that they can be easily reused in multiple applications.

The paper is structured as follows. In Sect. 2, we briefly present the syntax of Mediator and formalizations of the language entities. Then in Sect. 3. We introduce the formal semantics of Mediator. Section 4 provides a case study where a commonly used coordination algorithm *leader election* is modeled in Mediator. Section 5 concludes the paper and comes up with some future work we are going to work on.

2   Syntax of Mediator

In this section, we introduce the syntax of Mediator, represented by a variant of Extended Backus-Naur Form (known as EBNF) where:

- Terminal symbols are written in `monospaced fonts`.
- Non-terminal productions are encapsulated in ⟨*angle brackets*⟩.
- We use "?" to denote "zero or one occurence", "*" to denote "zero or more occurence" and "+" to denote "one or more occurence".

A Mediator *program* is defined as follows:

$$\langle program \rangle ::= (\ \langle typedef \rangle \mid \langle function \rangle \mid \langle automaton \rangle \mid \langle system \rangle\ )^*$$

*Typedef*s specify alias for given types. *Functions* define customized functions. *Systems* declare hierarchical structures of components and connections between them. Both components and connections are described by *automata* based on local variables and transitions.

2.1   Type System

Mediator provides a rich-featured type system to support various data types that are widely used in both formal modeling languages and programming languages.

Primitive Types. Table 1 shows the primitive types supported by Mediator, including: *integers and bounded integers, real numbers with arbitrary precision, boolean values, single characters (ASCII only)* and *finite enumerations.*

Table 1. Primitive data types

Name	Declaration	Term example
Integer	`int`	$-1,0,1$
Bounded integer	`int lowerBound .. upperBound`	$-1,0,1$
Real	`real`	`0.1, 1E-3`
Boolean	`bool`	`true, false`
Character	`char`	`'a', 'b'`
Enumeration	`enum item`$_1$`, ..., item`$_n$	`enumname.item`

Table 2. Composite data types (T denotes an arbitrary data type)

Name	Declaration
Tuple	`T`$_1$`,...,T`$_n$
Union	`T`$_1$`|...|T`$_n$
Array	`T [length]`
List	`T []`
Map	`map [T`$_{key}$`] T`$_{value}$
Struct	`struct { field`$_1$`:T`$_1$`,..., field`$_n$`:T`$_n$` }`
Initialized	`T`$_{base}$` init term`

Composite Types. Composite types can be used to construct complex data types from simpler ones. Several composite patterns are introduced as follows (Table 2):

- *Tuple.* The *tuple* operator ',' can be used to construct a finite tuple type with several base types.
- *Union.* The *union* operator '|' is designed to combine different types as a more complicated one.
- *Array* and *List.* An *array* $T[n]$ is a finite ordered collection containing exactly n elements of type T. Moreover, a *list* is an array of which the capacity is not specified, i.e. a list is a dynamic array.
- *Map.* A *map* $[T_{key}]\ T_{val}$ is a dictionary that maps a key of type T_{key} to a value of type T_{val}.
- *Struct.* A *struct* $\{field_1 : T_1, \cdots, field_n : T_n\}$ contains a finite number of fields, each has a unique identifier $field_i$ and a particular type T_i.
- *Initialized.* An initialized type is used to specify default value of a type T_{base} with `term`.

Parameter Types. A generalizable automaton or system that includes a template function or template component needs to be defined on many occasions. For example, a binary operator that supports various operations $(+,\times,$ etc.$)$, or an encrypted communication system that supports different encryption algorithms.

Parameter types make it possible to take functions, automata or systems as template parameters. Mediator supports two parameter types:

1. *An Interface*, denoted by `interface` (port_1:T_1,$\cdots$, port_n:T_n), defines a parameter that could be any *automaton* or *system* with exactly the same interface (i.e. number, types and directions of the ports are a perfect match). Interfaces are only used in templates of *systems*.
2. *A Function*, denoted by `func` (arg_1:T_1,$\cdots$, arg_n:T_n):T, defines a function that has the argument types $T_1,\cdots,T_n$ and result types T. Functions are permitted to appear in templates of *other functions, automata* and *systems*.

For simplicity, we use $Dom(T)$ to denote the value domain of type T, i.e. the set of all possible value of T.

Example 1 (Types Used in a Queue). A queue is a well-known data structure being used in various message-oriented middlewares. In this example, we introduce some type declarations and local variables used in an automaton `Queue` defining the queue structure. As shown in the following code fragment, we declare a singleton enumeration `NULL`, which contains only one element `null`. The buffer of a queue is in turn formalized as an array of `T` or `NULL`, indicating that the elements in the queue can be either an assigned item or empty. The head and tail pointers are defined as two bounded integers.

```
1   typedef enum {null} init null as NULL;
2   automaton <T:type,size:int> Queue(A:in T, B:out T) {
3       variables {
4           buf : ((T | NULL) init null) [size];
5           phead, ptail : int 0 .. (size - 1) init 0;
6       }
7       ...
8   }
```

2.2 Functions

Functions are used to encapsulate and reuse complex computation processes. In Mediator, the notion of *functions* is a bit different from most existing programming languages. Mediator functions include no control statements at all but assignments, and have access only to its local variables and arguments. This design makes functions' behavior more predictable. In fact, the behavior of functions in Mediator can be simplified into mathematical functions.

The abstract syntax tree of functions is as follows.

$$\langle funcDecl\rangle ::= \text{function } \langle template\rangle^? \langle identifier\rangle \langle funcInterface\rangle \text{ \{}$$
$$(\text{ variables } \{ \langle varDecl\rangle^* \})^?$$
$$\text{statements } \{ \langle assignStmt\rangle^* \langle returnStmt\rangle \}$$
$$\langle funcInterface\rangle ::= ((\langle identifier\rangle : \langle type\rangle)^*) : \langle type\rangle$$
$$\langle assignStmt\rangle ::= \langle term\rangle (, \langle term\rangle)^* := \langle term\rangle (, \langle term\rangle)^*$$
$$\langle returnStmt\rangle ::= \text{return } \langle term\rangle$$
$$\langle varDecl\rangle ::= \langle identifier\rangle : \langle type\rangle (\text{init } \langle term\rangle)^?$$

Basically, a function definition includes the following parts.

Template. A function may contain an optional template with a set of parameters. A parameter can be either a *type* parameter (decorated by **type**) or a *value* parameter (decorated by its type). Values of the parameters should be clearly specified during compilation. Once a parameter is declared, it can be referred in all the following language elements, e.g. parameter declarations, arguments, return types and statements.

Name. An identifier that indicates the name of this function.

Type. Type of a function is determined by the *number and types of arguments,* together with *the type of its return value.*

Body. Body of a function includes an optional set of local variables and a list of ordered (assignment or return) statements. In an assignment statement, local variables, parameters and arguments can be referenced, but only local variables are writable. The list of statements always ends up with a **return** statement.

Example 2 (Incline Operation on Queue Pointers). Incline operation of pointers are widely used in a *round-robin* queue, where storage are reused circularly. The **next** function shows how pointers in such queues (denoted by a bounded integer) are inclined.

```
1    function <size:int> next(pcurr:int 0..(size-1)) : int 0..(size-1) {
2        statements { return (pcurr + 1) }
3    }
```

2.3 Automaton: The Basic Behavioral Unit

Automata theory is widely used in formal verification, and its variations, finite-state machines for example, are also accepted by modeling tools like NI Lab-VIEW and Mathworks Simulink/Stateflow.

Here we introduce the notion of *automaton* as the basic behavior unit. Compared with other variations, an *automaton* in Mediator contains local variables and typed ports that support complicated behavior and powerful communication. The abstract syntax tree of *automaton* is as follows.

$$
\begin{aligned}
\langle automaton\rangle ::= {}& \texttt{automaton}\ \langle template\rangle\,^?\ \langle identifier\rangle\ (\ \langle port\rangle\,^*\ )\ \{ \\
& (\ \texttt{variables}\ \{\ \langle varDecl\rangle\,^*\ \}\ )^? \\
& \texttt{transitions}\ \{\ \langle transition\rangle\,^*\ \}\ \} \\
\langle port\rangle ::= {}& \langle identifier\rangle\ :\ (\ \texttt{in}\,|\,\texttt{out}\ )\ \langle type\rangle \\
\langle transition\rangle ::= {}& \langle guardedStmt\rangle\,|\,\texttt{group}\ \{\ \langle guardedStmt\rangle\,^*\ \} \\
\langle guardedStmt\rangle ::= {}& \langle term\rangle\ \texttt{->}\ (\ \langle stmt\rangle\,|\,\{\ \langle stmt\rangle\,^*\ \}\ ) \\
\langle stmt\rangle ::= {}& \langle assignStmt\rangle\,|\,\texttt{sync}\ \langle identifier\rangle\,^+
\end{aligned}
$$

Template. Compared with templates in functions, templates in automata provide support for parameters of *function type.*

Name. The identifier of an automaton.

Type. Type of an automaton is determined by the *number* and *types* of its ports. Type of a port contains its *direction* (either in or out) and its *data type*. For example, a port P that takes integer values as input is denoted by P:in int. To ensure the well-definedness of automata, ports are required to have *initialized* data types, e.g. int 0..1 init 0 instead of int 0..1.

Variables. Two classes of variables are used in an automaton definition. *Local variables* are declared in the *variables* segment, which can be referenced only in its owner automaton. *Port variables*, on the other hand, are shared variables that describe the status and values of ports.

Port variables are denoted as fields of ports. An arbitrary port P has two corresponding Boolean port variables P.reqRead and P.reqWrite indicating whether there is any pending *read* or *write* requests on P, and a data field P.value indicating the current value of P. When automata are combined, port variables are shared between automata to perform communications. To avoid data-conflict, we require that only reqRead and value fields of input ports, and reqWrite fields of output ports are writable. Informally, an automaton only requires data from its input port and writes data to its output port.

Transitions. In Mediator, behavior of an automaton is described by a list of guarded transitions (groups). A *transition* (denoted by *guard* -> *statements*) comprises two parts, a Boolean term *guard* that declares the activating condition of this transition, and a (sequence of) statement(s) describing how variables are updated when the transition is fired.

We have two types of statements supported in automata:

- *Assignment Statement* (var_1,...,var_n := term_1,...,term_n). Assignment statements update variables with new values where only local variables and writable port variables are assignable.
- *Synchronizing Statement* (sync port_1,...,port_n). Synchronizing statements are used as synchronizing *flags* when joining multiple automata. In a synchronizing statement, the order of ports being synchronized is arbitrary. For further details, please refer to Sect. 3.3.

A transition is called *external* iff. It synchronizes with its environment through certain ports or *internal* nodes with synchronizing statements. In such transitions, we require that *any assignment statements including reference to an input(output) port should be placed after(before) its corresponding synchronizing statement*.

We use $g \rightarrow S$ to denote a transition, where g is the guard formula and $S = [s_1, \cdots, s_n]$ is a sequence of statements.

Transitions in Mediator automata are literally ordered. Given a list of transitions $g_1 \rightarrow S_1, \cdots, g_n \rightarrow S_n$ where $\{g_{i_j}\}_{j=1,\cdots,m}$ is satisfied, only the transition $g_{min\{i_j\}} \rightarrow S_{min\{i_j\}}$ will be fired. In other words, $g_i \rightarrow S_i$ is fired iff. g_i is satisfied and for all $0 < j < i$, g_j is unsatisfied.

Example 3 (Transitions in Queue). For a queue, we use internal transitions to capture the modifications corresponding to the changes of its environment. For example, the automaton `Queue` tries to:

1. Read data from its input port A by setting `A.reqRead` to *true* when the buffer isn't full.
2. Write the earliest existing buffered data to its output port B when the buffer is not empty.

External transitions, on the other hand, mainly show the implementation details for the enqueue and dequeue operations.

```
1    // internal transitions
2    !A.reqRead && (buf[phead] == null) -> A.reqRead := true;
3    A.reqRead && (buf[phead] != null) -> A.reqRead := false;
4    !B.reqWrite && (buf[ptail] != null) -> B.reqWrite := true;
5    B.reqWrite && (buf[ptail] == null) -> B.reqWrite := false;
6
7    // enqueue operation (as an external transition)
8    (A.reqRead && A.reqWrite) -> {
9        sync A; // read data from input port A
10       buf[phead] := A.value; phead := next(phead);
11   }
12   // dequeue operation (as an external transition)
13   (B.reqRead && B.reqWrite) -> {
14       B.value := buf[ptail]; ptail := next(ptail);
15       sync B; // write data to output port B
16   }
```

If all transitions are organized with priority, the automata would be fully deterministic. However, in some cases non-determinism is still more than necessary. Consequently, we introduce the notion of *transition group* to capture non-deterministic behavior. A transition group t_G is formalized as a finite set of guarded transitions $t_G = \{t_1, \cdots, t_n\}$ where $t_i = g_i \to S_i$ is a single transition with guard g_i and a sequence of statements S_i.

Transitions encapsulated in a **group** are not ruled by priority. Instead, the group itself is literally ordered w.r.t. other groups and single transitions (basically, we can take all single transitions as a singleton transition group).

Example 4 (Another Queue Implementation). In Example 3, when both *enqueue* and *dequeue* operations are activated, *enqueue* will always be fired first. Such a queue may get stuff up immediately when requests start accumulating, and in turn lead to excessive memory usage. With the help of transition groups, here we show another non-deterministic implementation which solves this problem.

```
1    group {
2        (A.reqRead && A.reqWrite) -> {
3            sync A; buf[phead] := A.value; phead := next(phead);
4        }
5        (B.reqRead && B.reqWrite) -> {
6            B.value := buf[ptail]; ptail := next(ptail); sync B;
7        }
8    }
```

In the above code fragment, the two external transitions are encapsulated together as a transition group. Consequently, firing of the dequeue operation doesn't rely on deactivation of the enqueue operation.

We use a 3-tuple $A = \langle Ports, Vars, Trans_G \rangle$ to represent an automaton in Mediator, where $Ports$ is a set of ports, $Vars$ is a set of local variables (the set of port variables are denoted by $Adj(A)$, which can be obtained from $Ports$ directly) and $Trans_G = [t_{G_1}, \cdots, t_{G_n}]$ is a sequence of transition groups, where all single transitions are encapsulated as singleton transition groups.

2.4   System: The Composition Approach

Theoretically, automata and their product is capable to model various classical applications. However, modeling complex systems through a mess of transitions and tons of local variables could become a real disaster.

As mentioned before, Mediator is designed to help the programmers, even nonprofessionals, to enjoy the convenience of formal tools, which is exactly the reason why we introduce the notion of *system* as an *encapsulation mechanism*. Basically, a *system* is the textual representation of a hierarchical diagram where automata and smaller systems are organized as *component*s or *connection*s.

Example 5 (A Message-Oriented Middleware). A simple diagram of a message-oriented middleware [5] is provided in Fig. 1, where a queue works as a connector to coordinate the message producers and consumers.

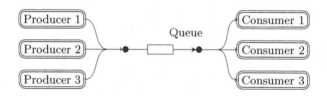

Fig. 1. A scenario where queue is used as message-oriented middleware

The abstract syntax tree of *system*s is as follows:

$$
\begin{aligned}
\langle system \rangle ::= {}& \texttt{system } \langle template \rangle^{?} \langle identifier \rangle \text{ (} \langle port \rangle^{*} \text{) } \{ \\
& \text{(internals } \langle identifier \rangle^{+})^{?} \\
& \text{(components } \{ \langle componentDecl \rangle^{*} \})^{?} \\
& \text{connections } \{ \langle connectionDecl \rangle^{*} \} \} \\
\langle componentDecl \rangle ::= {}& \langle identifier \rangle^{+} : \langle systemType \rangle \\
\langle connectionDecl \rangle ::= {}& \langle systemType \rangle \langle params \rangle \text{ (} \langle portName \rangle^{+})
\end{aligned}
$$

Template. In templates of systems, all the parameter types being supported include: *(a)* parameters of abstract type **type**, *(b)* parameters of primitive types and composite types, and *(c)* interfaces and functions.

Name and Type. Exactly the same as *name* and *type* of an automaton.

Components. In `components` segments, we can declare any entity of an *interface type* as components, e.g. an automaton, a system, or a parameter of interface type. Ports of a component can be referenced by `identifier.portName` once declared.

Connections. Connections, e.g. the queue in Fig. 1, are used to connect *(a) the ports of the system itself, (b) the ports of its components, and (c) the internal nodes.* We declare the connections in `connections` segments. Both components and connections are supposed to run as automata in parallel.

Internals. Sometimes we need to combine multiple connections to perform more complex coordination behavior. Internal nodes, declared in `internals` segments, are untyped identifiers which are capable to weld two ports with consistent data-flow direction. For example, in Fig. 1 the two internal nodes (denoted by •) are used to combine a *replicator*, a queue and a *merger* together to work as a multi-in-multi-out queue.

A system is denoted by a 4-tuple $S = \langle Ports, Entities, Internals, Links \rangle$ where *Ports* is a set of ports, *Entities* is a set of automata or systems (including both components and connections), *Internals* is a set of internal nodes and *Links* is a set of pairs, where each element of such a pair is either a port or an internal node. A link $\langle p_1, p_2 \rangle$ suggests that p_1 and p_2 are linked together. A well-defined system satisfies the following assumptions:

1. $\forall \langle p_1, p_2 \rangle \in Links$, data transfers from p_1 to p_2. For example, if $p_1 \in Ports$ is an input port, p_2 could be
   - an output port of the system ($p_2 \in Ports$),
   - an input port of some automaton $A_i \in Automata$ ($p_2 \in A_i.Ports$), or
   - an internal node ($p_2 \in Internals$).
2. $\forall n \in Internals, \exists! p_1, p_2$, s.t. $\langle p_1, n \rangle, \langle n, p_2 \rangle \in Links$ and p_1, p_2 have the same data type.

Example 6 (Model of the System in Fig. 1). In Fig. 1, a simple scenario is presented where a queue is used as a message-oriented middleware. To model this scenario, we need two automata *Producer* and *Consumer* (details are omitted due to space limit, and can be found at [1]) that produce or consume messages of type T.

```
1   automaton <T:type> Producer (OUT: out T) { ... }
2   automaton <T:type> Consumer (IN: in T) { ... }
3
4   system <T:type> middleware_in_use () {
5       components {
6           producer_1, producer_2, producer_3 : Producer<T>;
7           consumer_1, consumer_2, consumer_3 : Consumer<T>;
8       }
9       internals M1, M2 ;
10      connections {
11          Merger<T>(producer_1.OUT, producer_2.OUT, producer_3.OUT, M1);
12          Queue<T>(M1, M2);
13          Replicator<T>(M2, consumer_1.IN, consumer_2.IN, consumer_3.IN);
14      }
15  }
```

3   Semantics

In this section, we introduce the formal semantics of Mediator through the following steps. First we use the concept *configuration* to describe the state of an automaton. Next we show what the canonical forms of the transitions and automata are, and how to make them canonical. Finally, we define the formal semantics of automata as *labelled transition systems (LTS)*.

Instead of formalizing systems as LTS directly, we propose an algorithm that flattens the hierarchical structure of a system and generates a corresponding automaton.

3.1   Configurations

States of a Mediator automaton depend on the values of its *local variables* and *port variables*. First we introduce the definition of *evaluation* on a set of variables.

Definition 1 (Evaluation). *An evaluation of a set of variables V is defined as a function $v : V \to \mathbb{D}$ that satisfies $\forall x \in V, v(x) \in Dom(type(x))$. We denote the set of all possible evaluations of $Vars$ by $EV(Vars)$.*

Basically, an evaluation is a function that maps variables to one of its valid values, where we use $\mathbb{D}$ to denote the set of all values of all supported types. Now we can introduce *configuration* that snapshots an automaton.

Definition 2 (Configuration). *A configuration of an automaton $A = \langle Ports,$ $Vars, Trans_G \rangle$ is defined as a tuple (v_{loc}, v_{adj}) where $v_{loc} \in EV(Vars)$ is an evaluation on local variables, and $v_{adj} \in EV(Adj(A))$ is an evaluation on port variables. We use $Conf(A)$ to denote the set of all configurations of A.*

Now we can mathematically describe the language elements in an automaton:

- *Guard*s of an automaton A are represented by boolean functions on its configurations $g : Conf(A) \to Bool$.
- *Assignment Statement*s of A are represented by functions that map configurations to their updated ones $s_a : Conf(A) \to Conf(A)$.

3.2   Canonical Form of Transitions and Automata

Different statement combinations may have the same behavior. For example, a := b; c := d and a, c := b, d. Such irregular forms may lead to an extremely complicated and non-intuitive process when joining multiple automata. To simplify this process, we introduce the *canonical* form of transitions and automata as follows.

Definition 3 (Canonical Transitions). *A transition $t = g \to [s_1, \cdots, s_n]$ is canonical iff. $[s_1, \cdots, s_n]$ is a non-empty interleaving sequence of assignments and synchronizing statements which starts and ends with assignments.*

Suppose $g \to [s_1, \cdots, s_n]$ is a transition of automaton A, it can be made canonical through the following steps.

S1. If we find a continuous subsequence $s_i, \cdots, s_j$ (where s_k is an assignment statement for all $k = i, i+1, \cdots, j$, and $j > i$), we merge them as a single one. Since the assignment statements are formalized as functions $Conf(A) \to Conf(A)$, the subsequence $s_i, \cdots, s_j$ can be replaced by $s' = s_j \circ \cdots \circ s_i$[1].

S2. Keep on going with *S1* until there is no further subsequence to merge.

S3. Use identical assignments $id_{Conf(A)}$ to fill the gap between any adjacent synchronizing statements. Similarly, if the statements' list starts or ends with a synchronizing statement, we should also use $id_{Conf(A)}$ to decorate its head or tail.

It's clear that once we found such a continuous subsequence, the merging operation will reduce the number of statements. Otherwise it stops. It's clear that S is a finite set, and the algorithm always terminates within certain time.

Definition 4 (Canonical Automata). $A = \langle Ports, Vars, Trans_G \rangle$ *is a canonical automaton iff. (a) $Trans_G$ includes only one transition group and (b) all transitions in this group are canonical.*

Now we show for an arbitrary automaton $A = \langle Ports, Vars, Trans_G \rangle$, how $Trans_G$ is reformed to make A canonical. Suppose $Trans_G$ is a sequence of transition groups t_{G_i}, where the length of t_{G_i} is denoted by l_i,

$$[t_{G_1} = \{g_{11} \to S_{11}, \cdots, g_{1l_1} \to S_{1l_1}\}, \cdots, t_{G_n} = \{g_{n1} \to S_{n1}, \cdots, g_{nl_n} \to S_{nl_n}\}]$$

Informally speaking, once a transition in t_{G_i} is activated, all the other transitions in $t_{G_j} (j > i)$ are strictly prohibited from being fired. We use $activated(t_G)$ to denote the condition where at least one transition in t_G is enabled, formalized as

$$activated(t_G = \{g_1 \to S_1, \cdots, g_n \to S_n\}) = g_1 \vee \cdots \vee g_n.$$

To simplify the equations, we use $activated(t_{G_1}, \cdots, t_{G_{n-1}})$ to indicate that at least one group in $t_{G_1}, \cdots, t_{G_{n-1}}$ is activated. It's equivalent form is:

$$activated(t_{G_1}) \vee \cdots \vee activated(t_{G_{n-1}})$$

Then we can generate the new group of transitions with no dependency on priority as followings.

$$
\begin{aligned}
Trans'_G = [&g_{11} \to S_{11}, \cdots, g_{1l_1} \to S_{1l_1}, \\
&g_{21} \wedge \neg activated(t_{G_1}) \to S_{21}, \cdots, g_{2l_2} \wedge \neg activated(t_{G_1}) \to S_{2l_2}, \cdots \\
&g_{n1} \wedge \neg activated(t_{G_1}, \cdots, t_{G_{n-1}}) \to S_{n1}, \cdots, \\
&g_{nl_n} \wedge \neg activated(t_{G_1}, \cdots, t_{G_{n-1}}) \to S_{nl_n}]
\end{aligned}
$$

---

[1] The symbol $\circ$ denotes the composition operator on functions.

3.3   From System to Automaton

Mediator provides an approach to construct hierarchical system models from automata. In this section, we present an algorithm that flattens such a hierarchical system into a typical automaton.

For a system $S = \langle Ports, Entities, Internals, Links \rangle$, Algorithm 1 flattens it into an automaton $A_S = \langle Ports, Vars', Trans'_G \rangle$, where we assume that all the entities are canonical automata (they will be flattened recursively first if they are systems). The whole process is mainly divided into 2 steps:

1. Rebuild the structure of the flattened automaton, i.e. to integrate local variables and resolve the internal nodes.
2. Put the transitions together, including both internal transitions and external transitions according to the connections.

First of all, we refactor all the variables in all entities (in $Entities$) to avoid name conflicts, and add them to $Vars'$. Besides, all internal nodes are resolved in the target automaton, and be represented as

$$\{i\_field | i \in Internals, field \in \{\texttt{reqRead, reqWrite, value}\}\} \subseteq Vars'$$

Once all local variables needed are well prepared, we can merge the transitions for both *internal* and *external* ones.

- Internal transitions are easy to handle. Since they do not synchronize with other transitions, we directly put all the internal transitions in all entities into the flattened automaton, also as internal transitions.
- External transitions, on the other hand, have to synchronize with its corresponding external transitions in other entities. For example, when an automaton reads from an input port P_1, there must be another automaton which is writing to its output port P_2, where P_1 and P_2 are welded in the system. An example is presented as follows.

Example 7 (Synchronizing External Transitions). Consider two queues that cooperate on a shared internal node: Queue(A,B) and Queue(B,C). Obviously the dequeue operation of Queue(A,B) and enqueue operation of Queue(B,C) should be synchronized and scheduled. During the synchronization, the basic principle is to make sure that synchronizing statements on the same ports should be aligned strictly.

Dequeue Operation:	Enqueue Operation:	After Scheduling:

```
(B.reqRead && B.reqWrite)-> {   (B.reqRead && B.reqWrite)-> {   (B_reqRead && B_reqWrite)-> {
    B.value := buf[ptail];                                          B_value:=buf1[ptail1];
    ptail := next(ptail);                                          ptail1:=next(ptail1);
    sync B; <---- sync with -- --> sync B; <--- and goes to   --> B_reqWrite:=
                                                                      false,false;
                                                                   buf2[phead2]:=B_value;
                            buf[phead] := B.value;                 phead2:=next(phead2);
}                           phead := next(phead);         }
                        }
```

Algorithm 1. Flat a System into an Automaton

Require: A system $S = \langle Ports, Entities, Internals, Links \rangle$
Ensure: An automaton A
1: $A \leftarrow$ an empty automaton
2: $A.Ports \leftarrow S.Ports$
3: $Automata \leftarrow$ all the flattened automata of $S.Entities$
4: rename *local variables* in $Automata = \{A_1, \cdots, A_n\}$ to avoid duplicated names
5: **for** $l = \langle p_1, p_2 \rangle \in S.Links$ **do**
6:      **if** $p_1 \in S.Ports$ **then**
7:          replace all occurrance of p_2 with p_1
8:      **else**
9:          replace all occurrance of p_1 with p_2
10:     **end if**
11: **end for**
12: $ext\_trans \leftarrow \{\}$
13: **for** $i \leftarrow 1, 2, \cdots, n$ **do**
14:     add $A_i.Vars$ to $A.Vars$
15:     **for** $internal \in A_i.Ports$ **do**
16:         add $\{internal.\texttt{reqRead}, internal.\texttt{reqWrite}, internal.\texttt{value}\}$ to $A.Vars$
17:     **end for**
18:     add *all internal transitions* in $A_i.Trans_G$ to $A.Trans_G$
19:     add *all external transitions* in $A_i.Trans_G$ to ext_trans
20: **end for**
21: **for** $set\_trans \in \mathcal{P}(ext\_trans)$ **do**
22:     add $\texttt{Schedule}(S, set\_trans)$ to $A.Trans_G$ if it is not *null*
23: **end for**

During the synchronization, we refactor the local variables `ptail`, `phead` and `buf`, and transfer internal node B to a set of local variables. Synchronizing statement `sync B` is aligned between two transitions and in turn leads to the final result, where scheduled synchronizing statements are replaced by its local behavior – to reset its corresponding port variables.

We now formally present the flatting algorithms for systems. In the following we use $\mathcal{P}(A)$ to denote the powerset of A.

In Mediator *systems*, only port variables are shared between automata. During synchronization, the most important principle is to make sure assignments to port variables are performed before the port variables are referenced. Basically, this is a topological sorting problem on dependency graphs. A detailed algorithm is described in Algorithm 2. In this algorithm, we use

– $\bot$ and $\top$ to denote starting and ending of a transition's execution,
– $synchronizable(t_1, \cdots, t_n)$ to denote that the transitions are synchronizable, i.e. they come from different automaton and for each port being synchronized, there are exactly 2 transitions in $t_1, \cdots, t_n$ that synchronize it, and
– $reset\_stmt(p)$ to denote the corresponding statement that resets a port's status `p.reqRead`, `p.reqWrite := false, false`.

Algorithm 2. Schedule a Set of External Transitions

Require: A System S, a set of external canonical transitions $t_1, t_2, \cdots, t_n$
Ensure: A synchronized transition t

```
 1: if not synchronizable(t_1, ⋯ , t_n) then return t ← null
 2: t.g, t.S, G ← ⋀_i t_i.g, [ ], an empty graph ⟨V, E⟩
 3: for i ← 1, ⋯ , n do
 4:     add ⊥_i, ⊤_i to G.V
 5:     syncs, ext_syncs ← {⊥_i}, {}
 6:     for j ← 1, 3, ⋯ , len(t_i.S) do
 7:         add t_i.S_j to G.V
 8:         if ext_syncs ≠ {} then add 'sync ext_syncs' → t_i.S_j to G.E
 9:         for p ∈ syncs do
10:             add edge reset_stmt(p) → t_i.S_j to G.E
11:         end for
12:         syncs ← { all the synchronized ports in t_i.S_{j+1} } \S.Ports
13:         ext_syncs ← { all the synchronized ports in t_i.S_{j+1} } ∩ S.Ports
14:         if j < len(t_i.S) then
15:             for p ∈ syncs do
16:                 add reset_stmt(p) to G.V if is is not included yet
17:                 add edge t_i.S_j → reset_stmt(p) to G.E
18:             end for
19:             if ext_syncs ≠ {} then
20:                 add 'sync ext_syncs' to G.V
21:                 add edge t_i.S_j → 'sync ext_syncs' to G.E
22:             end if
23:         else
24:             add edge t_i.S_j → ⊤_i to G.E
25:         end if
26:     end for
27: end for
28: if G comprises a ring then t ← null
29: else t.S ← [ select all the statements in G.E using topological sort ]
```

Algorithm 2 may not always produce a valid synchronized transition. When the dependency graph has a *ring*, the algorithm fails due to *circular dependencies*. For example, transition g_1->{sync A;sync B;} and transition g_2->{sync B;sync A;} cannot be synchronized where both A, B need to be triggered first.

Topological sorting, as we all know, may generate different schedules for the same dependency graph. The following theorem shows that all the existing schedules are equivalent as transition statements.

Theorem 1 (Equivalence between Schedules). *If two sequences of assignment statements S_1, S_2 are generated from the same set of external transitions, they have exactly the same behavior (i.e. S_1 and S_2 will lead to the same result when they are executed under the same configuration).*

3.4   Automaton as Labelled Transition System

With all the language elements properly formalized, now we introduce the formal semantics of *automata* based on *labelled transition system*.

Definition 5 (Labelled Transition System). *A labelled transition system is a tuple* $(S, \Sigma, \rightarrow, s_0)$ *where S is a set of states with initial state $s_0 \in S$, Σ is a set of actions, and $\rightarrow \subseteq S \times \Sigma \times S$ is a set of transitions. For simplicity, we use* $s \xrightarrow{a} s'$ *to denote* $(s, a, s') \in \rightarrow$.

Suppose $A = \langle Ports, Vars, Trans_G \rangle$ is an automaton, its semantics can be captured by a LTS $\langle S_A, \Sigma_A, \rightarrow_A, s_0 \rangle$ where

- $S_A = Conf(A)$ is the set of all configurations of A.
- $s_0 \in S_A$ is the initial configuration where all variables (except for `reqReads` and `reqWrites`) are initialized with their default value, and all `reqReads` and `reqWrites` are initialized as `false`.
- $\Sigma_A = \{i\} \cup \mathcal{P}(Ports)$ is the set of all actions, where i denotes the internal action (i.e. no synchronization is performed).
- $\rightarrow_A \subseteq S_A \times \Sigma_A \times S_A$ is a set of transitions obtained by the following rules.

$$\frac{p \in P_{in}}{(v_{loc}, v_{adj}) \xrightarrow{i}_A (v_{loc}, v_{adj}[p.reqWrite \mapsto \neg p.reqWrite])} \text{ R-InputStatus}$$

$$\frac{p \in P_{in}, val \in Dom(Type(p.value))}{(v_{loc}, v_{adj}) \xrightarrow{i}_A (v_{loc}, v_{adj}[p.value \mapsto val])} \text{ R-InputValue}$$

$$\frac{p \in P_{out}}{(v_{loc}, v_{adj}) \xrightarrow{i}_A (v_{loc}, v_{adj}[p.reqRead \mapsto \neg p.reqRead])} \text{ R-OutputStatus}$$

$$\frac{\{g \rightarrow \{s\}\} \in Trans_G \text{ is internal}}{(v_{loc}, v_{adj}) \xrightarrow{i}_A s(v_{loc}, v_{adj})} \text{ R-Internal}$$

$$\frac{g \rightarrow S \in Trans_G \text{ is external}, [s_1, \cdots, s_n] \text{ are assignments in } S \quad p_1, \cdots, p_m \text{ are the synchronized ports}}{(v_{loc}, v_{adj}) \xrightarrow{\{p_1, \cdots, p_m\}}_A s_n \circ \cdots \circ s_1(v_{loc}, v_{adj})} \text{ R-External}$$

The first three rules describe the potential change of environment, i.e. the port variables. R-InputStatus and R-OutputStatus show that the reading status of an output port and writing status of an input port may be changed by the environment randomly. And R-InputValue shows that the value of an input port may also be updated by the environment.

The rule R-Internal specifies the internal transitions in $Trans_G$. As illustrated previously, an internal transition contains no synchronizing statement. So its canonical form comprises only one assignment s. Firing such a transition will simply apply s to the current configuration.

Meanwhile, the rule R-External specifies the external transitions, where the automaton interact with its environment. Fortunately, since all the environment changes are captured by the first three rules, we can simply regard the environment as another set of local variables. Consequently, the only difference between an internal transition and an external transition is that the later one may contain multiple assignments.

4 Case Study

In modern distributed computing frameworks (e.g. MPI [6] and ZooKeeper [9]), *leader election* plays an important role to organize multiple servers efficiently and consistently. This section shows how a classical leader election algorithm is modeled and reused to coordinate other components in Mediator.

In [7] the authors proposed a classical algorithm for a typical leader election scenario, as shown in Fig. 2. Distributed processes are organized as an *asynchronous unidirectional* ring where communication takes place only between adjacent processes and following certain direction (indicated by the arrows on edges in Fig. 2(a)).

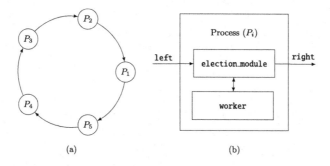

(a)   (b)

Fig. 2. (a) Topology of an asynchronous ring and (b) Structure of a process

The algorithm has the following steps. At first, each process sends a voting message containing its own *id* to its successor. When receives a voting message, the process will *(a)* forward the message to its successor if it contains a larger *id* than the process itself, or *(b)* ignore the message if it contains a smaller *id* than the process itself, or *(c)* take the process itself as a leader if it contains the same *id* with itself, and send an acknowledgement message to this successor, which will be spread over around the ring.

Here we formalize this algorithm through a more general approach. Leader election is encapsulated as the election_module. A computing module worker, attached to the election_module, is an implementation of the working process.

Two types of messages, `msgVote` and `msgLocal`, are supported when formalizing this architecture. Voting messages `msgVote` are transferred between the processes. A voting message carries two fields, *vtype* that declares the stage of leader election (either it is still voting or some process has already been acknowledged) and *id* is an identifier of the current leader (if it exists). On the other hand, `msgLocal` is used when a process communicates with its corresponding worker.

Example 8 (The Election Module). The following automaton shows how the election algorithm is implemented in Mediator. Due to the space limit, we omit some transitions here. A full version can be found at [1].

```
1    automaton <id:int> election_module ( left : in msgVote, right : out msgVote,
2        query : out msgLocal
3    ) {
4        variables {
5            leaderStatus : enum { pending, acknowledged } init pending;
6            buffer : (voteMsg | NULL) init {vtype: vote, id:id};
7            leaderId : (int | NULL) init null;
8        }
9        transitions {
10           (buffer != null)&&(buffer.vtype == vote)&&(buffer.id < id) -> {buffer := null;}
11           (buffer != null)&&(buffer.vtype == vote)&&(buffer.id == id) -> {buffer.vtype :=
                 ack;}
12           (buffer != null)&&(buffer.vtype == ack)&&(buffer.id < id) -> {
13               // restart voting if the acknowledged leader has a smaller id
14               buffer := { vtype: vote, id: id };
15           }
16           (buffer != null)&&(buffer.vtype == ack)&&(buffer.id >= id) -> {
17               leaderStatus := acknowledged;
18               leaderId := buffer.id;
19               buffer := buffer.id == id ? null : buffer;
20           }
21       }
22   }
```

The following code fragment encodes a parallel program containing 3 *worker*s and 3 *election_module*s to organize the *worker*s. In this example, we do not focus on the implementation details on *worker*s, but hope that any component with a proper interface could be embedded into this system instead.

```
1    system <worker: interface (query:in msgLocal)> parallel_instance() {
2        components {
3            E1 : election_module<1>;
4            E2 : election_module<2>;
5            E3 : election_module<3>;
6            C1, C2, C2 : worker;
7        }
8        connections {
9            Sync<msgVote>(E1.left, E2.right);
10           Sync<msgVote>(E2.right, E3.left);
11           Sync<msgVote>(E3.right, E1.left);
12
13           Sync<msgLocal>(C1,query, E1.query);
14           Sync<msgLocal>(C2,query, E2.query);
15           Sync<msgLocal>(C3,query, E3.query);
16       }
17   }
```

As we are modeling the leader election algorithm on a synchronous ring, only synchronous communication channels *Syncs* are involved in this example. The implementation details of `Sync` can be found in [1].

5   Conclusion and Future Work

A new modeling language Mediator is proposed in this paper to help with component-based software engineering through a formal way. With the basic behavior unit *automata* that captures the formal nature of components and connections, and *systems* for hierarchical composition, the language is easy-to-use for both formal method researchers and system designers.

This paper is a preface of a set of under-development tools. We plan to build a model checker for Mediator, and extend it through symbolic approach. An automatic code-generator is also being built to generate platform-specific codes like *Arduino* [13].

Acknowledgements. The work was partially supported by the National Natural Science Foundation of China under grant no. 61532019, 61202069 and 61272160.

References

1. A list of Mediator models. https://github.com/liyi-david/Mediator-Proposal
2. Abdulla, P.A., Deneux, J., Stålmarck, G., Ågren, H., Åkerlund, O.: Designing safe, reliable systems using scade. In: Margaria, T., Steffen, B. (eds.) ISoLA 2004. LNCS, vol. 4313, pp. 115–129. Springer, Heidelberg (2006). doi:10.1007/11925040_8
3. Amnell, T., Behrmann, G., Bengtsson, J., D'Argenio, P.R., David, A., Fehnker, A., Hune, T., Jeannet, B., Larsen, K.G., Möller, M.O., Pettersson, P., Weise, C., Yi, W.: UPPAAL - now, next, and future. In: Cassez, F., Jard, C., Rozoy, B., Ryan, M.D. (eds.) MOVEP 2000. LNCS, vol. 2067, pp. 99–124. Springer, Heidelberg (2001). doi:10.1007/3-540-45510-8_4
4. Arbab, F.: Reo: a channel-based coordination model for component composition. Math. Struct. Comput. Sci. **14**(3), 329–366 (2004)
5. Curry, E.: Message-oriented middleware. In: Mahmoud, Q. (ed.) Middleware for Communications, pp. 1–28. Wiley (2004)
6. Gropp, W., Lusk, E., Thakur, R.: Using MPI-2: Advanced Features of the Message-Passing Interface. MIT Press, Cambridge (1999)
7. Hagit, A., Jennifer, W.: Distributed Computing: Fundamentals, Simulations, and Advanced Topics. Wiley, Hoboken (2004)
8. Hahn, B., Valentine, D.T.: SIMULINK toolbox. In: Essential MATLAB for Engineers and Scientists, pp. 341–356. Academic Press (2016)
9. Junqueira, F.P., Reed, B.C., Serafini, M.: Zab: high-performance broadcast for primary-backup systems. In: Proceedings of DSN 2011, pp. 245–256. IEEE Compute Society (2011)
10. Kim, H., Lee, E.A., Broman, D.: A toolkit for construction of authorization service infrastructure for the internet of things. In: Proceedings of IoTDI 2017, pp. 147–158. ACM (2017)

11. Kwiatkowska, M., Norman, G., Parker, D.: PRISM 4.0: verification of probabilistic real-time systems. In: Gopalakrishnan, G., Qadeer, S. (eds.) CAV 2011. LNCS, vol. 6806, pp. 585–591. Springer, Heidelberg (2011). doi:10.1007/978-3-642-22110-1_47

12. Liu, Z., Morisset, C., Stolz, V.: rCOS: theory and tool for component-based model driven development. In: Arbab, F., Sirjani, M. (eds.) FSEN 2009. LNCS, vol. 5961, pp. 62–80. Springer, Heidelberg (2010). doi:10.1007/978-3-642-11623-0_3

13. Margolis, M.: Arduino Cookbook. O'Reilly Media Inc., Sebastopol (2011)

14. National Instruments: Labview. http://www.ni.com/zh-cn/shop/labview.html

15. Zou, L., Zhan, N., Wang, S., Fränzle, M., Qin, S.: Verifying simulink diagrams via a hybrid hoare logic prover. In: Proceedings of EMSOFT 2013, pp. 9:1–9:10. IEEE (2013)

A Component-Oriented Framework
for Autonomous Agents

Tobias Kappé[1]([⊠]), Farhad Arbab[2,3], and Carolyn Talcott[4]

[1] University College London, London, UK
tkappe@cs.ucl.ac.uk
[2] Centrum Wiskunde & Informatica, Amsterdam, The Netherlands
[3] LIACS, Leiden University, Leiden, The Netherlands
[4] SRI International, Menlo Park, USA

Abstract. The design of a complex system warrants a compositional methodology, i.e., composing simple components to obtain a larger system that exhibits their collective behavior in a meaningful way. We propose an automaton-based paradigm for compositional design of such systems where an *action* is accompanied by one or more *preferences*. At run-time, these preferences provide a natural fallback mechanism for the component, while at design-time they can be used to reason about the behavior of the component in an uncertain physical world. Using structures that tell us how to compose preferences and actions, we can compose formal representations of individual components or agents to obtain a representation of the composed system. We extend Linear Temporal Logic with two unary connectives that reflect the compositional structure of the actions, and show how it can be used to diagnose undesired behavior by tracing the falsification of a specification back to one or more culpable components.

1 Introduction

Consider the design of a software package that steers a crop surveillance drone. Such a system (in its simplest form, a single drone agent) should survey a field and relay the locations of possible signs of disease to its owner. There are a number of concerns at play here, including but not limited to maintaining an acceptable altitude, keeping an eye on battery levels and avoiding birds of prey. In such a situation, it is best practice to isolate these separate concerns into different modules — thus allowing for code reuse, and requiring the use of well-defined protocols in case coordination between modules is necessary. One would also like to verify that the designed system satisfies desired properties, such as "even on a conservative energy budget, the drone can always reach the charging station".

In the event that the designed system violates its verification requirements or exhibits behavior that does not conform to the specification, it is often useful to have an example of such behavior. For instance, if the surveillance drone fails to maintain its target altitude, an example of behavior where this happens could tell us that the drone attempted to reach the far side of the field and ran out of

© Springer International Publishing AG 2017
J. Proença and M. Lumpe (Eds.): FACS 2017, LNCS 10487, pp. 20–38, 2017.
DOI: 10.1007/978-3-319-68034-7_2

energy. Additionally, failure to verify an LTL-like formula typically comes with a counterexample — indeed, a counterexample arises from the automata-theoretic verification approach quite naturally [27]. Taking this idea of *diagnostics* one step further in the context of a compositional design, it would also be useful to be able to identify the components responsible for allowing a behavior that deviates from the specification, whether this behavior comes from a run-time observation or a design-time counterexample to a desired property. The designer then knows which components should be adjusted (in our example, this may turn out to be the route planning component), or, at the very least, rule out components that are not directly responsible (such as the wildlife evasion component).

In this paper, we propose an automata-based paradigm based on Soft Constraint Automata [1,18], called Soft Component Automata (SCAs[1]). An SCA is a state-transition system where transitions are labeled with actions and preferences. Higher-preference transitions typically contribute more towards the goal of the component; if a component is in a state where it wants the system to move north, a transition with action north has a higher preference than a transition with action south. At run-time, preferences provide a natural fallback mechanism for an agent: in ideal circumstances, the agent would perform only actions with the highest preferences, but if the most-preferred actions fail, the agent may be permitted to choose a transition of lower preference. At design-time, preferences can be used to reason about the behavior of the SCA in suboptimal conditions, by allowing all actions whose preference is bounded from below by a threshold. In particular, this is useful if the designer wants to determine the circumstances (i.e., threshold on preferences) where a property is no longer verified by the system.

Because the actions and preferences of an SCA reside in well-defined mathematical structures, we can define a composition operator on SCAs that takes into account the composition of actions as well as preferences. The result of composition of two SCAs is another SCA where actions and preferences reflect those of the operands. As we shall see, SCAs are amenable to verification against formulas in Linear Temporal Logic (LTL). More specifically, one can check whether the behavior of an SCA is contained in the behavior allowed by a formula of LTL.

Soft Component Automata are a generalization of Constraint Automata [3]. The latter can be used to coordinate interaction between components in a verifiable fashion [2]. Just like Constraint Automata, the framework we present blurs the line between *computation* and *coordination* — both are captured by the same type of automata. Consequently, this approach allows us to reason about these concepts in a uniform fashion: coordination is not separate in the model, it is effected by components which are inherently part of the model.

We present two contributions in this paper. First, we propose an compositional automata-based design paradigm for autonomous agents that contains enough information about actions to make agents behave in a robust manner — by which we mean that, in less-than-ideal circumstances, the agent has alternative actions available when its most desired action turns out to be impossible, which help it achieve some subset of goals or its original goals to a lesser degree.

---

[1] Here, we use the abbreviation *SCA* exclusively to refer to Soft *Component* Automata.

We also put forth a dialect of LTL that accounts for the compositional structure of actions and can be used to verify guarantees about the behavior of components, as well as their behavior in composition. Our second contribution is a method to trace errant behavior back to one or more components, exploiting the algebraic structure of preferences. This method can be used with both run-time and design-time failures: in the former case, the behavior arises from the action history of the automaton, in the latter case it is a counterexample obtained from verification.

In Sect. 2, we mention some work related to this paper; in Sect. 3 we discuss the necessary notation and mathematical structures. In Sect. 4, we introduce Soft Component Automata, along with a toy model. We discuss the syntax and semantics of the LTL-like logic used to verify properties of SCAs in Sect. 5. In Sect. 6, we propose a method to extract which components bear direct responsibility for a failure. Our conclusions comprise Sect. 7, and some directions for further work appear in Sect. 8. To save space, the proofs appear in the technical report accompanying this paper [17].

2   Related Work

The algebraic structure for preferences called the *Constraint Semiring* was proposed by Bistarelli et al. [4,5]. Further exploration of the compositionality of such structures appears in [10,13,18]. The structure we propose for modeling actions and their compositions is an algebraic reconsideration of *static constructs* [14].

The automata formalism used in this paper generalizes *Soft Constraint Automata* [1,3]. The latter were originally proposed to give descriptions of Web Services [1]; in [18], they were used to model fault-tolerant, compositional autonomous agents. Using preference values to specify the behavior of autonomous agents is also explored from the perspective of rewriting logic in the *Soft Agent Framework* [25,26]. Recent experiments with the Soft Agent Framework show that behavior based on soft constraints can indeed contribute robustness [20].

Sampath et al. [24] discuss methods to detect unobservable errors based on a model of the system and a trace of observable events; others extended this approach [9,22] to a multi-component setting. Casanova et al. [8] wrote about fault localisation in a system where some components are inobservable, based on which computations (tasks involving multiple components) fail. In these paradigms, one tries to find out where a *runtime fault* occurs; in contrast, we try to find out which component is responsible for *undesired behavior*, i.e., behavior that is allowed by the system but not desired by the specification.

A general framework for fault ascription in concurrent systems based on *counterfactuals* is presented in [11,12]. Formal definitions are given for failures in a given set of components to be necessary and/or sufficient cause of a system violating a given property. Components are specified by sets of sets of events (analogous to actions) representing possible correct behaviors. A parallel (asynchronous) composition operation is defined on components, but there is no notion of composition of events or explicit interaction between components. A system is given by a global behavior (a set of event sets) together with a set of system component specifications. The global behavior, which must be provided separately, includes component events, but may also have other events, and may violate component specifications (hence the faulty components). In our approach, global behavior is obtained by component composition. Undesired behavior may be local to a component or emerge as the result of interactions.

In LTL, a counterexample to a negative result arises naturally if one employs automata-based verification techniques [21, 27]. In this paper, we further exploit counterexamples to gain information about the component or components involved in violating the specification. The application of LTL to Constraint Automata is inspired by an earlier use of LTL for Constraint Automata [2].

Some material in this paper appeared in the first author's master's thesis [16].

3   Preliminaries

If Σ is a set, then 2^Σ denotes the set of subsets of Σ, i.e., the *powerset* of Σ. We write Σ^* for the set of *finite words* over Σ, and if $\sigma \in \Sigma^*$ we write $|\sigma|$ for the *length* of σ. We write $\sigma(n)$ for the n-th letter of σ (starting at 0). Furthermore, let Σ^ω denote the set of functions from $\mathbb{N}$ to Σ, also known as *streams* over Σ [23]. We define for $\sigma \in \Sigma^\omega$ that $|\sigma| = \omega$ (the smallest infinite ordinal). Concatenation of a stream to a finite word is defined as expected. We use the superscript ω to denote infinite repetition, writing $\sigma = \langle 0, 1 \rangle^\omega$ for the parity function; we write Σ^π for the set of *eventually periodic* streams in Σ^ω, i.e., $\sigma \in \Sigma^\omega$ such that there exist $\sigma_h, \sigma_t \in \Sigma^*$ with $\sigma = \sigma_h \cdot \sigma_t^\omega$. We write $\sigma^{(k)}$ with $k \in \mathbb{N}$ for the k-th *derivative* of σ, which is given by $\sigma^{(k)}(n) = \sigma(k + n)$.

If S is a set and $\odot : S \times S \to S$ a function, we refer to $\odot$ as an *operator on S* and write $p \odot q$ instead of $\odot(p, q)$. We always use parentheses to disambiguate expressions if necessary. To model composition of actions, we need a slight generalization. If $R \subseteq S \times S$ is a relation and $\odot : R \to S$ is a function, we refer to $\odot$ as a *partial operator on S up to R*; we also use infix notation by writing $p \odot q$ instead of $\odot(p, q)$ whenever pRq. If $\odot : R \to S$ is a partial operator on S up to R, we refer to $\odot$ as *idempotent* if $p \odot p = p$ for all $p \in S$ such that pRp, and *commutative* if $p \odot q = q \odot p$ whenever $p, q \in S$, pRq and qRp. Lastly, $\odot$ is *associative* if for all $p, q, r \in S$, pRq and $(p \odot q)Rr$ if and only if qRr and $pR(q \odot r)$, either of which implies that $(p \odot q) \odot r = p \odot (q \odot r)$. When $R = S \times S$, we recover the canonical definitions of idempotency, commutativity and associativity.

A *constraint semiring*, or *c-semiring*, provides a structure on preference values that allows us to *compare* the preferences of two actions to see if one is preferred over the other as well as *compose* preference values of component actions to find out the preference of their composed action. A c-semiring [4,5] is a tuple $\langle \mathbb{E}, \bigoplus, \otimes, \mathbf{0}, \mathbf{1} \rangle$ such that (1) $\mathbb{E}$ is a set, called the *carrier*, with $\mathbf{0}, \mathbf{1} \in \mathbb{E}$, (2) $\bigoplus : 2^\mathbb{E} \to \mathbb{E}$ is a function such that for $e \in \mathbb{E}$ we have that $\bigoplus \emptyset = \mathbf{0}$ and $\bigoplus \mathbb{E} = \mathbf{1}$, as well as $\bigoplus \{e\} = e$, and for $\mathcal{E} \subseteq 2^\mathbb{E}$, also $\bigoplus \{\bigoplus(E) : E \in \mathcal{E}\} = \bigoplus \bigcup \mathcal{E}$ (the *flattening property*), and (3) $\otimes : \mathbb{E} \times \mathbb{E} \to \mathbb{E}$ is a commutative and associative operator, such that for $e \in \mathbb{E}$ and $E \subseteq \mathbb{E}$, it holds that $e \otimes \mathbf{0} = \mathbf{0}$ and

$e \otimes \mathbf{1} = e$ as well as $e \otimes \bigoplus E = \bigoplus \{e \otimes e' : e' \in E\}$. We denote a c-semiring by its carrier; if we refer to $\mathbb{E}$ as a c-semiring, associated symbols are denoted $\bigoplus_{\mathbb{E}}, \mathbf{0}_{\mathbb{E}}$, et cetera. We drop the subscript when only one c-semiring is in context.

The operator $\bigoplus$ of a c-semiring $\mathbb{E}$ induces an idempotent, commutative and associative binary operator $\oplus : \mathbb{E} \times \mathbb{E} \to \mathbb{E}$ by defining $e \oplus e' = \bigoplus(\{e, e'\})$. The relation $\leq_{\mathbb{E}} \subseteq \mathbb{E} \times \mathbb{E}$ is such that $e \leq_{\mathbb{E}} e'$ if and only if $e \oplus e' = e'$; $\leq_{\mathbb{E}}$ is a partial order on $\mathbb{E}$, with $\mathbf{0}$ and $\mathbf{1}$ the minimal and maximal elements [4]. All c-semirings are complete lattices, with $\bigoplus$ filling the role of the least upper bound operator [4]. Furthermore, $\otimes$ is *intensive*, meaning that for any $e, e' \in \mathbb{E}$, we have $e \otimes e' \leq e$ [4]. Lastly, when $\otimes$ is idempotent, $\otimes$ coincides with the greatest lower bound [4].

Models of a c-semiring include $\mathbb{W} = \langle \mathbb{R}_{\geq 0} \cup \{\infty\}, \inf, \hat{+}, \infty, 0 \rangle$ (the *weighted semiring*), where inf is the infimum and $\hat{+}$ is arithmetic addition generalized to $\mathbb{R}_{\geq 0} \cup \{\infty\}$. Here, $\leq_{\mathbb{W}}$ coincides with the obvious definition of the order $\geq$ on $\mathbb{R}_{\geq 0} \cup \{\infty\}$. Composition operators for c-semirings exist, such as product composition [6] and (partial) lexicographic composition [10]. We refer to [18] for a self-contained discussion of these composition techniques.

4   Component Model

We now discuss our component model for the construction of autonomous agents.

4.1   Component Action Systems

Observable behavior of agents is the result of the actions put forth by their individual components; we thus need a way to talk about how actions compose. For example, in our crop surveillance drone, the following may occur:

- The component responsible for taking pictures wants to take a snapshot, while the routing component wants to move north. Assuming the camera is capable of taking pictures while moving, these actions may compose into the action "take a snapshot while moving north". In this case, actions compose *concurrently*, and we say that the latter action *captures* the former two.
- The drone has a single antenna that can be used for GPS and communications, but not both at the same time. The component responsible for relaying pictures has finished its transmission and wants to release its lock on the antenna, while the navigation component wants to get a fix on the location and requests use of the antenna. In this case, the actions "release privilege" and "obtain privilege" compose *logically*, into a "transfer privilege" action.
- The routing component wants to move north, while the wildlife avoidance component notices a hawk approaching from that same direction, and thus wants to move south. In this case, the intentions of the two components are contradictory; these component actions are *incomposable*, and some resolution mechanism (e.g., priority) will have to decide which action takes precedence.

All of these possibilities are captured in the definition below.

Definition 1. *A* Component Action System (CAS) *is a tuple* $\langle \Sigma, \odot, \boxdot \rangle$, *such that* Σ *is a finite set of* actions, $\odot \subseteq \Sigma \times \Sigma$ *is a reflexive and symmetric relation and* $\boxdot : \odot \to \Sigma$ *is an idempotent, commutative and associative operator on* Σ *up to* $\odot$ *(i.e.,* $\boxdot$ *is an operator defined only on elements of* Σ *related by* $\odot$*). We call* $\odot$ the composability relation, *and* $\boxdot$ the composition operator.

Every CAS $\langle \Sigma, \odot, \boxdot \rangle$ induces a relation $\sqsubseteq$ on Σ, where for $a, b \in \Sigma$, $a \sqsubseteq b$ if and only if there exists a $c \in \Sigma$ such that a and c are composable $(a \odot c)$ and they compose into b ($a \boxdot c = b$). One can easily verify that $\sqsubseteq$ is a preorder; accordingly, we call $\sqsubseteq$ the *capture preorder* of the CAS.

As with c-semirings, we may refer to a set Σ as a CAS. When we do, its composability relation, composition operator and preorder are denoted by $\odot_\Sigma$, $\boxdot_\Sigma$ and $\sqsubseteq_\Sigma$. We drop the subscript when there is only one CAS in context.

We model incomposability of actions by omitting them from the composability relation; i.e., if south is an action that compels the agent to move south, while north drives the agent north, we set south $\not\odot$ north. Note that $\odot$ is not necessarily transitive. This makes sense in the scenarios above, where snapshot is composable with south as well as north, but north is incomposable with south. Moreover, incomposability carries over to compositions: if south $\odot$ snapshot and south $\not\odot$ north, also (south $\boxdot$ snapshot) $\not\odot$ north. This is formalized in the following lemma.

Lemma 1. *Let* $\langle \Sigma, \odot, \boxdot \rangle$ *be a CAS and let* $a, b, c \in \Sigma$. *If* $a \odot b$ *but* $a \not\odot c$, *then* $(a \boxdot b) \not\odot c$. *Moreover, if* $a \not\odot c$ *and* $a \sqsubseteq b$, *then* $b \not\odot c$.

The composition operator facilitates concurrent as well as logical composition. Given actions obtain, release and transfer, with their interpretation as in the second scenario, we can encode that obtain and release are composable by stipulating that obtain $\odot$ release, and say that their (logical) composition involves an exchange of privileges by choosing obtain $\boxdot$ release = transfer. Furthermore, the capture preorder describes our intuition of capturing: if snapshot and move are the actions of the first scenario, with snapshot $\odot$ north, then snapshot, north $\sqsubseteq$ snapshot $\boxdot$ north.

Port Automata [19] contain a model of a CAS. Here, actions are sets of symbols called *ports*, i.e., elements of 2^P for some finite set P. Actions $\alpha, \beta \in 2^P$ are compatible when they agree on a fixed set $\gamma \subseteq P$, i.e., if $\alpha \cap \gamma = \beta \cap \gamma$, and their composition is $\alpha \cup \beta$. Similarly, we also find an instance of a CAS in *(Soft) Constraint Automata* [1,3]; see [16] for a full discussion of this correspondence.

4.2 Soft Component Automata

Having introduced the structure we impose on actions, we are now ready to discuss the automaton formalism that specifies the sequences of actions that are allowed, along with the preferences attached to such actions.

Definition 2. *A* Soft Component Automaton (SCA) *is a tuple* $\langle Q, \Sigma, \mathbb{E}, \to, q^0, t \rangle$ *where* Q *is a finite set of* states, *with* $q^0 \in Q$ *the* initial state, Σ *is a*

CAS and $\mathbb{E}$ *is a c-semiring with* $t \in \mathbb{E}$, *and* $\rightarrow \subseteq Q \times \Sigma \times \mathbb{E} \times Q$ *is a finite relation called the* transition relation. *We write* $q \xrightarrow{a,\,e} q'$ *when* $\langle q, a, e, q' \rangle \in \rightarrow$.

An SCA models the actions available in each state of the component, how much these actions contribute towards the goal and the way actions transform the state. The threshold value restricts the available actions to those with a preference bounded from below by the threshold, either at run-time, or at design-time when one wants to reason about behaviors satisfying some minimum preference.

We stress here that the threshold value is purposefully defined as part of an SCA, rather than as a parameter to the semantics in Sect. 4.4. This allows us to speak of the preferences of an individual component, rather than a threshold imposed on the whole system; instead, the threshold of the system arises from the thresholds of the components, which is especially useful in Sect. 6.

We depict SCAs in a fashion similar to the graphical representation of finite state automata: as a labeled graph, where vertices represent states and the edges transitions, labeled with elements of the CAS and c-semiring. The initial state is indicated by an arrow without origin. The CAS, c-semiring and threshold value will always be made clear where they are germane to the discussion.

An example of an SCA is A_{e}, drawn in Fig. 1; its CAS contains the incomposable actions charge, discharge$_1$ and discharge$_2$, and its c-semiring is the weighted semiring $\mathbb{W}$. This particular SCA can model the component of the crop surveillance drone responsible for keeping track of the amount of energy remaining in the system; in state q_n (for $n \in \{0, 1, \ldots, 4\}$), the drone has n units of energy left, meaning that in states q_1 to q_4, the component can spend one unit of energy through discharge$_1$, and in states q_2 to q_4, the drone can consume two units of energy through discharge$_2$. In states q_0 to q_3, the drone can try to recharge through charge.[2] Recall that, in $\mathbb{W}$, higher values reflect a lower preference (a higher *weight*); thus, charge is preferred over discharge$_1$.

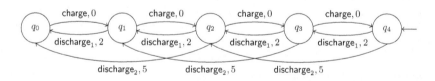

Fig. 1. A component modeling energy management, A_{e}.

Here, A_{e} is meant to describe the possible behavior of the energy management component only. Availability of the actions within the *total model* of the drone (i.e., the composition of all components) is subject to how actions compose with those of other components; for example, the availability of charge may

---

[2] This is a rather simplistic description of energy management. We remark that a more detailed description is possible by extending SCAs with *memory cells* [15] and using a memory cell to store the energy level. In such a setup, a state would represent a *range* of energy values that determines the components disposition regarding resources.

depend on the state of the component modelling position. Similarly, preferences attached to actions concern energy management only. In states q_0 to q_3, the component prefers to top up its energy level through charge, but the preferences of this component under composition with some other component may cause the composed preferences of actions composed with charge to be different. For instance, the total model may prefer executing an action that captures $discharge_2$ over one that captures charge when the former entails movement and the latter does not, especially when survival necessitates movement.

Nevertheless, the preferences of A_e affect the total behavior. For instance, the weight of spending one unit of energy (through $discharge_1$) is lower than the weight of spending two units (through $discharge_2$). This means that the energy component prefers to spend a small amount of energy before re-evaluating over spending more units of energy in one step. This reflects a level of care: by preferring small steps, the component hopes to avoid situations where too little energy is left to avoid disaster.

4.3 Composition

Composition of two SCAs arises naturally, as follows.

Definition 3. *Let* $A_i = \langle Q_i, \Sigma, \mathbb{E}, \rightarrow_i, q_i^0, t_i \rangle$ *be an SCA for* $i \in \{0,1\}$. *The (parallel) composition of* A_0 *and* A_1 *is the SCA* $\langle Q, \Sigma, \mathbb{E}, \rightarrow, q^0, t_0 \otimes t_1 \rangle$, *denoted* $A_0 \bowtie A_1$, *where* $Q = Q_0 \times Q_1$, $q^0 = \langle q_0^0, q_1^0 \rangle$, $\otimes$ *is the composition operator of* $\mathbb{E}$, *and* $\rightarrow$ *is the smallest relation satisfying*

$$\frac{q_0 \xrightarrow{a_0,\, e_0}_0 q_0' \qquad q_1 \xrightarrow{a_1,\, e_1}_1 q_1' \qquad a_0 \odot a_1}{\langle q_0, q_1 \rangle \xrightarrow{a_0 \,\boxdot\, a_1,\; e_0 \otimes e_1} \langle q_0', q_1' \rangle}$$

In a sense, composition is a generalized product of automata, where composition of actions is mediated by the CAS: transitions with composable actions manifest in the composed automaton, as transitions with composed action and preference.

Composition is defined for SCAs that share CAS and c-semiring. Absent a common CAS, we do not know which actions compose, and what their compositions are. However, composition of SCAs with different c-semirings does make sense when the components model different concerns (e.g., for our crop surveillance drone, "minimize energy consumed" and "maximize covering of snapshots"), both contributing towards the overall goal. Earlier work on Soft Constraint Automata [18] explored this possibility. The additional composition operators proposed there can easily be applied to Soft Component Automata.

A state q of a component may become unreachable after composition, in the sense that no state composed of q is reachable from the composed initial state. For example, in the total model of our drone, it may occur that any state representing the drone at the far side of the field is unreachable, because the energy management component prevents some transition for lack of energy.

To discuss an example of SCA composition, we introduce the SCA A_s in Fig. 2, which models the concern of the crop surveillance drone that it should take a snapshot of every location before moving to the next. The CAS of A_s includes the pairwise incomposable actions pass, move and snapshot, and its c-semiring is the weighted c-semiring $\mathbb{W}$. We leave the threshold value t_s undefined for now. The purpose of A_s is reflected in its states: q_Y (respectively q_N) represents that a snapshot of the current location was (respectively was not) taken since moving there. If the drone moves to a new location, the component moves to q_N, while q_Y is reached by taking a snapshot. If the drone has not yet taken a snapshot, it prefers to do so over moving to the next spot (missing the opportunity).[3]

Fig. 2. A component modeling the desire to take a snapshot at every location, A_s.

We grow the CAS of A_e and A_s to include the actions move, move_2, snapshot and snapshot_1 (here, the action α_i is interpreted as "execute action α and account for i units of energy spent"), and $\odot$ is the smallest reflexive, commutative and transitive relation such that the following hold: $\text{move} \odot \text{discharge}_2$ (moving costs two units of energy), $\text{snapshot} \odot \text{discharge}_1$ (taking a snapshot costs one unit of energy) and $\text{pass} \odot \text{charge}$ (the snapshot state is unaffected by charging). We also choose $\text{move} \boxdot \text{discharge}_2 = \text{move}_2$, $\text{snapshot} \boxdot \text{discharge}_1 = \text{snapshot}_1$ and $\text{pass} \boxdot \text{charge} = \text{charge}$. The composition of A_e and A_e is depicted in Fig. 3.

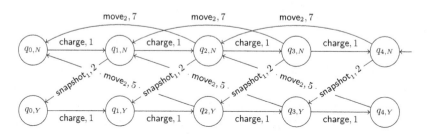

Fig. 3. The composition of the SCAs A_e and A_s, dubbed $A_{e,s}$: a component modeling energy and snapshot management. We abbreviate pairs of states $\langle q_i, q_j \rangle$ by writing $q_{i,j}$.

The structure of $A_{e,s}$ reflects that of A_e and A_s; for instance, in state $q_{2,Y}$ two units of energy remain, and we have a snapshot of the current location. The same holds for the transitions of $A_{e,s}$; for example, $q_{2,N} \xrightarrow{\text{snapshot}_1,\ 2} q_{1,Y}$ is the result of composing $q_2 \xrightarrow{\text{discharge}_1,\ 2} q_1$ and $q_N \xrightarrow{\text{snapshot},\ 0} q_Y$.

---

[3] A more detailed description of such a component could count the number of times the drone has moved without taking a snapshot first, and assign the preference of doing so again accordingly.

Also, note that in $A_{e,s}$ the preference of the $\mathsf{move_2}$-transitions at the top of the figure is lower than the preference of the diagonally-drawn $\mathsf{move_2}$-transitions. This difference arises because the component transition in A_s of the former is $q_N \xrightarrow{\mathsf{move},\ 2} q_N$, while that of the latter is $q_Y \xrightarrow{\mathsf{move},\ 0} q_N$. As such, the preferences of the component SCAs manifest in the preferences of the composed SCA.

The action $\mathsf{snapshot_1}$ is not available in states of the form $q_{i,Y}$, because the only action available in q_Y is pass, which does not compose into $\mathsf{snapshot_1}$.

4.4   Behavioral Semantics

The final part of our component model is a description of the behavior of SCAs. Here, the threshold determines which actions have sufficient preference for inclusion in the behavior. Intuitively, the threshold is an indication of the amount of flexibility allowed. In the context of composition, lowering the threshold of a component is a form of compromise: the component potentially gains behavior available for composition. Setting a lower threshold makes a component more permissive, but may also make it harder (or impossible) to achieve its goal.

The question of where to set the threshold is one that the designer of the system should answer based on the properties and level of flexibility expected from the component; Sect. 5 addresses the formulation of these properties, while Sect. 6 talks about adjusting the threshold.

Definition 4. *Let* $A = \langle Q, \Sigma, \mathbb{E}, \rightarrow, q^0, t \rangle$ *be an SCA. We say that a stream* $\sigma \in \Sigma^\omega$ *is a* behavior *of* A *when there exist streams* $\mu \in Q^\omega$ *and* $\nu \in \mathbb{E}^\omega$ *such that* $\mu(0) = q^0$, *and for all* $n \in \mathbb{N}$, $t \leq \nu(n)$ *and* $\mu(n) \xrightarrow{\sigma(n),\ \nu(n)} \mu(n+1)$. *The set of behaviors of* A, *denoted by* $L(A)$, *is called the* language *of* A.

We note the similarity between the behavior of an SCA and that of Büchi-automata [7]; we elaborate on this in the accompanying technical report [17].

To account for states that lack outgoing transitions, one could include implicit transitions labelled with halt (and some appropriate preference) to an otherwise unreachable "halt state", with a halt self-loop. Here, we set for all $\alpha \in \Sigma$ that $\mathsf{halt} \circledcirc \alpha$ and $\mathsf{halt} \boxdot \alpha = \mathsf{halt}$. To simplify matters, we do not elaborate on this.

Consider $\sigma = \langle \mathsf{snapshot}, \mathsf{move}, \mathsf{move} \rangle^\omega$ and $\tau = \langle \mathsf{snapshot}, \mathsf{move}, \mathsf{pass} \rangle^\omega$. We can see that when $t_s = 2$, both are behaviors of A_s; when $t_s = 1$, τ is a behavior of A_s, while σ is not, since every second move-action in σ has preference 2. More generally, if A and A' are SCAs over c-semiring $\mathbb{E}$ that only differ in their threshold values $t, t' \in \mathbb{E}$, and $t \leq t'$, then $L(A') \subseteq L(A)$. In the case of A_e, the threshold can be interpreted as a bound on the amount of energy to be spent in a single action; if $t_e < 5$, then behaviors with $\mathsf{discharge_2}$ do not occur in $L(A_e)$.

Interestingly, if A_1 and A_2 are SCAs, then $L(A_1 \bowtie A_2)$ is not uniquely determined by $L(A_1)$ and $L(A_2)$. For example, suppose that $t_e = 4$ and $t_s = 1$, and consider $L(A_{e,s})$, which contains $\langle \mathsf{snapshot} \rangle \cdot \langle \mathsf{move}, \mathsf{snapshot}, \mathsf{charge}, \mathsf{charge}, \mathsf{charge} \rangle^\omega$ even though the corresponding stream of component actions in A_e, i.e., the stream $\langle \mathsf{discharge_1} \rangle \cdot \langle \mathsf{discharge_2}, \mathsf{discharge_1}, \mathsf{charge}, \mathsf{charge}, \mathsf{charge} \rangle^\omega$ is not contained in $L(A_e)$. This is a consequence of a more general observation for c-semirings, namely that $t \leq e$ and $t' \leq e'$ is sufficient but not necessary to derive $t \otimes t' \leq e \otimes e'$.

5   Linear Temporal Logic

We now turn our attention to verifying the behavior of an agent, by means of a simple dialect of Linear Temporal Logic (LTL). The aim of extending LTL is to reflect the compositional nature of the actions. This extension has two aspects, which correspond roughly to the relations $\sqsubseteq$ and $\circledcirc$: reasoning about behaviors that *capture* (i.e., are composed of) other behaviors, and about behaviors that are *composable* with other behaviors. For instance, consider the following scenarios:

(i) We want to verify that under certain circumstances, the drone performs a series of actions where it goes north before taking a snapshot. This is useful when, for this particular property, we do not care about other actions that may also be performed while or as part of going north, for instance, whether or not the drone engages in communications while moving.

(ii) We want to verify that every behavior of the snapshot-component is composable with some behavior that eventually recharges. This is useful when we want to abstract away from the action that allows recharging, i.e., it is not important which particular action composes with charge.

Our logic aims to accommodate both scenarios, by providing two new connectives: $\succ\phi$ describes every behavior that captures a behavior validating ϕ, while $\circledcirc\,\phi$ holds for every behavior composable with a behavior validating ϕ.

5.1   Syntax and Semantics

The syntax of the LTL dialect we propose for SCAs contains atoms, conjunctions, negation, and the "until" and "next" connectives, as well as the unary connectives $\circledcirc$ and $\succ$. Formally, given a CAS Σ, the language $\mathcal{L}_\Sigma$ is generated by the grammar

$$\phi, \psi ::= \top \mid a \in \Sigma \mid \phi \wedge \psi \mid \phi\,U\,\psi \mid X\phi \mid \neg\phi \mid \succ\phi \mid \circledcirc\,\phi$$

As a convention, unary connectives take precedence over binary connectives. For example, $\succ\phi\,U\,\neg\psi$ should be read as $(\succ\phi)\,U\,(\neg\psi)$. We use parentheses to disambiguate formulas where this convention does not give a unique bracketing.

The semantics of our logic is given as a relation $\models_\Sigma$ between Σ^ω and $\mathcal{L}_\Sigma$; to be precise, $\models_\Sigma$ is the smallest such relation that satisfies the following rules

$$\frac{\sigma \in \Sigma^\omega}{\sigma \models_\Sigma \top} \qquad \frac{\sigma \in \Sigma^\omega}{\sigma \models_\Sigma \sigma(0)} \qquad \frac{\sigma \models_\Sigma \phi \qquad \sigma \models_\Sigma \psi}{\sigma \models_\Sigma \phi \wedge \psi}$$

$$\frac{n \in \mathbb{N} \qquad \forall k < n.\ \sigma^{(k)} \models_\Sigma \phi \qquad \sigma^{(n)} \models_\Sigma \psi}{\sigma \models_\Sigma \phi\,U\,\psi} \qquad \frac{\sigma^{(1)} \models_\Sigma \phi}{\sigma \models_\Sigma X\phi}$$

$$\frac{\sigma \not\models_\Sigma \phi}{\sigma \models_\Sigma \neg\phi} \qquad \frac{\sigma \models_\Sigma \phi \qquad \sigma \sqsubseteq^\omega \tau}{\tau \models_\Sigma \succ\phi} \qquad \frac{\sigma \models_\Sigma \phi \qquad \sigma \circledcirc^\omega \tau}{\tau \models_\Sigma \circledcirc\,\phi}$$

in which $\sqsubseteq^\omega$ and $\odot^\omega$ are the pointwise extensions of the relations $\sqsubseteq$ and $\odot$, i.e., $\sigma \sqsubseteq^\omega \tau$ when, for all $n \in \mathbb{N}$, it holds that $\sigma(n) \sqsubseteq \tau(n)$, and similarly for $\odot^\omega$.

Although the atoms of our logic are formulas of the form $\phi = a \in \Sigma$ that have an exact matching semantics, in general one could use predicates over Σ. We chose not to do this to keep the presentation of examples simple.

The semantics of $\odot$ and $\succ$ match their descriptions: if $\sigma \in \Sigma^\omega$ is described by ϕ (i.e., $\sigma \models_\Sigma \phi$) and $\tau \in \Sigma^\omega$ captures this σ at every action (i.e., $\sigma \sqsubseteq^\omega \tau$), then τ is a behavior described by $\succ\phi$ (i.e., $\tau \models_\Sigma \succ\phi$). Similarly, if $\rho \in \Sigma^\omega$ is described by ϕ (i.e., $\rho \models_\Sigma \phi$), and this ρ is composable with $\sigma \in \sigma^\omega$ at every action (i.e., $\sigma \odot^\omega \rho$), then ρ is described by $\odot\phi$ (i.e., $\rho \models_\Sigma \odot\phi$).

As usual, we obtain disjunction ($\phi \vee \psi$), implication ($\phi{\rightarrow}\psi$), "always" ($\square\phi$) and "eventually" ($\Diamond\phi$) from these connectives. For example, $\Diamond\phi$ is defined as $\top U \phi$, meaning that, if $\sigma \models_\Sigma \Diamond\phi$, there exists an $n \in \mathbb{N}$ such that $\sigma^{(n)} \models_\Sigma \phi$. The operator $\odot$ has an interesting dual that we shall consider momentarily.

We can extend $\models_\Sigma$ to a relation between SCAs (with underlying c-semiring $\mathbb{E}$ and CAS Σ) and formulas in $\mathcal{L}_\Sigma$, by defining $A \models_\Sigma \phi$ to hold precisely when $\sigma \models_\Sigma \phi$ for all $\sigma \in L(A)$. In general, we can see that fewer properties hold as the threshold t approaches the lowest preference in its semiring, as a consequence of the fact that decreasing the threshold can only introduce new (possibly undesired) behavior. Limiting the behavior of an SCA to some desired behavior described by a formula thus becomes harder as the threshold goes down, since the set of behaviors exhibited by that SCA is typically larger for lower thresholds.

We view the tradeoff between available behavior and verified properties as essential and desirable in the design of robust autonomous systems, because it represents two options available to the designer. On the one hand, she can make a component more accommodating in composition (by lowering the threshold, allowing more behavior) at the cost of possibly losing safety properties. On the other hand, she can restrict behavior such that a desired property is guaranteed, at the cost of possibly making the component less flexible in composition.

Example: no wasted moves. Suppose we want to verify that the agent never misses an opportunity to take a snapshot of a new location. This can be expressed by

$$\phi_{\mathsf{w}} = \succ\square(\mathsf{move}{\rightarrow}X(\neg\mathsf{move}\, U\, \mathsf{snapshot}))$$

This formula reads as "every behavior captures that, at any point, if the current action is a move, then it is followed by a sequence where we do not move until we take a snapshot". Indeed, if $t_e \otimes t_s = 5$, then $A_{\mathsf{e,s}} \models_\Sigma \phi_{\mathsf{w}}$, since in this case every behavior of $A_{\mathsf{e,s}}$ captures that between move-actions we find a snapshot-action. However, if $t_e \otimes t_s = 7$, then $A_{\mathsf{e,s}} \not\models_\Sigma \phi_{\mathsf{w}}$, since $\langle\mathsf{move}_2, \mathsf{move}_2, \mathsf{charge}, \mathsf{charge}, \mathsf{charge}, \mathsf{charge}\rangle^\omega$ would be a behavior of $A_{\mathsf{e,s}}$ that does not satisfy ϕ_{w}, as it contains two successive actions that capture move.[4]

---

[4] Recall that move_2 is the composition of move and $\mathsf{discharge}_2$, i.e., $\mathsf{move} \sqsubseteq \mathsf{move}_2$.

This shows the primary use of $\succ$, which is to verify the behavior of a component in terms of the behavior contributed by subcomponents.

Example: verifying a component interface. Another application of the operator ⊚ is to verify properties of the behavior composable with a component. Suppose we want to know whether all behaviors composable with a behavior of A validate ϕ. Such a property is useful, because it tells us that, in composition, A filters out the behaviors of the other operand that do not satisfy ϕ. Thus, if every behavior that composes with a behavior of A indeed satisfies ϕ, we know something about the behavior *imposed* by A in composition. Perhaps surprisingly, this use can be expressed using the ⊚-connective, by checking whether $A \models_\Sigma \neg \otimes \neg \phi$ holds; for if this is the case, then for all $\sigma, \tau \in \Sigma^\omega$ with σ a behavior of A and $\sigma \otimes^\omega \tau$, we know that $\sigma \not\models_\Sigma \otimes \neg\phi$, thus in particular $\tau \not\models_\Sigma \neg\phi$ and therefore $\tau \models_\Sigma \phi$.

More concretely, consider the component A_e. From its structure, we can tell that the action charge must be executed at least once every five moves. Thus, if τ is composable with a behavior of A_e, then τ must also execute some action composable with charge once every five moves. This claim can be encoded by

$$\phi_c = \neg \otimes \neg \Box \left(X \otimes \text{charge} \vee X^2 \otimes \text{charge} \vee \cdots \vee X^5 \otimes \text{charge} \right)$$

where X^n denotes repeated application of X. If $A_e \models_\Sigma \phi_c$, then every behavior of A_e is incomposable with behavior where, at some point, one of the next five actions is not composable with with charge. Accordingly, if $\sigma \in \Sigma^\omega$ is composable with some behavior of A_e, then, at every point in σ, one of the next five actions must be composable with charge. All behaviors that fail to meet this requirement are excluded from the composition.

5.2   Decision Procedure

We developed a procedure to decide whether $A \models_\Sigma \phi$ holds for a given SCA A and $\phi \in \mathcal{L}_\Sigma$. To save space, the details of this procedure, which involve relating SCAs to Büchi-automata, appear in the accompanying technical report; the main results are summarized below.

Proposition 1. *Let $\phi \in \mathcal{L}_\Sigma$. Given an SCA A and CAS Σ, the question whether $A \models_\Sigma \phi$ is decidable. In case of a negative answer, we obtain a stream $\sigma \in \Sigma^\pi$ such that $\sigma \in L(A)$ but $\sigma \not\models_\Sigma \phi$. The total worst-case complexity is bounded by a stack of exponentials in $|\phi|$, i.e., $2^{\cdot^{\cdot^{\cdot^{|\phi|}}}}$, whose height is the maximal nesting depth of $\succ$ and ⊚ in ϕ, plus one.*

This complexity is impractical in general, but we suspect that the nesting depth of $\succ$ and ⊚ is at most two for almost all use cases. We exploit the counterexample in Sect. 6.

6   Diagnostics

Having developed a logic for SCAs as well as its decision procedure, we investigate how a designer can cope with undesirable behavior exhibited by the agent, either as a run-time behavior σ, or as a counterexample σ to a formula found at design-time (obtained through Proposition 1). The tools outlined here can be used by the designer to determine the right threshold value for a component given the properties that the component (or the system at large) should satisfy.

6.1   Eliminating Undesired Behavior

A simple way to counteract undesired behavior is to see if the threshold can be raised to eliminate it — possibly at the cost of eliminating other behavior. For instance, in Sect. 5.1, we saw a formula ϕ_w such that $A_{e,s} \not\models_\Sigma \phi_w$, with counterexample $\sigma = \langle \mathsf{move}_2, \mathsf{move}_2, \mathsf{charge}, \mathsf{charge}, \mathsf{charge}, \mathsf{charge} \rangle^\omega$, when $t_e \otimes t_s = 7$. Since all move_2-labeled transitions of $A_{e,s}$ have preference 7, raising[5] $t_e \otimes t_s$ to 5 ensures that σ is not present in $L(A_{e,s})$; indeed, if $t_e \otimes t_s = 5$, then $A_{e,s} \models_\Sigma \phi_w$. We should be careful not to raise the threshold too much: if $t_e \otimes t_s = 0$, then $L(A_{e,s}) = \emptyset$, since every behavior of $A_{e,s}$ includes a transition with a non-zero weight — with threshold $t_e \otimes t_s = 0$, $A_{e,s} \models_\Sigma \psi$ holds for *any* ψ.

In general, since raising the threshold does not add new behavior, this does not risk adding additional undesired behavior. The only downside to raising the threshold is that it possibly eliminates desirable behavior. We define the *diagnostic preference* of a behavior as a tool for finding such a threshold.

Definition 5. *Let $A = \langle Q, \Sigma, \mathbb{E}, \rightarrow, q^0, t \rangle$ be an SCA, and let $\sigma \in \Sigma^\pi \cup \Sigma^*$. The diagnostic preference of σ in A, denoted $d_A(\sigma)$, is calculated as follows:*

1. *Let Q_0 be $\{q^0\}$, and for $n < |\sigma|$ set $Q_{n+1} = \{q' : q \in Q_n, q \xrightarrow{\sigma(n),\, e} q'\}$.*
2. *Let $\xi \in \mathbb{E}^\pi \cup \mathbb{E}^*$ be the stream such that $\xi(n) = \bigoplus \{e : q \in Q_n, q \xrightarrow{\sigma(n),\, e} q'\}$.*
3. *$d_A(\sigma) = \bigwedge \{\xi(n) : n \leq |\sigma|\}$, with $\bigwedge$ the greatest lower bound operator of $\mathbb{E}$.*

Since σ is finite or eventually periodic, and Q is finite, ξ is also finite or eventually periodic. Consequently, $d_A(\sigma)$ is computable.

Lemma 2. *Let $A = \langle Q, \Sigma, \mathbb{E}, \rightarrow, q^0, t \rangle$ be an SCA, and let $\sigma \in \Sigma^\pi \cup \Sigma^*$. If $\sigma \in L(A)$, or σ is a finite prefix of some $\tau \in L(A)$, then $t \leq_\mathbb{E} d_A(\sigma)$.*

Since $d_A(\sigma)$ is a necessary upper bound on t when σ is a behavior of A, it follows that we can exclude σ from $L(A)$ if we choose t such that $t \not\leq_\mathbb{E} d_A(\sigma)$. In particular, if we choose t such that $d_A(\sigma) <_\mathbb{E} t$, then $\sigma \notin L(A)$. Note that this may not always be possible: if $d_A(\sigma)$ is $\mathbf{1}$ then such a t does not exist.

Note that there may be another threshold (i.e., not obtained by Lemma 2), which may also eliminate fewer desirable behaviors. Thus, while this lemma gives helps to choose a threshold to exclude some behaviors, it is not a definitive guide. The accompanying technical report [17] contains a concrete example.

---

[5] Recall that $7 \leq_w 5$, so 5 is a "higher" threshold in this context.

6.2 Localizing Undesired Behavior

One can also use the diagnostic preference to identify the components that are involved in allowing undesired behavior. Let us revisit the first example from Sect. 5.1, where we verified that every pair of move-actions was separated by at least one snapshot action, as described in ϕ_w. Suppose we choose $t_e = 10$ and $t_s = 1$; then $t_e \otimes t_s = 11$, thus $\sigma = \langle \text{move}_2, \text{charge}, \text{charge} \rangle^\omega \in L(A_s)$, meaning $A_{e,s} \not\models_\Sigma \phi_w$. By Lemma 2, we find that $11 = t_{e,s} = t_e \otimes t_s \leq_W d_{A_{e,s}}(\sigma) = 7$. Even if A_s's threshold were as strict as possible (i.e., $t_s = 0 = 1_W$), we would find that $t_e \otimes t_s \leq_W d_{A_{e,s}}(\sigma)$, meaning that we cannot eliminate σ by changing t_s only. In some sense, we could say that t_e is responsible for σ.[6]

More generally, let $(A_i)_{i \in I}$ be a finite family of automata over the c-semiring $\mathbb{E}$ with thresholds $(t_i)_{i \in I}$. Furthermore, let $A = \bowtie_{i \in I} A_i$ and let ψ be such that $A \not\models_\Sigma \psi$, with counterexample behavior σ. Suppose now that for some $J \subseteq I$, we have $\bigotimes_{i \in J} t_i \leq_E d_A(\sigma)$. Since $\otimes$ is intensive, we furthermore know that $\bigotimes_{i \in I} t_i \leq_E \bigotimes_{i \in J} t_i$. Therefore, at least one of t_i for $i \in J$ must be adjusted to exclude the behavior σ from the language of $\bowtie_{i \in I} A_i$.

We call $(t_i)_{i \in J}$ *suspect* thresholds: *some* t_i for $i \in I$ must be adjusted to eliminate σ; by extension, we refer to J as a *suspect subset* of I. Note that I may have distinct and disjoint suspect subsets. If $J \subseteq I$ is disjoint from every suspect subset of I, then J is called *innocent*. If J is innocent, changing t_j for some $j \in J$ (or even t_j for all $j \in J$) alone does not exclude σ. Finding suspect and innocent subsets of I thus helps in finding out which thresholds need to change in order to exclude a specific undesired behavior.

Function FindSuspect *(I)*:
    $M := \emptyset$;
    foreach $i \in I$ **do**
        if $I \setminus \{i\}$ *is suspect* **then**
            $M := M \cup \text{FindSuspect}(I \setminus \{i\})$;
        end
    end
    if $M = \emptyset$ **then**
        return $\{I\}$;
    else
        return M;
    end
end

Algorithm 1. Algorithm to find minimal suspect subsets.

---

[6] Arguably, A_e as a whole may not be responsible, because modifying the preference of the move-loop on q_N in A_s can help to exclude the undesired behavior as well. In our framework, however, the threshold is a generic property of any SCA, and so we use it as a handle for talking about localizing undesired behaviors to component SCAs.

Algorithm 1 gives pseudocode to find minimal suspect subsets of a suspect set I; we argue correctness of this algorithm in Theorem 1; for a proof, see [17].

Theorem 1. *If I is suspect and $d_A(\sigma) < 1$, then* FindSuspect(I) *contains exactly the minimal suspect subsets of I.*

In the case where $d_A(\sigma) = 1$, it is easy to see that $\{\{i\} : i \in I\}$ is the set of minimal suspect subsets of I.

In the worst case, every subset of I is suspect, and therefore the only minimal suspect subsets are the singletons; in this scenario, there are $O(|I|!)$ calculations of a composed threshold value. Using memoization to store the minimal suspect subsets of every $J \subseteq I$, the complexity can be reduced to $O(2^{|I|})$.

While this complexity makes the algorithm seem impractical (I need not be a small set), we note that the case where all components are individually responsible for allowing a certain undesired behavior should be exceedingly rare in a system that was designed with the violated concern in mind: it would mean that *every component* contains behavior that ultimately composes into the undesired behavior — in a sense, *facilitating* behavior that counteracts their interest.

7   Discussion

In this paper, we proposed a framework that facilitates the construction of autonomous agents in a compositional fashion. We furthermore considered an LTL-like logic for verification of the constructed models that takes their compositional nature into account, and showed the added value of operators related to composition in verifying properties of the interface between components. We also provided a decision procedure for the proposed logic.

The proposed agents are "soft", in that their actions are given preferences, which may or may not make the action feasible depending on the threshold preference. The designer can *decrease* this threshold to allow for more behavior, possibly to accommodate the preferences of another component, or *increase* it to restrict undesired behavior observed at run-time or counterexamples to safety assertions found at design-time. We considered a simple method to raise the threshold enough to exclude a given behavior, but which may overapproximate in the presence of partially ordered preferences, possibly excluding desired behavior.

In case of a composed system, one can also find out which component's thresholds can be thought of as *suspect* for allowing a certain behavior. This information can give the designer a hint on how to adjust the system — for example, if the threshold of an energy management component turns out to be suspect for the inclusion of undesired behavior, perhaps the component's threshold needs to be more conservative with regard to energy expenses to avoid the undesired behavior. We stress that responsibility may be assigned to a *set* of components as a whole, if their composed threshold is suspect for allowing the undesired behavior, which is possible when preferences are partially ordered.

8   Further Work

Throughout our investigation, the tools for verification and diagnosis were driven by the compositional nature of the framework. As a result, they apply not only to the "grand composition" of all components of the system, but also to subcomponents (which may themselves be composed of sub-subcomponents). What is missing from this picture is a way to "lift" verified properties of subcomponents to the composed system, possibly with a side condition on the interface between the subcomponent where the property holds and the subcomponent representing the rest of the system, along the lines of the interface verification in Sect. 5.1.

If we assume that agents have low-latency and noiseless communication channels, one can also think of a multi-agent system as the composition of SCAs that represent each agent. As such, our methods may also apply to verification and diagnosis of multi-agent systems. However, this assumption may not hold. One way to model this could be to insert "glue components" that mediate the communication between agents, by introducing delay or noise. Another method would be to introduce a new form of composition for loosely coupled systems.

Finding an appropriate threshold value also deserves further attention. In particular, a method to adjust the threshold value *at run-time*, would be useful, so as to allow an agent to relax its goals as gracefully as possible if its current goal appears unachievable, and raise the bar when circumstances improve.

Lastly, the use soft constraints for autonomous agents is also being researched in a parallel line of work [25], which employs rewriting logic. Since rewriting logic is backed by powerful tools like Maude, with support for soft constraints [28], we aim to reconcile the automata-based perspective with rewriting logic.

Acknowledgements. The authors would like to thank Vivek Nigam and the anonymous FACS-referees for their valuable feedback. This work was partially supported by ONR grant N00014-15-1-2202.

References

1. Arbab, F., Santini, F.: Preference and similarity-based behavioral discovery of services. In: ter Beek, M.H., Lohmann, N. (eds.) WS-FM 2012. LNCS, vol. 7843, pp. 118–133. Springer, Heidelberg (2013). doi:10.1007/978-3-642-38230-7_8
2. Baier, C., Blechmann, T., Klein, J., Klüppelholz, S., Leister, W.: Design and verification of systems with exogenous coordination using vereofy. In: Margaria, T., Steffen, B. (eds.) ISoLA 2010. LNCS, vol. 6416, pp. 97–111. Springer, Heidelberg (2010). doi:10.1007/978-3-642-16561-0_15
3. Baier, C., Sirjani, M., Arbab, F., Rutten, J.: Modeling component connectors in Reo by constraint automata. Sci. Comput. Program. **61**, 75–113 (2006)
4. Bistarelli, S. (ed.): Semirings for Soft Constraint Solving and Programming. LNCS, vol. 2962. Springer, Heidelberg (2004). doi:10.1007/b95712
5. Bistarelli, S., Montanari, U., Rossi, F.: Constraint solving over semirings. In: Proceedings of the International Joint Conference on Artificial Intelligence (IJCAI), pp. 624–630 (1995)

6. Bistarelli, S., Montanari, U., Rossi, F.: Semiring-based constraint satisfaction and optimization. J. ACM **44**(2), 201–236 (1997)
7. Büchi, J.R.: On a decision method in restricted second order arithmetic. In: Proceedings of Logic, Methodology and Philosophy of Science, pp. 1–11. Stanford University Press, Stanford (1962)
8. Casanova, P., Garlan, D., Schmerl, B.R., Abreu, R.: Diagnosing unobserved components in self-adaptive systems. In: Proceedings of Software Engineering for Adaptive and Self-Managing Systems (SEAMS), pp. 75–84 (2014)
9. Debouk, R., Lafortune, S., Teneketzis, D.: Coordinated decentralized protocols for failure diagnosis of discrete event systems. Discrete Event Dyn. Syst. **10**(1–2), 33–86 (2000)
10. Gadducci, F., Hölzl, M., Monreale, G.V., Wirsing, M.: Soft constraints for lexicographic orders. In: Castro, F., Gelbukh, A., González, M. (eds.) MICAI 2013. LNCS, vol. 8265, pp. 68–79. Springer, Heidelberg (2013). doi:10.1007/978-3-642-45114-0_6
11. Goessler, G., Astefanoaei, L.: Blaming in component-based real-time systems. In: Proceedings of Embedded Software (EMSOFT), pp. 7:1–7:10 (2014)
12. Gössler, G., Stefani, J.-B.: Fault ascription in concurrent systems. In: Ganty, P., Loreti, M. (eds.) TGC 2015. LNCS, vol. 9533, pp. 79–94. Springer, Cham (2016). doi:10.1007/978-3-319-28766-9_6
13. Hölzl, M.M., Meier, M., Wirsing, M.: Which soft constraints do you prefer? Electr. Notes Theor. Comput. Sci. **238**(3), 189–205 (2009)
14. Hüttel, H., Larsen, K.G.: The use of static constructs in a model process logic. In: Meyer, A.R., Taitslin, M.A. (eds.) Logic at Botik 1989. LNCS, vol. 363, pp. 163–180. Springer, Heidelberg (1989). doi:10.1007/3-540-51237-3_14
15. Jongmans, S.T., Kappé, T., Arbab, F.: Constraint automata with memory cells and their composition. Sci. Comput. Program. **146**, 50–86 (2017)
16. Kappé, T.: Logic for Soft Component Automata. Master's thesis, Leiden University, Leiden, The Netherlands (2016). http://liacs.leidenuniv.nl/assets/Masterscripties/CS-studiejaar-2015-2016/Tobias-Kappe.pdf
17. Kappé, T., Arbab, F., Talcott, C.: A component-oriented framework for autonomous agents (2017). https://arxiv.org/abs/1708.00072
18. Kappé, T., Arbab, F., Talcott, C.L.: A compositional framework for preference-aware agents. In: Proceedings of Workshop on Verification and Validation of Cyber-Physical Systems (V2CPS), pp. 21–35 (2016)
19. Koehler, C., Clarke, D.: Decomposing port automata. In: Proceedings ACM Symposium on Applied Computing (SAC), pp. 1369–1373 (2009)
20. Mason, I.A., Nigam, V., Talcott, C., Brito, A.: A framework for analyzing adaptive autonomous aerial vehicles. In: Proceedings of Workshop on Formal Co-Simulation of Cyber-Physical Systems (CoSim) (2017)
21. Muller, D.E., Saoudi, A., Schupp, P.E.: Weak alternating automata give a simple explanation of why most temporal and dynamic logics are decidable in exponential time. In: Proceedings of Symposium on Logic in Computer Science (LICS), pp. 422–427 (1988)
22. Neidig, J., Lunze, J.: Decentralised Diagnosis of Automata Networks. IFAC Proceedings Volumes, vol. 38(1), pp. 400–405 (2005)
23. Rutten, J.J.M.M.: A coinductive calculus of streams. Math. Struct. Comput. Sci. **15**(1), 93–147 (2005)
24. Sampath, M., Sengupta, R., Lafortune, S., Sinnamohideen, K., Teneketzis, D.: Failure diagnosis using discrete-event models. IEEE Trans. Contr. Sys. Techn. **4**(2), 105–124 (1996)

25. Talcott, C.L., Arbab, F., Yadav, M.: Soft agents: exploring soft constraints to model robust adaptive distributed cyber-physical agent systems. In: Software, Services, and Systems – Essays Dedicated to Martin Wirsing on the Occasion of His Retirement from the Chair of Programming and Software Engineering, pp. 273–290 (2015)
26. Talcott, C., Nigam, V., Arbab, F., Kappé, T.: Formal specification and analysis of robust adaptive distributed cyber-physical systems. In: Bernardo, M., De Nicola, R., Hillston, J. (eds.) SFM 2016. LNCS, vol. 9700, pp. 1–35. Springer, Cham (2016). doi:10.1007/978-3-319-34096-8_1
27. Vardi, M.Y.: An automata-theoretic approach to linear temporal logic. In: Moller, F., Birtwistle, G. (eds.) Logics for Concurrency. LNCS, vol. 1043, pp. 238–266. Springer, Heidelberg (1996). doi:10.1007/3-540-60915-6_6
28. Wirsing, M., Denker, G., Talcott, C.L., Poggio, A., Briesemeister, L.: A rewriting logic framework for soft constraints. Electr. Notes Theor. Comput. Sci. **176**(4), 181–197 (2007)

Coordination of Dynamic Software Components with JavaBIP

Anastasia Mavridou[1(✉)], Valentin Rutz[2], and Simon Bliudze[3]

[1] Institute for Software Integrated Systems, Vanderbilt University, Nashville, USA
anastasia.mavridou@vanderbilt.edu
[2] Microsoft Corporation, Dublin, Ireland
[3] Ecole Polytechnique Fédérale de Lausanne, Lausanne, Switzerland

Abstract. JavaBIP allows the coordination of software components by clearly separating the functional and coordination aspects of the system behavior. JavaBIP implements the principles of the BIP component framework rooted in rigorous operational semantics. Recent work both on BIP and JavaBIP allows the coordination of static components defined prior to system deployment, i.e., the architecture of the coordinated system is fixed in terms of its component instances. Nevertheless, modern systems, often make use of components that can register and deregister dynamically during system execution. In this paper, we present an extension of JavaBIP that can handle this type of dynamicity. We use first-order interaction logic to define synchronization constraints based on component types. Additionally, we use directed graphs with edge coloring to model dependencies among components that determine the validity of an online system. We present the software architecture of our implementation, provide and discuss performance evaluation results.

1 Introduction

We have previously introduced JavaBIP [9,10] that allows coordinating software components exogenously, i.e., without requiring access to component source code. JavaBIP relies on the following observations. Domain specific components have states (e.g., idle, working) that are known to component users with domain expertise. Furthermore, components always provide APIs that allow programs to invoke operations (e.g., suspend or resume) in order to change their state, or to be notified when a component changes its state spontaneously. Thus, component behavior can be easily represented by Finite State Machines (FSMs).

JavaBIP brings the BIP principles into a more general software engineering context than that of embedded systems, in which code generation might not be desirable due to continuous code updates. Thus, to use JavaBIP, instead of generating Java code from the BIP modeling language, developers must provide—for the relevant components—the corresponding FSMs in the form of annotated Java classes. The FSMs describe the protocol that must be respected to access a shared resource or use a service provided by a component. FSM transitions

J. Proença and M. Lumpe (Eds.): FACS 2017, LNCS 10487, pp. 39–57, 2017.
DOI: 10.1007/978-3-319-68034-7_3

are associated with calls to API functions, which force a component to take an action, or with event notifications that allow reacting to external events.

For component coordination, JavaBIP provides two primitive mechanisms: (1) multi-party synchronizations of component transitions and (2) asynchronous event notifications. The latter embodies the reactive programming paradigm. In particular, JavaBIP extends the Actor model [1], since event notifications can be used to emulate asynchronous messages, while providing the synchronization of component transitions as a primitive mechanism gives developers a powerful and flexible tool to manage coordination. The synchronization of component transitions is managed by a runtime called JavaBIPEngine, which, for simplicity, we call "engine" in the rest of the paper. Notice that in a completely asynchronous system the engine is not needed.

JavaBIP clearly separates system-wide coordination policies from component behavior. Synchronization constraints, defining the possible synchronizations among transitions of different components i.e., the set of possible component *interactions*, are specified independently from the design of individual components in dedicated XML files. This separation of functional and coordination aspects greatly reduces the burden of system complexity. Finally, integration with the BIP framework, through a JavaBIP-to-BIP code generation tool, allows the use of existing deadlock-detection and model checking tools [7,8] ensuring the correctness of JavaBIP systems.

The previous implementation of JavaBIP [10] was static. To coordinate a system, the full set of components had be registered before starting the engine. No components could be added on-the-fly and, most importantly, if a failure occurred in a single component, the engine execution had to stop and the full set of constraints had to be computed anew. Notice that none of the current BIP implementations [5,6,11] allows to add or remove components on-the-fly, including DyBIP presented in [12] that allows dynamically changing the set of interactions among a fixed set of components at runtime. This might be problematic, since modern systems, e.g., large banking systems or modular smartphones, make use of components that can register and deregister during system execution.

To allow dynamicity in JavaBIP, we use first-order interaction logic to describe synchronization constraints on component types. As a result, a developer can write synchronization constraints without knowing the exact number of components in the system. Thus, component instances of known types, i.e., types for which synchronization constraints exist, can register at runtime without any additional input from the developer. To optimize JavaBIP performance, we have introduced a notion of system validity: *a system is valid if and only if its set of possible interactions is not empty*. The notion of validity allows the engine to be started and stoped automatically at runtime by just checking the status of the system. By stopping the engine if the system is invalid, we eliminate any processing time needed by the engine. To check system validity, we use directed graphs with edge coloring to model component synchronization dependencies.

Notice that the introduced notion of validity is only relevant for the engine: in an invalid system components can still communicate asynchronously.

We have extended the interface and implementation of the engine to register, deregister, and pause a component at runtime. The difference between pausing and deregistering a component is as follows. If a component deregisters, then the engine clears all the associated data and references to this component; other components cannot synchronize with the deregistered component unless it registers anew. If a component is paused, other components cannot synchronize with it but the engine keeps all associated data and references to it; the paused component can start synchronizing with other components by simply informing the engine that it is back on track.

The rest of the paper is structured as follows. Section 2 describes our motivating case study. Section 3 presents the JavaBIP framework and the macronotation used to specify JavaBIP synchronization constraints on component types. Section 4 presents the notion of JavaBIP system validity and the construction of validity graphs. Section 5 describes the implemented software architecture and presents performance results. Section 6 discusses related work. Section 7 summarizes the results and future work directions.

2   Motivating Case Study

Modular phones require application layer specifications that can handle dynamic device insertion and removal at runtime. In the rest of the paper, we refer to the phone's devices as *modules*. In this case study, we model in JavaBIP some of the application layer protocols offered by Google's Greybus specification[1].

Figure 1 illustrates the composite component types, of the case study. Greybus requires that exactly one application processor (AP) is present in the system

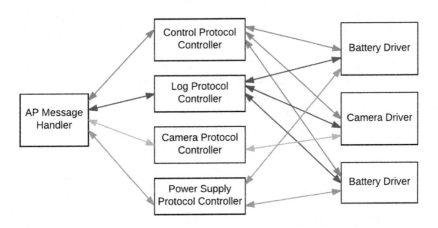

Fig. 1. Modular phone architecture.

---

[1] https://github.com/projectara/greybus-spec

```
Application Layer ::= (AP Message Handler).(Controller)⁺.(Driver)*
AP Message Handler ::= (AP Request Worker).(AP Response Worker).
                        (AP Message Worker).(AP Receiver Fifo)
Controller ::= (Control Protocol Controller).(Log Protocol Controller).
            (Camer Protocol Controller).(Power Supply Protocol Controller)
Driver ::= (Battery Driver)*.(Camera Driver)*
Camera Driver ::= (Control Connect Handler).(Control Disconnect Handler).
            (Log Handler).(Camera Capture Handler).(Camera Stream Handler)
Battery Driver ::= (Control Connect Handler).(Control Disconnect Handler).
                        (Log Handler).(Power Supply Handler)
```

Fig. 2. Hierarchical decomposition of the `Application Layer` into components.

for storing user data and executing applications. We consider two types of modules that can be inserted on the phone's frame at runtime: (1) power supply modules, e.g., batteries and (2) cameras. Any number of instances of these two types can be inserted or removed from the phone at runtime. Figure 1 presents an example configuration of a phone, in which two battery and one camera modules are connected. These modules communicate with the AP through dedicated device class connection protocols: the *camera*, *power supply*, and *log* protocols. The latter can be used by any module to send human-readable debug log messages to AP. Additionally, AP uses the *control protocol* to perform basic initialization and configuration actions with other modules. If no power supply or camera modules are connected, the system configuration would consist of the AP Message Handler, Control Protocol Controller, the Log Protocol Controller, Camera Protocol Controller, and the Power Supply Protocol Controller composite components. The grammar in Fig. 2 shows how to obtain the desired systems as the incremental composition of components. Operators . (dot), ·* and ·⁺ are used as usual to denote composition and repetition. Notice that Fig. 1 illustrates only one of the possible system configurations that are described by the grammar in Fig. 2. A detailed description of the system's componentization and interaction model can be found in [31].

A Greybus protocol defines a number of Greybus operations, which are *request-response pairs* of remote procedure calls from one module to another. The bi-directional arrows in Fig. 1 represent Greybus operations. For instance, the AP very often needs to retrieve information from other modules. This requires that a message requesting information be paired with a response message containing the information requested. In many cases, Greybus operations need to be performed in a specific order. Additionally, the access to shared resources such as memory and logging services needs to be controlled among modules. We enforce action flow of Greybus operations, as well as controlled access to the phone's shared resources with JavaBIP. We developed the case study using the WebGME-BIP design studio[2], the complete system exceeds 2000 lines of code.

---

[2] https://github.com/anmavrid/webgme-bip.

3   The JavaBIP Component Framework

JavaBIP implements the BIP (Behavior-Interaction-Priority) coordination mechanism [5], for coordination of concurrent components. In BIP, the behavior of components is described by Finite State Machines (FSMs) having transitions labeled with *ports* and extended with data stored in local variables. Ports form the interface of a component and are used to define its interactions with other components. They can also export part of the local variables, allowing access to the component's data. Component coordination is defined in BIP by means of *interaction models*, i.e., sets of interactions. Interactions are sets of ports that define allowed synchronizations among components.

JavaBIP takes as input the *system specification*, which is provided by the user and consists of the following:

- A *behavior specification* for each component type, which is an FSM extended with ports and data provided as an annotated Java class.
- The *glue specification*, which is the interaction model of the system, is provided as an XML file. It specifies how the transitions of different component types must be synchronized, i.e., synchronization constrains.
- The optional *data-wire specification*, which is the data transfer model of the system, is provided as an XML file. It specifies which and how data are exchanged among component types.

For property analysis, the system specification can be automatically translated into an equivalent model of the system in the BIP language. This model can then be verified for deadlock freedom or other properties, using DFinder [7], ESST or nuXmv [8]. Other analyses can be performed using any tool for which a model transformation from BIP is available.

3.1   Glue Specification

The glue specification is defined in JavaBIP through a macro-notation, similar to the one introduced in [12], based on first-order interaction logic. This notation imposes synchronization constraints based on component types rather than on component instances, which allows a developer to write a glue specification without knowing the exact number of components in the system. Instances of component types for which synchronization constraints exist in the glue specification can be dynamically registered or deregistered at runtime without requiring additional input or changes in the glue specification. We briefly present the JavaBIP Require/Accept macro-notation used for the glue specification. The JavaBIP Require/Accept macro-notation was previously presented in [10]. We also refer the interested reader to [31], where we present in detail the propositional interaction logic, the first-order extension and the Require/Accept macro-notation.

Consider a port p of a component type T, which labels one or more transitions of T. The associated synchronization constraint to all transitions of T labeled by p is the conjunction of two constraints: the *causal* and *acceptance* constraints.

Two macros are used: (1) the **Require** macro and (2) the **Accept** macro to define the causal and acceptance constraints, respectively. Next, we describe the meaning of the two macros through representative examples. The generalization of the above definitions to more complex macros is straightforward, but cumbersome. Therefore we omit it here.

The Require Macro is used to specify ports required for synchronization. Let $T^1, T^2 \in \mathcal{T}$ be two component types. The macro

$$T_1.p \ \textbf{Require} \ T_2.q$$

means that, to participate in an interaction, each of the ports p of component instances of type T_1 requires synchronization with *precisely one* of the ports q of component instances of type T_2. Notice that the cardinality of required component instances is explicit: should two instances of the same port type be required, this is specified by explicitly putting the required port type twice, e.g.,

$$T_1.p \ \textbf{Require} \ T_2.q \ T_2.q \,,$$

and so on for higher cardinalities. We call *effect* what is specified in the left-hand side of **Require** (e.g., $T_1.p$) and *cause* what is specified in the right-hand side (e.g., $T_2.q \ T_2.q$). A cause consists of a set of *OR-causes*, where each OR-cause is a set of ports. For p to participate in an interaction, all the ports belonging to at least one of the OR-causes must synchronize. For instance,

$$T_1.p \ \textbf{Require} \ T_2.q \ T_2.q \ ; \ T_2.r$$

means that p requires either the synchronization of two instances of q or one instance of r. Notice the semicolon that separates the two OR-causes.

The Accept Macro defines optional ports for synchronization, i.e., it defines the boundary of interactions. This is expressed by explicitly excluding from interactions all the ports that are not accepted. Let $T^1, T^2 \in \mathcal{T}$ be two component types. The following:

$$T_1.p \ \textbf{Accept} \ T_2.q$$

means that p accepts the synchronization of instances of q but does not accept instances of any other port types.

4   Defining System Validity

In the previous, static JavaBIP implementation, a developer had to first register all components to the engine and then start the engine manually. Since, in the presented implementation, components may register or deregister on-the-fly, we introduce a notion of validity so that depending on whether there are enough registered components, the engine can automatically start or stop its execution. We start by formally defining components, BIP systems and valid BIP systems.

Definition 1 (BIP Component). *A BIP component B is an FSM represented by a triple $(Q, P, \rightarrow)$, where Q is a set of states, P is a set of communication ports, $\rightarrow \subseteq Q \times P \times Q$ is a set of transitions, each labeled by a port.*

Below, we use the common notation, writing $q \xrightarrow{p} q'$ instead of $(q, p, q') \in \rightarrow$.

Definition 2 (BIP System). *A BIP system is defined by a composition operator parameterized by a set of interactions $\gamma \subseteq 2^P$. $\mathcal{B}_n = \gamma(B_1, \dots, B_n)$ is an FSM represented by a triple $(Q, \gamma, \rightarrow)$, where $Q = \prod_{i=1}^{n} Q_i$ and $\rightarrow$ is the least set of transitions satisfying the following rule:*

$$\frac{a = \{p_i\}_{i \in I} \in \gamma \qquad \forall i \in I : q_i \xrightarrow{p_i} q_i' \qquad \forall i \notin I : q_i = q_i'}{(q_1, \dots, q_n) \xrightarrow{a} (q_1', \dots, q_n')}$$

The inference rule says that a BIP system, consisting of n components, can execute an interaction $a \in \gamma$, iff for each port $p_i \in a$, the corresponding component B_i, can execute a transition labeled with p_i; the states of components that do not participate in the interaction remain the same. The set of possible interactions of a BIP system is defined in JavaBIP by the glue specification, i.e., the set of Require and Accept macros. We write $B : T$ to denote a component B of type T. We denote by $\mathcal{T}$ the set of all component types of a BIP system.

Definition 3 extends Definition 2 to describe a valid BIP system. System validity is defined from the perspective of starting/stopping the engine execution. Notice that even if a system is not valid according to Definition 3, JavaBIP components can communicate in an asynchronous manner.

Definition 3 (Valid BIP System). *A BIP system $(Q, \gamma, \rightarrow)$ is valid iff $\gamma \neq \emptyset$.*

Remark 1. In Definitions 1 and 2, for the sake of simplicity, we omit the presentation of data-related aspects. However, it should be noted that the full JavaBIP [10] allows data variables within components. In such cases, component transitions can be guarded by Boolean predicates on data variables. Notice that in Definition 3 we do not consider guards. This is a design choice that we made. The result of guard evaluation might easily change multiple times throughout the system lifecycle, e.g., based on the components internal state or on component interaction. Thus, it is undesirable to base engine execution on such often recurring changes, which could actually result in increasing the engine's overhead.

Definition 3 says that a BIP system is valid if and only if there are enough registered components such that the interaction set of the system is not empty. To determine the validity of a system, we use directed graphs with edge coloring to model dependencies among components. The generation of the validity graph is based on the Require macros of the glue specification, since these define the minimum number of required interactions among the components. The complete glue specification is used by the engine for orchestrating component execution.

Definition 4 (Validity graph). *A labelled graph $G = (\mathcal{T}, E, c)$ is the validity graph of a set of Require macros iff:*

1. the vertex set T is the set of component types defined in the Require macros;
2. the edge set E contains a directed edge (T_1, T_2) iff there exists a Require macro that contains T_1 in the effect and T_2 in an OR-cause;
3. for each edge $(T_1, T_2) \in E$, the counter $c : E \rightarrow \mathbb{Z}$ is initialized with the cardinality of T_2 in the corresponding OR-cause.

The edges of the graph are colored such that: 1) all edges corresponding to an OR-cause of a Require macro are colored the same; 2) edges corresponding to different OR-causes are colored differently.

Clearly, there always exists a validity graph for any set of Require macros. Note that the outgoing edges of two different vertices may have the same color.

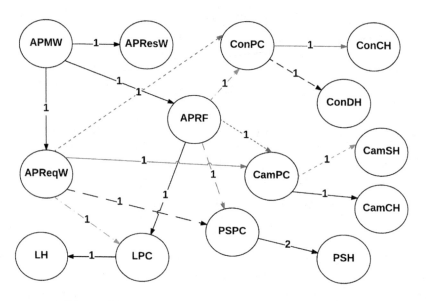

Fig. 3. Validity graph of the Modular Phone case study.

Figure 3 shows part of the validity graph of the case study (the full graph can be found in [31]). There are 13 vertices, each one representing an atomic component type from Fig. 2. Due to space limitations, we substituted the full names with their acronyms. For instance, we substituted AP Message Handler by APMW. In case of acronym conflicts, we added more letters, e.g., we substituted AP Request Worker by APReqW, and AP Response Worker by APResW.

Let us now consider two of the Require macros of the case study (the full set of Require and Accept macros can be found in [31]).

```
PSPC.snd  Require PSH.rcv PSH.rcv
APRF.snd  Require ConPC.rvc; CamPC.rcv; PSPC.rcv; LPC.rcv
```

Since, component type `Power Supply Protocol Controller` requires synchronization with two instances of component type `Power Supply Handler`, there is an edge from vertex PSPC to vertex PSH labeled by a counter initialized to 2. Furthermore, component type `AP Receiver Fifo` requires synchronization either with an instance of component type `Control Protocol Controller` or an instance of component type `Camera Protocol Controller` or an instance of `Power Supply Protocol Controller` or an instance of `Logger Protocol Controller`. Thus, there are four outgoing edges from vertex APRF, each labeled by a counter initialized to 1 and colored by a different color, to vertices ConPC, CamPC, PSPC, and LPC, respectively. In Fig. 3, edges with different colors are also represented by different line styles.

Definition 5 (Dynamic change in validity graph). *In the event of a dynamic change, a validity graph is updated as follows:*

1. *If a component instance of type T is registered, the counters of all incoming edges of vertex T are decremented by 1.*
2. *If a component instance of type T is deregistered or paused, the counters of all incoming edges of vertex T are incremented by 1.*

Proposition 1 (Determining system validity). *Consider a BIP system and a corresponding validity graph. The BIP system is valid iff for at least one vertex of the validity graph, an instance of the vertex's corresponding type is registered and the counters of all outgoing edges of at least one color are equal to or less than 0.*

Example 1. Figure 4 presents the changes in the validity graph of Fig. 3[3], after the registration of an instance of each of the APMW, APResW, APRF, and PSH component types. System validity will be guaranteed if at least one instance of a component type contained in one of the red dashed boxes gets registered.

To start and stop the engine, we determine first whether the system is valid by using Proposition 1. Nevertheless, we do not need to check system validity every time a component registers/deregisters/pauses. Corollaries 1 and 2 define such cases. The proofs of Proposition 1 and Corollaries 1 and 2 can be found in [31].

Corollary 1. *If a BIP system $\mathcal{B}_n$ is valid and a component is registered, then the new BIP system $\mathcal{B}_{n+1}$ is also valid.*

Corollary 2. *If a BIP system $\mathcal{B}_n$ is invalid and a component is deregistered or paused, then the new BIP system $\mathcal{B}_{n-1}$ is also invalid.*

---

[3] The complete validity graph of the case study can be found in [31].

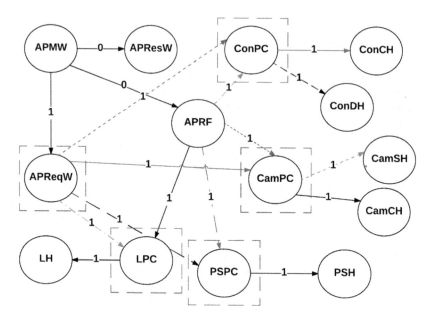

Fig. 4. Changes in validity graph when adding/removing components.

5   Implementation

Next, we discuss the implementation of the dynamic JavaBIP extension, during which the implementation of the JavaBIP engine has significantly changed. Let us consider first the interface of the JavaBIP engine, i.e., `BIPEngine`. In the static implementation, `BIPEngine` consisted of the following functions: (1) `register` used by a developer to register a component to the engine; (2) `inform` used by a component to inform the engine of its current state and enabled transitions; (3) `specifyGlue` used by a developer to send the glue specification to engine; (4) `start` used by a developer to start the engine thread and (5) `stop` used by a developer to stop the engine.

We updated `BIPEngine` as follows. Function `start` was removed, since the engine thread is now started automatically based on whether enough components are registered to form a valid system. We added two functions: (1) `deregister` used by a developer or the component itself (e.g., in the case of a failure) to deregister from the engine and (2) `pause` used by a developer or the component (e.g., in the case that the component is going to communicate asynchronously with other components for an amount of time) to pause synchronizations with other components. Function `register` was considerably updated, as well as function `stop` which can also be called internally by the engine in the case of an invalid system. The remaining functions were not modified. Figure 5 shows the software architecture of the JavaBIP engine. The arrows labeled `register`, `deregister`, `stop`, `specifyGlue`, and `pause` represent calls to the `BIPEngine` functions.

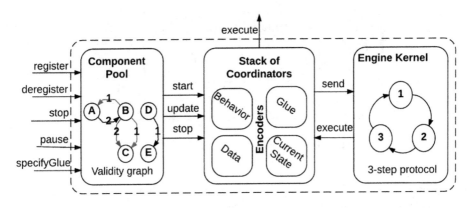

Fig. 5. Dynamic JavaBIP Engine software architecture.

The `ComponentPool` object was added, which is used as an interface to the validity graph described in Definition 4. The `ComponentPool` starts the core engine (comprising a stack of coordinators and the engine kernel), when the system becomes valid, and stops it, when the system becomes invalid. System validity is checked whenever a component is registered, deregistered or paused, excluding the cases described in Corollaries 1 and 2. Whenever a component is registered or deregistered without affecting the validity of the system, the `Component Pool` sends an update registration/deregistration event to the core engine.

The engine composes and solves the various constraints of the system. Its implementation is based on Binary Decision Diagrams (BDDs) [2], which are efficient data structures to store and manipulate Boolean formulas.[4] The imposed constraints encode information about the behavior, glue, data, and current state of the components. Current state constraints allow us to compute the enabled transitions of the component. For each type of constraints, we discuss which parts must be recomputed when registering components at runtime. There is no need to recompute these constraints when a component is paused or deregistered. Whenever constraints are recomputed, the Coordinators send these to the kernel.

The formulas that define the behavior, glue, data, and current state constraints were presented in [10]. Figure 6 summarizes the constraint computation. The white color indicates that the constraint is computed only once at system initialization. The light gray indicates that the constraint is recomputed when a component is registered. The dark gray color indicates that the constraint is recomputed during each execution cycle.

The *behavior constraint* of a component includes its ports and states. For each port, a Boolean port variable is created. Similarly, for each state, a Boolean state variable is created. Behavior constraints are built using these port and state variables. The *total behavior constraint* is computed as the conjunction of all component behavior constraints. When a component is registered, its behavior

---

[4] We have used the JavaBDD package, available at http://javabdd.sourceforge.net.

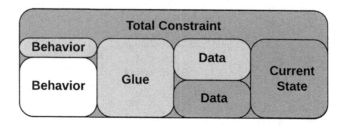

Fig. 6. Constraint computation phases.

constraint is computed and conjuncted to the total behavior constraint. When a component is deregistered, its port variables are set to *false*.

The *glue constraint* is computed by interpreting the Require and Accept macros of the glue specification. The same Boolean port variables that were previously created for the behavior constraints are used for the glue constraint as well. The glue constraint must be recomputed, in a valid system, every time a new component is registered.

For the *data constraint*, additional data variables have to be created. The data constraints represent how data is exchanged among components, i.e., which components are providing data and which components are consuming data. For each pair of components exchanging data, a data variable is created. When a component is registered, the data constraints that involve the newly arrived components are recomputed. Components exchange data at the beginning of each execution cycle of the system. Based on the exchanged data, components may disable some of the possible interactions. As a result, a subset of data constraints is recomputed at each execution cycle.

The *current state constraint* of a component is computed when a component informs of its disabled transitions due to guard evaluation. The *total current state BDD* is the conjunction of the current state constraints of all registered components. During engine execution, i.e., in a valid system, the total current state constraint is computed at each execution cycle of the engine and is further conjuncted with the total behavior constraint, the glue constraint, and the total data constraint.

The execution of a JavaBIP valid system is driven by the engine kernel applying the following protocol in a cyclic manner:

1. Upon reaching a state, all component constraints are sent to the kernel;
2. The kernel computes the *total constraint*, which is the conjunction of the total behavior, glue, current state and data constraints. Thus, it computes the possible interactions satisfying the total system constraint and picks one of them;
3. The kernel notifies the Coordinators of its decision by calling `execute`, which then notify the components to execute the necessary transitions.

Notice that a component can be registered during any step of the engine protocol. The engine, however will only include the newly registered component in the BDD computation at the beginning of the next cycle. System validity is checked, when a component is paused or deregistered. If the system remains valid and the engine is executing the second or third step of the engine protocol, the engine sets the port variables of this component to *false* and recomputes the possible interactions.

5.1 Performance Results

We show performance results for the modular phone case study. The experiments were performed on a 3.1 GHz Intel Core i7 with 8GB RAM. We started with 5 registered components and registered up to 45 additional components. The JavaBIP models are available online[5]. Table 1 summarizes the engine's computation times and the BDD Manager peak memory usage for various numbers of components. We present and discuss three different engine times: (1) the time needed to perform a complete engine execution cycle (three-step protocol run by the Engine kernel); (2) the time needed to (partially) recompute the behavior, glue, and data BDD constraints due to the registration of a new component; (3) the time needed to add or remove a component from the component tool and check the validity of the system.

The first column shows the number of components in the system, after the registration or deregistration of a component. For instance, 10 means that a new component was registered and the total number of components in the system is now 10. The number of components is also decreased in two cases, when it is equal to 11 and equal to 29. This means that a component was deregistered or paused and the total number of components in the system is 11 or 29, respectively.

The second column shows the average engine execution time of the first 1000 engine cycles after a component registration or deregistration. The system becomes valid and the engine is started upon the registration of the 12th component. As a result, the engine execution times are equal to 0 for the first two rows of the table. If the engine had been started, for instance, after the registration of the 5th component (without the system being valid), the engine would have needed < 1 ms per execution cycle. This means that an overhead of seconds or minutes could have been added in the system's execution if more than a certain number of engine execution cycles (e.g., 100000) had been performed by the time the system became valid.

The third column of Table 1 shows the amount of time needed to recompute the behavior, glue, and data constraints of the system due to a component registration. The first two rows are equal to 0 since the system is invalid and thus, no BDD computation is required. If the engine had been started before the system became valid, the BDDs would have been recomputed upon the registration of each new component. For instance, after the registration of the 5th component, the engine would have needed 13 ms and after the registration of the 11th component, the engine would have needed additional 49 ms to recompute the BDDs.

---

[5] https://github.com/sbliudze/javabip-itest.

The fifth column shows the peak memory usage of the BDD manager after a component registration or deregistration.

Finally, the fourth column of Table 1 presents the amount of time needed to add or remove a component from the component pool and check for system validity. The time needed is very low, in some cases even less than 1 ms. These were the cases that system validity was not checked due to the results of Corollaries 1 and 2. The system became valid when the 12th component was registered. This required the maximum amount of time (3.654 ms), since the full graph was checked for validity, and then the core engine thread was started. Next, a component was deregistered, the system became invalid again, and the engine thread was stopped. The amount of time needed by the component pool was 2.908 ms.

Table 1. Engine times and BDD Manager peak memory usage. Times are in milliseconds and memory usage is in Megabytes.

Number of components	Time: Engine execution cycle	Time: BDD (re)computation	Time: Component pool	Memory
5	0	0	2.078	0
10	0	0	2.186	0
12	< 1	63	3.654	0.059
11	0	0	2.908	0.057
20	< 1	151	< 1	0.083
25	1.149	194	< 1	0.099
30	1.247	239	< 1	0.129
29	1.241	0	2.451	0.121
40	1.399	283	< 1	0.199
50	1.896	337	< 1	0.254

6   Related Work

Dynamicity in BIP has been studied by several authors [12,15,20]. In [12], the authors present the Dy-BIP framework that allows dynamic reconfiguration of connectors among the ports of the system. They use *history variables* to allow sequences of interactions with the same instance of a given component type. JavaBIP can emulate history variables using data. In contrast, our focus is on dynamicity due to the creation and deletion of components that is often encountered in modern software systems that are not restricted to the embedded systems domain. Additionally, the interface-based design and the modular software architecture of JavaBIP allow us to easily extend the JavaBIP implementation.

Our approach is closest to [15,21]. In [15], two extensions of the BIP model are defined: reconfigurable—similar to Dy-BIP—and dynamic, allowing dynamic replication of components. They focus on the operational semantics of the two extensions and their properties, by studying their encodability in BIP and Place/Transition Petri nets (P/T Nets). Composition is defined through interaction models, without considering structured connectors. In contrast, our work focuses mostly on the connectivity among components, defined by Require/Accept relations. In [21], the BIP coordination mechanisms are implemented by a set of connector combinators in Haskell and Scala. Functional BIP provides combinators for managing connections in a dynamically evolving set of components. However, as in [15], such evolution must be managed by explicit actions of existing components. In contrast, the JavaBIP approach allows components to be created independently, only requiring that they be subsequently registered with the JavaBIP engine.

The Reo coordination language [33]—which realizes component coordination through circuit-like connectors built of channels and nodes—provides dedicated primitives for reconfiguring connectors by creating new channels (Ch), and manipulating channel ends and nodes (split, join, hide and forget). A number of papers study reconfiguration of Reo connectors. In particular, [18] provides a framework for model checking reconfigurable circuits, whereas [26] and [27] take the approach based on graph transformation techniques. The main difference between connector reconfiguration in Reo and dynamicity in JavaBIP is that, in Reo, reconfiguration operations are performed on constituent elements of the connector. Thus, in principle, such operations can affect *ongoing* interactions. This is not possible in JavaBIP, since interactions are completely atomic.

In [16,34], the authors study adaptation of open component-based systems. The underlying component and composition model inherits from the work of Arnold on synchronization vectors [4] and thereby is very close to that of BIP and other frameworks, e.g., [23]. The authors focus on fixing several types of mismatch situations, among which *name mismatch*, which occurs when the names of the sending and receiving events do not coincide (CCS and π-calculus are used to describe component behavior), and *independent evolution*, which occurs when an event on a particular interface does not have an equivalent in its counterparts interface. Contrary to BIP, synchronization and data transfer concerns are not fully separate in [16,34], since they rely on *send-receive* primitives. Thus, they use multiparty synchronization exclusively to allow broadcasting. The goal of both static and dynamic adaptation is to resolve the mismatches, based on a user-specified mapping, while avoiding deadlocks. Our work in this paper differs insofar as the BIP synchronization mechanism is blocked *anyway* (communication through direct message passing can still proceed) if the necessary components have not been registered. Thus, our main concern is not avoiding deadlock, but reducing the coordination overhead induced by the engine.

Three main types of formalisms have been studied in the literature for the specification of dynamic architectures and architecture styles [13]: (1) graph grammars, (2) process algebras, and (3) logics. Graph grammars have been used to specify reconfiguration in a dynamic architecture through the use of graph rewriting rules. Representative approaches include the Le Métayer approach [28], where nodes plus CSP-like behavior specifications are components and edges are connectors. A different way of representing software architectures with graph grammars can be found in [24], where hyperedges with CCS labels are components and nodes are communication ports. Other graph-based approaches are summarized in [14]. None of these approaches offers tool support.

Additionally, process algebras have been used to define dynamic architectures as part of several architecture description languages (ADLs). For instance, π-calculus [32] was used in Darwin [29] and LEDA [17], CCS was used in PiLar [19], and CSP was used in Dynamic Wright [3]. In comparison with our approach, Darwin and PiLar support only binary bindings (connectors), while in Dynamic Wright and LEDA there is no clear distinction between behavior and coordination since connectors can have behavior.

Logic has also been used for the specification of dynamic software architectures and architecture styles. Alloy's first-order logic [25] was used in [22] for the specification of dynamic architectures, while the Alloy Analyzer tool was used to analyze these specifications. JavaBIP specifications can also be analyzed [7,8], however, the main focus of JavaBIP is runtime coordination, which is not offered in [22]. Configuration logics [30] were proposed for the specification of architecture styles, which however, in their current form do not capture dynamic change.

7   Conclusion and Future Work

We presented an extension of the JavaBIP framework for coordination of software components that can register, deregister and pause at runtime. To handle this type of dynamicity, JavaBIP uses a macro-notation based on first-order interaction logic that allows specifying synchronization constraints on component types. This way, a developer is not required to know the exact number of components that need to be coordinated when specifying the synchronization constraints of a system. We introduced a notion of system validity that is used to start and stop the JavaBIP engine automatically at runtime depending on whether there are enough registered components in the system so that there is at least one possible interaction. In the previous, static JavaBIP implementation, developers had to manually start and stop the engine. Starting and stopping the engine in an automatic way helps optimize JavaBIP performance since it eliminates the engine's overhead in the case of an invalid system.

JavaBIP implements the principles of the BIP component framework rooted in rigorous operational semantics. Notice, however, that currently none of the other BIP engine implementations can handle dynamic insertion and deletion of components at runtime. The functionality of pausing a component at runtime increases the incrementality of the JavaBIP engine. In our previous, static implementation, the engine had to wait for all registered components to inform in each cycle before making any computations. As a result, a single component could introduce a long delay in the system execution. In the current implementation, when a component is paused, the engine does not wait for it to inform, but rather computes the set of enabled interaction in the system that involve only the non-paused components. JavaBIP is an open-source tool[6].

Future work includes increasing the incrementality of the engine in the following way: the engine does not have to wait for all non-paused components to inform but rather checks whether there is an enabled interaction among the components that have already informed and orders its execution. To check the enableness of interactions we plan to reuse the notion of validity graphs introduced in this paper and extend it with additional information on component ports. Additionally, we plan on extending the engine functionality to handle registration of new component types and synchronization patterns.

References

1. Agha, G.: Actors: A Model of Concurrent Computation in Distributed Systems. MIT Press, Cambridge (1986)
2. Akers, S.B.: Binary decision diagrams. IEEE Trans. Comput. **C-27**(6), 509–516 (1978)
3. Allen, R., Douence, R., Garlan, D.: Specifying and analyzing dynamic software architectures. In: Astesiano, E. (ed.) FASE 1998. LNCS, vol. 1382, pp. 21–37. Springer, Heidelberg (1998). doi:10.1007/BFb0053581
4. Arnold, A.: Synchronized behaviours of processes and rational relations. Acta Informatica **17**, 21–29 (1982)
5. Basu, A., Bensalem, S., Bozga, M., Combaz, J., Jaber, M., Nguyen, T.-H., Sifakis, J.: Rigorous component-based system design using the BIP framework. IEEE Softw. **28**(3), 41–48 (2011)
6. Basu, A., Bozga, M., Sifakis, J.: Modeling heterogeneous real-time components in BIP. In: 4th IEEE International Conference on Software Engineering and Formal Methods (SEFM 2006), pp. 3–12, September 2006, Invited talk
7. Bensalem, S., Bozga, M., Nguyen, T.-H., Sifakis, J.: D-Finder: a tool for compositional deadlock detection and verification. In: Bouajjani, A., Maler, O. (eds.) CAV 2009. LNCS, vol. 5643, pp. 614–619. Springer, Heidelberg (2009). doi:10.1007/978-3-642-02658-4_45
8. Bliudze, S., Cimatti, A., Jaber, M., Mover, S., Roveri, M., Saab, W., Wang, Q.: Formal verification of infinite-state BIP models. In: Finkbeiner, B., Pu, G., Zhang, L. (eds.) ATVA 2015. LNCS, vol. 9364, pp. 326–343. Springer, Cham (2015). doi:10.1007/978-3-319-24953-7_25
9. Bliudze, S., Mavridou, A., Szymanek, R., Zolotukhina, A.: Coordination of software components with BIP: application to OSGi. In: Proceedings of the 6th International Workshop on Modeling in Software Engineering, MiSE 2014, pp. 25–30. ACM, New York (2014)
10. Bliudze, S., Mavridou, A., Szymanek, R., Zolotukhina, A.: Exogenous coordination of concurrent software components with JavaBIP. Software: Practice and Experience (2017). Early view: http://dx.doi.org/10.1002/spe.2495
11. Bonakdarpour, B., Bozga, M., Jaber, M., Quilbeuf, J., Sifakis, J.: From high-level component-based models to distributed implementations. In: Proceedings of the Tenth ACM International Conference on Embedded Software, EMSOFT 2010, pp. 209–218. ACM, New York (2010)

---

[6] github.com/sbliudze/javabip-core, github.com/sbliudze/javabip-engine.

12. Bozga, M., Jaber, M., Maris, N., Sifakis, J.: Modeling dynamic architectures using Dy-BIP. In: Gschwind, T., De Paoli, F., Gruhn, V., Book, M. (eds.) SC 2012. LNCS, vol. 7306, pp. 1–16. Springer, Heidelberg (2012). doi:10.1007/978-3-642-30564-1_1

13. Bradbury, J.S., Cordy, J.R., Dingel, J., Wermelinger, M.: A survey of self-management in dynamic software architecture specifications. In: Proceedings of the 1st ACM SIGSOFT Workshop on Self-Managed Systems, WOSS 2004, pp. 28–33. ACM, New York (2004)

14. Bruni, R., Bucchiarone, A., Gnesi, S., Melgratti, H.: Modelling dynamic software architectures using typed graph grammars. Electron. Notes Theoret. Comput. Sci. **213**(1), 39–53 (2008)

15. Bruni, R., Melgratti, H., Montanari, U.: Behaviour, interaction and dynamics. In: Iida, S., Meseguer, J., Ogata, K. (eds.) Specification, Algebra, and Software. LNCS, vol. 8373, pp. 382–401. Springer, Heidelberg (2014). doi:10.1007/978-3-642-54624-2_19

16. Cámara, J., Salaün, G., Canal, C.: Composition and run-time adaptation of mismatching behavioural interfaces. J. Univ. Comput. Sci. **14**(13), 2182–2211 (2008)

17. Canal, C., Pimentel, E., Troya, J.M.: Specification and refinement of dynamic software architectures. In: Donohoe, P. (ed.) Software Architecture. ITIFIP, vol. 12, pp. 107–125. Springer, Boston (1999). doi:10.1007/978-0-387-35563-4_7

18. Clarke, D.: A basic logic for reasoning about connector reconfiguration. Fundamenta Informaticae **82**(4), 361–390 (2008)

19. Cuesta, C.E., de la Fuente, P., Barrio-Solárzano, M.: Dynamic coordination architecture through the use of reflection. In: Proceedings of the 2001 ACM Symposium on Applied Computing, pp. 134–140. ACM (2001)

20. Di Giusto, C., Stefani, J.-B.: Revisiting glue expressiveness in component-based systems. In: De Meuter, W., Roman, G.-C. (eds.) COORDINATION 2011. LNCS, vol. 6721, pp. 16–30. Springer, Heidelberg (2011). doi:10.1007/978-3-642-21464-6_2

21. Edelmann, R., Bliudze, S., Sifakis, J., Functional, B.I.P.: Embedding connectors in functional programming languages. J. Logical Algebraic Methods Program. (2017) (Under review)

22. Georgiadis, I., Magee, J., Kramer, J.: Self-organising software architectures for distributed systems. In: Proceedings of the First Workshop on Self-Healing Systems, pp. 33–38. ACM (2002)

23. Henrio, L., Madelaine, E., Zhang, M.: A theory for the composition of concurrent processes. In: Albert, E., Lanese, I. (eds.) FORTE 2016. LNCS, vol. 9688, pp. 175–194. Springer, Cham (2016). doi:10.1007/978-3-319-39570-8_12

24. Hirsch, D., Inverardi, P., Montanari, U.: Graph grammars and constraint solving for software architecture styles. In: Proceedings of the Third International Workshop on Software Architecture, pp. 69–72. ACM (1998)

25. Jackson, D.: Alloy: a lightweight object modelling notation. ACM Trans. Softw. Eng. Methodol. (TOSEM) **11**(2), 256–290 (2002)

26. Koehler, C., Costa, D., Proença, J., Arbab, F.: Reconfiguration of Reo connectors triggered by dataflow. ECEASST **10** (2008)

27. Krause, C., Maraikar, Z., Lazovik, A., Arbab, F.: Modeling dynamic reconfigurations in Reo using high-level replacement systems. Sci. Comput. Program. **76**(1), 23–36 (2011)

28. Le Métayer, D.: Describing software architecture styles using graph grammars. IEEE Trans. Softw. Eng. **24**(7), 521–533 (1998)

29. Magee, J., Kramer, J.: Dynamic structure in software architectures. ACM SIGSOFT Softw. Eng. Notes **21**(6), 3–14 (1996)

30. Mavridou, A., Baranov, E., Bliudze, S., Sifakis, J.: Configuration logics: modeling architecture styles. J. Logical Algebraic Methods Program. **86**(1), 2–29 (2017)
31. Mavridou, A., Rutz, V., Bliudze, S.: Coordination of dynamic software components with JavaBIP. Technical report (2017), https://arxiv.org/abs/1707.09716
32. Milner, R., Parrow, J., Walker, D.: A calculus of mobile processes, I. Inf. Comput. **100**(1), 1–40 (1992)
33. Papadopoulos, G.A., Arbab, F.: Configuration and dynamic reconfiguration of components using the coordination paradigm. Future Gener. Comput. Syst. **17**(8), 1023–1038 (2001)
34. Poizat, P., Salaün, G.: Adaptation of open component-based systems. In: Bonsangue, M.M., Johnsen, E.B. (eds.) FMOODS 2007. LNCS, vol. 4468, pp. 141–156. Springer, Heidelberg (2007). doi:10.1007/978-3-540-72952-5_9

A Formal Model of Parallel Execution on Multicore Architectures with Multilevel Caches

Shiji Bijo, Einar Broch Johnsen, Ka I Pun[✉], and Silvia Lizeth Tapia Tarifa

Department of Informatics, University of Oslo, Oslo, Norway
{shijib,einarj,violet,sltarifa}@ifi.uio.no

Abstract. The performance of software running on parallel or distributed architectures can be severely affected by the location of data. On shared memory multicore architectures, data movement between caches and main memory is driven by tasks executing in parallel on different cores and by a protocol to ensure cache coherence, such as MSI. This paper integrates MSI in a formal model to capture such data movement from an application perspective. We develop an executable model which integrates cache coherent data movement between different cache levels and main memory, for software described by task-level data access patterns. The proposed model is generic in the number of cache levels and cores, and abstracts from the concrete communication medium. We show that the model guarantees expected correctness properties for the MSI protocol, in particular data consistency. This paper further presents a proof of concept implementation of the proposed model in rewriting logic, which allows different choices for a program's underlying hardware architecture to be specified and compared.

1 Introduction

Multicore architectures enhance the performance of software applications by executing programs in parallel on multiple cores, and by exploiting a hierarchy of cache memory which allows quick access to recently used data, but comes at a price of managing multiple co-existing copies of the same data. The cost of accessing data from a core depends on where the data is located and how it is used by tasks executing on other cores. To fully benefit from multicore architectures, it is essential to understand how software applications interact with these architectures at runtime; i.e., we need to understand multicore architectures from the programmers' perspective. For example, the benefits from developing lock-free algorithms may be severely reduced by bad data locality and unexpected cache misses [18].

Software developers targeting multicore architectures need to answer questions about data locality, data access, and data movement: Is the data organized

---

Supported by the EU project FP7-612985 *UpScale: From Inherent Concurrency to Massive Parallelism through Type-based Optimizations* (www.upscale-project.eu) and the *SIRIUS Centre for Scalable Data Access* (www.sirius-labs.no).

J. Proença and M. Lumpe (Eds.): FACS 2017, LNCS 10487, pp. 58–77, 2017.
DOI: 10.1007/978-3-319-68034-7_4

in the most convenient way to allow efficient data access for the application? Are the organization and ordering of tasks optimal with respect to a given data layout? How does a given data layout fit with the target cache hierarchy? These questions are important for software quality, but they are difficult to answer in an intuitive and straightforward way. Formal models of program execution may help answer such questions, but models of parallel programs today generally abstract from caches in multicore architectures and only assume single copies of data in shared memory [9,14,16,34] (i.e., they assume that threads have direct access to memory). On the other hand, formal models of hardware architecture and consistency protocols, such as cache coherence, focus on low-level correctness, but completely abstract from the programming level [11,12,21,32,33]. Consequently, neither programming nor hardware models provide much guidance for software developers in making efficient use of cache memory. In the context of shared memory multicore computing, it seems interesting to integrate models of parallel program execution with models of hardware architecture. Such an integration opens for reasoning about data movement when parallel applications access data from shared memory multicore architectures.

To address the problem described above, our aim for this paper is to develop a formal model of parallel programs executing on *shared* memory multicore architectures with multilevel caches. For simplicity, we focus on programs specified in terms of their *data access patterns*, rather than on the programs themselves. These data access patterns describe how tasks running on a core interact with memory in terms of read and write accesses. The formalization is inspired by programming language semantics; we develop an operational semantics of parallel computation for these data access patterns, which accounts for data movement and data consistency in an architecture with many cores and associated multilevel caches.

The purpose of this work is not to evaluate the specifics of a concrete hardware architecture, but rather to formally describe program execution in a setting with multiple and consistent copies of the same data in shared memory and in caches. Consequently, we integrate a cache coherence protocol directly into the operational semantics of our formal model, while abstracting from the concrete communication medium (e.g., a bus or a ring). This protocol acts as an orchestrator between parallel executions on different cores, by restricting data access to the memory components of the shared memory architecture to ensure consistency. Cache coherence is orthogonal to weak memory models and associated program reordering [1]; in fact, most cache coherence protocols guarantee sequential consistency. Whereas work on weak memory models (e.g., [2]) focus on the possible values of program variables, our work completely abstracts from the data being manipulated. The presented model of multicore architecture with multilevel caches guarantees desirable properties for the program, such as the preservation of the program order for the data access patterns, the absence of data races, and that cores always access the most recent data value. The technical contributions of this paper are:

1. a formal, operational model of execution on multicore architectures with multilevel caches for tasks describing data access patterns with loops, choice and spawn;
2. correctness properties for this formal model, expressed as invariants over an arbitrary number of cores and an arbitrary number of multilevel caches; and
3. a proof of concept implementation of the model in the rewriting tool Maude [8].

This work is part of a line of research by the authors. Whereas previous work [3,4] studied the much simpler setting of statically given, purely sequential data access patterns and single-level caches, this paper addresses data access patterns with dynamically spawned tasks with loops and branching, and multilevel caches.

Paper overview. Section 2 briefly reviews background concepts on shared memory multicore architectures, Sect. 3 presents our abstract formal model of multicore architecture with multilevel caches and shared memory, Sect. 4 summarizes the proven correctness properties of this model, Sect. 5 presents a proof of concept implementation and an example, Sect. 6 discusses the related work, and Sect. 7 concludes the paper.

2 An Overview of Shared Memory Multicore Architectures

We briefly discuss basic concepts of multicore architectures, for further details see, e.g., [10,15,28,35]. The components of multicore architectures are parallel processing units called *cores* for executing tasks, a main memory for data storage, and memory units called *caches* which give the cores rapid access to recently used data. Each core has a hierarchically structured memory system, organized in terms of size, speed, and distance: the L_1 cache is the smallest, fastest, and closest to the core and the L_m cache is the slowest, largest, and furthest away. The memory systems of the cores are connected via a communication medium for inter-core communication with a given topology such bus, ring, or mesh. A *cache hit* expresses that data required by the core is found in its caches, a *cache miss* that the data needs to be fetched from main memory. The hierarchy can be generalized to architectures in which caches may be shared between cores.

Data is stored in main memory as *words*, each with a unique reference. Multiple continuous words constitute a *block*, which has a distinct memory address. Cache memory is organized in cache lines, which store memory blocks. During program execution, cores access data in memory as a word using its reference, but the cache fetches the entire memory block containing the required word and stores it in a cache line. Blocks in cache lines may need to be evicted to give space for newly fetched blocks. The choice of which block to evict depends on the cache line organization, the so-called *associativity*, and the *replacement policy*. In *k-way* set associative caches, cache memory is organized as sets of *k*-cache lines and a memory block can go anywhere in a particular set. *Fully associative* caches treat the entire cache memory as a single set. A *direct mapped* cache consists of singleton sets; thus, a particular block can only go to one specific cache line. If the set in which a new block should be placed is full, a block is evicted to free space using a replacement policy such as random, FIFO or LRU (Least Recently Used).

Multilevel caches can be organized in several ways. For *inclusive caches*, blocks in level i cache are also included in all lower level caches j ($j > i$). Consequently, the last-level cache contains blocks in all other caches in the hierarchy. For *exclusive caches*, it is guaranteed that data exists in at most one of the caches in the hierarchy. With *NINE* (non-inclusive non-exclusive), neither inclusive nor exclusive policy is enforced; i.e., memory blocks in a cache may or may not be in the corresponding lower-level caches.

A *memory consistency model* [1] for cache-based architectures combines a (weak or strong) local memory model with a cache coherence protocol. Cache coherence protocols ensure the consistency of data between the caches of different cores. The local memory model and the cache coherence protocol are traditionally completely orthogonal: a weak memory model may be built on top of a cache coherence protocol which (normally) guarantees sequential consistency between caches. The cost of sequential consistency is that writing to non-exclusive cache lines need to be broadcast. *Invalidation-based protocols* inform other affected caches when a core performs a write operation. The most common invalidation-based protocols are MSI and its extensions (e.g., MESI and MOESI). In MSI, a cache line can be in one of three states: modified, shared or invalid. A *modified* state indicates that the block in that cache line has the most recently updated data and that all other copies are *invalid* (including the copy in main memory), while a *shared* state indicates that all copies of the block have consistent data (including the copy in main memory). These protocols broadcast messages in the communication medium. Following the standard nomenclature, messages of the form *Rd* request read access to a memory block while messages of the form *RdX* request exclusive read access to a memory block (for writing purposes), and thereby invalidating other copies of the same block in other caches.

3   A Formal Model of Execution on Shared Memory Multicore Architectures

This section presents our formal model of program execution on shared memory multicore architectures with multilevel caches. We first discuss the abstractions introduced in the model, then its syntax, and finally the operational semantics of the formal model.

3.1   Abstractions in the Formal Model

We consider a model of multicore architectures with a communication medium that abstracts from concrete topologies but ensures cache coherency using the MSI protocol. The architecture is illustrated in Fig. 1a. A *node* consists of a core and its hierarchy of private caches. Each core in the model executes tasks scheduled from a shared task pool, which can easily be extended to a more advanced

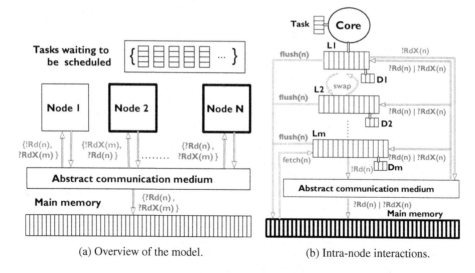

(a) Overview of the model.   (b) Intra-node interactions.

Fig. 1. The structure of the formal model of multicore architectures (Color figure online)

scheduler. To communicate with the other components, the node broadcasts request messages $!Rd(n)$ and $!RdX(n)$ via the medium to read or write to a block with address n, respectively.

The structure of a single node comprises a core with multiple levels of exclusive caches $L_1, L_2, \cdots, L_m$, as illustrated by Fig. 1b. Each cache L_i has a data instruction queue D_i for *flush* and *fetch* instructions, which move blocks of data from or to main memory or between caches. Red lines capture messages broadcast by the node to the others via the medium, blue lines capture messages received by main memory and by components in each node, and green lines capture data transfer between components.

To read data from a block n, the core looks for n by traversing its local caches in the hierarchical order (i.e., from the first level L_1 to the last level, here L_m). If we get a *cache miss*, the last-level cache broadcasts a *read request* $!Rd(n)$ via the communication medium to the other nodes and main memory. The last-level cache *fetches* the block when it is available in main memory. Eviction is required if the last-level cache is full. From a cache L_i, block n is propagated to the first level L_1 through intermediate caches. The block is transferred from L_i to L_{i-1} if the cache has free space; otherwise a block is selected from L_{i-1} and *swapped* with n in L_i. Writing to a block n is only allowed if it is in shared or modified state in the first-level cache, which then broadcasts an *invalidation request* $!RdX(m)$ through the medium to all other nodes, to obtain exclusive access.

Let $?Rd(n)$ and $?RdX(n)$ denote the reception of read and invalidation requests by a cache or by main memory (the blue lines in Fig. 1b); they are the duals of the broadcast requests discussed above. If a cache receives a read request $?Rd(n)$ and it has the block in modified state, the cache *flushes* the block to main memory (the green lines in Fig. 1b); if the cache receives an invalidation request $?RdX(n)$ and it has the block in shared state, the cache line will be *invalidated*; the requests are discarded otherwise. For simplicity, we abstract from the actual data stored in memory blocks, let blocks transfer between nodes via the main memory, and without compromising the validity of the model, we assume that a cache line has the same size as a memory block. We model read and invalidation requests in the communication medium to be instantaneous; this is justified by message transfer being an order of magnitude faster than data transfer, and by the focus of the work is on data movement. We can then match dual labels in a labelled transition system to coordinate messages in a transition, as commonly done in process algebra, abstracting from the concrete communication medium. By lifting this matching of dual labels to sets of labels, we capture a *true concurrency* execution model for an arbitrary number of cores in the proposed operational semantics.

3.2   The Syntax of Data Access Patterns and Runtime Configurations

The syntax of the formal model is shown in Fig. 2. A configuration *Config* consists of a main memory M, shared between multiple nodes with cores $\overline{CR}$ and caches $\overline{Ca}$, and a set of tasks $\overline{T}$ to be executed. A core CR with identifier Cid has runtime statements rst to be executed. A cache Ca has a memory M, an identifier Lev, and a sequence of data instructions dst to be performed. In a cache identifier $lev(Cid, Lid, flag)$, Cid indicates to which core the cache belongs, $Lid \in \mathbb{N}^+$ the level of the cache, and *flag* whether it is at the last level in the node. Lid is unique within each node. A memory $M : n \rightharpoonup st$ maps addresses n to status tags st. The status tags mo, sh, and inv refer to the three states in the MSI protocol, respectively. Note that blocks in main memory can only be in sh or inv state. The task table $Tb : T \rightharpoonup dap$ maps task identifiers T to *data access patterns dap*. These are sequences of basic operations **read**(r) and **write**(r) to read from and write to a memory reference r, **commit**(r) to flush r to main memory, and control flow statements $dap_1 \sqcap dap_2$ to select either dap_1 or dap_2 for execution, dap^* to repeat the execution of dap zero or many times, and **spawn**(T) to add dap to the pool of tasks to be scheduled, where dap is the data access pattern corresponding to task T in the task table. To ensure data consistency, the statement **commit** is used at the end of each tasks to flush the entire cache after task execution. Since the task table is statically given, we assume it is always available and not represent it explicitly in the configurations.

The cores execute *runtime statements rst*, which extend *dap* with the additional control statements **readBl**(r) and **writeBl**(r) to indicate that the core is blocked due to a cache miss. Each cache performs *data instructions dst*, which are sequences of **fetch**(n) to fetch a block n from the next level cache or from main memory, **flush**(n) to flush the modified copy of n to the main memory, and **flush** to flush all modified copies in the cache. The instruction **fetch**(n)

Syntactic categories.	Definitions.	
$Lid \in Int$	$Config$	$::= M \circ \overline{T} \circ \overline{Ca} \circ \overline{CR}$
$Cid \in CoreId$	$CR \in Core$	$::= Cid \bullet rst$
$n \in Address$	$Ca \in Cache$	$::= Lev \bullet M \bullet dst$
$T \in TaskId$	$Lev \in CacheId$	$::= lev(Cid, Lid, flag)$
$M \in Memory$	$st \in Status$	$::= \{mo, sh, inv\}$
$Tb \in TaskTable$	$rst \in RuntimeLang$	$::= dap \mid rst; rst \mid \mathbf{readBl}(r) \mid \mathbf{writeBl}(r)$
	$dap \in AccessPatterns$	$::= \varepsilon \mid dap; dap \mid \mathbf{read}(r) \mid \mathbf{write}(r) \mid \mathbf{commit}(r)$
		$\mid \mathbf{commit} \mid dap \sqcap dap \mid dap^* \mid \mathbf{skip} \mid \mathbf{spawn}(T)$
	$dst \in DataLang$	$::= \varepsilon \mid dst; dst \mid \mathbf{fetch}(n) \mid \mathbf{flush}(n) \mid \mathbf{fetchBl}(n)$
		$\mid \mathbf{flush}$

Fig. 2. Syntax for the formal model of multicore architectures, where over-bar denotes sets (e.g., $\overline{CR}$), n represents memory addresses and r references

is replaced by $\mathbf{fetchBl}(n)$ when the cache is suspended, waiting for block n to arrive in the next level cache.

3.3 An Operational Semantics of Parallel Execution on Multicore Architectures

We define a parallel model of task execution, which expresses true concurrency in the multicore setting, by means of a structural operational semantics (SOS) [29], and use labels on transitions to synchronize read and invalidation requests. The semantics consists of a local and a global level. The *local level* captures local transitions in main memory, task execution in each core and intra-node communications to ensure data consistency between different components. The *global level* captures transitions involving data transfer between caches and main memory, broadcasting of messages, scheduling of tasks, and enforces data consistency by restricting how labels match in the composition rules. Multiple nodes may request different memory blocks at the same time by parallel instantaneous broadcast, using possibly empty sets of labels. The formal syntax for the label mechanism is as follows:

$$W ::= \,!Rd(n) \mid !RdX(n) \quad Q ::= \,?Rd(n) \mid ?RdX(n)$$
$$S ::= \emptyset \mid \{W\} \mid S \cup S \quad R ::= \emptyset \mid \{Q\} \mid R \cup R$$

where S and R represent possibly empty sets of sent and received requests, respectively.

Let $Config \xrightarrow{*} Config'$ denote an execution starting from $Config$ which produces $Config'$ by repeatedly applying rules at the global level, which in turn apply rules at the local level for each component. In an *initial configuration*, all blocks in main memory M have status tag sh, all cores are idle (i.e., rst is ε), all caches are empty and have no data instructions in dst, and the task pool in $\overline{T}$ names a single task, representing the main block of a program. A configuration $Config'$ is *reachable* if there is an execution $Config \xrightarrow{*} Config'$ starting from an initial configuration *Config*. For brevity, we do not discuss the full operational semantics here, but focus on a representative subset of the rules; the full semantics can be found in the accompanying technical report [5].

Local Semantics. The local semantics reflects the execution of statements, the interactions between caches in a node, and how the local state changes in each cache line by following the finite state controller that enforces the MSI protocol during the execution. A representative selection of local transition rules for a node and for main memory is given in Figs. 3 and 4. Let the function $addr(r)$ return the block address n containing reference r, the predicate $first(Lev)$ is true when Lev is the first level cache, $last(Lev)$ is true when Lev is at the last level, and the function $status(M, n)$ returns the status of block n in map M.

$$(\text{PRRD}_1)$$

$$\frac{first(Lev) = true \quad Cid(Lev) = c \quad n = addr(r) \quad status(M,n) = sh \vee status(M,n) = mo}{(Lev \bullet M \bullet dst) \circ (c \bullet \textbf{read}(r); rst\ ) \rightarrow (Lev \bullet M \bullet dst) \circ (c \bullet\ rst\ )}$$

$$(\text{PRRD}_2)$$

$$\frac{first(Lev) = true \quad Cid(Lev) = c \quad n = addr(r) \quad status(M,n) = inv \vee n \notin dom(M)}{(Lev \bullet\ M \bullet dst\ ) \circ (c \bullet \textbf{read}(r); rst\ ) \rightarrow (Lev \bullet\ M[n \mapsto \bot] \bullet dst; \textbf{fetch}(n)\ ) \circ (c \bullet\ \textbf{readBl}(r); rst\ )}$$

$$(\text{PRWR}_2)$$

$$\frac{first(Lev) = true \quad Cid(Lev) = c \quad n = addr(r) \quad status(M,n) = sh}{(Lev \bullet\ M\ \bullet dst) \circ (c \bullet \textbf{write}(r); rst\ ) \xrightarrow{!RdX(n)} (Lev \bullet\ M[n \mapsto mo]\ \bullet dst) \circ (c \bullet\ rst\ )}$$

Fig. 3. Local semantics of task execution in a core and the first level cache

Figure 3 shows a representative selection of transition steps involving a core and its first level cache. Reading reference r succeeds in rule PRRD_1 if the block containing r is available in the first-level cache. Otherwise, rule PRRD_2 adds a **fetch**(n) instruction to the end of the data instructions dst of the first level cache and blocks further execution of the core with the statement **readBl**(r). Execution may proceed once the block n is copied into the cache with status sh. Repeated invalidation may occur if the cache line gets invalidated by another core while the core is still blocked, which entails reapplying rule PRRD_2. Writing to reference r succeeds if the associated memory block has mo status in the first-level cache. If the cache line is in shared state, the core broadcasts $!RdX(n)$ request, which appears as a label in rule PRWR_2, to get exclusive access. If the cache line is invalid (or the block is not in the cache), the core needs to fetch the block from main memory and execution is blocked by the statement **writeBl**(r), similar to reading in rule PRRD_2. The rules for the other rst statements are standard.

Figure 4 shows rules which are local to the cache hierarchy: rules LC-HIT_1 and LC-MISS_1 capture the interactions between two adjacent levels of caches,

$$(\text{LC-Hit}_1)$$

$$Cid(Lev_i) = Cid(Lev_j) \quad status(M_j, n) = s_j \quad s_j \in \{sh, mo\}$$
$$\frac{Lid(Lev_j) = Lid(Lev_i) + 1 \quad select(M_i, n) = n_i \quad status(M_i, n_i) = s_i}{}$$

$$(Lev_i \bullet \; M_i \bullet \mathbf{fetch}(n); dst_i \;) \circ (Lev_j \bullet \; M_j \; \bullet dst_j) \rightarrow$$
$$(Lev_i \bullet \; M_i[n_i \mapsto \perp, n \mapsto s_j] \bullet dst_i \;) \circ (Lev_j \bullet \; M_j[n \mapsto \perp, n_i \mapsto s_i] \; \bullet dst_j)$$

$$(\text{LC-Miss}_1)$$

$$\frac{status(M_j, n) = inv \vee n \notin dom(M_j) \quad Lid(Lev_j) = Lid(Lev_i) + 1 \quad Cid(Lev_i) = Cid(Lev_j)}{}$$

$$(Lev_i \bullet M_i \bullet \; \mathbf{fetch}(n); dst_i \;) \circ (Lev_j \bullet \; M_j \bullet dst_j \;) \rightarrow$$
$$(Lev_i \bullet M_i \bullet \; \mathbf{fetchBl}(n); dst_i \;) \circ (Lev_j \bullet \; M_j[n \mapsto \perp] \bullet dst_j; \mathbf{fetch}(n) \;)$$

$$(\text{LLC-Miss})$$

$$\frac{last(Lev) = true \quad status(M, n) = inv \vee n \notin dom(M)}{}$$

$$(Lev \bullet M \bullet \; \mathbf{fetch}(n); dst \;) \xrightarrow{!Rd(n)} (Lev \bullet M[n \mapsto \perp] \bullet \; \mathbf{fetchBl}(n); dst \;)$$

(Inv-One-Line)	(Flush-One-Line)
$status(M, n) = sh$	$status(M, n) = mo$

$$Lev \bullet \; M \; \bullet dst \xrightarrow{?RdX(n)} Lev \bullet \; M[n \mapsto inv] \; \bullet dst \qquad Lev \bullet M \bullet \; dst \xrightarrow{?Rd(n)} Lev \bullet M \bullet \; \mathbf{flush}(n); dst$$

Fig. 4. Local semantics between caches in a core

while the rest describes the transition steps local to a cache. Rule LC-Hit$_1$ captures the case where cache Lev_i needs to fetch block n and finds it in sh or mo state in the next level cache. The function $select(M_i, n)$ determines the address where the block should be placed, based on a cache associativity and a replacement policy. If eviction is needed, block n from Lev_j will be swapped with the selected block in Lev_i in rule LC-Hit$_1$. Otherwise, n is transferred to Lev_i and removed from Lev_j since the model considers exclusive caches. Setting a block n to $\perp$ in memory M, denoted as $M[n \mapsto \perp]$, means that n is removed from M. Rule LC-Miss$_1$ shows how fetch instructions are propagated to lower levels in the cache hierarchy. If the block cannot be found in any local cache, we have a *cache miss*: execution is blocked by the instruction $\mathbf{fetchBl}(n)$, and a read request $!Rd(n)$ will be broadcast, represented by a label in rule LLC-Miss.

If a cache receives an invalidation request $?RdX(n)$ for a block n and has this block with status sh, the cache changes the status to inv in rule Inv-One-Line. If a cache receives a read request $?Rd(n)$ and has block n with status mo, rule Flush-One-Line appends a $\mathbf{flush}$-instruction to dst to prioritize the flushing of the modified copy (to avoid deadlock caused by cyclic waiting for modified data to be flushed to main memory). The received messages are ignored in all other cases. The main memory ignores read requests, but responds to invalidate requests by changing the status of a block to inv as in the rule Inv-Main-Memory, defined as $M \xrightarrow{?RdX(n)} M[n \mapsto inv]$.

Global Semantics. The global semantics represents the abstract communication medium: it captures interactions between different components in the configuration and ensures data coherency between caches and main memory. A representative selection of global transition rules is given in Fig. 5. Rules FLUSH and FETCH$_1$ capture the data movement between a cache and the main memory. A cache at any level can flush data to main memory. Rule FLUSH updates a block in main memory with the modified copy in the cache and sets the status to *sh* both in the cache and main memory. However, only the last-level cache can fetch data from main memory. Rule FETCH$_1$ copies the data to the cache if no eviction is required. If eviction is needed and the block chosen by the *select* function has status *mo*, it will be flushed before the requested block can be fetched.

The remaining rules in Fig. 5 handle interactions between different components in the architecture. Rule SYNCH$_1$ captures global synchronization for a non-empty set S. In this rule, different read and invalidation requests are being broadcast, and to maintain data consistency, the different components must process these requests at the same time. Note that to apply rule SYNCH$_1$, S must contain at most one request per address, which is ensured by the predicate $\bigcap allAddrIn(S) = \emptyset$, and the set of receiving labels R is generated as the *dual* of S. For synchronization, the transition is decomposed into a premise for main memory with labels R, and another premise for the cores with labels S.

$$
\frac{\text{(FLUSH)} \qquad status(M_j,n) = mo}{M_i \circ (Lev \bullet \ M_j \ \bullet \mathbf{flush}(n); dst) \to \ M_i[n \mapsto sh] \circ (Lev \bullet \ M_j[n \mapsto sh] \ \bullet dst)}
$$

$$
\frac{\text{(FETCH}_1\text{)} \qquad last(Lev) = true \quad select(M_j,n) = n \quad status(M_i,n) = sh}{M_i \circ (Lev \bullet \ M_j \ \bullet \mathbf{fetchBl}(n); dst) \to \ M_i \circ (Lev \bullet \ M_j[n \mapsto sh] \ \bullet dst)}
$$

$$
\frac{\text{(SYNCH}_1\text{)} \quad S \neq \emptyset \quad \bigcap allAddrIn(S) = \emptyset \quad R = dual(S) \quad M \xrightarrow{R} M' \quad \overline{Ca} \circ \overline{CR} \xrightarrow{S} \overline{Ca'} \circ \overline{CR'}}{M \circ \overline{T} \circ \overline{Ca} \circ \overline{CR} \xrightarrow{S} M' \circ \overline{T} \circ \overline{Ca'} \circ \overline{CR'}}
$$

$$
\frac{\text{(ASYNCH)} \quad \overline{CR} = \overline{CR}_1 \uplus \overline{CR}_2 \uplus \overline{CR}_3 \quad \overline{Ca} = \overline{Ca}_1 \uplus \overline{Ca}_2 \uplus \overline{Ca}_3 \uplus \overline{Ca}_4}{M \circ \overline{Ca}_1 \to M' \circ \overline{Ca'}_1 \quad \overline{Ca}_2 \to \overline{Ca'}_2 \quad \overline{T} \circ \overline{CR}_2 \to \overline{T'} \circ \overline{CR'}_2}
$$
$$
\frac{belongs(\overline{Ca}_3, \overline{CR}_3) \quad \overline{Ca}_3 \circ \overline{CR}_3 \to \overline{Ca'}_3 \circ \overline{CR'}_3}{\overline{CR'} = \overline{CR}_1 \cup \overline{CR'}_2 \cup \overline{CR'}_3 \quad \overline{Ca'} = \overline{Ca'}_1 \cup \overline{Ca'}_2 \cup \overline{Ca'}_3 \cup \overline{Ca}_4}
$$
$$
M \circ \overline{T} \circ \overline{Ca} \circ \overline{CR} \xrightarrow{\emptyset} M' \circ \overline{T'} \circ \overline{Ca'} \circ \overline{CR'}
$$

$$
\frac{\text{(SYNCH}_2\text{)} \quad belongs(\overline{Ca}_1, \overline{CR}_1) \quad belongs(\overline{Ca}_2, \overline{CR}_2) \quad S = S_1 \uplus S_2 \quad R_1 = dual(S_1) \quad R_2 = dual(S_2)}{\overline{Ca}_1 \circ \overline{CR}_1 \xrightarrow{S_1 \cup R_2 \cup R} \overline{Ca'}_1 \circ \overline{CR'}_1 \quad \overline{Ca}_2 \circ \overline{CR}_2 \xrightarrow{S_2 \cup R_1 \cup R} \overline{Ca'}_2 \circ \overline{CR'}_2}
$$
$$
\overline{Ca}_1 \circ \overline{CR}_1 \circ \overline{Ca}_2 \circ \overline{CR}_2 \xrightarrow{S \cup R} \overline{Ca'}_1 \circ \overline{CR'}_1 \circ \overline{Ca'}_2 \circ \overline{CR'}_2
$$

$$
\frac{\text{(TASK-SPAWN)} \quad \overline{T'} = \overline{T} \cup \{T\} \quad \overline{T'} \circ \overline{CR} \to \overline{T''} \circ \overline{CR'}}{\overline{T} \circ \overline{CR} \circ (\ Cid \bullet \mathbf{spawn}(T); dap\ ) \to \ \overline{T''} \circ \overline{CR'} \circ (\ Cid \bullet dap\ )}
$$

$$
\frac{\text{(TASK-SCHEDULER)} \quad \overline{T'} = \overline{T} \backslash \{T\} \quad dap = Tb(T) \quad \overline{T'} \circ \overline{CR} \to \overline{T''} \circ \overline{CR'}}{\overline{T} \circ \overline{CR} \circ (\ Cid \bullet \varepsilon\ ) \to \ \overline{T''} \circ \overline{CR'} \circ (\ Cid \bullet dap; \mathbf{commit}\ )}
$$

Fig. 5. Global semantics for cache coherent multicore architectures. The disjoint union operator $\uplus$ is defined as $X_1 \uplus X_2 = X_1 \cup X_2$ such that $X_1 \cap X_2 = \emptyset$

Rule SYNCH-2 distributes labels over cores by recursively decomposing S into sets of sending and receiving labels for sets of cores $\overline{CR}_1$ and $\overline{CR}_2$, such that each set eventually contains at most one W label (either $!Rd(n)$ or $!RdX(n)$) to match transitions in the local rules. The predicate $belongs(\overline{Ca}, \overline{CR})$ expresses that any cache in $\overline{Ca}$ belongs to exactly one of the cores in $\overline{CR}$. The recursive decomposition of S repeats until the dual labels have been generated for each single node. The rule ensures that the sender of a message W does not receive its dual Q. Rule ASYNCH captures parallel transitions when the label set is empty. These transitions can be local to individual nodes, parallel memory accesses, or scheduling of new tasks. TASK-SPAWN adds a new task identifier to the task queue and TASK-SCHEDULER looks up in the task table with the task identifier T and schedules the corresponding task to a core. Adding the statement **commit** to the end of the scheduled task ensures that all modified data is flushed before the next task is executed on the same core. Note that parallel spawning/scheduling in one transition is allowed by rules ASYNCH and TASK-SCHEDULER.

4   Correctness of the Model

For the proposed model, we consider standard correctness properties for data consistency and cache coherency, based on the literature [10,36], including the preservation of program order in each core, absence of data races and no access to stale data. The preservation of these properties by our semantics ensures that the model correctly captures cache coherent data movement triggered by the underlying parallel architecture with any number of cores and caches, using our formalization of the MSI protocol for data consistency. For brevity, the full proofs have been omitted in this paper, and can be found in the accompanying technical report [5].

To formulate and prove these properties, we extend the syntax of Sect. 3.2 with monitoring information. For *data consistency*, the memory mapping M is extended with version numbers k, therefore $M : n \rightharpoonup \langle k, st \rangle$ such that k is incremented every time there is a **flush** operation in n. For *program order*, we add local histories h to the cores, which log all successful read and write operations executed so far by the current task; therefore, the syntax of a core is modified to $(c \bullet rst) : h$, expressing that the core with identifier c is executing the task rst starting after history h. The history h is extended in the semantics by the rules which correspond to successful operations. The syntax of the global configuration is also extended with global history H as $M \circ \overline{T} \circ \overline{Ca} \circ \overline{CR} : H$, where H records the concurrent executions in all cores $\overline{CR}$ in the architecture in terms of a sequence of sets of successful operations. The monitoring extensions do not influence execution in the operational semantics; i.e., the applicability of the rules is not affected by these extensions (the details are omitted for brevity, see [5]).

We now formalize the denotational meaning of the *rst*-statements of our syntax, in terms of sets of local histories. Let ϵ denote the empty history, ";" the concatenation operator, and   the reflexive prefix relation on histories.

Let $R(c,n)$ and $W(c,n)$ denote successful read and write operations to address n by core c, respectively.

Definition 1. *Let c be a core identifier and let $addr(r) = n$. The denotational meaning $[\![rst]\!]_c$ of a task rst is defined inductively as follows:*

$$[\![\textbf{read}(r)]\!]_c = \{R(c,n)\}$$
$$[\![\textbf{readBl}(r)]\!]_c = \{R(c,n)\}$$
$$[\![\textbf{write}(r)]\!]_c = \{W(c,n)\}$$
$$[\![\textbf{writeBl}(r)]\!]_c = \{W(c,n)\}$$
$$[\![(dap_1 \sqcap dap_2)]\!]_c = [\![dap_1]\!]_c \cup [\![dap_2]\!]_c$$
$$[\![(rst_1; rst_2)]\!]_c = \{\tau_1; \tau_2 | \tau_1 \in [\![rst_1]\!]_c, \tau_2 \in [\![rst_2]\!]_c\}$$

$$[\![\textbf{commit}(r)]\!]_c = \{\epsilon\}$$
$$[\![\textbf{commit}]\!]_c = \{\epsilon\}$$
$$[\![\textbf{skip}]\!]_c = \{\epsilon\}$$
$$[\![\textbf{spawn}(T)]\!]_c = \{\epsilon\}$$
$$[\![dap^*]\!]_c = [\![dap; dap^*]\!]_c \cup [\![\textbf{skip}]\!]_c$$

Intuitively, $[\![rst]\!]_c$ reflects the possible program orders in terms of read and write accesses when executing *rst* directly on main memory. The following lemma and corollary show that executions in a core preserve this program order.

Lemma 1. *If $(c \bullet rst) : \epsilon \to^* (c \bullet rst') : h$, then $\{h; \tau \mid \tau \in [\![rst']\!]_c\} \subseteq [\![rst]\!]_c$.*

Proof (sketch). Starting with an empty history ϵ, $(c \bullet rst) : \epsilon \to^* (c \bullet rst') : h$ describes a core c executing *rst* reaches *rst'* with history h by making zero or more transition steps, where h is a sequence of successful read and write access generated during the execution. The proof is by induction on the transition steps local in a core, partially captured in Fig. 3.   □

Corollary 1 (Program order). *If $(c \bullet rst) : h_1 \to^* (c \bullet rst') : h_1; h_2$, where h_2 is the sequence of events produced by the transition step(s) from rst to rst', then $h_2 h$ for some $h \in [\![rst]\!]_c$.*

Proof (sketch). Since h_2 is the sequence of events produced by the transition step(s) from *rst* to *rst'*, we get $\{h_2; \tau \mid \tau \in [\![rst']\!]_c\} \subseteq [\![rst]\!]_c$ by Lemma 1. Thus, $h_2 h$ for some $h \in [\![rst]\!]_c$.   □

Corollary 1 establishes the local program order of the operations of each individual core. Hence, the model's formalization of the MSI protocol preserves *sequential consistency* [19] in the sense that the result of any execution on the proposed model of multicore architectures is equivalent to the result of executing the operations of all cores in some sequential order. The next lemma captures the absence of data races when accessing a block from main memory.

Lemma 2 (No data races). *Let Ca_x be the cache $(Lev_x \bullet M_x \bullet dst_x)$. The conjunction of the following properties holds for all reachable configurations $M \circ \overline{T} \circ \overline{Ca} \circ \overline{CR} : H$:*

(a) $\forall n \in dom(M).(status(M,n) = inv \Leftrightarrow \exists\ Ca_i \in \overline{Ca}.\ status(M_i, n) = mo)$

(b) $\forall n \in dom(M).\ (status(M,n) = inv \Leftrightarrow (\exists\ Ca_i \in \overline{Ca}.\ status(M_i, n) = mo)$
$\qquad \wedge \forall\ Ca_j \in \overline{Ca} \backslash Ca_i\ .\ (status(M_j, n) = inv\ \vee n \notin dom(M_j)))$

(c) $\forall n \in dom(M).\ status(M,n) = sh \Leftrightarrow \forall\ Ca_i \in \overline{Ca}.\ status(M_i, n) \neq mo$

(d) $\forall\ Ca_i \in \overline{Ca}\ , \forall n \in dom(M_i).\ (status(M_i, n) = sh \Rightarrow status(M,n) = sh)$

Proof (sketch). The lemma can be proven by showing that these properties are invariants preserved by all transition steps:

$$M \circ \overline{T} \circ \overline{Ca} \circ \overline{CR} : H \xrightarrow{S} M' \circ \overline{T}' \circ \overline{Ca}' \circ \overline{CR}' : H' \tag{1}$$

where S is a set of sending messages, handled by ASYNCH, SYNCH$_1$ and SYNCH$_2$ in Fig. 5. Remember that the caches are exclusive in each core, and in order to apply SYNCH$_1$, S must contain at most one message for each block address n. The proof proceeds by case distinction on the rules for the transition steps. □

Lemma 2 ensures that there is at most one modified copy of a memory block among the cores. This guarantees single write access and parallel read accesses to memory blocks. The next lemma shows that shared copies of a memory block in different cores always have the same version number. Let function $version(M, n)$ return the version number of block address n in M.

Lemma 3 (Consistent shared copies). *Let $M \circ \overline{T} \circ \overline{Ca} \circ \overline{CR} : H$ be a reachable configuration and assume that $status(M, n) = sh$. If $(Lev_i \bullet M_i \bullet dst_i) \in \overline{Ca}$ such that $status(M_i, n) = sh$ for any cache, then $version(M, n) = version(M_i, n)$.*

Proof (sketch). The invariant trivially holds for transition rules that are for two caches residing in the same core, or local in either a single cache or the main memory as the transitions do not modify the version number of a block address. The proof then proceeds by cases for the transition steps dealing with fetching/flushing a memory block from/to the main memory by a cache, e.g., the rules FLUSH and FETCH$_1$ in Fig. 5. □

To show that cores in our formal model never access stale values in a memory block, we first define *the most recent value* of a memory block as follows:

Definition 2 (Most recent value). *Let $M \circ \overline{T} \circ \overline{Ca} \circ \overline{CR} : H$ be a global configuration, n a memory location, and $Ca_i \in \overline{Ca}$ a cache such that $Ca_i = (Lev_i \bullet M_i \bullet dst_i)$. Then $M_i(n)$ has the most recent value if the following holds:*

(a) If $M_i(n) = \langle k, sh \rangle$, then $M(n) = \langle k, sh \rangle$
    and $\forall (Lev_j \bullet M_j \bullet dst_j) \in \overline{Ca} \backslash Ca_i. status(M_j, n) = sh \Rightarrow M_j(n) = \langle k, sh \rangle$.
(b) If $status(M_i, n) = mo$, then $status(M, n) = inv$
    and $\forall (Lev_j \bullet M_j \bullet dst_j) \in \overline{Ca} \backslash Ca_i. status(M_j, n) = inv$.

With Lemma 3 and Definition 2, we can show that if a core succeeds to access a memory block, it will always get the most recent value.

Lemma 4 (No access to stale data). *Let $M \circ \overline{T} \circ \overline{Ca} \circ \overline{CR} : H$ be a reachable configuration such that $CR_i = (c_i \bullet rst_i) : h_i$ for $CR_i \in \overline{CR}$, $Ca_i = (Lev_i \bullet M_i \bullet dst_i)$ for $Ca_i \in \overline{Ca}$ and $belongs(Ca_i, CR_i)$. Consider a block address n and an event $e \in \{R(c_i, n), W(c_i, n)\}$.*

If $Ca_i \circ CR_i : h_i \to Ca_i' \circ CR_i' : (h_i; e)$ or $Ca_i \circ CR_i : h_i \xrightarrow{!RdX(n)} Ca_i' \circ CR_i' : (h_i; e)$, then $M_i(n)$ has the most recent value.

Proof (sketch). For the core CR_i to make *successful* read or write accesses to block address n in its local cache (i.e., to generate an event $R(c_i, n)$ or $W(c_i, n)$), CR_i applies the rules which capture the interactions between the core and its first level cache. The proof therefore proceeds by cases for these rules, a subset of which is shown in Fig. 3.

Consider, for example, the rule PRRD$_1$, where the status of n is either *mo* or *sh*. If $status(M_i, n) = mo$, it follows from Lemma 2(a) and (b) that $M_i(n)$ has the most recent copy according to Definition 2(b). If $M_i(n) = \langle k, sh \rangle$, it follows from Lemma 2(d) that $status(M, n) = sh$, and consequently from Lemma 2(c) that $\forall Ca_j \in \overline{Ca}.\ status(M_j, n) \neq mo$ where $Ca_j = (Lev_j \bullet M_j \bullet dst_j)$. Then we need to consider all caches $Lev_g \bullet M_g \bullet dst_g \in \overline{Ca}$ where $status(M_g, n) = sh$. From Lemma 3, we get $version(M_i, n) = k = version(M, n) = version(M_g, n)$, which satisfies Definition 2(a). This concludes the case. The other rules can be proven analogously.   □

5 Proof of Concept Implementation

To show the proposed model executable and to observe the behavior of different configurations, we have developed a proof of concept implementation[1] in Maude [8], a rewriting logic [24]. The Maude framework allows us to build an executable implementation of the operational semantics where transition rules are implemented as conditional rewrite rules of the form crl [*label*]: $t \to t'$ if *cond*, which transforms a term which matches a pattern t into a term of the corresponding pattern t', and as conditional equations of the form ceq $t = t'$ if *cond* for modelling the instantaneous communication of the label mechanism and the implementation of different auxiliary functions. The main differences and challenges between our operational semantics and the Maude implementation of the model are rather technical: while the former is not explicit with respect to parameters (e.g., the number of cores and caches, the size of caches, cache associativity, replacement policies and memory layout), the latter requires them to be explicit such that the model with a particular configuration, containing an explicit parallel architecture and a number of parallel tasks that are specified by the user, can be executed. This enables behavior of various configurations to be observed and compared. Another important difference is that while our semantics captures true concurrency by using the label mechanism, the Maude framework only allows interleaving. Therefore, one parallel and global step in the semantics will be translated into one or more interleaving steps in the Maude proof of concept implementation. Such translation does not affect the properties discussed in Sect. 4.

The proof of concept implementation in Maude is complementary to the proposed semantics because it allows specifying and comparing configurations in which the design choices for the underlying hardware architecture are different, such as the number of cores, cache levels, the data layout in main memory,

---

[1] The proof of concept implementation in Maude and the complete example scenarios can be downloaded from http://folk.uio.no/shijib/multilevel.zip.

the cache associativity and replacement policy. Exploring such design decisions is beneficial for the development of software for multicore systems, where hardware features and data layout influence data movement, and consequently the performance of an application. Using a simple example, we illustrate how to observe the impact of the number of caches and the data layout on data movement, captured by weighted penalties associated with accessing data from memory other than the first level cache.

```
task T1{(read(r0);read(r5);write(r10);read(r15);write(r20);read(r25);read(r30);write(r35);
        read(r40);write(r45);read(r50);write(r55);write(r60);read(r65);write(r70);read(r75);
        write(r80);read(r85);write(r3);read(r8);write(r13);read(r18);write(r23);write(r28);
        write(r4);read(r9);write(r14);read(r19);write(r24);read(r29);read(r30);write(r85);
        read(r30);write(r40);read(r30);write(r40);write(r8);read(r3);write(r8);read(r3);
        write(r28); write(r23))*}

task T2{(read(r1);read(r6);read(r11);write(r16);read(r21);write(r26);read(r31);read(r36);
        write(r41);read(r46);write(r51);read(r56);read(r61);read(r66);write(r71);read(r76);
        write(r81);read(r86);read(r33);write(r38);read(r43);write(r48);write(r53);read(r58);
        read(r34);write(r39);read(r44);write(r49);read(r54);write(r59);read(r33);write(r38);
        read(r33);write(r38);write(r53);read(r58);read(r11);write(r16);read(r11);write(r16);
        write(r21);write(r26);read(r71);read(r66);write(r61);write(r16))*}

task T3{(read(r2);write(r7);read(r12);write(r17);read(r22);read(r27);write(r32);read(r37);
        write(r42);read(r47);read(r52);read(r57);read(r62);write(r67);read(r72);read(r77);
        write(r82);read(r87);write(r63);read(r68);write(r73);write(r78);read(r83);write(r88);
        write(r64);read(r69);write(r74);write(r79);read(r84);read(r89);write(r32);read(r37);
        write(r42);read(r47);read(r52);read(r57);read(r67);read(r62);read(r67);read(r62);
        read(r77);read(r82);read(r63);read(r47);read(r63);write(r87))*}

main{spawn(T1);spawn(T2);spawn(T3)}
```

Fig. 6. An example of the data access patterns of a program

Example: Observing the Impact of Multilevel Caches and Data Layout
Consider a program that has been abstracted into the data access patterns shown in Fig. 6. We want to compare different scenarios for running this program, using our proof of concept implementation. We consider three architectures with three cores C1, C2 and C3, varying in the number of caches per core. We are going to observe a parallel execution where C1, C2 and C3 execute the tasks T1, T2 and T3, respectively, and consider nine scenarios in which for each of the three architectures, there are three different data layouts. For simplicity, we here consider the results after running the loop of each task a finite number of times, in this case, 20.

In the first architecture, we have a single level cache L1 in each core; in the second architecture, we have two levels of cache L1, L2, as depicted in Fig. 7; and in the third architecture, we have three levels of cache L1, L2, L3. To easily compare the data access in the different levels of cache and in main memory, we associate weighted penalties to accesses from different levels of memory. For simplicity in this example, we use order of magnitude differences and associate penalties 1,10,100, and 1000 with accesses from L1, L2, L3 and main memory, respectively. Cache associativity has been set up as direct mapped, 2-way

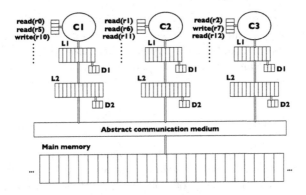

Fig. 7. An example of a parallel architecture with 3 cores and 2 level caches.

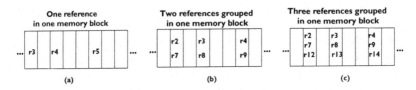

Fig. 8. Different data layouts to be setup in the example

associativity and 3-way associativity for L1, L2, L3, respectively. We additionally consider three different data layouts, depicted in Fig. 8. In the first layout (Fig. 8a) the tasks need to access different memory blocks for each reference, in the second (Fig. 8b) we group two references together in one block, and in the third (Fig. 8c) we group three references together.

Figure 9 summarises the results of executing the model in the Maude proof of concept implementation, for the nine considered scenarios. Observe that when we have spread data, that is, the different references reside in different memory blocks, the scenarios where cores have a single level of cache need to perform many evictions and fetch operations to access data from main memory. This increases the access time, as reflected by the accumulated the penalty.

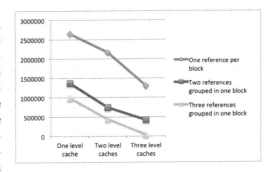

Fig. 9. Accumulated penalties of the nine different scenarios

In the scenarios where cores have three levels of cache, the penalty is substantially lower, although the access patterns are the same as the scenarios of single level caches. This is because it requires fewer evictions and operations for the cores to fetch or flush data from or to main memory, although there are still penalties from swapping data between the different cache levels. Thus, the scenarios in the example confirm the expected behavior of the model proposed in this paper, and we can observe the impact of data layout on data movement and the relation between data movement and the number of caches.

6   Related Work

Work on analysis of multicore architectures typically include simulation of cache coherence protocols and formal techniques analyzing their correctness. Simulation tools for cache coherence protocols evaluate their performance and efficiency on different architectures (e.g., gems [22] and gem5 [6]). These tools perform evaluations of, e.g., the cache hit/miss ratio and response time, by running benchmark programs written as low-level read and write instructions to memory. Advanced simulators such as Graphite [25] and Sniper [7] run programs on distributed clusters to simulate executions on multicore architectures with thousands of cores, where the simulations do not consider the data movements in the architecture. In contrast, our work provides a formal model capturing the interactions that trigger data transfer between different components, and shows the potential impacts on such movement with respect to data layout and the number of caches by a proof of concept implementation of the model in Maude. The worst-case response times of concurrent programs running on multicore architectures with shared caches can also be analyzed [20].

Both operational and axiomatic formal models have been used to capture the impact of parallel executions on shared memory under relaxed memory models. They include abstract calculi [9], memory models for programming languages such as Java [16], and machine-level instruction sets for concrete processors such as POWER [21,32] and x86 [33], and for programs executing under total store order (TSO) architectures [14,34]. This work on weak memory models abstracts from caches, and is as such largely orthogonal to our work which does not consider the reordering of source-level syntax.

Cache coherence protocols have also been analyzed in the setting of automata, and (parametrized) model checking (e.g., [11,27,30]) has been used to abstract from a specific number of cores when proving the correctness of the protocols (e.g., [12,13,37]). For instance, Maude's model checker has recently been used to verify the correctness of configurations of the MSI and ESI protocols [23, 31]. In contrast, our work, which also considers cache coherent movement of data, focuses on formally capturing the movement of data as a consequence of the interaction between cores, caches and shared memory during the parallel execution of programs, rather than on protocol verification.

7   Conclusions and Future Work

Software is increasingly designed to run on multicore architectures, where data locality, data access, and data movement crucially influence the performance of the parallel execution. We believe that formal models that capture how parallel programs interact with memory, may help software developers understand how data access influences the behavior of parallel tasks executing on multicore architectures with shared memory, and thereby improve data locality and better avoid expensive cache misses. For this purpose, we combine abstract models of parallel program execution with models of shared memory multicore architecture, to capture data movement when parallel programs access data on such architectures. This paper develops a formal executable model of multicore architectures with multilevel caches from a program perspective rather than a hardware perspective, and addresses dynamically spawned data access patterns. The formal model is given as an operational semantics for data access patterns executing in parallel on different cores, and ensures data consistency by embodying the MSI cache coherence protocol. We have shown that the model guarantees correctness properties concerning data consistency, to ensure that we correctly capture data movement triggered by the cache coherence protocol. We provide a proof of concept implementation of the model, and show by example how choices for a program's data layout in combination with the underlying hardware architecture affect data movement.

This work opens several interesting directions for future work, including extensions required for richer programming languages. For data structures and dynamically allocated memory (e.g., object creation), the model could be extended with type layouts and alloc (e.g., [26]). We are currently considering the extraction of data access patterns from models in ABS [17] and we are implementing a more powerful simulation tool. Other directions of future work include shared caches and locking mechanisms which allow atomic blocks and synchronization between data access patterns to be modeled. Finally, models as developed in this paper could serve as a foundation to study the effects of program specific optimizations of data layout and scheduling.

References

1. Adve, S.V., Gharachorloo, K.: Shared memory consistency models: a tutorial. IEEE Comput. **29**(12), 66–76 (1996)
2. Alglave, J., Maranget, L., Tautschnig, M., Cats, H.: Modelling, simulation, testing, and data mining for weak memory. ACM Trans. Program. Lang. Syst. **36**(2), 7:1–7:74 (2014)
3. Bijo, S., Johnsen, E.B., Pun, K.I., Tapia Tarifa, S.L.: A Maude framework for cache coherent multicore architectures. In: Lucanu, D. (ed.) WRLA 2016. LNCS, vol. 9942, pp. 47–63. Springer, Cham (2016). doi:10.1007/978-3-319-44802-2_3
4. Bijo, S., Johnsen, E.B., Pun, K.I., Tapia Tarifa, S.L.: An operational semantics of cache coherent multicore architectures. In: Proceedings of Symposium Applied Computing (SAC). ACM (2016)
5. Bijo, S., Johnsen, E.B., Pun, K.I., Tapia Tarifa, S.L.: A formal model of parallel execution in multicore architectures with multilevel caches (long version). Res. rep., Department of Informatics, University of Oslo (2017). http://violet.at.ifi.uio.no/papers/mc-rr.pdf

6. Binkert, N., et al.: The gem5 simulator. SIGARCH Comput. Archit. News **39**(2), 1–7 (2011)
7. Carlson, T.E., Heirman, W., Eeckhout, L.: Sniper: exploring the level of abstraction for scalable and accurate parallel multi-core simulation. In: Proceedings of High Performance Computing, Networking, Storage and Analysis (SC), pp. 52:1–52:12. ACM (2011)
8. Clavel, M., Durán, F., Eker, S., Lincoln, P., Martí-Oliet, N., Meseguer, J., Talcott, C. (eds.): All About Maude - A High-Performance Logical Framework, How to Specify, Program and Verify Systems in Rewriting Logic. LNCS, vol. 4350. Springer, Heidelberg (2007)
9. Crary, K., Sullivan, M.J.: A calculus for relaxed memory. In: Proceedings of Principles of Programming Languages (POPL), pp. 623–636. ACM (2015)
10. Culler, D.E., Gupta, A., Singh, J.P.: Parallel Computer Architecture: A Hardware/Software Approach. Morgan Kaufmann, San Francisco (1997)
11. Delzanno, G.: Constraint-based verification of parameterized cache coherence protocols. Formal Meth. Syst. Des. **23**(3), 257–301 (2003)
12. Dill, D.L., Drexler, A.J., Hu, A.J., Yang, C.H.: Protocol verification as a hardware design aid. In: Proceedings of Computer Design on VLSI in Computer Processors (ICCD). IEEE (1992)
13. Dill, D.L., Park, S., Nowatzyk, A.G.: Formal specification of abstract memory models. In: Proceedings of Symposium Research on Integrated Systems, pp. 38–52. MIT Press (1993)
14. Dongol, B., Travkin, O., Derrick, J., Wehrheim, H.: A high-level semantics for program execution under total store order memory. In: Liu, Z., Woodcock, J., Zhu, H. (eds.) ICTAC 2013. LNCS, vol. 8049, pp. 177–194. Springer, Heidelberg (2013). doi:10.1007/978-3-642-39718-9_11
15. Hennessy, J.L., Patterson, D.A.: Computer Architecture: A Quantitative Approach. Morgan Kaufmann, San Francisco (2011)
16. Jagadeesan, R., Pitcher, C., Riely, J.: Generative operational semantics for relaxed memory models. In: Gordon, A.D. (ed.) ESOP 2010. LNCS, vol. 6012, pp. 307–326. Springer, Heidelberg (2010). doi:10.1007/978-3-642-11957-6_17
17. Johnsen, E.B., Hähnle, R., Schäfer, J., Schlatte, R., Steffen, M.: ABS: a core language for abstract behavioral specification. In: Aichernig, B.K., Boer, F.S., Bonsangue, M.M. (eds.) FMCO 2010. LNCS, vol. 6957, pp. 142–164. Springer, Heidelberg (2011). doi:10.1007/978-3-642-25271-6_8
18. Kandemir, M., et al.: Improving locality using loop and data transformations in an integrated framework. In: Proceedings of ACM/IEEE International Symposium on Microarchitecture (1998)
19. Lamport, L.: How to make a multiprocessor computer that correctly executes multiprocess programs. IEEE Trans. Comput. **28**(9), 690–691 (1979)
20. Li, Y., Suhendra, V., Liang, Y., Mitra, T., Roychoudhury, A.: Timing analysis of concurrent programs running on shared cache multi-cores. In: Proceedings of Real-Time Systems Symposium (RTSS), pp. 57–67. IEEE (2009)
21. Mador-Haim, S., Maranget, L., Sarkar, S., Memarian, K., Alglave, J., Owens, S., Alur, R., Martin, M.M.K., Sewell, P., Williams, D.: An axiomatic memory model for POWER multiprocessors. In: Madhusudan, P., Seshia, S.A. (eds.) CAV 2012. LNCS, vol. 7358, pp. 495–512. Springer, Heidelberg (2012). doi:10.1007/978-3-642-31424-7_36
22. Martin, M.M.K., et al.: Multifacet's general execution-driven multiprocessor simulator (GEMS) toolset. SIGARCH Comput. Archit. News **33**(4), 92–99 (2005)

23. Martín, Ó., Verdejo, A., Martí-Oliet, N.: Model checking TLR* guarantee formulas on infinite systems. In: Iida, S., Meseguer, J., Ogata, K. (eds.) Specification, Algebra, and Software. LNCS, vol. 8373, pp. 129–150. Springer, Heidelberg (2014). doi:10.1007/978-3-642-54624-2_7

24. Meseguer, J.: Conditional rewriting logic as a unified model of concurrency. Theor. Comput. Sci. **96**(1), 73–155 (1992)

25. Miller, J.E., et al.: Graphite: a distributed parallel simulator for multicores. In: Proceedings of the High-Performance Computer Architecture (HPCA), pp. 1–12. IEEE (2010)

26. Nita, M., Grossman, D., Chambers, C.: A theory of platform-dependent low-level software. In: Proceedings of the Principles of Programming Languages (POPL), pp. 209–220. ACM (2008)

27. Pang, J., Fokkink, W., Hofman, R.F.H., Veldema, R.: Model checking a cache coherence protocol of a Java DSM implementation. J. Log. Algeb. Prog. **71**(1), 1–43 (2007)

28. Patterson, D.A., Hennessy, J.L.: Computer Organization and Design: The Hardware/Software Interface. Morgan Kaufmann (2013)

29. Plotkin, G.D.: A structural approach to operational semantics. J. Log. Algeb. Prog. **60–61**, 17–139 (2004)

30. Pong, F., Dubois, M.: Verification techniques for cache coherence protocols. ACM Comput. Surv. **29**(1), 82–126 (1997)

31. Ramírez, S., Rocha, C.: Formal verification of safety properties for a cache coherence protocol. In: Proceedings of the Colombian Computing Conference (10CCC), pp. 9–16. IEEE (2015)

32. Sarkar, S., Sewell, P., Alglave, J., Maranget, L., Williams, D.: Understanding POWER multiprocessors. In: Proceedings of PLDI, pp. 175–186. ACM (2011)

33. Sewell, P., Sarkar, S., Owens, S., Nardelli, F.Z., Myreen, M.O.: X86-TSO: A rigorous and usable programmer's model for x86 multiprocessors. Commun. ACM **53**(7), 89–97 (2010)

34. Smith, G., Derrick, J., Dongol, B.: Admit your weakness: verifying correctness on TSO architectures. In: Lanese, I., Madelaine, E. (eds.) FACS 2014. LNCS, vol. 8997, pp. 364–383. Springer, Cham (2015). doi:10.1007/978-3-319-15317-9_22

35. Solihin, Y.: Fundamentals of Parallel Multicore Architecture. Chapman & Hall/CRC (2015)

36. Sorin, D.J., Hill, M.D., Wood, D.A.: A Primer on Memory Consistency and Cache Coherence. Morgan & Claypool, San Francisco (2011)

37. Yu, X., Vijayaraghavan, M., Devadas, S.: A proof of correctness for the Tardis cache coherence protocol. CoRR, abs/1505.06459 (2015)

Guarded Terms for Rewriting Modulo SMT

Kyungmin Bae[1]([✉]) and Camilo Rocha[2]

[1] Pohang University of Science and Technology, Pohang, South Korea
kmbae@postech.ac.kr
[2] Pontificia Universidad Javeriana, Cali, Colombia

Abstract. Rewriting modulo SMT is a novel symbolic technique to model and analyze infinite-state systems that interact with a nondeterministic environment. It seamlessly combines rewriting modulo equational theories, SMT solving, and model checking. One of the main challenges of this technique is to cope with the symbolic state-space explosion problem. This paper presents guarded terms, an approach to deal with this problem for rewriting modulo SMT. Guarded terms can encode many symbolic states into one by using SMT constraints as part of the term structure. This approach enables the reduction of the symbolic state space by limiting branching due to concurrent computation, and the complexity and size of constraints by distributing them in the term structure. A case study of an unbounded and symbolic priority queue illustrates the approach.

1 Introduction

The specification and verification effort in component-based software engineering can be improved using symbolic approaches. They can make available symbolic analysis techniques and tools with the promise of taming the many complexities involved in component-based systems, including real-time and cyber-physical systems. Symbolic techniques can be used to verify the functionality offered by software components for *any* possible input and communication interleaving. Rewriting modulo SMT [19] is a novel symbolic technique to model and analyze infinite-state systems that interact with a nondeterministic environment. It is a symbolic specification and verification method for rewriting logic [14], a general logical framework in which many component-based systems, such as AADL [3] and Ptolemy II [4], can be naturally specified [15].

Rewriting modulo SMT seamlessly combines rewriting modulo equational theories, SMT solving, and model checking. In rewriting modulo SMT, states are represented as symbolic constrained terms $(t\,;\phi)$ with t a term with variables ranging over the *built-ins* (the sorts handled by the SMT solver) and ϕ a SMT-solvable formula. State transitions are symbolic rewrite steps between constrained terms. In one rewrite step from $(t_1\,;\phi_1)$ to $(t_2\,;\phi_2)$, possibly infinitely many instances of t_1 can be rewritten to instances of t_2; namely, those ground instances of t_1 that satisfy the constraint ϕ_1 result in a ground instance of t_2 satisfying the constraint ϕ_2. In general, a n-step symbolic rewrite from $(t_1\,;\phi_1)$

© Springer International Publishing AG 2017
J. Proença and M. Lumpe (Eds.): FACS 2017, LNCS 10487, pp. 78–97, 2017.
DOI: 10.1007/978-3-319-68034-7_5

to $(t_n \,;\phi_n)$ captures *all* possible traces with n transitions from ground instances of t_1 satisfying ϕ_1 to *all* ground instances of t_n satisfying ϕ_n. By being complete, the symbolic rewrite relation will capture any ground trace satisfying these conditions, if any exists. This is one of the reasons why rewriting modulo SMT is well-suited for symbolically proving (or disproving) safety properties of rewrite theories.

Rewriting modulo SMT can be used to analyze existential reachability properties of infinite-state systems such as invariant and deadlock freedom properties. Moreover, it can be efficiently implemented by performing matching (instead of the more costly unification) for the term t and querying the SMT solver for the satisfiability of ϕ, for a given symbolic state $(t\,;\phi)$ at each rewrite step. However, the effective application of this technique comes with new challenges in terms of scalability: namely, the symbolic state-space explosion problem. For instance, the symbolic semantics of PLEXIL [18,19] – a synchronous language developed by NASA to support autonomous spacecraft operations –, which uses rewriting modulo SMT, is nondeterministic despite the fact that its ground counterpart is deterministic [12]. Therefore, in the symbolic rewriting logic semantics of PLEXIL, the state space can grow very large and the constraints become complex, making the formal analysis task time-consuming or unfeasible.

This paper presents *guarded terms*, a technique with the potential to reduce the symbolic state space and the complexity of constraints in the rewriting modulo SMT approach. A guarded term can be seen as a choice operator that is part of the term structure in a constrained term. Guarded terms generalize constrained terms by allowing t in a symbolic state $(t\,;\phi)$ to have, e.g., a guarded term $u_1|_\psi \vee u_2|_{\neg\psi}$ as a subterm. This means that when the constraint $\phi \wedge \psi$ is satisfiable, $(t\,;\phi)$ represents those ground instances of t in which the subterm $u_1|_\psi \vee u_2|_{\neg\psi}$ is replaced by u_1. Analogously, when $\phi \wedge \neg\psi$ is satisfiable, $(t\,;\phi)$ represents those ground instances of t in which the subterm $u_1|_\psi \vee u_2|_{\neg\psi}$ is replaced by u_2. Therefore, the guarded term can actually encode both alternatives without the need for two constrained terms. The greater potential of guarded terms can better be seen when they are composed in parallel or nested, thus enabling the succinct encoding of several constrained terms into one guarded term.

Guarded terms are particularly useful in rewriting modulo SMT in many situations for reducing: (i) the symbolic state space by implicitly encoding branching in the term structure, and (ii) the complexity and size of constraints by distributing them in several parts of the term structure. The effectiveness of the approach is illustrated with a case study of an unbounded and symbolic priority queue that, with the help of guarded terms, enables automatic reachability analysis of the CASH scheduling algorithm [7].

The rest of the paper is organized as follows. Section 2 overviews rewriting logic and rewriting modulo SMT. Section 3 presents guarded terms and their main properties. Section 4 introduces the case study on the CASH algorithm. Finally, Sect. 5 discusses related work and presents some concluding remarks. The examples used throughout the paper, and the proofs omitted in Sect. 3 can be found in [5].

2   Rewriting Logic and Rewriting Modulo SMT in a Nutshell

This section briefly explains order-sorted rewriting logic and rewriting modulo SMT, summarizing Sects. 2–5 in [19]. Rewriting logic [14] is a semantic framework that unifies a wide range of models of concurrency. Maude [11] is a language and tool to support the formal specification and analysis of concurrent systems in rewriting logic. Rewriting modulo SMT [19] is a symbolic technique to model and analyze reachability properties of infinite-state systems in rewriting logic, that can be executed in Maude by querying decision procedures available from SMT technology.

2.1   Order-Sorted Rewrite Theories

An *order-sorted signature* Σ is a tuple $\Sigma = (S, \leq, F)$ with a finite poset of sorts $(S, \leq)$ and set of function symbols F typed with sorts in S, which can be subsort-overloaded. The *set of function symbols of sort* $w \in S^*$ in Σ is denoted by Σ_w. The binary relation $\equiv_\leq$ denotes the equivalence relation $(\leq \cup \geq)^+$ generated by $\leq$ on S and its point-wise extension to strings in S^*. The expression $[s]$ denotes the connected component of s, that is, $[s] = [s]_{\equiv_\leq}$. A *top sort* in Σ is a sort $s \in S$ such that for all $s' \in [s]$, $s' \leq s$.

For $X = \{X_s\}_{s \in S}$ an S-indexed family of disjoint variable sets with each X_s countably infinite, the *set of terms of sort* s and the *set of ground terms of sort* s are denoted, respectively, by $T_\Sigma(X)_s$ and $T_{\Sigma,s}$; similarly, $T_\Sigma(X)$ and T_Σ denote, respectively, the set of terms and the set of ground terms.

A *substitution* is an S-indexed mapping $\theta : X \longrightarrow T_\Sigma(X)$ that is different from the identity only for a finite subset of X, and such that $\theta(x) \in T_\Sigma(X)_s$ if $x \in X_s$, for any $x \in X$ and $s \in S$. A substitution θ is called *ground* if and only if $\theta(x) \in T_\Sigma$ or $\theta(x) = x$ for any $x \in X$. The application of a substitution θ to a term t is denoted by θt and the composition (in diagrammatic order) of two substitutions θ_1 and θ_2 is denoted by $\theta_1 \theta_2$, so that $\theta_1 \theta_2 t$ denotes $\theta_1(\theta_2 t)$.

A *rewrite theory* is a tuple $\mathcal{R} = (\Sigma, E \uplus B, R)$ with: (i) $(\Sigma, E \uplus B)$ an order-sorted equational theory with signature Σ, E a set of equations over T_Σ, and B a set of structural axioms – disjoint from the set of equations E – over T_Σ for which there is a finitary matching algorithm (e.g., associativity, commutativity, and identity, or combinations of them); and (ii) R a finite set of rewrite rules over T_Σ.

Intuitively, $\mathcal{R}$ specifies a concurrent system whose states are elements of the set $T_{\Sigma/E \uplus B}$ of Σ-terms modulo $E \uplus B$ and whose concurrent transitions are axiomatized by the rules R according to the inference rules of rewriting logic [6]. In particular, for $t, u \in T_\Sigma$ representing states of the concurrent system described by $\mathcal{R}$, a transition from t to u is captured by a formula of the form $t \rightarrow_\mathcal{R} u$; the symbol $\rightarrow_\mathcal{R}$ denotes the binary rewrite relation induced by R over $T_{\Sigma/E \uplus B}$ and $\mathcal{T}_\mathcal{R} = (T_{\Sigma/E \uplus B}, \rightarrow_\mathcal{R})$ denotes the *initial reachability model* of $\mathcal{R}$. The expressions $\mathcal{T}_{\Sigma/E \uplus B}$ and $=_{E \uplus B}$ denote, respectively, the *initial algebra* of $(\Sigma, E \uplus B)$ and the congruence induced by $(\Sigma, E \uplus B)$ on Σ-terms.

Example 1. Consider a system with states in the top sort *Conf* of the form $C_1 \parallel C_2$, with C_1 and C_2 multisets of integer numbers. Each state has sort *Conf*, an integer has sort *Int*, and a multiset of integers has sort *Channel*. Multiset union is denoted by juxtaposition, and it is associative, commutative, and has identity *none* (which denotes the empty collection). Integer number addition and the "less-than" total order relation on integers are denoted with the usual function symbols.

The symbol $\stackrel{n}{=}$ represents the "modulo n congruence" binary relation over integers (i.e., a shorthand for $x \equiv y \mod n$). The system consists of the following three rewrite rules, where I_1, I_2 range over integers and C_1, C_2 over multisets of integers:

$$I_1 \, I_2 \, C_1 \parallel C_2 \;\rightarrow\; I_1 \, C_1 \parallel (I_1 + I_2 + 1) \, C_2 \quad \text{if } 0 < I_1 \wedge 0 < I_2 \wedge (I_1 + I_2 \stackrel{3}{=} 0)$$

$$I_1 \, I_2 \, C_1 \parallel C_2 \;\rightarrow\; I_1 \, C_1 \parallel C_2 \quad \text{if } 0 < I_1 \wedge 0 < I_2 \wedge \neg (I_1 + I_2 \stackrel{3}{=} 0)$$

$$I_1 \parallel I_2 \, C_2 \;\rightarrow\; none \parallel I_2 \, C_2 \quad \text{if } 0 < I_1 \wedge 0 < I_2 \wedge (I_1 + I_2 \stackrel{17}{=} 0)$$

In this system, integers move from the left channel to the right channel. By the first rule, an intenger I_2 is removed from the left channel and the integer $I_1 + I_2 + 1$ is added to the right channel, for any I_1 and I_2 in the left channel, whenever I_1 and I_2 are at least 1, and $I_1 + I_2$ is a multiple of 3. By the second rule, an integer I_2 is removed from the left channel, for any I_1 and I_2 in the left channel, whenever I_1 and I_2 are at least 1, and $I_1 + I_2$ is not a multiple of 3. By the third rule, an integer I_1 is removed from the left channel, for any I_1 in the left channel and I_2 in the right channel, whenever I_1 is the only number in the left channel, I_1 and I_2 are at least 1, and $I_1 + I_2$ is a multiple of 17.

This system can be executed by rewriting in Maude as follows. Given a rewrite rule $l \rightarrow r$ **if** *cond*, with $l, r \in T_\Sigma(X)_{Conf}$, a ground term $t \in T_{\Sigma, Conf}$ rewrites to a ground term $u \in T_{\Sigma, Conf}$ (i.e., $t \rightarrow_{\mathcal{R}} u$) if and only if there is a ground substitution σ such that t and u are respectively substitution instances of l and r modulo $=_{E \uplus B}$ (i.e., $\sigma l =_{E \uplus B} t$ and $\sigma r =_{E \uplus B} u$), and the condition $\sigma cond$ holds. For example, by the first rule and $\sigma = \{I_1 \mapsto 1, I_2 \mapsto 2, C_1 \mapsto 3\,4, C_2 \mapsto none\}$, follows $1\,2\,3\,4 \parallel none \rightarrow_{\mathcal{R}} 1\,3\,4 \parallel 4$.

By being executable in Maude, automatic state-space search capabilities can be used, e.g., to identify potential deadlocks in this system. A Maude search command searches for states that are reachable from a *ground* initial state and match the search pattern and satisfy the search condition. Starting from the initial state $1\,2\,3\,4 \parallel none$, the following search command checks if there is a deadlock state with a nonempty left channel that can not be further rewritten (and this command finds no solution):

```
search [1]    1 2 3 4 || none   =>!   C1 || C2   such that C1 =/= none .
```

In this command, [1] specifies the maximum number (in this case, 1) of solutions that the command should return, and =>! means that only non-reducible states with respect to $\rightarrow_{\mathcal{R}}$ are to be considered as solutions to the query.

2.2 Rewriting Modulo SMT

Rewriting modulo SMT is illustrated using a symbolic version of Example 1. In this version, a symbolic state is given by a *constrained term* $(t \,; \phi)$, with $t \in T_\Sigma(X_0)_{Conf}$ and $\phi \in QF_{\Sigma_0}(X_0)$, where $X_0 \subseteq X$ denotes the set of variables ranging over the built-ins, $\Sigma_0 \subseteq \Sigma$ denotes the signature of the built-in sorts, and $QF_{\Sigma_0}(X_0)$ denotes the set of quantifier-free formulas over Σ_0 with variables in X_0.

Example 2. In the symbolic version of the system, the built-in sorts are *Bool* and *Int*, and the non-built-in sorts are *Channel* and *Conf*. There are three rewrite rules with variables I_1, I_2 of sort *Int*, variables C_1, C_2 of sort *Channel*, and ϕ_1, ϕ_2 of sort *Bool*:

$$(I_1 \; I_2 \; C_1 \parallel C_2 \,; \phi_1) \; \rightarrow \; (I_1 \; C_1 \parallel (I_1 + I_2 + 1) \; C_2 \,; \phi_1 \wedge \phi_2)$$
$$\textbf{if} \quad \phi_2 := 0 < I_1 \; \wedge \; 0 < I_2 \; \wedge \; (I_1 + I_2 \overset{3}{=} 0) \; \wedge \; sat(\phi_1 \wedge \phi_2)$$
$$(I_1 \; I_2 \; C_1 \parallel C_2 \,; \phi_1) \; \rightarrow \; (I_1 \; C_1 \parallel C_2 \,; \phi_1 \wedge \phi_2)$$
$$\textbf{if} \quad \phi_2 := 0 < I_1 \; \wedge \; 0 < I_2 \; \wedge \; \neg(I_1 + I_2 \overset{3}{=} 0) \; \wedge \; sat(\phi_1 \wedge \phi_2)$$
$$(I_1 \parallel I_2 \; C_2 \,; \phi_1) \; \rightarrow \; (none \parallel I_2 \; C_2 \,; \phi_2)$$
$$\textbf{if} \quad \phi_2 := 0 < I_1 \; \wedge \; 0 < I_2 \; \wedge \; (I_1 + I_2 \overset{17}{=} 0) \; \wedge \; sat(\phi_1 \wedge \phi_2)$$

These rules are similar to the ones in Example 1. The key observation in this version is that conditions are treated as constraints, accumulated in the system state, and queried for satisfiability with the help of the function *sat* (an interface to the SMT-solver to check whether ϕ is satisfiable or not). A *matching condition* [11] of the form $t := u$ is a syntactic variant of the equational condition $t = u$ mathematically interpreted as an ordinary equation. Operationally, a matching condition behaves like a 'let' construct in functional programming languages so that $t := u$ introduces t in the rule as the result of reducing u to canonical form with the oriented equations modulo the axioms.

Definition 1. *Given a rewrite rule $(l \,; \phi_l) \rightarrow (r \,; \phi_r)$ if ϕ, with $l, r \in T_\Sigma(X)_{Conf}$ and $\phi \in QF_{\Sigma_0}(X_0)$, a constrained term $(t \,; \phi_t) \in T_\Sigma(X_0)_{Conf} \times QF_{\Sigma_0}(X_0)$ symbolically rewrites to a constrained term $(u \,; \phi_u) \in T_\Sigma(X_0)_{Conf} \times QF_{\Sigma_0}(X_0)$ (denoted by $(t \,; \phi_t) \rightsquigarrow_\mathcal{R} (u \,; \phi_u)$) if and only if there is a substitution θ such that:*

(a) $\theta l =_{E \uplus B} t$ and $\theta r =_{E \uplus B} u$,
(b) $\mathcal{T}_{\Sigma / E \uplus B} \models (\phi_l \wedge \theta\phi) \Leftrightarrow \phi_u$, and
(c) ϕ_u is $\mathcal{T}_{\Sigma / E \uplus B}$-satisfiable.

The symbolic relation $\rightsquigarrow_\mathcal{R}$ is defined as a topmost rewrite relation, where all rewrites take place at the top of the term, induced by R modulo $E \uplus B$ on $T_\Sigma(X_0)$ with extra bookkeeping of constraints.

Condition (a) can be solved by matching as in the definition of $\rightarrow_\mathcal{R}$ above. Condition (b) can be met by setting ϕ_u to be $\phi_l \wedge \theta\phi$, as in the above matching conditions. However, Condition (c) cannot – in general – be dealt with by rewriting.

The reason is that such a condition can be an inductive theorem of $T_{\Sigma/E \uplus B}$. Instead, these conditions are checked with the help of decision procedures available from an SMT solver via the function *sat*. Observe that, up to the choice of the semantically equivalent φ_u for which a fixed strategy such as the one suggested above can be assumed, the symbolic relation $\leadsto_\mathcal{R}$ is deterministic in the sense of being determined by the rule and the substitution θ (here it is assumed that variables in the rules are disjoint from the ones in the target terms). The reader is referred to [19] for details about rewriting modulo SMT.

Example 3. Consider the constrained term $(A \; B \; C \; D \parallel none; true)$, with four variables $A, B, C, D \in X_{Int}$. Notice that $(A \; B \; C \; D \parallel none; true)$ symbolically rewrites in one step to $(A \; C \; D \parallel A + B + 1; 0 < A \wedge 0 < B \wedge (A + B \overset{3}{=} 0))$.

Rewriting modulo SMT can be used for solving existential reachability goals in the initial model $T_\mathcal{R}$ of a rewrite theory $\mathcal{R}$ modulo built-ins $\mathcal{E}_0$. In general, for any constrained term $(t; \phi)$ where t is a state term with sort *Conf* and ϕ is a constraint, $[\![t]\!]_\phi$ is the *denotation* of $(t; \phi)$ consisting of all ground instances of t that satisfy ϕ; formally $[\![t]\!]_\phi = \{t' \in T_{\Sigma, Conf} \mid (\exists \sigma : X \longrightarrow T_\Sigma) \, t' = \sigma t \wedge T_{\Sigma/E \uplus B} \models \sigma \phi\}$. The type of *existential reachability* question that rewriting modulo SMT can solve can now be formulated: are there some states in $[\![t]\!]_\phi$ from which is possible to reach some state in $[\![u]\!]_\psi$? Answering this question can be especially useful for symbolically proving or disproving safety properties of $\mathcal{R}$, such as inductive invariants or deadlock freedom of $T_\mathcal{R}$: when $[\![u]\!]_\psi$ is a set of *bad* states, the idea is to know whether reaching a state in $[\![u]\!]_\psi$ is possible.

Consider the following existential query, where $\mathcal{R}$ is the rewrite theory presented in Example 1 (i.e., the one without symbolic constraints):

$$T_\mathcal{R} \models (\exists I, C_1, C_2) \; I \, (I + 1) \, (I + 2) \, (I + 3) \parallel none \longrightarrow_\mathcal{R}^* \; C_1 \parallel C_2 \wedge I > 0$$
$$\wedge \; C_1 \neq none \wedge \text{``}C_1 \parallel C_2 is \longrightarrow_\mathcal{R}\text{-}irreducible\text{''}.$$

This query asks if it is possible to find an initial state consisting of four consecutive positive integers in the left channel and no number on the right channel that leads to an irreducible state where there are still numbers in the left channel. This is the same type of deadlock freedom property discussed before, namely, the one in which bad states are those irreducible ones in which the channel has at least one number.

Answering this query in the negative proves that $\mathcal{R}$ is deadlock free for any initial state satisfying the initial pattern. Since I ranges over an infinite domain, this question cannot be solved directly via rewriting and would require, e.g., inductive reasoning over $\longrightarrow_\mathcal{R}$. However, the following Maude *search* command can be issued in Maude to find a proof (or a counterexample) for the symbolic rewrite relation $\leadsto_\mathcal{R}$:

```
search [1] { I  I+1 I+2 I+3 || none , I > 0 }
       =>! { C1 || C2, Phi } such that C1 =/= none .
```

Executed as it is, this command times out after 5 min. As shown in the next section, with the help of guarded terms, the exact same search command terminates in less than 1 second without finding a witness, therefore proving the deadlock freedom of $\mathcal{T}_\mathcal{R}$ from states satisfying the pattern I $(I+1)$ $(I+2)$ $(I+3)$ $\|$ *none*.

3   Guarded Terms

Guarded terms generalize constrained terms with heterogeneous patterns and nested structures. Guarded terms succinctly represent various terms by choices of subterms that are guarded by a constraint. These subterms represent possible realizations, namely, those instances in which the constraints are true. The proofs of lemmas and theorems presented in this section can be found in [5].

3.1   Syntax

Consider the constrained terms $(t_1 ; \phi_1), \ldots, (t_n ; \phi_n)$ with the terms $t_1, \ldots, t_n$ of the same sort. First, a guarded term can be built by combining these constrained terms in parallel as $(t_1 ; \phi_1) \vee \cdots \vee (t_n ; \phi_n)$, semantically representing the union of the sets $[\![t_1]\!]_{\phi_1}, \ldots, [\![t_n]\!]_{\phi_n}$ of ground terms. Second, guarded terms can be *nested* so that the terms t_i may include guarded terms as subterms. For example, if f and g are unary and binary function symbols, respectively, then the term $f((t_1 ; \phi_1) \vee (f(g((t_3 ; \phi_3), t_4)); \phi_2))$ is a guarded term. The guarded subterm $g((t_3 ; \phi_3), t_4)$ encodes the ground instances $\theta g(t_3, t_4)$ in which $\theta \phi_3$ is true, for any ground substitution θ.

In order to avoid confusion between the syntax of constrained terms and guarded terms, $(t ; \phi)$ will be written as $t|_\phi$. With this convention, the above-mentioned guarded terms can be written as $t_1|_{\phi_1} \vee \cdots \vee t_n|_{\phi_n}$ and $f(t_1|_{\phi_1} \vee f(g(t_3|_{\phi_3}, t_4))|_{\phi_2})$. The syntax of guarded terms is formally presented in Definition 2.

Definition 2. *Given a signature Σ, the set of guarded terms of sort s is the smallest set $\overline{T}_\Sigma(X)_s$ satisfying the following conditions:*

- $T_\Sigma(X)_s \subseteq \overline{T}_\Sigma(X)_s$;
- $f(t_1, \ldots, t_n) \in \overline{T}_\Sigma(X)_s$, if $f \in \Sigma_{s_1 \ldots s_n, s}$ and $t_i \in \overline{T}_\Sigma(X)_{s_i}$ for $1 \leq i \leq n$;
- $t|_\phi \in \overline{T}_\Sigma(X)_s$, if $t \in \overline{T}_\Sigma(X)_s$ and ϕ is a constraint; and
- $t_1 \vee t_2 \in \overline{T}_\Sigma(X)_s$ for guarded terms $t_1, t_2 \in \overline{T}_\Sigma(X)_s$ of sort s.

A signature $G(\Sigma)$ for guarded terms can be built by adding new sorts and function symbols to the underlying signature Σ as follows:

- a new sort $g(s)$ with a subsort relation $s < g(s)$ for each sort s;
- an operator $f : g(s_1) \cdots g(s_m) \longrightarrow g(s)$ for each operator $f : s_1 \cdots s_m \longrightarrow s$;
- a guard operator $\_|\_ : g(s) \times Bool \longrightarrow g(s)$ for each sort s; and
- an union operator $\_\vee\_ : g(s) \times g(s) \longrightarrow g(s)$ for each sort s,

where constraints have sort *Bool* (in the built-in subsignature $\Sigma_0 \subseteq \Sigma$) and sort $g(s_1)$ is a subsort of $g(s_2)$ whenever s_1 is a subsort of s_2. By construction, a guarded term $u \in \overline{T}_\Sigma(X)_s$ of sort s is a $G(\Sigma)$-term of sort $g(s)$.

Lemma 1. *Given an order-sorted signature* Σ, *a guarded term* u *of sort* s *in* $\overline{T}_\Sigma(X)$ *is a term of sort* $g(s)$ *in* $T_{G(\Sigma)}(X)$, *and vice versa.*

Example 4. In the example in Sect. 2, a term $I + J + 1$ is added to the right-hand side of the first rule if the condition $I + J \overset{3}{=} 0$ holds. A one-step symbolic rewrite step with this rule involves two cases: either $I + J \overset{3}{=} 0$ holds or not. Thus, n-rewrite steps with this rule can yield 2^n different symbolic states. For example, from the term $A\ B\ C\ \|\ none$, where A, B, C are integer variables, symbolic rewriting up to three steps generates:

$$
\begin{array}{ll}
A\ B\ C\ \|\ none & A\ B\ C\ \|\ (A+B+1)\ (B+C+1) \\
A\ B\ C\ \|\ (A+B+1) & A\ B\ C\ \|\ (A+B+1)\ (C+A+1) \\
A\ B\ C\ \|\ (B+C+1) & A\ B\ C\ \|\ (B+C+1)\ (C+A+1) \\
A\ B\ C\ \|\ (C+A+1) & A\ B\ C\ \|\ (A+B+1)\ (B+C+1)\ (C+A+1).
\end{array}
$$

A set of terms can be succinctly encoded as a guarded term. Consider guarded terms of the form $elm(I, J)$ defined as $elm(I, J) = I + J + 1|_{I+J \overset{3}{=} 0} \vee \emptyset|_{I+J \overset{3}{\neq} 0}$. The guarded term $elm(I_1, J_1)\ elm(I_2, J_2)\ \cdots\ elm(I_N, J_N)$ can encode the 2^n symbolic states that can be reached in n-rewrite steps with respect to the satisfaction of the n conditions $I_i + J_i \overset{3}{=} 0$, for $1 \leq i \leq N$. For example, the set of terms reachable from $A\ B\ C\ \|\ none$ in three steps can be encoded as: $A\ B\ C\ \|\ elm(A, B)\ elm(B, C)\ elm(C, A)$.

3.2   Semantics

A guarded term u represents a (possibly infinite) set of ground terms, denoted by $[\![u]\!]$. Intuitively, $[\![u|_\phi]\!]$ is the set of all ground instances of u that satisfy the constraint ϕ, and $[\![u_1 \vee u_2]\!]$ is the union of the sets $[\![u_1]\!] \cup [\![u_2]\!]$.

To formally define the semantics of guarded terms, *ground* guarded terms are first considered. The ground semantics in Definition 3 is straightforward, because the constraints in ground guarded terms can be determined as either *true* or *false* in the underlying built-in algebra $\mathcal{T}_{\mathcal{E}_0}$. Specifically, a ground guarded term $u|_\phi$ represents either $[\![u]\!]$ if ϕ is satisfiable in $\mathcal{T}_{\mathcal{E}_0}$ or the empty set if ϕ is not satisfiable in $\mathcal{T}_{\mathcal{E}_0}$.

Definition 3. *Given a ground guarded term* $u \in \overline{T}_\Sigma$, *the set* $[\![u]\!] \subseteq T_\Sigma$ *of ground terms represented by* u *is inductively defined as follows:*

$$[\![t]\!] = \{t' \in T_\Sigma \mid t' =_E t\}\ \text{if } t \in T_\Sigma,$$

$$[\![f(u_1, \ldots, u_n)]\!] = \{t \in [\![f(t_1, \ldots, t_n)]\!] \mid t_i \in [\![u_i]\!], 1 \leq i \leq n\},$$

$$[\![u|_\phi]\!] = \begin{cases} [\![u]\!] & \text{if } \mathcal{T}_{\mathcal{E}_0} \models \phi \\ \emptyset & \text{if } \mathcal{T}_{\mathcal{E}_0} \not\models \phi, \end{cases}$$

$$[\![u_1 \vee u_2]\!] = [\![u_1]\!] \cup [\![u_2]\!].$$

Example 5. Recall the guarded terms in Example 4. The ground guarded term

$$u = (3+1+1|_{3+1\overset{3}{=}0} \vee \emptyset|_{3+1\overset{3}{\neq}0}) \; (5+4+1|_{5+4\overset{3}{=}0} \vee \emptyset|_{5+4\overset{3}{\neq}0})$$

represents the set $\llbracket u \rrbracket = \{t' \mid t' =_E \emptyset \; (5+4+1)\}$, because $3+1 \overset{3}{\neq} 0$ and $5+4 \overset{3}{=} 0$. Note that $5+4+1 \in \llbracket u \rrbracket$, since $5+4+1 =_E \emptyset \; (5+4+1)$.

The semantics of guarded terms in general, introduced by Definition 4, is based on the semantics of ground guarded terms. Each ground instance θu of a guarded term u under a ground substitution θ defines the set $\llbracket \theta u \rrbracket$ of ground terms. The set $\llbracket u \rrbracket$ is the union of all the sets given by the ground instances of the guarded term u.

Definition 4. *Given a guarded term $u \in \overline{T}_\Sigma(X)$, the set of all ground terms represented by u is defined as $\llbracket u \rrbracket = \{t \in T_\Sigma \mid (\exists \theta : X \longrightarrow T_\Sigma) \, t \in \llbracket \theta u \rrbracket\}$.*

It is worth noting that the semantics of non-ground guarded terms cannot be defined in the same way as the case of ground guarded terms. Specifically, the second condition $\llbracket f(u_1, \ldots, u_n) \rrbracket = \{t \in \llbracket f(t_1, \ldots, t_n) \rrbracket \mid t_i \in \llbracket u_i \rrbracket, 1 \le i \le n\}$ in Definition 3 for ground guarded terms is generally *not* applicable to non-ground guarded terms. For example, consider an unsorted signature Σ with two different constants c and d. Notice that $\llbracket f(x|_{x \neq y}, y|_{x=y}) \rrbracket = \emptyset$, but $\llbracket x|_{x \neq y} \rrbracket = \{c, d\}$ and $\llbracket y|_{x=y} \rrbracket = \{c, d\}$.

Example 6. Consider the nested guarded terms in Example 4. The guarded term

$$(I_1 + J_1 + 1|_{I_1+J_1\overset{3}{=}0} \vee \emptyset|_{I_1+J_1\overset{3}{\neq}0}) \; (I_2 + J_2 + 1|_{I_2+J_2\overset{3}{=}0} \vee \emptyset|_{I_2+J_2\overset{3}{\neq}0})$$

represents the set of terms for ground substitution $\{I_i \mapsto x_i, J_i \mapsto y_i \mid i = 1,2\}$ as follows:

$$\llbracket (x_1 + y_1 + 1) \; (x_2 + y_2 + 1) \rrbracket \quad \text{if } x_1 + y_1 \overset{3}{=} 0 \wedge x_2 + y_2 \overset{3}{=} 0,$$

$$\llbracket \emptyset \; (x_2 + y_2 + 1) \rrbracket \quad \text{if } x_1 + y_1 \overset{3}{\neq} 0 \wedge x_2 + y_2 \overset{3}{=} 0,$$

$$\llbracket (x_1 + y_1 + 1) \; \emptyset \rrbracket \quad \text{if } x_1 + y_1 \overset{3}{=} 0 \wedge x_2 + y_2 \overset{3}{\neq} 0,$$

$$\llbracket \emptyset \; \emptyset \rrbracket \quad \text{if } x_1 + y_1 \overset{3}{\neq} 0 \wedge x_2 + y_2 \overset{3}{\neq} 0.$$

Each one of these cases includes an infinite number of ground terms because there are an infinite number of ground substitutions that satisfy each guard. It can be easily seen that the number of cases increases exponentially: if the number of elements is n, the number of different cases is 2^n.

The notion of constrained terms in Sect. 2 can be seen as a special case of guarded terms since the denotation $\llbracket t \rrbracket_\phi$ of $(t; \phi)$ coincides with the semantics of $t|_\phi$.

Lemma 2. *Given a Σ-term $t \in T_\Sigma(X)$ and a constraint ϕ, $\llbracket t \rrbracket_\phi = \llbracket t|_\phi \rrbracket$ holds.*

3.3   Equivalence

Guarded terms u_1 and u_2 are called *equivalent*, written $u_1 \equiv u_2$, if they represent the same set of ground terms, that is, $[\![u_1]\!] = [\![u_2]\!]$. For example, guarded terms that are identical up to variable renaming are equivalent, since they have the same set of ground instances. Guarded terms are called *ground equivalent*, written $u_1 \equiv_g u_2$, if their ground instances by the same substitution are equivalent. The ground equivalence $u_1 \equiv_g u_2$ implies $u_1 \equiv u_2$, but the converse may not hold.[1]

Definition 5. *Let $u_1, u_2 \in \overline{T}_\Sigma(X)$:*

1. $u_1 \equiv u_2$ *iff* $[\![u_1]\!] = [\![u_2]\!]$.
2. $u_1 \equiv_g u_2$ *iff* $[\![\theta u_1]\!] = [\![\theta u_2]\!]$, *for every ground substitution* $\theta : X \longrightarrow T_\Sigma$.

The semantics of $\vee$ is associative and commutative with respect to ground equivalence, because its is defined as a set union operation. From now on, the expression $u_1 \vee \cdots \vee u_n$ will be written without parentheses using this fact.

Corollary 1 (Associativity and Commutativity of $\vee$). *If $u_1, u_2, u_3 \in \overline{T}_\Sigma(X)$, then*

1. $u_1 \vee u_2 \equiv_g u_2 \vee u_1$.
2. $(u_1 \vee u_2) \vee u_3 \equiv_g u_1 \vee (u_2 \vee u_3)$.

The ground equivalence $\equiv_g$ between guarded terms is a *congruence* as shown in Lemma 3. On the contrary, the equivalence $\equiv$ violates the congruence rules. Specifically, u and its variable renaming σu satisfy $u \equiv \sigma u$, but $u|_\phi$ and $(\sigma u)|_\phi$ are not equivalent.[2]

Lemma 3 (Congruence of Ground Equivalence). *If $u, v \in \overline{T}_\Sigma(X)$ and $u \equiv_g v$, then:*

- $\sigma u \equiv_g \sigma v$ *for a substitution* $\sigma : X \longrightarrow T_\Sigma(X)$.
- $f(u_1, \ldots, u, \ldots, u_n) \equiv_g f(u_1, \ldots, v, \ldots, u_n)$.
- $u|_\phi \equiv_g v|_\phi$.
- $u_1 \vee \cdots \vee u \vee \cdots \vee u_n \equiv_g u_1 \vee \cdots \vee v \vee \cdots \vee u_n$.

Guarded terms with different syntactic structures can be ground equivalent (and thus they are also equivalent by definition). Lemma 4 identifies some properties of ground equivalence between guarded terms.

Lemma 4 (Ground Equivalence Rules)

- $\left(\bigvee_{i=1}^n u_i \right)\big|_\phi \equiv_g \bigvee_{i=1}^n (u_i|_\phi)$

---

[1] As an example, $0|_{x=0} \equiv 0|_{x=1}$, because $[\![0|_{x=0}]\!] = [\![0|_{x=1}]\!] = \{0\}$. But $0|_{x=0} \not\equiv_g 0_{x=1}$, because $[\![\theta(0|_{x=0})]\!] = \{0\}$ and $[\![\theta(0|_{x=1})]\!] = \emptyset$ for $\theta = \{x \mapsto 0\}$, provided that $0 \neq 1$.

[2] For example, $0|_{x=0} \equiv 0_{y=0}$ but $(0|_{x=0})|_{x=1} \not\equiv (0|_{y=0})|_{x=1}$, because $[\![(0|_{x=0})|_{x=1}]\!] = \emptyset$ and $[\![(0|_{y=0})|_{x=1}]\!] = \{0\}$, provided that 0 and 1 are different.

$$- f(u_1, \ldots (\bigvee_{i=1}^n u_j^i) \ldots, u_n) \equiv_g \bigvee_{i=1}^n f(u_1, \ldots u_j^i \ldots, u_n)$$
$$- (u|_\varphi)|_\phi \equiv_g u|_{\varphi \wedge \phi}$$
$$- f(u_1, \ldots u_j|_\phi \ldots, u_n) \equiv_g f(u_1, \ldots u_j \ldots, u_n)|_\phi$$

Guarded terms can be simplified using these equivalence rules. For example,

$$f(u_1 \vee u_2, v_1 \vee v_2) \equiv_g f(u_1, v_1 \vee v_2) \vee f(u_2, v_1 \vee v_2) \equiv_g \bigvee_{i,j \in \{1,2\}} f(u_i, v_j),$$
$$f(u|_\phi, v|_\psi) \equiv_g f(u, v)|_\phi|_\psi \equiv_g f(u, v)|_{\phi \wedge \psi}.$$

By repeatedly applying the equivalences in Lemma 4, a (ground) equivalent guarded term that is a combination of normal constrained terms can be obtained.

Theorem 1 (Standard Form). *Every $u \in \overline{T}_\Sigma(X)$ is ground equivalent to a guarded term in* standard form *$t_1|_{\phi_1} \vee t_2|_{\phi_2} \vee \cdots \vee t_n|_{\phi_n}$, with terms $t_1, \ldots, t_n \in T_\Sigma(X)$.*

A guarded term in standard form has a flat structure in which parallel combinations $\vee$ and constraints ϕ appear only at the top. However, a *nested* guarded term can be exponentially smaller than an equivalent one in the standard form. For example, a nested guarded term $f(u_1 \vee v_1, \ldots, u_n \vee v_n)$ of size $O(n)$ is equivalent to its standard form $\bigvee_{w_i \in \{u_i, v_i\}} f(w_1, \ldots, w_n)$ of size $O(2^n)$.

This explains why guarded terms are very useful for succinctly representing the symbolic state space.

Example 7. Consider the nested guarded term in Example 6. The guarded term

$$(I_1 + J_1 + 1|_{I_1 + J_1 \overset{3}{=} 0} \vee \emptyset|_{I_1 + J_1 \overset{3}{\neq} 0}) \, (I_2 + J_2 + 1|_{I_2 + J_2 \overset{3}{=} 0} \vee \emptyset|_{I_2 + J_2 \overset{3}{\neq} 0})$$

is equivalent to the following guarded term in the standard form:

$$(I_1 + J_1 + 1)\,(I_2 + J_2 + 1)|_{I_1 + J_1 \overset{3}{=} 0 \wedge I_2 + J_2 \overset{3}{=} 0} \vee \emptyset\,(I_2 + J_2 + 1)|_{I_1 + J_1 \overset{3}{\neq} 0 \wedge I_2 + J_2 \overset{3}{=} 0} \vee$$
$$(I_1 + J_1 + 1)\,\emptyset|_{I_1 + J_1 \overset{3}{=} 0 \wedge I_2 + J_2 \overset{3}{\neq} 0} \vee \emptyset\,\emptyset|_{I_1 + J_1 \overset{3}{\neq} 0 \wedge I_2 + J_2 \overset{3}{\neq} 0},$$

where each case is expressed as a single disjunct. As explained in Example 6, since the number of cases increases exponentially, the size of the standard form also increases exponentially with respect to the size of the original one.

3.4   Rewriting with Guarded Terms

In principle, one-step rewrite $u \rightarrow u'$ between guarded terms u and u' represents a one-step rewrite $t \rightarrow t'$ between the corresponding terms $t \in [\![u]\!]$ and $t' \in [\![u']\!]$. The next task is to consider *guarded rewrite rules* of the form $l \rightarrow r$ **if** ϕ, where l and r are guarded terms, in order to define rewriting between guarded terms. Using Lemma 1, it can be assumed that l and r are $G(\Sigma)$-terms in the extended signature $G(\Sigma)$. Also, following the ideas of rewriting modulo SMT, rewriting with guarded terms is topmost.

Definition 6. *A guarded rewrite rule is a triple $l \rightarrow r$ **if** ϕ with two guarded terms $l, r \in T_{G(\Sigma)}(X)_{g(State)}$ of top sort State and a constraint ϕ.*

As usual, rewriting by guarded rules happens modulo a set of equations E. To be semantically correct regarding guarded terms, a set of equations E should preserve the semantics of guarded terms (i.e., if $u =_E \theta l$, then $u \equiv \theta l$), which is generally not true.[3] But structural axioms meet this condition as stated in Lemma 5. These structural axioms are very useful to specify component-based systems [11]; e.g., the formal specification of the case study in Sect. 4 frequently uses these axioms. From this point on it is assumed that E only includes structural axioms.

Lemma 5. *Given a set of equations B that only includes identity, associativity, and commutativity, $u =_B v$ implies $u \equiv_g v$ for guarded terms $u, v, \in T_{G(\Sigma)}(X)$.*

Definition 7 introduces the ground rewrite relation $\rightarrow_\mathcal{R}$ for guarded rewrite rules. A ground rewrite relation $u \rightarrow_\mathcal{R} u'$ holds by a guarded rule $l \rightarrow r$ **if** ϕ, whenever u is an instance of l, u' is an instance of $r|_\phi$, and both $\llbracket u \rrbracket$ and $\llbracket u' \rrbracket$ are not empty.

Definition 7. *For ground guarded terms $u, u' \in T_{G(\Sigma),g(State)}$, a ground rewrite relation $u \rightarrow_\mathcal{R} u'$ holds if and only if for a guarded rule $l \rightarrow r$ **if** ϕ and a ground substitution $\theta : X \longrightarrow T_{G(\Sigma)}$, it holds that: $u =_E \theta l$, $u' =_E \theta r|_{\theta \phi}$, $\llbracket u \rrbracket \neq \emptyset$, and $\llbracket u' \rrbracket \neq \emptyset$.*

The symbolic rewrite relation $\rightsquigarrow_\mathcal{R}$ by guarded rules is introduced in Definition 8. The last condition in this definition states that there is at least one ground instance $\theta u \rightarrow_\mathcal{R} \theta u'$ and also implies that $\mathcal{T}_{\mathcal{E}_0} \models \sigma \phi$ holds (because $u' =_E \sigma r|_{\sigma \phi}$ includes $\sigma \phi$).

Definition 8. *A symbolic rewrite relation $u \rightsquigarrow_\mathcal{R} u'$ holds for $u, u' \in T_{G(\Sigma)}(X)$ if and only if for a guarded rule $l \rightarrow r$ **if** ϕ and a substitution $\sigma : X \longrightarrow T_{G(\Sigma)}(X)$: $u =_E \sigma l$, $u' =_E \sigma r|_{\sigma \phi}$, and $(\exists \theta : X \rightarrow T_{G(\Sigma)}) \llbracket \theta u \rrbracket \neq \emptyset \wedge \llbracket \theta u' \rrbracket \neq \emptyset$.*

Consider a ground rewrite $u \rightarrow_\mathcal{R} u'$, which is ground equivalent to its standard expansion $u_1 \vee \cdots \vee u_n \rightarrow_\mathcal{R} u'_1 \vee \cdots \vee u'_m$, where u's standard form is $u_1 \vee \cdots \vee u_n$ and u''s standard form is $u'_1 \vee \cdots \vee u'_m$. This intuitively represents a set of ground rewrite relations $\{u_i \rightarrow u'_j \mid 1 \leq i \leq n, 1 \leq j \leq m\}$. This idea can be used to define a standard expansion of a guarded rewrite rule.

Definition 9 (Standard Expansion). *Consider a guarded rule $l \rightarrow r$ **if** ϕ such that l's standard form is $\bigvee_{i=1}^{n} l_i|_{\psi_i^l}$ and r's standard form is $\bigvee_{j=1}^{m} r_j|_{\psi_j^r}$. A standard expansion of $l \rightarrow r$ **if** ϕ is a collection of ordinary rewrite rules*

$$S(l \rightarrow r \text{ if } \phi) = \{l_i \rightarrow r_j \text{ if } \phi \wedge \psi_i^l \wedge \psi_j^r \mid 1 \leq i \leq n, 1 \leq j \leq m\}.$$

---

[3] Consider a set of equations E that replace any constraint in a guarded term by its negation. Then, $0|_{false} \equiv_E 0|_{\neg false}$, but clearly $\llbracket 0|_{false} \rrbracket \neq \llbracket 0|_{\neg false} \rrbracket$.

A guarded rewrite rule $l \to r$ **if** ϕ is related to its standard expansion (in terms of simulation). For each ground rewrite by a guarded rewrite rule, there exists a corresponding ground rewrite by its standard expansion. This means that reachability analysis can be effectively performed using guarded rewrite rules.

Theorem 2 (Simulation of Standard Expansion). *Consider a set R of guarded rewrite rules and its standard expansion $\hat{R} = \bigcup_{l \to r \text{ if } \phi \in R} S(l \to r \text{ if } \phi)$. For ground guarded terms $u, u' \in T_{G(\Sigma)}$, $u \to_{\mathcal{R}} u' \implies t \to_{\hat{R}} t'$ holds for any $t \in [\![u]\!]$ and $t' \in [\![u']\!]$.*

However, ground rewriting by a guarded rule may not capture all of ground rewriting by its standard expansion. Consider a guarded term $f(0) \vee g(0)$ and a guarded rewrite rule $f(x) \vee g(s(x)) \to f(x)$ **if** $x < 1$. Clearly, $f(0) \vee g(0)$ cannot be rewritten since it is not equal to any ground instance of $f(x) \vee g(s(x))$. But a ground instance of the rule $f(0) \vee g(s(0)) \to f(0)$ **if** $0 < 1$ suggests that $f(0) \to_{\mathcal{R}} f(0)$ holds. The notion of *admissible guarded terms* with respect to a guarded rewrite rule is introduced.

Definition 10. *A guarded term $u \in T_{G(\Sigma)}(X)$ is admissible for a rule $l \to r$ **if** ϕ if and only if $[\![u]\!] \cap [\![l]\!] \neq \emptyset \iff u =_E \sigma l$ for a substitution $\sigma : X \longrightarrow T_{\Sigma}(X)$.*

The admissibility requirements can be checked by using the standard form of guarded terms. In order to check $[\![u]\!] \cap [\![l]\!] \neq \emptyset$, u's standard form $\bigvee_i u_i|_{\phi_i}$ and l's standard form $\bigvee_j l_j|_{\psi_j}$ can be both computed, and then check if $\theta u_i =_E \theta l_j$ for a ground substitution θ such that $T_{\mathcal{E}_0} \models \theta \phi_i \wedge \theta \psi_j$. If no such substitution exists, then clearly $[\![u]\!] \cap [\![l]\!] = \emptyset$. This problem can be determined by E-unification. If $[\![u]\!] \cap [\![l]\!] \neq \emptyset$, it suffices to check if $u =_E \sigma l$ for a substitution σ, which can be determined by E-matching.

For admissible guarded terms, a symbolic rewrite relation exactly captures a ground rewrite relation as stated in Theorem 3. First, the notion of admissible terms is extended to guarded rewrite rules. A guarded rewrite rule $l \to r$ **if** ϕ is admissible for a set R of guarded rewrite rules if and only if the right side r is admissible for every rule in R. A set R of guarded rewrite rules is admissible if and only if every guarded rewrite rule in R is admissible for every rule in R.

Theorem 3 (Symbolic Guarded Rewriting). *Let R be a set of admissible guarded rules, $\theta : X \longrightarrow T_{G(\Sigma)}$ be a ground substitution, and $u, u' \in T_{G(\Sigma)}(X)$ be admissible guarded terms. Then: (i) If $u \rightsquigarrow_{\mathcal{R}} u'$, then $\theta u \to_{\mathcal{R}} \theta u'$ whenever $[\![\theta u]\!] \neq \emptyset$ and $[\![\theta u']\!] \neq \emptyset$. (ii) If $\theta u \to_{\mathcal{R}} w'$ for $w' \in T_{G(\Sigma)}$, then $u \rightsquigarrow_{\mathcal{R}} u'$ and $[\![w']\!] \subseteq [\![u']\!]$ for some u'.*

Example 8. Consider the following guarded rewrite rules:

$$I_1 \, I_2 \, C_1 \parallel C_2 \to I_1 \, C_1 \parallel (I_1 + I_2 + 1)|_{(I_1+I_2)\overset{3}{=}0} \vee \emptyset|_{(I_1+I_2)\overset{3}{\neq}0}) \, C_2 \text{ if } 0 < I_1 \wedge 0 < I_2$$

$$I_1 \parallel (I_2|_B \vee C_1|_{\neg B}) \, C_2 \to \emptyset \parallel (I_2|_B \vee C_1|_{\neg B}) \, C_2 \text{ if } B \wedge 0 < I_1 \wedge 0 < I_2 \wedge I_1 + I_2 \overset{17}{=} 0.$$

These rules are admissible, because each state is a pair $D_1 \parallel D_2$, constraints only appear in D_2, and the left-hand side of each rule defines the most general pattern for D_2. By Theorem 2, these rules are related to the standard expansion:

$$I_1\ I_2\ C_1 \parallel C_2 \rightarrow I_1\ C_1 \parallel I_1 + I_2 + 1\ C_2 \quad \text{if } 0 < I_1 \wedge 0 < I_2 \wedge (I_1 + I_2) \overset{3}{=} 0$$

$$I_1\ I_2\ C_1 \parallel C_2 \rightarrow I_1\ C_1 \parallel \emptyset\ C_2 \quad \text{if } 0 < I_1 \wedge 0 < I_2 \wedge (I_1 + I_2) \overset{3}{\neq} 0$$

$$I_1 \parallel I_2\ C_2 \rightarrow \emptyset \parallel I_2\ C_2 \text{ if } B \wedge 0 < I_1 \wedge 0 < I_2 \wedge I_1 + I_2 \overset{17}{=} 0 \wedge B$$

$$I_1 \parallel C_1\ C_2 \rightarrow \emptyset \parallel C_1\ C_2 \text{ if } B \wedge 0 < I_1 \wedge 0 < I_2 \wedge I_1 + I_2 \overset{17}{=} 0 \wedge \neg B$$

The last rule can be discarded because its condition is always unsatisfiable (containing both B and $\neg B$). Thanks to Theorems 2 and 3, the above guarded rewrite rules can be used to perform reachability analysis from an admissible symbolic state.

The use of guarded terms for the symbolic specification in Sect. 2.2 results in the search command proving the deadlock-freedom property that had previously timed-out:

```
search [1]  { I  I+1 I+2 I+3 || none, I > 0 }
      =>!  { C1 | C2, Phi } such that C1 =/= none = true .
No solution.
states: 265  rewrites: 37516 in 702ms cpu (704ms real)
```

This means that for *any* collection of 4 consecutive positive integers in the left channel, the system will eventually reach a state without numbers in this channel.

4   A Case Study

This section shows how the number of symbolic states can be dramatically reduced by slightly introducing guarded terms in the existing symbolic specification of CASH in [19]. The CASH algorithm was first formally specified and analyzed in Real-Time Maude using explicit-state methods [17], and symbolically analyzed using rewriting modulo SMT to deal with an infinite number of states [19]. Due to the symbolic state space explosion problem and the complexity of the accumulated constraints, some reachability properties of interest were previously beyond the reach of rewriting modulo SMT in [19], but can now be analyzed using guarded terms.

4.1   Symbolic States Using Guarded Terms

In CASH, each task has a given period and a given worst-case execution time. When an instance of a task is completed before its worst-case execution time, the unused processor time is added to a global queue of unused budgets. Another task can then use these unused execution times as well as its own execution budget, instead of just wasting them. In addition to capacity sharing, tasks are scheduled according to standard preemptive EDF scheduling: the task with the shortest time remaining until its deadline has the priority and can preempt the currently executing task. The reader is referred to [7,17] for details about the CASH algorithm.

In rewriting logic specification, an object of class C is represented as a term $<O: C|att_1: v_1, \ldots, att_1: v_n>$ of sort *Object*, where O is the identifier, and $v_1, \ldots, v_n$ are the values of the attributes $att_1, \ldots, att_n$ [11]. A system state, called a *configuration*, is declared as a multiset of these objects. Multiset union for configurations is given by a juxtaposition operator that is associative and commutative and having the `none` multiset as its identity element.

In the CASH specification, the configuration consists of a number of servers (i.e., tasks) and a global queue. A server state consists of six attributes: the maximum budget, period, internal state (`idle`, `waiting`, or `executing`), time executed, budget time used, and time to deadline. These variables are modeled as nonnegative integers. Specifically, for internal states, 0 denotes `idle`, 1 denotes `waiting`, and 2 denotes `executing`. A server object with name O is modeled as a term of sort *Object* and has the form

```
< O : server | maxBudget : m,    period : p,        state : s,
               timeExecuted : e, usedOfBudget : u, timeToDeadline : d >
```

A global object contains the global queue of unused budgets, the availability of the processor, and a flag to denote whether any deadline has been missed. Both availability and deadline missed flags are modeled as Boolean values. A global object with name G is modeled as a term of sort *Object* and has the form

```
< G : global | cq : queue, available : a, deadline-miss : b >
```

A global queue is a priority queue of unused budgets. Each item in a queue is a pair (`deadline:` i `budget:` i') of deadline i and budget i'. An item with the smallest deadline has the highest priority. In [17,19], a global queue is specified as a sorted list. Instead, in this work the queue is modeled as a *multiset* of items in order to symbolically define queue operations using only SMT constraints. For example, consider a queue

$$cq \equiv (\texttt{deadline:} \ i_1 \ \texttt{budget:} \ i'_1) \ \ldots \ (\texttt{deadline:} \ i_n \ \texttt{budget:} \ i'_n)$$

with n items. The operation to peek the highest-priority element is defined by:

$$peek(cq) = (\texttt{deadline:} \ i_k \ \texttt{budget:} \ i'_k) \iff \bigwedge_{j=1}^{n} i_k \leq i_j.$$

Guarded terms are used in the new symbolic specification in a number of ways. First, each variable in a server state or a global object can be guarded by constraints. For example, the guarded term $0_\phi \vee 1_{\neg\phi}$ denotes an internal state of a server which is either 0, if the condition ϕ holds, or 1, otherwise. Second, each item in a server state can be guarded by constraints. In a similar way to the example in Sect. 2, the guarded term $(\texttt{deadline:} \ i \ \texttt{budget:} \ i')|_\phi \vee emptyQueue|_{\neg\phi}$ denotes an item which is either present if the condition ϕ is satisfiable, or absent otherwise.

Some syntactic sugar is defined to succinctly write these guarded terms as follows: $\phi \ ? \ i : j$ denotes the guarded term $i_\phi \vee j_{\neg\phi}$, for $i, j \in \mathbb{Z}$, and $(e \ \mathtt{const}\colon \phi)$ denotes the guarded term $e|_\phi \vee e|_{\neg\phi}$, for each item e in the priority queue. For example, the following expression includes both types of guarded terms:

```
(deadline: I3 >= 1 ? I3 - 1 : 0  budget: I2 >= 1 ? 1 : 0  const: I2 > 1).
```

4.2 Symbolic Transitions Using Guarded Rewrite Rules

The symbolic transitions of the CASH algorithm are specified by 13 conditional rewrite rules in [19], which are adapted from the Real-Time Maude specification in [17]. The rule conditions specify constraints solvable by the SMT decision procedure, together with some extra conditions to generate constraints by rewriting. This section highlights some of the rules to explain how to remove symbolic branching using guarded terms. The reader is referred to [5] for the full description of all (guarded) rewrite rules.

Rule stopExecuting1. This rule specifies when one server completes execution while another server is waiting. The waiting server with the least time remaining until its deadline starts executing, and any budget left is added to the global queue. Previously, this behavior was specified by two rewrite rules in [19], depending on whether any budget remains. However, with guarded terms only one rewrite rule is needed:[4,5,6]

```
{< G   : global | cq : CQ, AtSG >
 < O   : server | state : St,          usedOfBudget : T,
                  maxBudget : NZT,      timeToDeadline : T1,
                  timeExecuted : NZT1,  period : NZT2, AtS >
 < O'  : server | state : St', timeToDeadline : T2, AtS' > REST}
=> {< G  : global | cq : (deadline: T1  budget: (NZT monus T)
                         const: (NZT > T)) CQ, AtSG >
 < O   : server | state : idle,        usedOfBudget : NZT,
                  maxBudget : NZT,      timeToDeadline : T1,
                  timeExecuted : NZT1,  period : NZT2, AtS >
 < O'  : server | state : executing, timeToDeadline : T2, AtS' > REST}
if ALL := ...  /\  (St === executing) /\  (St' === waiting)  /\  (NZT > 0)
/\ (NZT1 > 0)  /\  (NZT2 > 0)  /\  (T >= 0)  /\  ((NZT monus T) <= T1)
/\ (T1 >= 0)  /\  (T2 >= 0)  /\  nextDeadlineWaiting(ALL,O,T2)
```

The guarded term `(deadline: T1 budget: (NZT monus T) const: (NZT > T))`, which is only present in the priority queue if the condition `NZT > T` is satisfiable, is written in the `global` object in the right hand side of the rewrite rule. Unlike [19], no constraints are yet added regarding the "position" of the newly added item in

---

[4] The specification of `ALL` has been omitted in the rule. `ALL` represents the entire configuration in the left hand side.

[5] The `monus` operator is defined by: $a \ \mathtt{monus} \ b = \max(a - b, 0)$.

[6] The function `nextDeadlineWaiting(ALL,O,T2)` returns a constraint stating that the `timeToDeadline` of all servers, except `O`, is at least `T2`.

the queue, because: (i) the item may be absent if its constraint is not satisfiable, and (ii) the priority queue is specified as a multiset with symbolic constraints.

Rule tickExecutingSpareCapacity. This rule models time elapse when a server is executing a spare capacity, specified as one guarded rewrite rule below.[7] The left hand side of the rule contains the guarded term (deadline: I1 budget: I2 const: iB). The condition iB in the rule condition specifies that the item is present in the queue. The condition aboveOrEqualDeadline(I1,CQ) states that all deadlines in CQ are at least I1, that is, that the item is indeed the one with the highest priority.

```
    {< G : global | cq : (deadline: I1 budget: I2 const: iB) CQ, AtSG >
     < O : server | state : St,
                   timeExecuted : T1,    timeToDeadline : T2, AtS > REST}
=> { delta-global( < G : global | cq : (deadline: I1 budget: (I2 + (- 1))
                   const: (iB and (I2 > 1))) CQ, AtSG >, 1)
      delta-servers(< O : server | state : executing,      timeExecuted : T1,
                   timeToDeadline : T2, AtS > REST, 1, false)}
if ALL := ...   /\  (St === executing)  /\  (T1 >= 0) /\  (T2 >= 0)
/\ iB  /\  (I1 >= 1)  /\  (I2 >= 1)  /\  (T2 >= 1)  /\  (I1 <= T2)
/\ mte-server(ALL,O,1)   /\   noDeadlineMiss(ALL)
/\ aboveOrEqualDeadline(I1,CQ)
```

4.3   Symbolic Reachability Analysis

The goal is to symbolically analyze if missed deadlines exist for variant of) the CASH algorithm from an infinite set of initial configurations containing two servers s_1 and s_2. Suppose that server s_i (for $i = 1, 2$) has maximum budget b_i and period p_i such that $0 \leq b_i < p_i$. No deadline misses are guaranteed only when the processor utilization is less than or equal to 100% (i.e., $b_1/p_1 + b_2/p_2 \leq 1$) [7]. A counterexample exists if there is no constraint on the initial configurations. Indeed, the previous work [19] can find a symbolic counterexample that violates this constraint using rewriting module SMT.

A more interesting problem is to check the existence of missed deadlines of the *variant* of the CASH algorithm [17], that uses a different scheduling strategy, when $b_1/p_1 + b_2/p_2 \leq 1$ is satisfied. Using explicit-state model checking, it is shown in [17] that the variant can have a counterexample, even though $b_1/p_1 + b_2/p_2 \leq 1$ is satisfied. Since this constraint is non-linear, it is beyond the capabilities of state-of-the-art SMT solvers. But by fixing p_1 and p_2, say $p_1 = 5$ and $p_2 = 7$, the constraint becomes linear and symbolic analysis can be performed using existing SMT solvers.

Here an infinite set of initial configurations with two servers s_1 and s_2 is considered. Server s_i (for $i = 1, 2$) has maximum budget b_i and period p_i such that $0 \leq b_i < p_i$, and has the constraint $b_1/p_1 + b_2/p_2 \leq 1$. A symbolic state

---

[7] The functions delta-global and delta-servers model the time lapse; that is, variables in servers and the queue are accordingly increased or decreased (by 1) based on the current state.

can be modeled as term init(b_1, p_1, b_2, p_2). The previous work in [19] cannot deal with this problem due to the symbolic state space explosion; it generates nearly one billion symbolic states and does not terminate for a few days. On the other hand, the new specification using guarded terms can successfully find a counterexample from init$(b_1, 5, b_2, 7)$:

```
search [1] init(I0,5,I2,7)
        =>* {B:Bool , < g : global | deadline-miss : true, AtS > Cnf} .
Solution 1 (state 590751)
states: 590752  rewrites: 1910935222 in 5513748ms cpu (5513848ms real)
B --> not I0 < 0 and not I2 + -5 < 0 and not 1 + - I0 < 0 and not 7 + -
    I2 < 0 and not 35 + - (I2 * 5) + - (I0 * 7) < 0 and (not 7 + - I2 < 0 or
    I2 + -1 < 0) and (not 12 + - I2 < 0 or I2 < 0) and (not 17 + - I2 < 0 or
    I2 < 0) and - I0 < 0 and I2 + -7 < 0 and I0 + -5 < 0 and 4 + - I2 < 0
Cnf --> < s1 : server | maxBudget : I0, period : 5, state : 2,
            usedOfBudget : 0, timeToDeadline : 0, timeExecuted : 5 >
        < s2 : server | maxBudget : I2, period : 7, state : 0,
            usedOfBudget : I2, timeToDeadline : 7, timeExecuted : 2 >
AtS --> cq : deadline: 7 budget: not I2 < 0 ? I2 + -5 : -5
            const: (not I2 < 0 and 5 + - I2 < 0), available : false
```

The counterexample is found at search depth 23, which could not be reached without guarded terms. A sequence of symbolic rewrites to reach this counterexample can be obtained by Maude's show path command. In the counterexample, B represents the accumulated constraint whose satisfiable assignment gives a concrete counterexample. The queue cq has the single item if the constraint (not I2 < 0 and 5 + - I2 < 0) is satisfied; otherwise, cq is empty. For example, B has the satisfiable assignment I0 = 1 and I2 = 5, which is found by an SMT solver, and in this case the queue cq is empty. An explicit search with these concrete values in the *ground* rewriting logic semantics of CASH gives an expected result as follows:

```
search [1] init(1,5,5,7)
        =>* {true, < g : global | deadline-miss : true, AtS > Cnf} .
Solution 1 (state 107393)
states: 107394  rewrites: 36507422 in 29543ms cpu (29699ms real)
Cnf --> < s1 : server | maxBudget : 1, period : 5, state : 2,
            usedOfBudget : 0, timeToDeadline : 0, timeExecuted : 5 >
        < s2 : server | maxBudget : 5, period : 7, state : 0,
            usedOfBudget : 5, timeToDeadline : 7, timeExecuted : 2 >
AtS --> cq : emptyQueue, available : false
```

5   Related Work and Concluding Remarks

SMT-based reachability analysis has been used in software component testing and verification of infinite-state systems [9]. SMT-CBMC [1] and Corral [13] use bounded model checking, with unbounded types represented by built-in variables. KLEE [8] is used for symbolic execution and constraint solving, finding possible inputs that will cause a programming artifact to crash. The IC3

SMT-based model checker [10] uses over- and under-approximation techniques to efficiently handle symbolic transitions on infinite sets of states. What all these approaches have in common is the effort in developing advanced techniques and tools to speed up the reachability analysis process based on SMT-solving. Guarded terms are a technique to speed up and often attain convergence of the reachability analysis process for rewriting modulo SMT. It complements narrowing-based reachability analysis [2,16], another symbolic technique combining narrowing modulo theories and model checking.

This paper presented *guarded terms*, a technique with the potential to reduce the symbolic state space and the complexity of constraints in the rewriting modulo SMT approach. Rewriting modulo SMT [19] is a novel symbolic technique to model and analyze reachability properties of infinite-state systems. This is a technique in the realm of rewriting logic that can greatly improve the specification and verification of reachability properties of open systems such as real-time and cyber-physical systems. Guarded terms generalize the constrained terms of rewriting modulo SMT by allowing a term in a symbolic state to have constrained subterms: these subterms can be seen as a choice operator that is part of the term structure. They can be composed in parallel and be nested, thus enabling the succinct encoding of several constrained terms into one guarded term. The potential of guarded terms for reducing the symbolic state-space, and the complexity and size of constraints has been illustrated by a running example and a case study. The latter is an improvement of a previously developed case study where guarded terms enable the analysis of reachability properties of the CASH scheduling algorithm [7].

As future work, the plan is to explore the use of guarded terms in improving the symbolic rewriting logic semantics of PLEXIL [18,19], and in specifying the symbolic rewriting logic semantics of other real-time and cyber-physical systems. Other SMT techniques, including state subsumption, backwards reachability, k-induction, and interpolants, should certainly be studied for rewriting modulo SMT. Another perspective is to use guarded terms for improving narrowing-based reachability analysis.

Acknowledgments. The first author was supported by the Basic Science Research Program through the National Research Foundation of Korea (NRF) funded by the Ministry of Education (2016R1D1A1B03935275). The second author has been supported in part by the EPIC project funded by the Administrative Department of Science, Technology and Innovation of Colombia (Colciencias) under contract 233-2017.

References

1. Armando, A., Mantovani, J., Platania, L.: Bounded model checking of software using SMT solvers instead of SAT solvers. Softw. Tools Technol. Transf. **11**(1), 69–83 (2009)
2. Bae, K., Escobar, S., Meseguer, J.: Abstract logical model checking of infinite-state systems using narrowing. In: RTA. LIPIcs, vol. 21, pp. 81–96. Schloss Dagstuhl (2013)

3. Bae, K., Ölveczky, P.C., Meseguer, J.: Definition, semantics, and analysis of Multirate Synchronous AADL. In: Jones, C., Pihlajasaari, P., Sun, J. (eds.) FM 2014. LNCS, vol. 8442, pp. 94–109. Springer, Cham (2014). doi:10.1007/978-3-319-06410-9_7

4. Bae, K., Ölveczky, P.C., Feng, T.H., Lee, E.A., Tripakis, S.: Verifying hierarchical Ptolemy II discrete-event models using Real-Time Maude. Sci. Comput. Program. **77**(12), 1235–1271 (2012)

5. Bae, K., Rocha, C.: A Note on Guarded Terms for Rewriting Modulo SMT, July 2017. http://sevlab.postech.ac.kr/~kmbae/rew-smt

6. Bruni, R., Meseguer, J.: Semantic foundations for generalized rewrite theories. Theoret. Comput. Sci. **360**(1–3), 386–414 (2006)

7. Caccamo, M., Buttazzo, G., Sha, L.: Capacity sharing for overrun control. In: RTSS, pp. 295–304. IEEE (2000)

8. Cadar, C., Dunbar, D., Engler, D.R.: KLEE: unassisted and automatic generation of high-coverage tests for complex systems programs. In: OSDI, pp. 209–224 (2008)

9. Cadar, C., Sen, K.: Symbolic execution for software testing: three decades later. Commun. ACM **56**(2), 82–90 (2013)

10. Cimatti, A., Griggio, A.: Software model checking via IC3. In: Madhusudan, P., Seshia, S.A. (eds.) CAV 2012. LNCS, vol. 7358, pp. 277–293. Springer, Heidelberg (2012). doi:10.1007/978-3-642-31424-7_23

11. Clavel, M., Durán, F., Eker, S., Lincoln, P., Martí-Oliet, N., Meseguer, J., Talcott, C.: All About Maude - A High-Performance Logical Framework: How to Specify, Program and Verify Systems in Rewriting Logic. LNCS, vol. 4350. Springer, Heidelberg (2007)

12. Dowek, G., Muñoz, C., Rocha, C.: Rewriting logic semantics of a plan execution language. Electron. Proc. Theor. Comput. Sci. **18**, 77–91 (2010)

13. Lal, A., Qadeer, S., Lahiri, S.: Corral: a solver for reachability modulo theories. Technical report MSR-TR-2012-9, Microsoft Research, January 2012

14. Meseguer, J.: Conditional rewriting logic as a unified model of concurrency. Theoret. Comput. Sci. **96**(1), 73–155 (1992)

15. Meseguer, J.: Twenty years of rewriting logic. J. Logic Algebraic Program. **81**(7–8), 721–781 (2012)

16. Meseguer, J., Thati, P.: Symbolic reachability analysis using narrowing and its application to verification of cryptographic protocols. High.-Ord. Symbolic Comput. **20**(1–2), 123–160 (2007)

17. Ölveczky, P.C., Caccamo, M.: Formal simulation and analysis of the CASH scheduling algorithm in Real-Time Maude. In: Baresi, L., Heckel, R. (eds.) FASE 2006. LNCS, vol. 3922, pp. 357–372. Springer, Heidelberg (2006). doi:10.1007/11693017_26

18. Rocha, C.: Symbolic Reachability Analysis for Rewrite Theories. Ph.D. thesis, University of Illinois, December 2012

19. Rocha, C., Meseguer, J., Muñoz, C.: Rewriting modulo SMT and open system analysis. J. Log. Algebraic Methods Program. **86**(1), 269–297 (2017)

On Weighted Configuration Logics

Paulina Paraponiari and George Rahonis[(⊠)]

Department of Mathematics, Aristotle University of Thessaloniki,
54124 Thessalonki, Greece
{parapavl,grahonis}@math.auth.gr

Abstract. We introduce and investigate a weighted propositional configuration logic over a commutative semiring. Our logic, which is proved to be sound and complete, is intended to serve as a specification language for software architectures with quantitative features. We extend the weighted configuration logic to its first-order level and succeed in describing architecture styles equipped with quantitative characteristics. We provide interesting examples of weighted architecture styles. Surprisingly, we can construct a formula, in our logic, which describes a classical problem of a different nature than that of software architectures.

Keywords: Software architectures · Configuration logics · Semirings · Weighted configuration logics

1 Introduction

Architecture is a critical issue in design and development of complex software systems. Whenever the construction of a software system is based on a "good" architecture, then the system satisfies most of its functional and quality requirements. But what are the characteristics of a "good" architecture and how one can design it? Despite the huge progress on software architecture, over almost three decades, the field remains relatively immature (cf. [5] for an excellent presentation of the progress of software architecture). Several fundamental matters still remain open, for instance the distinction between architectures and their properties. Recently in [11], the relation among architectures and architecture styles has been studied. An architecture style describes a family of "similar" architectures, i.e., architectures with the same types of components and topologies. The authors introduced the propositional configuration logic (*PCL* for short) which was proved sufficient to describe architectures: the meaning of every *PCL* formula is a configuration set, and every architecture can be represented by a configuration on the set of its components. The first-order and second-order extensions of *PCL* described perfectly the concept of architecture styles. Therefore, *PCL* and its first- and second-order extensions constitute logics for the specification of architecture styles and hence, an important contribution to rigorous systems design (cf. [14]).

In this paper we introduce and investigate a weighted *PCL* over a commutative semiring $(K, \oplus, \otimes, 1, 0)$. Our work is motivated as follows. *PCL* and its

© Springer International Publishing AG 2017
J. Proença and M. Lumpe (Eds.): FACS 2017, LNCS 10487, pp. 98–116, 2017.
DOI: 10.1007/978-3-319-68034-7_6

first- and second-order extensions of [11] describe qualitative features of architectures and architecture styles. Weighted *PCL* describes quantitative features of architectures, and weighted first-order configuration logic describes quantitative features of architecture styles. For instance, the costs of the interactions among the components of an architecture, the time needed, the probability of the implementation of a concrete interaction, etc. Our weighted *PCL* consists of the *PCL* of [11] which is interpreted in the same way, and a copy of it which is interpreted quantitatively. This formulation has the advantage that practitioners can use the *PCL* exactly as they are used to, and the copy of it for the quantitative interpretation. The semantics of weighted *PCL* formulas are polynomials with values in the semiring K. The semantics of (unweighted) *PCL* formulas take only the values 1 and 0 corresponding to *true* and *false*, respectively. Weighted logics have been considered so far in other set-ups. More precisely, the weighted *MSO* logic over words, trees, pictures, nested words, timed words, and graphs (cf. [1]), the weighted *FO* logic [8–10], the weighted *LTL* (cf. for instance [3] and the references in that paper), the weighted *LDL* [3], as well as the weighted *MSO* logic and *LDL* over infinite alphabets [13], and the weighted μ-calculus and CTL [7].

The main contributions of our work are the following. We prove that for every weighted *PCL* formula we can effectively construct an equivalent one in full normal form which is unique up to the equivalence relation. Furthermore, our weighted *PCL* is sound and complete. Both the aforementioned results hold also for *PCL* and this shows the robustness of the theory of *PCL*. We prove several properties for the weighted first-order configuration logic and in addition for its Boolean counterpart of [11]. We present as an example the weighted *PCL* formula describing the Master/Slave architecture with quantitative features. According to the underlying semiring, we get information for the cost, probability, time, etc. of the implementation of an interaction between a Master and a Slave. We construct a weighted first-order configuration logic formula for the Publish/Subscribe architecture style with additional quantitative characteristics. Surprisingly, though *PCL* was mainly developed as a specification language for architectures, we could construct a weighted *PCL* formula describing the well-known travelling salesman problem.

Apart from this introduction the paper contains 5 sections. In Sect. 2 we present preliminary background needed in the sequel. In Sect. 3 we introduce the weighted proposition interaction logic which describes quantitative interactions among the components of an architecture. Then, in Sect. 4 we introduce the weighted *PCL* and investigate the main properties of the semantics of weighted *PCL* formulas. Section 5 is devoted to the construction of the unique full normal form (modulo the equivalence relation) equivalent to a given weighted *PCL* formula. Furthermore, it contains the results for the soundness and completeness of the weighted *PCL*. In Sect. 6, we extend the weighted *PCL* to its first-order level. We prove several properties for weighted first-order configuration logic formulas as well as for first-order configuration logic formulas of [11]. Finally, in the conclusion, we list several open problems for future research. Due to space limitations we skip detailed proofs of our results. We refer the interested reader to the full version of our paper on arXiv [12].

2 Preliminaries

A *semiring* $(K, \oplus, \otimes, 0, 1)$ consists of a set K, two binary operations $\oplus$ and $\otimes$ and two constant elements 0 and 1 such that $(K, \oplus, 0)$ is a commutative monoid, $(K, \otimes, 1)$ is a monoid, multiplication distributes over addition, and $0 \otimes k = k \otimes 0 = 0$ for every $k \in K$. If the monoid $(K, \otimes, 1)$ is commutative, then the semiring is called commutative. The semiring is denoted simply by K if the operations and the constant elements are understood. The result of the empty product as usual equals to 1. The semiring K is called (additively) idempotent if $k \oplus k = k$ for every $k \in K$. The following algebraic structures are well-known semirings: the semiring $(\mathbb{N}, +, \cdot, 0, 1)$ of natural numbers, the Boolean semiring $B = (\{0, 1\}, +, \cdot, 0, 1)$, the tropical or min-plus semiring $\mathbb{R}_{\min} = (\mathbb{R}_+ \cup \{\infty\}, \min, +, \infty, 0)$ where $\mathbb{R}_+ = \{r \in \mathbb{R} \mid r \geq 0\}$, the arctical or max-plus semiring $\mathbb{R}_{\max} = (\mathbb{R}_+ \cup \{-\infty\}, \max, +, -\infty, 0)$, the Viterbi semiring $([0, 1], \max, \cdot, 0, 1)$ used in probability theory, and every bounded distributive lattice with the operations sup and inf, especially the fuzzy semiring $F = ([0, 1], \max, \min, 0, 1)$. Trivially all the previous semirings are commutative, and all but the first one are idempotent.

Let Q be a set. A *formal series* (or simply *series*) *over Q and K* is a mapping $s : Q \to K$. The *support of s* is the set $\mathrm{supp}(s) = \{q \in Q \mid s(q) \neq 0\}$. A series with finite support is called also a *polynomial*. We denote by $K\langle\langle Q \rangle\rangle$ the class of all series over Q and K, and by $K\langle Q \rangle$ the class of all polynomials over Q and K. Let $s, r \in K\langle\langle Q \rangle\rangle$ and $k \in K$. The *sum* $s \oplus r$, the *products with scalars* ks and sk, and the *Hadamard product* $s \otimes r$ are defined elementwise, respectively by $s \oplus r(v) = s(v) \oplus r(v)$, $ks(v) = k \otimes s(v)$, $sk(v) = s(v) \otimes k$, $s \otimes r(v) = s(v) \otimes r(v)$ for every $v \in Q$. Trivially, if the series s, r are polynomials, then the series $s \oplus r, ks, sk, s \otimes r$ are also polynomials.

Throughout the paper K will denote a commutative semiring.

3 Weighted Propositional Interaction Logic

In this section, we introduce the weighted propositional interaction logic. For this, we need to recall first the propositional interaction logic [11].

Let P be a nonempty finite set of *ports*. We let $I(P) = \mathcal{P}(P) \setminus \{\emptyset\}$, where $\mathcal{P}(P)$ denotes the power set of P. Every set $a \in I(P)$ is called an *interaction*. The syntax of *propositional interaction logic* (*PIL* for short) formulas over P is given by the grammar

$$\phi ::= true \mid p \mid \overline{\phi} \mid \phi \vee \phi$$

where $p \in P$. As usual, we set $\overline{\overline{\phi}} = \phi$ for every *PIL* formula ϕ and $false = \overline{true}$. Then, the conjunction of two *PIL* formulas ϕ, ϕ' is defined by $\phi \wedge \phi' = \overline{(\overline{\phi} \vee \overline{\phi'})}$. A *PIL* formula of the form $p_1 \wedge \ldots \wedge p_n$ where $n > 0$ and $p_i \in P$ or $\overline{p_i} \in P$ for every $1 \leq i \leq n$, is called a *monomial*. We shall simply denote a monomial $p_1 \wedge \ldots \wedge p_n$ by $p_1 \ldots p_n$.

Let ϕ be a *PIL* formula and a an interaction. We write $a \models_i \phi$ iff the formula ϕ evaluates to *true* by letting $p = true$ for every $p \in a$, and $p = false$ otherwise. It should be clear that $a \not\models_i false$ for every $a \in I(P)$. For every interaction a we define its characteristic monomial $m_a = \bigwedge_{p \in a} p \wedge \bigwedge_{p \notin a} \bar{p}$. Then, for every interaction a' we trivially get $a' \models_i m_a$ iff $a' = a$.

Throughout the paper P will denote a nonempty finite set of ports.

Definition 1. *The syntax of formulas of the* weighted *PIL over P and K is given by the grammar*

$$\varphi :: = k \mid \phi \mid \varphi \oplus \varphi \mid \varphi \otimes \varphi$$

where $k \in K$ and ϕ denotes a PIL formula.

We denote by $PIL(K, P)$ the set of all weighted *PIL* formulas φ over P and K. Next, we represent the semantics of formulas $\varphi \in PIL(K, P)$ as polynomials $\|\varphi\| \in K \langle I(P) \rangle$[1]. For the semantics of *PIL* formulas ϕ we use the satisfaction relation as defined above. In this way, we ensure that the semantics of *PIL* formulas ϕ gets only the values 0 and 1.

Definition 2. *Let $\varphi \in PIL(K, P)$. The semantics of φ is a polynomial $\|\varphi\| \in K \langle I(P) \rangle$. For every $a \in I(P)$ the value $\|\varphi\| (a)$ is defined inductively as follows:*

$$\|k\| (a) = k, \qquad\qquad \|\varphi \oplus \psi\| (a) = \|\varphi\| (a) \oplus \|\psi\| (a),$$

$$\|\phi\| (a) = \begin{cases} 1 & \text{if } a \models_i \phi \\ 0 & \text{otherwise} \end{cases}, \qquad \|\varphi \otimes \psi\| (a) = \|\varphi\| (a) \otimes \|\psi\| (a).$$

A polynomial $s \in K \langle I(P) \rangle$ is called *PIL-definable* if there is a formula $\varphi \in PIL(K, P)$ such that $s = \|\varphi\|$.

Remark 1. The reader should note that the semantics of the weighted *PIL* formulas $\phi \vee \phi$ and $\phi \oplus \phi$, where ϕ is a *PIL* formula, are different. Indeed assume that $a \in I(P)$ is such that $a \models_i \phi$. Then, by our definition above, we get $\|\phi \vee \phi\| (a) = 1$ whereas $\|\phi \oplus \phi\| (a) = 1 \oplus 1$.

Next we present an example of a weighted *PIL* formula.

Example 1. We recall from [11] the Master/Slave architecture for two masters M_1, M_2 and two slaves S_1, S_2 with ports m_1, m_2 and s_1, s_2, respectively. The monomial

$$\phi_{i,j} = s_i \wedge m_j \wedge \overline{s_{i'}} \wedge \overline{m_{j'}}$$

for every $1 \leq i, i', j, j' \leq 2$ with $i \neq i'$ and $j \neq j'$, defines the binary interaction between the ports s_i and m_j (Fig. 1).

For every $1 \leq i, j \leq 2$ we consider the weighted *PIL* formula $\varphi_{i,j} = k_{i,j} \otimes \phi_{i,j}$ where $k_{i,j} \in K$. Hence, $k_{i,j}$ can be considered, according to the underlying semiring, as the "cost" for the implementation of the interaction $\phi_{i,j}$. For instance if K is the Viterbi semiring, then the value $k_{i,j} \in [0, 1]$ represents the probability of the implementation of the interaction between the ports s_i and m_j.

---

[1] Since P is finite, the domain of $\|\varphi\|$ is finite and in turn its support is also finite.

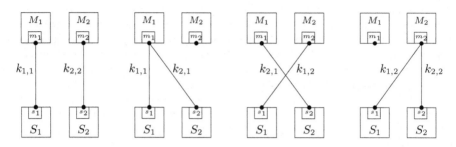

Fig. 1. Weighted Master/Slave architecture.

4   Weighted Propositional Configuration Logic

In this section, we introduce and investigate the weighted propositional configuration logic. Firstly, we recall the propositional configuration logic of [11]. More precisely, the syntax of *propositional configuration logic* (*PCL* for short) formulas over P is given by the grammar

$$f:: = true \mid \phi \mid \neg f \mid f \sqcup f \mid f + f$$

where ϕ denotes a *PIL* formula. The operators $\neg$, $\sqcup$, and $+$ are called *complementation, union,* and *coalescing,* respectively. We define also the *intersection* $\sqcap$ and *implication* $\implies$ operators, respectively as follows: $f_1 \sqcap f_2 := \neg(\neg f_1 \sqcup \neg f_2)$, and $f_1 \implies f_2 := \neg f_1 \sqcup f_2$. To avoid any confusion, every *PCL* formula which is a *PIL* formula will be called an *interaction formula*. We let $C(P) = \mathcal{P}(I(P)) \setminus \{\emptyset\}$. For every *PCL* formula f and $\gamma \in C(P)$ we define the satisfaction relation $\gamma \models f$ inductively on the structure of f as follows:

$\gamma \models true,$ $\qquad\qquad\qquad \gamma \models f_1 \sqcup f_2$ iff $\gamma \models f_1$ or $\gamma \models f_2,$
$\gamma \models \phi$ iff $a \models_i \phi$ for every $a \in \gamma,$ $\gamma \models \neg f$ iff $\gamma \not\models f,$
$\gamma \models f_1 + f_2$ iff there exist $\gamma_1, \gamma_2 \in C(P)$ such that
$$\gamma = \gamma_1 \cup \gamma_2, \text{ and } \gamma_1 \models f_1 \text{ and } \gamma_2 \models f_2.$$

The *closure* $\sim f$ of every *PCL* formula f, and the *disjunction* $f_1 \vee f_2$ of two *PCL* formulas f_1 and f_2 are defined, respectively by $\sim f := f + true$ and $f_1 \vee f_2 := f_1 \sqcup f_2 \sqcup (f_1 + f_2)$. Two *PCL* formulas f, f' are called *equivalent,* and we denote it by $f \equiv f'$, whenever $\gamma \models f$ iff $\gamma \models f'$ for every $\gamma \in C(P)$. We shall need the following lemma.

Lemma 1. *Let ϕ be a PIL formula. Then $\phi + \phi \equiv \phi$.*

Next we introduce our weighted *PCL*.

Definition 3. *The syntax of formulas of the weighted PCL over P and K is given by the grammar*

$$\zeta:: = k \mid f \mid \zeta \oplus \zeta \mid \zeta \otimes \zeta \mid \zeta \uplus \zeta$$

where $k \in K$, f denotes a PCL formula, and $\uplus$ denotes the coalescing operator *among weighted PCL formulas.*

Again, as for *PCL* formulas, to avoid any confusion, every weighted *PCL* formula which is a weighted *PIL* formula will be called a *weighted interaction formula*. We denote by $PCL(K, P)$ the set of all weighted *PCL* formulas over P and K. We represent the semantics of formulas $\zeta \in PCL(K, P)$ as polynomials $\|\zeta\| \in K\langle C(P)\rangle$. For the semantics of *PCL* formulas we use the satisfaction relation as defined previously.

Definition 4. *Let* $\zeta \in PCL(K, P)$. *The semantics of* ζ *is a polynomial* $\|\zeta\| \in K\langle C(P)\rangle$. *For every* $\gamma \in C(P)$ *the value* $\|\zeta\|(\gamma)$ *is defined inductively as follows:*

$$\|k\|(\gamma) = k, \qquad\qquad \|\zeta_1 \oplus \zeta_2\|(\gamma) = \|\zeta_1\|(\gamma) \oplus \|\zeta_2\|(\gamma),$$

$$\|f\|(\gamma) = \begin{cases} 1 & \text{if } \gamma \models f \\ 0 & \text{otherwise} \end{cases}, \qquad \|\zeta_1 \otimes \zeta_2\|(\gamma) = \|\zeta_1\|(\gamma) \otimes \|\zeta_2\|(\gamma),$$

$$\|\zeta_1 \uplus \zeta_2\|(\gamma) = \bigoplus\nolimits_{\gamma = \gamma_1 \cup \gamma_2} \left(\|\zeta_1\|(\gamma_1) \otimes \|\zeta_2\|(\gamma_2)\right).$$

Since the semantics of every weighted *PCL* formula is defined on $C(P)$, the sets γ_1 and γ_2 in $\|\zeta_1 \uplus \zeta_2\|(\gamma)$ are nonempty. A polynomial $s \in K\langle C(P)\rangle$ is called *PCL-definable* if there is a formula $\zeta \in PCL(K, P)$ such that $s = \|\zeta\|$. Two weighted *PCL* formulas ζ_1, ζ_2 are called equivalent, and we write $\zeta_1 \equiv \zeta_2$ whenever $\|\zeta_1\| = \|\zeta_2\|$.

The *closure* $\sim\zeta$ of every weighted *PCL* formula $\zeta \in PCL(K, P)$, and the *disjunction* $\zeta_1 \curlyvee \zeta_2$ of two weighted *PCL* formulas $\zeta_1, \zeta_2 \in PCL(K, P)$ are determined, respectively, by the following macros:

- $\sim\zeta := \zeta \uplus 1$,
- $\zeta_1 \curlyvee \zeta_2 := \zeta_1 \oplus \zeta_2 \oplus (\zeta_1 \uplus \zeta_2)$.

Trivially, $\|\sim\zeta\|(\gamma) = \bigoplus_{\gamma' \subseteq \gamma} \|\zeta\|(\gamma')$ for every $\gamma \in C(P)$.

For every *PCL* formula f over P and every weighted *PCL* formula $\zeta \in PCL(K, P)$, we consider also the macro:

- $f \implies \zeta := \neg f \oplus (f \otimes \zeta)$.

Then for $\gamma \in C(P)$, we get $\|f \implies \zeta\|(\gamma) = \|\zeta\|(\gamma)$ if $\gamma \models f$, and $\|f \implies \zeta\|(\gamma) = 1$ otherwise.

Example 2 (Example 1 continued). The four possible configurations of the Master/Slave architecture for two masters M_1, M_2 and two slaves S_1, S_2 with ports m_1, m_2 and s_1, s_2, respectively, are given by the *PIL* formula

$$(\phi_{1,1} \sqcup \phi_{1,2}) + (\phi_{2,1} \sqcup \phi_{2,2}).$$

We consider the weighted *PCL* formula

$$\zeta = \sim\left((\varphi_{1,1} \oplus \varphi_{1,2}) \uplus (\varphi_{2,1} \oplus \varphi_{2,2})\right).$$

Then for $\gamma \in C(\{m_1, m_2, s_1, s_2\})$ we get that $\|\zeta\|(\gamma)$ equals to

$$\bigoplus_{\gamma' \subseteq \gamma} \left(\bigoplus_{\gamma' = \gamma_1 \cup \gamma_2} \left((\|\varphi_{1,1}\|(\gamma_1) \oplus \|\varphi_{1,2}\|(\gamma_1)) \otimes (\|\varphi_{2,1}\|(\gamma_2) \oplus \|\varphi_{2,2}\|(\gamma_2))\right)\right).$$

Let us assume that $\gamma = \{\{s_1, m_1\}, \{s_1, m_2\}, \{s_2, m_1\}, \{s_2, m_2\}\}$. Then for $K = \mathbb{R}_{\min}$ the value $\|\zeta\|(\gamma)$ gets the form

$$\min_{\gamma' \subseteq \gamma} \left(\min_{\gamma' = \gamma_1 \cup \gamma_2} \left(\min \left(\|\varphi_{1,1}\|(\gamma_1), \|\varphi_{1,2}\|(\gamma_1) \right) + \min \left(\|\varphi_{2,1}\|(\gamma_2), \|\varphi_{2,2}\|(\gamma_2) \right) \right) \right)$$

which is the minimum "cost" of all the implementations of the Master/Slave architecture.

If $K = \mathbb{R}_{\max}$, then $\|\zeta\|(\gamma)$ equals to

$$\max_{\gamma' \subseteq \gamma} \left(\max_{\gamma' = \gamma_1 \cup \gamma_2} \left(\max \left(\|\varphi_{1,1}\|(\gamma_1), \|\varphi_{1,2}\|(\gamma_1) \right) + \max \left(\|\varphi_{2,1}\|(\gamma_2), \|\varphi_{2,2}\|(\gamma_2) \right) \right) \right)$$

which is the maximum "cost" of all the implementations of the Master/Slave architecture.

Finally assume K to be the Viterbi semiring. Then the value $k_{i,j}$ in $\varphi_{i,j}$ for every $1 \leq i, j \leq 2$, can be considered as the probability of the implementation of the interaction $\phi_{i,j}$. Hence, $\|\zeta\|(\gamma)$ equals to

$$\max_{\gamma' \subseteq \gamma} \left(\max_{\gamma' = \gamma_1 \cup \gamma_2} \left(\max \left(\|\varphi_{1,1}\|(\gamma_1), \|\varphi_{1,2}\|(\gamma_1) \right) \cdot \max \left(\|\varphi_{2,1}\|(\gamma_2), \|\varphi_{2,2}\|(\gamma_2) \right) \right) \right)$$

and represents the maximum probability of all the implementations of the Master/Slave architecture.

The next proposition summarizes several properties of our weighted *PCL* formulas.

Proposition 1. *Let* $\zeta_1, \zeta_2, \zeta_3 \in PCL(K, P)$. *Then*
(i) $(\zeta_1 \uplus \zeta_2) \uplus \zeta_3 \equiv \zeta_1 \uplus (\zeta_2 \uplus \zeta_3)$.   *(iv)* $\zeta_1 \uplus (\zeta_2 \oplus \zeta_3) \equiv (\zeta_1 \uplus \zeta_2) \oplus (\zeta_1 \uplus \zeta_3)$.
(ii) $\zeta_1 \uplus 0 \equiv 0$.   *(v)* $\sim(\zeta_1 \oplus \zeta_2) \equiv \sim\zeta_1 \oplus \sim\zeta_2$.
(iii) $\zeta_1 \uplus \zeta_2 \equiv \zeta_2 \uplus \zeta_1$.   *(vi)* $\sim(\zeta_1 \uplus \zeta_2) \equiv \sim\zeta_1 \otimes \sim\zeta_2$.
If in addition K *is idempotent, then*
(vii) $\sim(\zeta_1 \uplus \zeta_2) \equiv \sim\zeta_1 \uplus \sim\zeta_2$.   *(viii)* $\sim\sim\zeta_1 \equiv \sim\zeta_1$.
(ix) $\zeta_1 \curlyvee (\zeta_2 \oplus \zeta_3) \equiv (\zeta_1 \curlyvee \zeta_2) \oplus (\zeta_1 \curlyvee \zeta_3)$.

We aim to show that $\otimes$ does not distribute, in general, over $\uplus$. For this, we consider the semiring $(\mathbb{N}, +, \cdot, 0, 1)$ of natural numbers, the set of ports $P = \{p, q\}$ and the formulas $\zeta, \zeta_1, \zeta_2 \in PCL(\mathbb{N}, P)$ determined, respectively by $\zeta = 5 \oplus pq$, $\zeta_1 = pq \otimes 6$, and $\zeta_2 = pq \otimes 3$. We let $\gamma = \{\{p, q\}\}$ and by straightforward computations we get $\|\zeta \otimes (\zeta_1 \uplus \zeta_2)\|(\gamma) = 108$ and $\|(\zeta \otimes \zeta_1) \uplus (\zeta \otimes \zeta_2)\|(\gamma) = 648$. Hence $\zeta \otimes (\zeta_1 \uplus \zeta_2) \not\equiv (\zeta \otimes \zeta_1) \uplus (\zeta \otimes \zeta_2)$. Nevertheless, this is not the case whenever ζ is a *PIL* formula. More precisely, we state the subsequent proposition.

Proposition 2. *Let* ϕ *be a PIL formula over* P *and* $\zeta_1, \zeta_2 \in PCL(K, P)$. *Then*

$$\phi \otimes (\zeta_1 \uplus \zeta_2) \equiv (\phi \otimes \zeta_1) \uplus (\phi \otimes \zeta_2).$$

As it is already mentioned (cf. [11]), configuration logic has been developed as a fundamental platform to describe architecture styles. In the next example we show that weighted PCL in fact can formulate other types of problems.

Example 3. We consider the travelling salesman problem for 5 cities $C_1, C_2, C_3,$ $C_4, C_5,$ and assume C_1 to be the origin city. We aim to construct a weighted PCL formula, whose semantics computes the shortest distance of all the routes that visit every city exactly once and return to the origin city. We consider a port c_i for every city C_i ($1 \leq i \leq 5$), hence $P = \{c_i \mid 1 \leq i \leq 5\}$. For every $1 \leq i, j, k, m, n \leq 5$ which are assumed to be pairwise disjoint, we define the monomials $\phi_{i,j}$ over P by

$$\phi_{i,j} = c_i c_j \bar{c}_k \bar{c}_m \bar{c}_n.$$

The interaction formulas $\phi_{i,j}$ represent the connection between the cities C_i and C_j. It should be clear that $\phi_{i,j} = \phi_{j,i}$ for every $1 \leq i \neq j \leq 5$. Assume that $K = \mathbb{R}_{\min}$ and for every $1 \leq i \neq j \leq 5$ we consider the weighted interaction formula

$$\varphi_{i,j} = k_{i,j} \otimes \phi_{i,j}$$

with $k_{i,j} \in \mathbb{R}_+$, where the values $k_{i,j}$ represent the distance between the cities C_i and C_j. Now we define the weighted PCL formula $\zeta \in PCL(\mathbb{R}_{\min}, P)$ as follows:

$$\zeta \equiv \sim \begin{pmatrix} (\varphi_{1,2} \uplus \varphi_{2,3} \uplus \varphi_{3,4} \uplus \varphi_{4,5} \uplus \varphi_{5,1}) \oplus (\varphi_{1,2} \uplus \varphi_{2,3} \uplus \varphi_{3,5} \uplus \varphi_{5,4} \uplus \varphi_{4,1}) \oplus \\ (\varphi_{1,2} \uplus \varphi_{2,4} \uplus \varphi_{4,5} \uplus \varphi_{5,3} \uplus \varphi_{3,1}) \oplus (\varphi_{1,2} \uplus \varphi_{2,5} \uplus \varphi_{5,4} \uplus \varphi_{4,3} \uplus \varphi_{3,1}) \oplus \\ (\varphi_{1,2} \uplus \varphi_{2,5} \uplus \varphi_{5,3} \uplus \varphi_{3,4} \uplus \varphi_{4,1}) \oplus (\varphi_{1,2} \uplus \varphi_{2,4} \uplus \varphi_{4,3} \uplus \varphi_{3,5} \uplus \varphi_{5,1}) \oplus \\ (\varphi_{1,3} \uplus \varphi_{3,2} \uplus \varphi_{2,4} \uplus \varphi_{4,5} \uplus \varphi_{5,1}) \oplus (\varphi_{1,3} \uplus \varphi_{3,2} \uplus \varphi_{2,5} \uplus \varphi_{5,4} \uplus \varphi_{4,1}) \oplus \\ (\varphi_{1,3} \uplus \varphi_{3,5} \uplus \varphi_{5,2} \uplus \varphi_{2,4} \uplus \varphi_{4,1}) \oplus (\varphi_{1,3} \uplus \varphi_{3,4} \uplus \varphi_{4,2} \uplus \varphi_{2,5} \uplus \varphi_{5,1}) \oplus \\ (\varphi_{1,4} \uplus \varphi_{4,2} \uplus \varphi_{2,3} \uplus \varphi_{3,5} \uplus \varphi_{5,1}) \oplus (\varphi_{1,4} \uplus \varphi_{4,3} \uplus \varphi_{3,2} \uplus \varphi_{2,5} \uplus \varphi_{5,1}) \end{pmatrix}.$$

Then for $\gamma = \{\{c_i, c_j\} \mid 1 \leq i \neq j \leq 5\}$, it is not difficult to see that the value $\|\zeta\|(\gamma)$ is the shortest distance of all the routes starting at C_1, visit every city exactly once, and return to C_1.

A weighted PCL formula can be constructed for the travelling salesman problem for any number n of cities. Indeed, assume the cities $C_1, \ldots, C_n$ with origin C_1. By preserving the above notations, we consider, for every $1 \leq i \neq j \leq n$, the interaction formula

$$\phi_{i,j} = c_i c_j \wedge \bigwedge_{k \in [n] \setminus \{i,j\}} \bar{c}_k$$

where $[n] = \{1, \ldots, n\}$, and the weighted interaction formula

$$\varphi_{i,j} = k_{i,j} \otimes \phi_{i,j}$$

with $k_{i,j} \in \mathbb{R}_+$, where the value $k_{i,j}$ represents the distance between the cities C_i and C_j. The required weighted PCL formula $\zeta \in PCL(\mathbb{R}_{\min}, P)$ is determined now as follows:

$$\zeta \equiv \sim \bigoplus_{\{i_1, \ldots, i_n\} \in \mathcal{CS}_n} \biguplus_{1 \leq j \leq n-1} \varphi_{i_j, i_{j+1}}$$

where $\mathcal{CS}_n$ denotes the set of all cyclic permutations of the first n positive integers such that clock-wise and anti-clock-wise cyclic permutations have been identified. It should be noted that $\text{card}(\mathcal{CS}_n) = (n-1)!/2$. Then for $\gamma \in C(P)$ defined similarly as above, i.e., $\gamma = \{\{c_i, c_j\} \mid 1 \leq i \neq j \leq n\}$, the value $\|\zeta\|(\gamma)$ is the shortest distance of all the routes starting at C_1, visit every city exactly once, and return to C_1.

5   A Full Normal Form for Weighted *PCL* formulas

In the present section, we show that for every weighted *PCL* formula $\zeta \in PCL(K, P)$ we can effectively compute an equivalent formula of a special form. For this, we will use a corresponding result from [11]. More precisely, in that paper the authors proved that for every *PCL* formula f over P there exists a unique equivalent *PCL* formula of the form $\bigsqcup_{i \in I} \sum_{i \in J_i} m_{i,j}$ which is called *full normal form* (cf. Thm. 4.43. in [11]). The index sets I and J_i, for every $i \in I$, are finite and $m_{i,j}$'s are *full monomials*, i.e., monomials involving all ports from P. Hence, a full monomial is a monomial of the form $\bigwedge_{p \in P_+} p \wedge \bigwedge_{p \in P_-} \overline{p}$ where $P_+ \cup P_- = P$ and $P_+ \cap P_- = \emptyset$. We show that we can also effectively build a unique full normal form for every weighted *PCL* formula. Uniqueness is up to the equivalence relation. Then we will use this result to state that our weighted *PCL* is complete.

Definition 5. *A weighted PCL formula* $\zeta \in PCL(K, P)$ *is said to be in* full normal form *if there are finite index sets* I *and* J_i *for every* $i \in I$, $k_i \in K$ *for every* $i \in I$, *and full monomials* $m_{i,j}$ *for every* $i \in I$ *and* $j \in J_i$ *such that*

$$\zeta = \bigoplus_{i \in I} \left(k_i \otimes \sum_{j \in J_i} m_{i,j} \right).$$

By our definition above, for every full normal form we can construct an equivalent one satisfying the following statements:

(i) $j \neq j'$ implies $m_{i,j} \not\equiv m_{i,j'}$ for every $i \in I$, $j, j' \in J_i$, and
(ii) $i \neq i'$ implies $\sum_{j \in J_i} m_{i,j} \not\equiv \sum_{j \in J_{i'}} m_{i',j}$ for every $i, i' \in I$.

Indeed, for the first one, if $m_{i,j} \equiv m_{i,j'}$ for some $j \neq j'$, then since $m_{i,j}, m_{i,j'}$ are interaction formulas, by Lemma 1, we can replace the coalescing $m_{i,j} + m_{i,j'}$ with $m_{i,j}$. For (ii), let us assume that $\sum_{j \in J_i} m_{i,j} \equiv \sum_{j \in J_{i'}} m_{i',j}$ for some $i \neq i'$. Then, we can replace the sum $\left(k_i \otimes \sum_{j \in J_i} m_{i,j} \right) \oplus \left(k_{i'} \otimes \sum_{j \in J_{i'}} m_{i',j} \right)$ with the equivalent one $(k_i \oplus k_{i'}) \otimes \sum_{j \in J_i} m_{i,j}$. Hence, in the sequel, we assume that every full normal form satisfies Statements (i) and (ii).

We intend to show that for every weighted *PCL* formula $\zeta \in PCL(K, P)$ we can effectively construct an equivalent weighted *PCL* formula $\zeta' \in PCL(K, P)$ in full normal form. Moreover, ζ' will be unique up to the equivalence relation. We shall need a sequence of preliminary results. All index sets occurring in the sequel are finite.

Lemma 2. *Let $k_1, k_2 \in K$ and $\zeta_1, \zeta_2 \in PCL(K, P)$. Then*

$$(k_1 \otimes \zeta_1) \uplus (k_2 \otimes \zeta_2) \equiv (k_1 \otimes k_2) \otimes (\zeta_1 \uplus \zeta_2).$$

Lemma 3. *Let J be an index set and m_j a full monomial for every $j \in J$. Then, there exists a unique $\overline{\gamma} \in C(P)$ such that for every $\gamma \in C(P)$ we have $\left\| \sum_{j \in J} m_j \right\| (\gamma) = 1$ if $\gamma = \overline{\gamma}$ and $\left\| \sum_{j \in J} m_i \right\| (\gamma) = 0$ otherwise.*

Proposition 3. *Let f be a PCL formula over P. Then there exist finite index sets I and J_i for every $i \in I$, and full monomials $m_{i,j}$ for every $i \in I$ and $j \in J_i$ such that*

$$f \equiv \bigoplus_{i \in I} \sum_{j \in J_i} m_{i,j} \equiv \bigoplus_{i \in I} \left(1 \otimes \sum_{j \in J_i} m_{i,j} \right).$$

In particular

$$true \equiv \bigoplus_{\emptyset \neq N \subseteq M} \sum_{m \in N} m$$

where M is the set of all full monomials over P such that for every $m, m' \in M$, if $m \neq m'$, then $m \not\equiv m'$.

Lemma 4. *Let m_i, m'_j be full monomials for every $i \in I$ and $j \in J$. Then*

$$\left(\sum_{i \in I} m_i \right) \otimes \left(\sum_{j \in J} m'_j \right) \equiv \begin{cases} \sum_{i \in I} m_i & \text{if } \sum_{i \in I} m_i \equiv \sum_{j \in J} m'_j \\ 0 & \text{otherwise.} \end{cases}$$

Theorem 1. *Let K be a commutative semiring and P a set of ports. Then for every weighted PCL formula $\zeta \in PCL(K, P)$ we can effectively construct an equivalent weighted PCL formula $\zeta' \in PCL(K, P)$ in full normal form. Furthermore, ζ' is unique up to the equivalence relation.*

Proof (Sketch). We prove our theorem by induction on the structure of weighted *PCL* formulas ζ over P and K. Firstly, we show our claim for $\zeta = k$ with $k \in K$ and $\zeta = f$ where f is a *PCL* formula, using Proposition 3. Next, we consider weighted *PCL* formulas $\zeta_1, \zeta_2 \in PCL(K, P)$ and assume that $\zeta'_1 = \bigoplus_{i_1 \in I_1} \left(k_{i_1} \otimes \sum_{j_1 \in J_{i_1}} m_{i_1, j_1} \right)$, $\zeta'_2 = \bigoplus_{i_2 \in I_2} \left(k_{i_2} \otimes \sum_{j_2 \in J_{i_2}} m_{i_2, j_2} \right)$ are respectively their equivalent full normal forms. Then, we prove our claim for the case $\zeta = \zeta_1 \oplus \zeta_2$, $\zeta = \zeta_1 \otimes \zeta_2$, and $\zeta = \zeta_1 \uplus \zeta_2$ using Lemmas 2-4. Finally, it remains to show that ζ' is unique up to the equivalence relation. This is proved in a straightforward way using Statements (i) and (ii). □

A construction of the full normal form $\zeta' \in PCL(K, P)$ of every weighted *PCL* formula $\zeta \in PCL(K, P)$ can be done using our Theorem 1, and the Abstract

Syntax Tree $(\text{AST})^2$, in a similar way as it is done in [11]. More precisely, in our case the leaves are labelled also by elements of the semiring K, and the nodes are labelled by additional symbols, namely the operators $\oplus$, $\otimes$, and $\uplus$. Whenever a node w of the AST is labelled by a symbol k, $\oplus$, $\otimes$, or $\uplus$, with $k \in K$, then every node of the path from the root to w is labelled by a symbol $\oplus$, $\otimes$, or $\uplus$.

Example 4 (Example 1 continued). We shall compute the full normal form of the weighted *PCL* formula

$$\zeta = \sim ((\varphi_{1,1} \oplus \varphi_{1,2}) \uplus (\varphi_{2,1} \oplus \varphi_{2,2}))$$

which formalizes the weighted Master/Slave architecture for two masters M_1, M_2 and two slaves S_1, S_2 with ports m_1, m_2 and s_1, s_2, respectively. We have

$$\zeta = \sim ((\varphi_{1,1} \oplus \varphi_{1,2}) \uplus (\varphi_{2,1} \oplus \varphi_{2,2}))$$
$$\equiv (((k_{1,1} \otimes k_{2,1}) \otimes (\phi_{1,1} + \phi_{2,1})) \oplus ((k_{1,2} \otimes k_{2,1}) \otimes (\phi_{1,2} + \phi_{2,1}))$$
$$\oplus ((k_{1,1} \otimes k_{2,2}) \otimes (\phi_{1,1} + \phi_{2,2})) \oplus ((k_{1,2} \otimes k_{2,2}) \otimes (\phi_{1,2} + \phi_{2,2}))) \uplus 1$$

$$\equiv \left(\bigoplus_{\emptyset \neq N \subseteq M} (k_{1,1} \otimes k_{2,1}) \otimes \left(\phi_{1,1} + \phi_{2,1} + \sum_{m \in N} m \right) \right)$$

$$\oplus \left(\bigoplus_{\emptyset \neq N \subseteq M} (k_{1,2} \otimes k_{2,1}) \otimes \left(\phi_{1,2} + \phi_{2,1} + \sum_{m \in N} m \right) \right)$$

$$\oplus \left(\bigoplus_{\emptyset \neq N \subseteq M} (k_{1,1} \otimes k_{2,2}) \otimes \left(\phi_{1,1} + \phi_{2,2} + \sum_{m \in N} m \right) \right)$$

$$\oplus \left(\bigoplus_{\emptyset \neq N \subseteq M} (k_{1,2} \otimes k_{2,2}) \otimes \left(\phi_{1,2} + \phi_{2,2} + \sum_{m \in N} m \right) \right)$$

since $1 \equiv \bigoplus_{\emptyset \neq N \subseteq M} (1 \otimes \sum_{m \in N} m)$, where M is the set of all full monomials over P such that for every $m, m' \in M$, if $m \neq m'$, then $m \not\equiv m'$.

In the sequel, we intend to show that our weighted *PCL* is sound and complete. For this, we need firstly to introduce the notions of soundness and completeness for the weighted *PCL*. Let $\Sigma = \{\zeta_1, \ldots, \zeta_n\}$ be a set of weighted *PCL* formulas. Then we say that Σ *proves* the weighted *PCL* formula ζ and we write $\Sigma \vdash \zeta$ if ζ is derived by the formulas in Σ, using the axioms of *PCL* [11] and the equivalences of Propositions 1 and 2. Furthermore, we write $\Sigma \models \zeta$ if $\zeta_1 \equiv \ldots \equiv \zeta_n \equiv \zeta$.

Definition 6. *Let K be a commutative semiring and P a set of ports.*

(i) The weighted PCL over P and K is sound if $\Sigma \vdash \zeta$ implies $\Sigma \models \zeta$ for every set of weighted PCL formulas Σ and weighted PCL formula ζ.

---

[2] We refer the reader to [11] for the definition of the Abstract Syntax Tree.

(ii) The weighted PCL over P and K is complete *if $\Sigma \models \zeta$ implies $\Sigma \vdash \zeta$ for every set of weighted PCL formulas Σ and weighted PCL formula ζ.*

Theorem 2. *Let K be a commutative semiring and P a set of ports. Then the weighted PCL over P and K is sound and complete.*

6   Weighted First-Order Configuration Logic

In this section, we equip our weighted *PCL* with first-order quantifiers and investigate the weighted first-order configuration logic. For this, we need to recall the first-order configuration logic from [11] for which, in addition, we prove several properties. We assume that $\mathcal{T} = \{T_1, \ldots, T_n\}$ is a finite set of component types such that instances of a component type have the same interface and behavior. We denote by C_T the set of all the components of type $T \in \mathcal{T}$, and we let $C_\mathcal{T} = \bigcup_{T \in \mathcal{T}} C_T$. A component c of type $T \in \mathcal{T}$ is denoted by $c : T$. The interface of every component type T has a distinct set of ports P_T. We set $P_\mathcal{T} = \bigcup_{T \in \mathcal{T}} P_T$. For every $B \subseteq C_\mathcal{T}$ we write P_B for the sets of ports of all the components in B. We denote by $c.p$ (resp. $c.P$) the port p (resp. the set of ports P) of component c. Furthermore, we assume that there is a universal component type U, such that every component or component set is of this type. Therefore, the set C_U is the set of all components of a model. Then, the syntax of *first-order configuration logic* (*FOCL* for short) formulas over $\mathcal{T}$ is given by the grammar

$$F ::= true \mid \phi \mid \neg F \mid F \sqcup F \mid F + F \mid \exists c : T(\Phi(c)).F \mid \sum c : T(\Phi(c)).F$$

where ϕ denotes an interaction formula, c a component variable and $\Phi(c)$ a set-theoretic predicate on c. We omit Φ, in an *FOCL* formula, whenever $\Phi = true$.

Let $B \subseteq C_\mathcal{T}$ be a set of component instances of types from $\mathcal{T}$ and $\gamma \in C(P_B)$. Let also F be an *FOCL* formula without free variables (i.e., variables that are not in the scope of any quantifier). We define the satisfaction relation $(B, \gamma) \models F$ inductively on the structure of F as follows:

$(B, \gamma) \models true$, $\qquad\qquad (B, \gamma) \models F_1 \sqcup F_2$ iff $(B, \gamma) \models F_1$ or $(B, \gamma) \models F_2$,

$(B, \gamma) \models \phi$ iff $\quad \gamma \models \phi$, $(B, \gamma) \models \neg F$ iff $(B, \gamma) \not\models F$,

$(B, \gamma) \models F_1 + F_2$ iff there exist $\gamma_1, \gamma_2 \in C(P_B)$ such that $\gamma = \gamma_1 \cup \gamma_2$, and
$$(B, \gamma_1) \models F_1 \text{ and } (B, \gamma_2) \models F_2,$$

$(B, \gamma) \models \exists c : T(\Phi(c)).F$ iff $\quad (B, \gamma) \models \bigsqcup_{c' : T \in B \wedge \Phi(c')} F[c'/c]$,

$(B, \gamma) \models \sum c : T(\Phi(c)).F$ iff $\quad \{c' : T \in B \mid \Phi(c')\} \neq \emptyset$ and
$$(B, \gamma) \models \sum_{c' : T \in B \wedge \Phi(c')} F[c'/c]$$

where $F[c'/c]$ is obtained by F, by replacing all occurrences of c by c'. We let

– $\forall c : T(\Phi(c)).F := \neg \exists c : T(\Phi(c)).\neg F$.

The subsequent results refer to properties of the *FOCL* formulas.

Proposition 4. *Let F, F_1, F_2 be FOCL formulas. Then the following statements hold true.*

(i) $\sim\sim F = \sim F$.

(ii) $F \implies \sim F$.

(iii) $\neg\sim\neg F \implies F$.

(iv) $\sim (F_1 \sqcup F_2) \equiv \sim F_1 \sqcup \sim F_2$.

(v) $\sim (F_1 + F_2) \equiv \sim F_1 + \sim F_2$.

(vi) $\sim \exists c : T(\Phi(c)).F \equiv \exists c : T(\Phi(c)).(\sim F)$.

(vii) $\sim \sum c : T(\Phi(c)).F \equiv \sum c : T(\Phi(c)).(\sim F) \equiv \forall c : T(\Phi(c)).(\sim F)$.

(viii) $\exists c : T(\Phi(c)).(F_1 \sqcup F_2) \equiv \exists c : T(\Phi(c)).F_1 \sqcup \exists c : T(\Phi(c)).F_2$.

(ix) $\forall c : T(\Phi(c)).(F_1 \wedge F_2) \equiv \forall c : T(\Phi(c)).F_1 \wedge \forall c : T(\Phi(c)).F_2$.

(x) $\sum c : T(\Phi(c)).(F_1 + F_2) \equiv \sum c : T(\Phi(c)).F_1 + \sum c : T(\Phi(c)).F_2$.

(xi) $(\sim \sum c : T(\Phi(c)).F_1) \wedge (\sim \sum c : T(\Phi(c)).F_2) \equiv \forall c : T(\Phi(c)).(\sim (F_1 + F_2))$.

Proposition 5. *Let F_1, F_2 be two FOCL formulas over T. Then*

(i) $\forall c : T(\Phi(c)).(F_1 + F_2) \implies \sum c : T(\Phi(c).F_1 + \sum c : T(\Phi(c).F_2$.

(ii) $\sum c : T(\Phi(c)).(F_1 \wedge F_2) \Rightarrow (\sum c : T(\Phi(c)).F_1) \wedge (\sum c : T(\Phi(c)).F_2)$.

The converse implications of both (i) and (ii) in Proposition 5 above do not in general hold.

Now we are ready to introduce the weighted *FOCL*.

Definition 7. *The syntax of formulas of the* weighted *FOCL over T and K is given by the grammar*

$$Z ::= k \mid F \mid Z \oplus Z \mid Z \otimes Z \mid Z \uplus Z \mid \bigoplus c : T(\Phi(c)).Z \mid$$

$$\bigotimes c : T(\Phi(c)).Z \mid \biguplus c : T(\Phi(c)).Z$$

where $k \in K$ and F denotes an FOCL formula.

We denote by $FOCL(K, T)$ the class of all weighted *FOCL* formulas over T and K. We represent the semantics of formulas $Z \in FOCL(K, T)$ as polynomials $\|Z\| \in K \langle \mathcal{P}(C_T) \times C(P_T) \rangle$. For the semantics of *FOCL* formulas we use the satisfaction relation as defined previously.

Definition 8. *Let $Z \in FOCL(K, T)$. The semantics $\|Z\|$ is a polynomial in $K \langle \mathcal{P}(C_T) \times C(P_T) \rangle$. For every $B \in \mathcal{P}(C_T)$ and $\gamma \in C(P_T)$ we let $\|Z\|(B, \gamma) = 0$ if $\gamma \notin C(P_B)$. Otherwise, the value $\|Z\|(B, \gamma)$ is defined inductively as follows:*

$\|k\|(B, \gamma) = k$, $\qquad\qquad \|Z_1 \oplus Z_2\|(B, \gamma) = \|Z_1\|(B, \gamma) \oplus \|Z_2\|(B, \gamma)$,

$\|F\|(B, \gamma) = \begin{cases} 1 & \text{if } (B, \gamma) \models F \\ 0 & \text{otherwise} \end{cases}$, $\quad \|Z_1 \otimes Z_2\|(B, \gamma) = \|Z_1\|(B, \gamma) \otimes \|Z_2\|(B, \gamma)$,

$\|Z_1 \uplus Z_2\|(B, \gamma) = \bigoplus_{\gamma = \gamma_1 \cup \gamma_2} (\|Z_1\|(B, \gamma_1) \otimes \|Z_2\|(B, \gamma_2))$,

$\|\bigoplus c : T(\Phi(c)).Z\|(B, \gamma) = \bigoplus_{c' : T \in B \wedge \Phi(c')} \|Z[c'/c]\|(B, \gamma)$,

$\|\bigotimes c : T(\Phi(c)).Z\|(B, \gamma) = \bigotimes_{c' : T \in B \wedge \Phi(c')} \|Z[c'/c]\|(B, \gamma)$,

$\|\biguplus c : T(\Phi(c)).Z\|(B, \gamma) = \bigoplus_{\gamma = \cup \gamma_{c'}, c' : T \in B \wedge \Phi(c')}$
$$\left(\bigotimes_{c' : T \in B \wedge \Phi(c')} \|Z[c'/c]\|(B, \gamma_{c'}) \right).$$

In the next proposition we establish the main properties of the weighted *FOCL* formulas.

Proposition 6. *Let* $Z, Z_1, Z_2 \in FOCL(K, \mathcal{T})$. *Then the following statements hold.*

(i) $\sim \bigoplus c : T(\Phi(c)).Z \equiv \bigoplus c : T(\Phi(c)).(\sim Z)$.

(ii) $\bigoplus c : T(\Phi(c)).(Z_1 \oplus Z_2) \equiv \bigoplus c : T(\Phi(c)).Z_1 \oplus \bigoplus c : T(\Phi(c)).Z_2$.

(iii) $\bigotimes c : T(\Phi(c)).(Z_1 \otimes Z_2) \equiv \bigotimes c : T(\Phi(c)).Z_1 \otimes \bigotimes c : T(\Phi(c)).Z_2$.

(iv) $\biguplus c : T(\Phi(c)).(Z_1 \uplus Z_2) \equiv (\biguplus c : T(\Phi(c)).Z_1) \uplus (\biguplus c : T(\Phi(c)).Z_2)$.

The subsequent examples constitute interesting applications of weighted *FOCL*. More precisely, in Example 5 we construct a weighted *FOCL* formula for the Master/Slave architecture for two Masters and three Slaves. In Example 2 we presented a weighted *PCL* formula for that architecture for two Masters and two Slaves. Nevertheless, that formula gets very complicated for several Masters and Slaves. On the contrary, the weighted *FOCL* formula of the next example can be easily modified for arbitrary numbers of Masters and Slaves and it is relatively simple. In Example 6 we built a formula for the Publish/Subscribe architecture style equipped with quantitative features.

Example 5 (Master/Slave architecture style). We intend to construct a weighted *FOCL* formula for two Masters and three Slaves. For this we need two types of components, namely M and S, for Masters and Slaves, respectively. Thus $\mathcal{T} = \{M, S\}$. We assume that every component of type M has only one port denoted by m and every component of type S has one port denoted by s, and we let $C_{\mathcal{T}} = \{b_1 : M, b_2 : M, d_1 : S, d_2 : S, d_3 : S\}$. We consider the weighted *FOCL* formula (with free variables c, c_1)

$$Z' = c.s \wedge c_1.m \otimes \left(\bigotimes_{\substack{i=1,2,3 \\ j=1,2}} ((c.s \equiv d_i.s \wedge c_1.m \equiv b_j.m) \implies k_{i,j}) \right) \otimes$$

$$\bigotimes c_2 : M(c_2 \neq c_1). \bigotimes c_3 : S(c_3 \neq c).(\overline{c_2.m} \wedge \overline{c_3.s})$$

and the weighted *FOCL* formula

$$Z = \sim \biguplus c : S. \left(\bigoplus c_1 : M.Z' \right).$$

Let $B = \{b_1 : M, b_2 : M, d_1 : S, d_2 : S, d_3 : S\}$ and $\gamma \in C(P_B)$. Then, by a straightforward computation, we can show that $\|Z\| (B, \gamma)$ equals to

$$\bigoplus_{\gamma' \subseteq \gamma} \left(\bigoplus_{\gamma' = \gamma_1 \cup \gamma_2 \cup \gamma_3} \left(\begin{pmatrix} \begin{pmatrix} k_{1,1} \otimes \|d_1.s \wedge b_1.m \wedge \overline{b_2.m} \wedge \overline{d_2.s} \wedge \overline{d_3.s}\| (\gamma_1) \oplus \\ k_{1,2} \otimes \|d_1.s \wedge b_2.m \wedge \overline{b_1.m} \wedge \overline{d_2.s} \wedge \overline{d_3.s}\| (\gamma_1) \end{pmatrix} \otimes \\ \begin{pmatrix} k_{2,1} \otimes \|d_2.s \wedge b_1.m \wedge \overline{b_2.m} \wedge \overline{d_1.s} \wedge \overline{d_3.s}\| (\gamma_2) \oplus \\ k_{2,2} \otimes \|d_2.s \wedge b_2.m \wedge \overline{b_1.m} \wedge \overline{d_1.s} \wedge \overline{d_3.s}\| (\gamma_2) \end{pmatrix} \otimes \\ \begin{pmatrix} k_{3,1} \otimes \|d_3.s \wedge b_1.m \wedge \overline{b_2.m} \wedge \overline{d_1.s} \wedge \overline{d_2.s}\| (\gamma_3) \oplus \\ k_{3,2} \otimes \|d_3.s \wedge b_2.m \wedge \overline{b_1.m} \wedge \overline{d_1.s} \wedge \overline{d_2.s}\| (\gamma_3) \end{pmatrix} \end{pmatrix} \right) \right).$$

Assume for instance that $K = \mathbb{R}_{\max}$ and let $\gamma = \{\{d_1.s, b_1.m\}, \{d_1.s, b_2.m\}, \{d_2.s, b_1.m\}, \{d_2.s, b_2.m\}, \{d_3.s, b_1.m\}, \{d_3.s, b_2.m\}\}$. Then the semantics $\|Z\| (B, \gamma)$

firstly computes the weights of all the patterns that occur according to the set B, and finally returns the maximum of those weights. The weighted *FOCL* formula Z can be easily modified for any number of Masters and Slaves. Indeed, one has just to change accordingly the weighted formula Z'.

Example 6 (Publish/Subscribe architecture style). Publish/Subscribe is a software architecture, relating *publishers* who send messages and receivers, called *subscribers* (cf. for instance [4,6]). The main characteristics of this architecture are as follows. The publishers characterize messages according to classes/topics but they do not know whether there is any subscriber who is interested in a concrete topic. Subscribers, on the other hand, express their interest in one or more topics and receive messages according to their interests in case such topics exist.

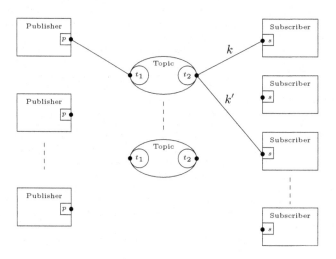

Fig. 2. Weighted Publish/Subscribe architecture.

There are three approaches to develop the Publish/Subscribe architecture, namely the *list-based*, the *broadcast-based*, and the *content-based*. Broadcast-based Publish/Subscribe and list-based Publish/Subscribe implementations can be broadly categorized as *topic-based* since they both use predefined subjects as many-to-many channels. More precisely, in a topic-based implementation, subscribers receive all messages published to the topics to which they subscribe, and all subscribers to a topic will receive the same messages. On the other hand, the publisher defines the topics of messages to which subscribers can subscribe. We intend to construct a weighted *FOCL* formula which formalizes the topic-based Publish/Subscribe architecture style. For this, we consider three types of components, the publishers, the topics and the subscribers denoted by the letters P, T, S, respectively. Hence, the set of component types is $\mathcal{T} = \{P, T, S\}$. The component P has one port p, T has two ports t_1 and t_2, and S has the port s. As it is mentioned above, the publishers do not have any knowledge of who and how many the subscribers are, and the same situation holds for the subscribers.

In other words the publishers and the subscribers do not have any connection. Furthermore, a subscriber can receive a message from a topic, if at least one publisher has sent a message to that particular topic. The architecture is illustrated in Fig. 2. Moreover, we should avoid interactions that transfer empty messages. The weights in our formula will represent the "priorities" that one subscriber gives to the topics. Next, we describe the required weighted $FOCL$ formula for the Publish/Subscribe architecture. Assume that we have a component of type P namely $c_3 : P$ and a component $c_2 : T$ of type T. If the publisher $c_3 : P$ will send a message to that topic $c_2 : T$, then this interaction is represented by the formula $c_3.p \wedge c_2.t_1$. However, we must ensure that no other components of type P, type T, or type S will interact. This case is obtained by the formula Z_1 below:

$$Z_1 = \forall d_1 : P(d_1 \neq c_3). \left(\begin{array}{l} \forall d_2 : T(d_2 \neq c_2). \\ \quad \left(\forall d_3 : S. \left(\overline{d_1.p} \wedge \overline{d_2.t_1} \wedge \overline{d_2.t_2} \wedge \overline{d_3.s} \wedge \overline{c_2.t_2} \right) \right) \end{array} \right).$$

Then the $FOCL$ formula

$$Z_2 = \sim (c_3.p \wedge c_2.t_1 \wedge Z_1)$$

characterizes interactions between a publisher and a topic. Assume now that a message has been sent to the component $c_2 : T$. Then this message can be sent to a subscriber $c_1 : S$ who has expressed interest in the same topic. This interaction is represented by the $FOCL$ formula $c_2.t_2 \wedge c_1.s$. Similarly, as in the previous case, in this interaction there must participate not any other subscribers, topics, or publishers. This case is implemented by the formula

$$Z_3 = \forall d_1 : P. \left(\forall d_2 : T(d_2 \neq c_2). \left(\begin{array}{l} \forall d_3 : S(d_3 \neq c_1). \\ \quad \overline{\left(d_1.p \wedge \overline{d_2.t_1} \wedge \overline{d_2.t_2} \wedge \overline{d_3.s} \wedge \overline{c_2.t_1} \right)} \end{array} \right) \right),$$

and thus we get

$$\sim (c_2.t_2 \wedge c_1.s \wedge Z_3).$$

However, the formula that characterizes an interaction between a topic and a subscriber is not yet complete. As it is mentioned above, each subscriber gives a certain priority to every topic that is interested in. So, in the last formula above we have also to "add" the corresponding weights. Therefore, we derive the weighted $FOCL$ formula Z_4 containing the priorities of two subscribers $s_1 : S$, $s_2 : S$ to the topics $r_1 : T$, $r_2 : T$, and $r_3 : T$ as follows:[3]

$$Z_4 = \bigotimes_{\substack{i=1,2,3 \\ j=1,2}} ((c_2.t_2 \equiv r_i.t_2 \wedge c_1.s \equiv s_j.s) \implies k_{i,j}).$$

We conclude to the following weighted $FOCL$ formula Z_5 which characterizes an interaction between a subscriber and a topic with its corresponding weight

$$Z_5 = (\sim (c_2.t_2 \wedge c_1.s \wedge Z_3)) \otimes Z_4.$$

---

[3] For simplicity we consider concrete numbers of subscribers and topics. Trivially, one can modify the weighted $FOCL$ formula Z_4 for arbitrarily many subscribers and topics.

Finally, in order to complete the formula that formalizes the Publish/Subscribe architecture style, we have to generalize the above procedure for every subscriber. Indeed, the required formula must check for every subscriber whether there exists a topic that the subscriber is interested in, and also if there exists a publisher that has sent a message to that topic, so that the subscriber can receive it. Therefore, we define the weighted $FOCL$ formula

$$Z = \bigotimes c_1 : S. \left(\bigoplus c_2 : T. \left(\bigoplus c_3 : P. (Z_2 \uplus Z_5) \right) \right)$$

which characterizes the Publish/Subscribe architecture style. Clearly Z can describe the Publish/Subscribe architecture for any number of subscribers by modifying accordingly the weighted $FOCL$ formula Z_4.

Assume, for instance, that $C_T = \{p_1 : P, p_2 : P, p_3 : P, p_4 : P, r_1 : T, r_2 : T, r_3 : T, s_1 : S, s_2 : S\}$ is the set of all the components, and K is the Viterbi semiring. Let also $B = \{p_1 : P, p_2 : P, r_1 : T, r_2 : T, r_3 : T, s_1 : S, s_2 : S\} \subseteq C_T$. Then for every $\gamma \in C(P_B)$ we get

$$\|Z\|(B,\gamma)$$

$$= \left\| \bigotimes c_1 : S. \left(\bigoplus c_2 : T. \left(\bigoplus c_3 : P. (Z_2 \uplus Z_5) \right) \right) \right\|(B,\gamma)$$

$$= \prod_{c_1':S\in B} \left\| \bigoplus c_2 : T. \left(\bigoplus c_3 : P.(Z_2 \uplus Z_5)[c_1'/c_1] \right) \right\|(B,\gamma)$$

$$= \prod_{c_1':S\in B} \left(\max_{c_2':T\in B} \left(\left\| \bigoplus c_3 : P.(Z_2 \uplus Z_5)[c_1'/c_1, c_2'/c_2] \right\| \right) \right)(B,\gamma)$$

$$= \prod_{c_1':S\in B} \left(\max_{c_2':T\in B} \left(\max_{c_3':P\in B} (\|(Z_2 \uplus Z_5)[c_1'/c_1, c_2'/c_2, c_3'/c_3]\|(B,\gamma)) \right) \right)$$

$$= \left(\max \left(\begin{array}{l} \max \left(\begin{array}{l} \|(Z_2 \uplus Z_5)[s_1/c_1, r_1/c_2, p_1/c_3]\|(B,\gamma), \\ \|(Z_2 \uplus Z_5)[s_1/c_1, r_1/c_2, p_2/c_3]\|(B,\gamma) \end{array} \right), \\ \max \left(\begin{array}{l} \|(Z_2 \uplus Z_5)[s_1/c_1, r_2/c_2, p_1/c_3]\|(B,\gamma), \\ \|(Z_2 \uplus Z_5)[s_1/c_1, r_2/c_2, p_2/c_3]\|(B,\gamma) \end{array} \right), \\ \max \left(\begin{array}{l} \|(Z_2 \uplus Z_5)[s_1/c_1, r_3/c_2, p_1/c_3]\|(B,\gamma), \\ \|(Z_2 \uplus Z_5)[s_1/c_1, r_3/c_2, p_2/c_3]\|(B,\gamma) \end{array} \right) \end{array} \right) \right).$$

$$\cdot \left(\max \left(\begin{array}{l} \max \left(\begin{array}{l} \|(Z_2 \uplus Z_5)[s_2/c_1, r_1/c_2, p_1/c_3]\|(B,\gamma), \\ \|(Z_2 \uplus Z_5)[s_2/c_1, r_1/c_2, p_2/c_3]\|(B,\gamma) \end{array} \right), \\ \max \left(\begin{array}{l} \|(Z_2 \uplus Z_5)[s_2/c_1, r_2/c_2, p_1/c_3]\|(B,\gamma), \\ \|(Z_2 \uplus Z_5)[s_2/c_1, r_2/c_2, p_2/c_3]\|(B,\gamma) \end{array} \right), \\ \max \left(\begin{array}{l} \|(Z_2 \uplus Z_5)[s_2/c_1, r_3/c_2, p_1/c_3]\|(B,\gamma), \\ \|(Z_2 \uplus Z_5)[s_2/c_1, r_3/c_2, p_2/c_3]\|(B,\gamma) \end{array} \right) \end{array} \right) \right).$$

Let $\gamma = \{\{p_1.p, r_1.t_1\}, \{p_1.p, r_3.t_1\}, \{p_2.p, r_1.t_1\}, \{r_1.t_2, s_1.s\}, \{r_2.t_2, s_2.s\}, \{r_3.t_2, s_2.s\}\}$. By straightforward computations we get $\|Z\|(B,\gamma) = k_{1,1} \cdot k_{3,2}$, which represents the greatest combination of priorities of the subscribers according to γ.

7   Conclusion

We introduced a weighted *PCL* over a commutative semiring K and investigated several properties of the class of polynomials obtained as semantics of this logic. For some of that properties we required our semiring to be idempotent. We proved that for every weighted *PCL* formula ζ we can effectively construct an equivalent one ζ' in full normal form. Furthermore, ζ' is unique up to the equivalence relation. This result implied that our logic is complete, and we showed that it is also sound. Weighted *PCL* describes nicely, architectures with quantitative characteristics. We extended the weighted *PCL* to weighted first-order configuration logic with which we could represent architecture styles equipped with quantitative features. We proved several properties for the class of polynomials definable by weighted first-order configuration logic. We also provided examples of weighted architecture styles. In our future work we will study decidability results and weighted second-order configuration logic. It is an open problem whether we can develop the theory of this paper by relaxing the commutativity property of the semiring K and thus obtaining our results for a larger class of semirings. Furthermore, it should be very interesting to investigate the weighted *PCL* and its first-order extension over more general weight structures which can describe further properties like average, limit inferior, limit superior, and discounting (cf. for instance [2]).

Acknowledgements. We should like to express our gratitude to Joseph Sifakis for useful discussions and to Anastasia Mavridou for clarifications on [11].

References

1. Droste, M., Kuich, W., Vogler, H. (eds.): Handbook of Weighted Automata. EATCS Monographs in Theoretical Computer Science. Springer, Heidelberg (2009). doi:10.1007/978-3-642-01492-5
2. Droste, M., Meinecke, I.: Weighted automata and weighted MSO logics for average and long-time behaviors. Inf. Comput. **220–221**, 44–59 (2012). doi:10.1016/j.ic.2012.10.001
3. Droste., M., Rahonis, G.: Weighted linear dynamic logic. In: GandALF 2016. EPTCS 226, pp. 149–163 (2016). doi:10.4204/EPTCS.226.11
4. Eugster, P., Felber, P., Guerraoui, R., Kermarrec, A.-M.: The many faces of Publish/Subscribe. ACM Comput. Surv. **35**(2), 114–131 (2003). doi:10.1145/857076.857078
5. Garlan, D.: Software architecture: a travelogue. In: FOSE 2014, pp. 29–39, ACM (2014). doi:10.1145/2593882.2593886
6. Hasan, S., O'Riain, S., Curry, E.: Approximate semantic matching of heterogeneous events. In: DEBS 2012, pp. 252–263, ACM (2012). doi:10.1145/2335484.2335512
7. Lluch-Lafuente, A., Montanari, U.: Quantitative μ-calculus and CTL over constraint semirings. Theoret. Comput. Sci. **346**, 135–160 (2005). doi:10.1016/j.entcs.2004.02.063
8. Mandrali, E.: Weighted Computability with Discounting, PhD Thesis. Aristotle University of Thessaloniki, Thessaloniki (2013)

9. Mandrali, E., Rahonis, G.: On weighted first-order logics with discounting. Acta Inform. **51**, 61–106 (2014). doi:10.1007/s00236-013-0193-3
10. Mandrali, E., Rahonis, G.: Weighted first-order logics over semirings. Acta Cybernet. **22**, 435–483 (2015). doi:10.14232/actacyb.22.2.2015.13
11. Mavridou, A., Baranov, E., Bliudze, S., Sifakis, J.: Configuration logics: modelling architecture styles. J. Logic Algebraic Methods Program. **86**, 2–29 (2016). doi:10.1016/j.jlamp.2016.05.002
12. Paraponiari, P., Rahonis, G.: On weighted configuration logics. arxiv:1704.04969v4
13. Pittou, M., Rahonis, G.: Weighted recognizability over infinite alphabets. Acta Cybernet. **23**, 283–317 (2017). doi:10.14232/actacyb.23.1.2017.16
14. Sifakis, J.: Rigorous systems design. Found. Trends Sig. Process **6**(4), 293–362 (2013). doi:10.1561/1000000034

Compositional Model Checking Is Lively

Sander de Putter and Anton Wijs[(✉)]

Eindhoven University of Technology, Eindhoven, Netherlands
{s.m.j.d.putter,a.j.wijs}@tue.nl

Abstract. Compositional model checking approaches attempt to limit state space explosion by iteratively combining behaviour of some of the components in the system and reducing the result modulo an appropriate equivalence relation. For an equivalence relation to be applicable, it should be a congruence for parallel composition where synchronisations between the components may be introduced. An equivalence relation preserving both safety and liveness properties is divergence-preserving branching bisimulation (DPBB). It is generally assumed that DPBB is a congruence for parallel composition, even in the context of synchronisations between components. However, so far, no such results have been published.

This work finally proves that this is the case. Furthermore, we discuss how to safely decompose an existing LTS network in components such that the re-composition is equivalent to the original LTS network. All proofs have been mechanically verified using the Coq proof assistant.

Finally, to demonstrate the effectiveness of compositional model checking with intermediate DPBB reductions, we discuss the results we obtained after having conducted a number of experiments.

1 Introduction

Model checking [3,9] is one of the most successful approaches for the analysis and verification of the behaviour of concurrent systems. However, a major issue is the so-called *state space explosion problem*: the state space of a concurrent system tends to increase exponentially as the number of parallel processes increases linearly. Often, it is difficult or infeasible to verify realistic large scale concurrent systems. Over time, several methods have been proposed to tackle the state space explosion problem. Prominent approaches are the application of some form of on-the-fly reduction, such as Partial Order Reduction [30] or Symmetry Reduction [7], and compositionally verifying the system, for instance using Compositional Reasoning [8] or Partial Model Checking [1,2].

The key operations in compositional approaches are the composition and decomposition of systems. First a system is decomposed into two or more components. Then, one or more of these components is manipulated (e.g., reduced). Finally, the components are re-composed. Comparison modulo an appropriate

This work is supported by ARTEMIS Joint Undertaking project EMC2 (grant nr. 621429).

J. Proença and M. Lumpe (Eds.): FACS 2017, LNCS 10487, pp. 117–136, 2017.
DOI: 10.1007/978-3-319-68034-7_7

equivalence relation is applied to ensure that the manipulations preserve properties of interest (for instance, expressed in the modal μ-calculus [19]). These manipulations are sound if and only if the equivalence relation is a congruence for the composition expression.

Two prominent equivalence relations are branching bisimulation and divergence-preserving branching bisimulation (DPBB) [13,15].[1] Branching bisimulation preserves safety properties, while DPBB preserves both safety and liveness properties.

In [14] it is proven that DPBB is the coarsest equivalence that is a congruence for parallel composition. However, compositional reasoning requires equivalences that are a congruence for parallel composition where new *synchronisations between parallel components* may be introduced, which is not considered by the authors. It is known that branching bisimulation is a congruence for parallel composition of synchronising Labelled Transition Systems (LTSs), this follows from the fact that parallel composition of synchronising LTSs can be expressed as a WB cool language [6]. However, obtaining such results for DPBB requires more work. To rigorously prove that DPBB is indeed a congruence for parallel composition of synchronising LTSs, a proof assistant, such as Coq [5], is required. So far, no results, obtained with or without the use of a proof assistant, have been reported.

A popular toolbox that offers a selection of compositional approaches is CADP [12]. CADP offers both *property-independent* approaches (e.g., compositional model generation, smart reduction, and compositional reasoning via behavioural interfaces) and *property-dependent* approaches (e.g., property-dependent reductions [25] and partial model checking [1]). The formal semantics of concurrent systems are described using *networks of LTSs* [22], or *LTS networks* for short. An LTS network consists of n LTSs representing the parallel processes. A set of synchronisation laws is used to describe the possible communication, i.e., synchronisation, between the process LTSs.

In this setting, this work considers parallel composition of synchronising LTS networks. Given two LTS networks $\mathcal{M}$ and $\mathcal{M}'$ of size n related via a DPBB relation B, another LTS network $\mathcal{N}$ of size m, and a parallel composition operator $\|_\sigma$ with a mapping σ that specifies synchronization between components, we show there is a DPBB relation C such that

$$\mathcal{M} \; B \; \mathcal{M}' \implies \mathcal{M} \|_\sigma \mathcal{N} \; C \; \mathcal{M}' \|_\sigma \mathcal{N}$$

This result subsumes the composition of individual synchronising LTSs via composition of LTS networks of size one. Moreover, generalization to composition of multiple LTS networks can be obtained via a reordering of the processes within LTS networks.

---

[1] It should be noted that a distinction can be made between divergence-sensitive branching bisimulation [28] and branching bisimulation with explicit divergence, also known as divergence-preserving branching bisimulation [13,15]. Contrary to the former, the latter distinguishes deadlocks and livelocks, and the latter is the coarsest congruence contained in the former.

Contributions. In this work, we prove that divergence-preserving branching bisimulation is a congruence for parallel composition of synchronising LTSs. Furthermore, we present a method to safely decompose an LTS network in components such that the composition of the components is equivalent to the original LTS network. The proofs have been mechanically verified using the Coq proof assistant and are available online.[2]

Finally, we discuss the effectiveness of compositionally constructing state spaces with intermediate DPBB reductions in comparison with the classical, non-compositional state space construction. The discussion is based on results we obtained after having conducted a number of experiments using the CADP toolbox. The authors of [11] report on experiments comparing the run-time and memory performance of three compositional verification techniques. As opposed to these experiments, our experiments concern the comparison of compositional and classical, non-compositional state space construction.

Structure of the paper. Related work is discussed in Sect. 2. In Sect. 3, we discuss the notions of LTS, LTS network, so-called LTS network admissibility, and DPBB. Next, the formal composition of LTS networks is presented in Sect. 4. We prove that DPBB is a congruence for the composition of LTS networks. Section 5 is on the decomposition of an LTS network. Decomposition allows the redefinition of a system as a set of components. In Sect. 6 we apply the theoretical results to a set of use cases comparing a compositional construction approach with non-compositional state space construction. In Sect. 7 we present the conclusions and directions for future work.

2   Related Work

Networks of LTSs are introduced in [21]. The authors mention that strong and branching bisimulations are congruences for the operations supported by LTS networks. Among these operations is the parallel composition with synchronisation on equivalent labels. A proof for branching bisimulation has been verified in PVS and a textual proof was written, but both the textual proof and the PVS proof have not been made public [23]. An axiomatisation for a rooted version of divergence-preserving branching bisimulation has been performed in a Master graduation project [33]. However, the considered language does not include parallel composition. In this paper, we formally show that DPBB is also a congruence for parallel composition with synchronisations between components. As DPBB is a branching bisimulation relation with an extra case for explicit divergence, the proof we present also formally shows that branching bisimulation is a congruence for parallel composition with synchronisations between components.

Another approach supporting compositional verification is presented in [22]. Given an LTS network and a component selected from the network the approach automatically generates an interface LTS from the remainder of the network.

---

[2] http://www.win.tue.nl/mdse/composition/DPBB_is_a_congruence_for_synchronizing _LTSs.zip.

This remainder of the network is called the environment. The interface LTS represents the synchronisation possibilities that are offered by the environment. This requires the construction and reduction of the system LTS of the environment. The advantage of this method is that transitions and states that do not contribute to the system LTS can be removed. In our approach only the system LTS of the considered component must be constructed. The environment is left out of scope until the components are composed.

Many process algebras support parallel composition with synchronisation on labels. Often a proof is given showing that some bisimulation is a congruence for these operators [10,20,24,26]. However, to the best of our knowledge no such proofs exist considering DPBB. Furthermore, if LTSs can be derived from their semantics (such as is the case with Structural Operational Semantics) then the fact that DPBB is a congruence for such a parallel composition can be directly derived from our results.

To generalize the congruence proofs a series of meta-theories have been proposed for algebras with parallel composition [6,34,35]. In [35] the *panth* format is proposed. They show that strong bisimulation is a congruence for algebras that adhere to the panth format. The focus of the work is on the expressiveness of the format. The author of [6] proposes *WB cool* formats for four bisimulations: weak bisimulation, rooted weak bisimulation, branching bisimulation, and rooted branching bisimulation. It is shown that these bisimulations are congruences for the corresponding formats. In [34] similar formats are proposed for eager bisimulation and branching bisimulation. Eager bisimulation is a kind of weak bisimulation wich is sensitive to divergence. The above mentioned formats do not consider DPBB. In our work we have shown that DPBB is a congruence for parallel composition of LTS networks and LTSs.

In earlier work, we presented decomposition for LTS transformation systems of LTS networks [36]. The work aims to verify the transformation of a component that may synchronise with other components. The paper proposes to calculate so called detaching laws which are similar to our interface laws. The approach can be modelled with our method. In fact, we show that the derivation of these detaching laws does not amount to a desired decomposition, i.e., the re-composition of the decomposition is *not* equivalent to the original system (see Example 3 discussed in Sect. 5).

A projection of an LTS network given a set of indices is presented in [12]. Their projection operator is similar to the consistent decomposition of LTS networks that we proposed. In fact, with a suitable operator for the reordering of LTS networks our decomposition operation is equivalent to their projection operator. The current paper contributes to these results that admissibility properties of the LTS network are indeed preserved for such consistent decompositions.

3   Preliminaries

In this section, we introduce the notions of LTS, LTS network, and divergence-preserving branching bisimulation of LTSs. The potential behaviour of processes is described by means of LTSs. The behaviour of a concurrent system is described by a *network of LTSs* [22], or *LTS network* for short. From an LTS network, a *system LTS* can be derived describing the global behaviour of the network. To compare the behaviour of these systems the notion of divergence-preserving branching bisimulation (DPBB) is used. DPBB is often used to reduce the state space of system specifications while preserving safety and liveness properties, or to compare the observable behaviour of two systems.

The semantics of a process, or a composition of several processes, can be formally expressed by an LTS as presented in Definition 1.

Definition 1 (Labelled Transition System). *An LTS $\mathcal{G}$ is a tuple $(\mathcal{S}_\mathcal{G}, \mathcal{A}_\mathcal{G}, \mathcal{T}_\mathcal{G}, \mathcal{I}_\mathcal{G})$, with*

- $\mathcal{S}_\mathcal{G}$ *a finite set of states;*
- $\mathcal{A}_\mathcal{G}$ *a set of action labels;*
- $\mathcal{T}_\mathcal{G} \subseteq \mathcal{S}_\mathcal{G} \times \mathcal{A}_\mathcal{G} \times \mathcal{S}_\mathcal{G}$ *a transition relation;*
- $\mathcal{I}_\mathcal{G} \subseteq \mathcal{S}_\mathcal{G}$ *a (non-empty) set of initial states.*

Action labels in $\mathcal{A}_\mathcal{G}$ are denoted by a, b, c, etc. Additionally, there is a special action label τ that represents internal, or hidden, system steps. A transition $(s, a, s') \in \mathcal{T}_\mathcal{G}$, or $s \xrightarrow{a}_\mathcal{G} s'$ for short, denotes that LTS $\mathcal{G}$ can move from state s to state s' by performing the a-action. The transitive reflexive closure of $\xrightarrow{a}_\mathcal{G}$ is denoted as $\xrightarrow{a}{}^*_\mathcal{G}$, and the transitive closure is denoted as $\xrightarrow{a}{}^+_\mathcal{G}$.

LTS Network. An LTS network, presented in Definition 2, describes a system consisting of a finite number of concurrent process LTSs and a set of synchronisation laws that define the possible interaction between the processes. We write $1..n$ for the set of integers ranging from 1 to n. A vector $\bar{v}$ of size n contains n elements indexed from 1 to n. For all $i \in 1..n$, $\bar{v}_i$ represents the ith element of vector $\bar{v}$. The *concatenation* of two vectors v and w of size n and m respectively is denoted by $v \parallel w$. In the context of composition of LTS networks, this concatenation of vectors corresponds to the parallel composition of the behaviour of the two vectors.

Definition 2 (LTS network). *An LTS network $\mathcal{M}$ of size n is a pair $(\Pi, \mathcal{V})$, where*

- Π *is a vector of n concurrent LTSs. For each $i \in 1..n$, we write $\Pi_i = (\mathcal{S}_i, \mathcal{A}_i, \mathcal{T}_i, \mathcal{I}_i)$.*
- $\mathcal{V}$ *is a finite set of synchronisation laws. A synchronisation law is a tuple $(\bar{v}, a)$, where $\bar{v}$ is a vector of size n, called the synchronisation vector, containing synchronising action labels, and a is an action label representing the result of successful synchronisation. We have $\forall i \in 1..n. \ \bar{v}_i \in \mathcal{A}_i \cup \{\bullet\}$, where $\bullet$ is a special symbol denoting that Π_i performs no action. The set of result actions of a set of synchronisation laws $\mathcal{V}$ is defined as $\mathcal{A}_\mathcal{V} = \{a \mid (\bar{v}, a) \in \mathcal{V}\}$.*

The explicit behaviour of an LTS network $\mathcal{M}$ is defined by its *system LTS* $\mathcal{G}_{\mathcal{M}}$ which is obtained by combining the processes in Π according to the synchronisation laws in $\mathcal{V}$ as specified by Definition 3. The LTS network model subsumes most hiding, renaming, cutting, and parallel composition operators present in process algebras. For instance, hiding can be applied by replacing the a component in a law by τ.

Definition 3 (System LTS). *Given an LTS network* $\mathcal{M} = (\Pi, \mathcal{V})$*, its* system LTS *is defined by* $\mathcal{G}_{\mathcal{M}} = (\mathcal{S}_{\mathcal{M}}, \mathcal{A}_{\mathcal{M}}, \mathcal{T}_{\mathcal{M}}, \mathcal{I}_{\mathcal{M}})$*, with*

- $\mathcal{I}_{\mathcal{M}} = \{\langle s_1, \ldots, s_n \rangle \mid s_i \in \mathcal{I}_i\}$*;*
- $\mathcal{T}_{\mathcal{M}}$ *and* $\mathcal{S}_{\mathcal{M}}$ *are the smallest relation and set, respectively, satisfying* $\mathcal{I}_{\mathcal{M}} \subseteq \mathcal{S}_{\mathcal{M}}$ *and for all* $\bar{s} \in \mathcal{S}_{\mathcal{M}}$, $a \in \mathcal{A}_{\mathcal{V}}$*, we have* $\bar{s} \xrightarrow{a}_{\mathcal{M}} \bar{s}'$ *and* $\bar{s}' \in \mathcal{S}_{\mathcal{M}}$ *iff there exists* $(\bar{v}, a) \in \mathcal{V}$ *such that for all* $i \in 1..n$:

$$
\begin{cases}
\bar{s}_i = \bar{s}_i' & \text{if } \bar{v}_i = \bullet \\
\bar{s}_i \xrightarrow{\bar{v}_i}_{\Pi_i} \bar{s}_i' & \text{otherwise}
\end{cases}
$$

- $\mathcal{A}_{\mathcal{M}} = \{a \mid \exists \bar{s}, \bar{s}' \in \mathcal{S}_{\mathcal{M}}.\bar{s} \xrightarrow{a}_{\mathcal{M}} \bar{s}'\}$.

In Fig. 1, an example of an LTS network $\mathcal{M} = (\langle \Pi_1, \Pi_2 \rangle, \mathcal{V})$ with four synchronisation laws is shown on the left, and the corresponding system TLS $\mathcal{G}_{\mathcal{M}}$ is shown on the right. Initial states are coloured black. The states of the system LTS $\mathcal{G}_{\mathcal{M}}$ are constructed by combining the states of Π_1 and Π_2. In this example, we have $\langle 1, 3 \rangle, \langle 1, 4 \rangle, \langle 2, 3 \rangle \in \mathcal{S}_{\mathcal{M}}$, of which $\langle 1, 3 \rangle$ is the single initial state of $\mathcal{G}_{\mathcal{M}}$.

The transitions of the system LTS in Fig. 1 are constructed by combining the transitions of Π_1 and Π_2 according to the set of synchronisation laws $\mathcal{V}$. Law $(\langle c, c \rangle, c)$ specifies that the process LTSs can synchronise on their c-transitions, resulting in c-transitions in the system LTS. Similarly, the process LTSs can synchronise on their d-transitions, resulting in a d-transition in $\mathcal{G}_{\mathcal{M}}$. Furthermore, law $(\langle a, \bullet \rangle, a)$ specifies that process Π_1 can perform an a-transition independently resulting in an a-transition in $\mathcal{G}_{\mathcal{M}}$. Likewise, law $(\langle \bullet, b \rangle, b)$ specifies that the b-transition can be fired independently by process Π_2. Because Π_1 does not partici-

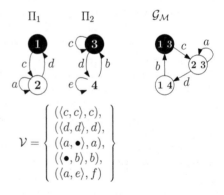

$$
\mathcal{V} = \begin{cases}
(\langle c, c \rangle, c), \\
(\langle d, d \rangle, d), \\
(\langle a, \bullet \rangle, a), \\
(\langle \bullet, b \rangle, b), \\
(\langle a, e \rangle, f)
\end{cases}
$$

Fig. 1. An LTS network $\mathcal{M} = (\Pi, \mathcal{V})$ (left) and its system LTS $\mathcal{G}_{\mathcal{M}}$ (right)

pate in this law, it remains in state $\langle 1 \rangle$ in $\mathcal{G}_{\mathcal{M}}$. The last law states that a- and e-transitions can synchronise, resulting in f-transitions, however, in this example the a- and e-transitions in Π_1 and Π_2 are never able to synchronise since state $\langle 2, 4 \rangle$ is unreachable.

An LTS network is called *admissible* if the synchronisation laws of the network do not synchronise, rename, or cut τ-transitions [22] as defined in Definition 4. The intuition behind this is that internal, i.e., hidden, behaviour should not be restricted by any operation. Partial model checking and compositional construction rely on LTS networks being admissible [12]. Hence, in this paper, we also restrict ourselves to admissible LTS networks when presenting our composition and decomposition methods.

Definition 4 (LTS network Admissibility). *An LTS network* $\mathcal{M} = (\Pi, \mathcal{V})$ *of length n is called admissible iff the following properties hold:*

1. $\forall (\bar{v}, a) \in \mathcal{V}, i \in 1..n.\ \bar{v}_i = \tau \implies \neg \exists j \neq i.\ \bar{v}_j \neq \bullet;$ *(no synchronisation of* τ *'s)*
2. $\forall (\bar{v}, a) \in \mathcal{V}, i \in 1..n.\ \bar{v}_i = \tau \implies a = \tau;$ *(no renaming of* τ *'s)*
3. $\forall i \in 1..n.\ \tau \in \mathcal{A}_i \implies \exists (\bar{v}, a) \in \mathcal{V}.\ \bar{v}_i = \tau.$ *(no cutting of* τ *'s)*

Divergence-Preserving Branching Bisimulation. To compare LTSs, we use DPBB, also called *branching bisimulation with explicit divergence* [13,15]. DPBB supports abstraction from actions and preserves both safety and liveness properties. To simplify proofs we use DPBB with the weakest divergence condition (D$_4$) presented in [15] as presented in Definition 5. This definition is equivalent to the standard definition of DPBB [15]. The smallest infinite ordinal is denoted by ω.

Definition 5 (Divergence-Preserving Branching bisimulation). *A binary relation B between two LTSs* $\mathcal{G}_1$ *and* $\mathcal{G}_2$ *is a* divergence-preserving branching bisimulation *iff for all* $s \in S_{\mathcal{G}_1}$ *and* $t \in S_{\mathcal{G}_2}$, *s B t implies:*

1. *if* $s \xrightarrow{a}_{\mathcal{G}_1} s'$ *then*
   (a) either $a = \tau$ *with* s' *B t;*
   (b) or $t \xrightarrow{\tau}{}^*_{\mathcal{G}_2} \hat{t} \xrightarrow{a}_{\mathcal{G}_2} t'$ *with* s *B* $\hat{t}$ *and* s' *B t'.*
2. *symmetric to 1.*
3. *if there is an infinite sequence of states* $(s^k)_{k \in \omega}$ *such that* $s = s^0$, $s^k \xrightarrow{\tau}_{\mathcal{G}_1} s^{k+1}$ *and* s^k *B t for all* $k \in \omega$, *then there exists a state* t' *such that* $t \xrightarrow{\tau}{}^+_{\mathcal{G}_2} t'$ *and* s^k *B t' for some* $k \in \omega$.
4. *symmetric to 3.*

Two states $s \in S_{\mathcal{G}_1}$ and $t \in S_{\mathcal{G}_2}$ are *divergence-preserving branching bisimilar*, denoted by $s \underline{\leftrightarrow}^{\Delta}_b t$, iff there is a DPBB relation B such that s B t. We say that two LTSs $\mathcal{G}_1$ and $\mathcal{G}_2$ are divergence-preserving branching bisimilar, denoted by $\mathcal{G}_1 \underline{\leftrightarrow}^{\Delta}_b \mathcal{G}_2$, iff $\forall s_1 \in \mathcal{I}_{\mathcal{G}_1}.\exists s_2 \in \mathcal{I}_{\mathcal{G}_2}.\ s_1 \underline{\leftrightarrow}^{\Delta}_b s_2$ and vice versa.

4   Composition of LTS Networks

This section introduces the compositional construction of LTS networks. Composition of process LTSs results in a system LTS that tends to grow exponentially when more processes are considered.

An LTS network can be seen as being composed of several *components*, each of which consists of a number of individual processes in parallel composition, with *intra-component* synchronisation laws describing how the processes inside a component should synchronise with each other. Furthermore, *inter-component* synchronisation laws define how the components as a whole should synchronise with each other. Compositional construction of a minimal version of the final system LTS may then be performed by first constructing the system LTSs of the different components, then minimising these, and finally combining their behaviour. Example 1 presents an example of a network with two components and an inter-component synchronisation law.

Example 1 (Component). Consider an LTS network $\mathcal{M} = (\Pi, \mathcal{V})$ with processes $\Pi = \langle \Pi_1, \Pi_2, \Pi_3 \rangle$ and synchronisation laws $\mathcal{V} = \{(\langle a, \bullet, \bullet \rangle, a), (\langle \bullet, b, b \rangle, b), (\langle c, c, c \rangle, c)\}$. We may split up the network in two *components*, say $\mathcal{M}_1 = (\langle \Pi_1 \rangle, \mathcal{V}_1)$ and $\mathcal{M}_{\{2,3\}} = (\langle \Pi_2, \Pi_3 \rangle, \mathcal{V}_{\{2,3\}})$. Then, $(\langle c, c, c \rangle, c)$ is an *inter-component law* describing synchronisation between $\mathcal{M}_1$ and $\mathcal{M}_{\{2,3\}}$. The component $\mathcal{M}_1$ consists of process Π_1, and the set of intra-component synchronisation laws $\mathcal{V}_1 = \{(\langle a, \bullet, \bullet \rangle, a)\}$ operating solely on Π_1. Similarly, component $\mathcal{M}_{\{2,3\}}$ consists of Π_2 and Π_3, and the set of intra-component synchronisation laws $\mathcal{V}_{\{2,3\}} = \{(\langle \bullet, b, b \rangle, b)\}$ operating solely on Π_2 and Π_3.

The challenge of compositional construction is to allow manipulation of the components while guaranteeing that the observable behaviour of the system as a whole remains equivalent modulo DPBB. Even though synchronisation laws of a component may be changed, we must somehow preserve synchronisations with the other components. Such a change of synchronisation laws occurs, for instance, when reordering the processes in a component, or renaming actions that are part of inter-component synchronisation laws.

In this paper, we limit ourselves to composition of two components: a left and a right component. This simplifies notations and proofs. However, the approach can be generalised to splitting networks given two sets of indices indicating which processes are part of which component, i.e., a projection operator can be used to project distinct parts of a network into components.

In the remainder of this section, first, we formalise LTS networks composition. Then, we show that admissibility is preserved when two admissible networks are composed. Finally, we prove that DPBB is a congruence for composition of LTS networks.

Composing LTS networks. Before defining the composition of two networks, we introduce a mapping indicating how the inter-component laws should be constructed from the interfaces of the two networks. An inter-component law can then be constructed by combining the interface vectors of the components and adding a result action. This is achieved through a given *interface mapping*, presented in Definition 6, mapping interface actions to result actions.

Definition 6 (Interface Mapping). *Consider LTS networks $\mathcal{M}_\Pi = (\Pi, \mathcal{V})$ and $\mathcal{M}_P = (P, \mathcal{W})$ of size n and m, respectively. An* interface mapping *between $\mathcal{M}_\Pi$ and $\mathcal{M}_P$ is a mapping $\sigma : \mathcal{A}_\mathcal{V} \setminus \{\tau\} \times \mathcal{A}_\mathcal{W} \setminus \{\tau\} \times \mathcal{A}_\sigma$ describing how the interface actions of $\mathcal{M}_\Pi$ should be combined with interface actions of $\mathcal{M}_P$, and* *what the action label should be resulting from successful synchronisation. The set $\mathcal{A}_\sigma$ is the set of actions resulting from successful synchronisation between Π and P. The actions mapped by σ are considered the interface actions.*

An interface mapping implicitly defines how inter-component synchronisation laws should be represented in the separate components. These local representatives are called the *interface synchronisation laws*. A mapping between $\mathcal{M}_\Pi = (\Pi, \mathcal{V})$ and $\mathcal{M}_\mathrm{P} = (\mathrm{P}, \mathcal{W})$ implies the following sets of interface synchronisation laws:

$$\mathcal{V}_\sigma = \{(\bar{v}, a) \in \mathcal{V} \mid \exists b, c.\ (a, b, c) \in \sigma\}$$

$$\mathcal{W}_\sigma = \{(\bar{w}, b) \in \mathcal{W} \mid \exists a, c.\ (a, b, c) \in \sigma\}$$

An interface synchronisation law makes a component's potential to synchronise with other components explicit. An interface synchronisation law has a synchronisation vector, called the *interface vector*, that may be part of inter-component laws. The result action of an interface synchronisation law is called an *interface action*. These notions are clarified further in Example 2.

Example 2 (Interface Vector and Interface Law). Let $\mathcal{M} = (\langle \Pi_1, \Pi_2, \Pi_3 \rangle, \mathcal{V})$ be a network with inter-component synchronisation law $(\langle a, a, b \rangle, c) \in \mathcal{V}$ and a component $M_{\{1,2\}} = (\langle \Pi_1, \Pi_2 \rangle, \mathcal{V}_{\{1,2\}})$. Then, $\langle a, a \rangle$ is an *interface vector* of $M_{\{1,2\}}$, and given a corresponding *interface action* α, the *interface law* is $(\langle a, a \rangle, \alpha)$.

Together the interface laws and interface mapping describe the possible synchronisations between two components, i.e., the interface laws and interface mapping describe inter-component synchronisation laws. Given two sets of laws $\mathcal{V}$ and $\mathcal{W}$ and an interface mapping σ, the inter-component synchronisation laws are defined as follows:

$$\sigma(\mathcal{V}, \mathcal{W}) = \{(\bar{v} \parallel \bar{w}, a) \mid (\bar{v}, \alpha) \in \mathcal{V} \wedge (\bar{w}, \beta) \in \mathcal{W} \wedge (\alpha, \beta, a) \in \sigma\}$$

The mapping partitions both $\mathcal{V}$ and $\mathcal{W}$ into two sets of synchronisation laws: the interface and non-interface synchronisation laws.

The application of the interface mapping, i.e., formal composition of two LTS networks, is presented in Definition 7. We show that a component may be exchanged with a divergence-preserving branching bisimilar component iff the interface actions are not hidden. In other words, the interfacing with the remainder of the networks is respected when the interface actions remain observable.

Definition 7 (Composition of LTS networks). *Consider LTS networks $\mathcal{M}_\Pi = (\Pi, \mathcal{V})$ of size n and $\mathcal{M}_\mathrm{P} = (\mathrm{P}, \mathcal{W})$ of size m. Let $\sigma : \mathcal{A}_\mathcal{V} \setminus \{\tau\} \times \mathcal{A}_\mathcal{W} \setminus \{\tau\} \times \mathcal{A}$ be an interface mapping describing the synchronisations between $\mathcal{M}_\Pi$ and $\mathcal{M}_\mathrm{P}$. The composition of $\mathcal{M}_\Pi$ and $\mathcal{M}_\mathrm{P}$, denoted by $\mathcal{M}_\Pi \parallel_\sigma \mathcal{M}_\mathrm{P}$, is defined as the LTS network $(\Pi \parallel \mathrm{P}, (\mathcal{V} \setminus \mathcal{V}_\sigma)^\bullet \cup {}^\bullet(\mathcal{W} \setminus \mathcal{W}_\sigma) \cup \sigma(\mathcal{V}, \mathcal{W}))$, where $(\mathcal{V} \setminus \mathcal{V}_\sigma)^\bullet = \{(\bar{v} \parallel \bullet^m, a) \mid (\bar{v}, a) \in \mathcal{V} \setminus \mathcal{V}_\sigma\}$ and ${}^\bullet(\mathcal{W} \setminus \mathcal{W}_\sigma) = \{(\bullet^n \parallel \bar{v}, a) \mid (\bar{v}, a) \in \mathcal{W} \setminus \mathcal{W}_\sigma\}$ are the sets of synchronisation laws $\mathcal{V} \setminus \mathcal{V}_\sigma$ padded with m $\bullet$'s and $\mathcal{W} \setminus \mathcal{W}_\sigma$ padded with n $\bullet$'s, respectively.*

As presented in Proposition 1, LTS networks that are composed (according to Definition 7) from two admissible networks are admissible as well. Therefore, composition of LTS networks is compatible with the compositional verification approaches of [12].

Proposition 1. *Let $\mathcal{M}_\Pi = (\Pi, \mathcal{V})$ and $\mathcal{M}_P = (P, \mathcal{W})$ be admissible LTS networks of length n and m, respectively. Furthermore, let $\sigma : \mathcal{A}_\mathcal{V}\backslash\{\tau\}\times\mathcal{A}_\mathcal{W}\backslash\{\tau\}\times\mathcal{A}$ be an interface mapping. Then, the network $\mathcal{M} = \mathcal{M}_\Pi \parallel_\sigma \mathcal{M}_P$, composed according to Definition 7, is also admissible.*

Proof. We show that $\mathcal{M}$ satisfies Definition 4:

- *No synchronisation and renaming of τ's.* Let $(\bar{v}, a) \in (\mathcal{V}\backslash\mathcal{V}_\sigma)^\bullet \cup {}^\bullet(\mathcal{W} \backslash \mathcal{W}_\sigma) \cup \sigma(\mathcal{V}, \mathcal{W})$ be a synchronisation law with $\bar{v}_i = \tau$ for some $i \in 1..(n + m)$. We distinguish two cases:
  - $(\bar{v}, a) \in (\mathcal{V} \backslash \mathcal{V}_\sigma)^\bullet \cup {}^\bullet(\mathcal{W}\backslash\mathcal{W}_\sigma)$. By construction of $(\mathcal{V} \backslash \mathcal{V}_\sigma)^\bullet$ and ${}^\bullet(\mathcal{W}\backslash\mathcal{W}_\sigma)$, and admissibility of $\mathcal{M}_\Pi$ and $\mathcal{M}_P$, we have $\forall j \in 1..n.\ \bar{v}_j \neq \bullet \implies i = j$, $\forall j \in (n+1)..(n+m).\ \bar{v}_j \neq \bullet \implies i = j$ and $a = \tau$. Hence, it holds that $\forall j \in 1..(n+m).\ \bar{v}_j \neq \bullet \implies i = j$ (no synchronisation of τ's) and $a = \tau$ (no renaming of τ's).
  - $(\bar{v}, a) \in \sigma(\mathcal{V}, \mathcal{W})$. By definition of $\sigma(\mathcal{V}, \mathcal{W})$, there are interface laws $(\bar{v}', \alpha') \in \mathcal{V}$ and $(\bar{v}'', \alpha'') \in \mathcal{W}$ such that $(\alpha', \alpha'', a) \in \sigma$. Hence, either $1 \leq i \leq n$ with $\bar{v}'_i = \tau$ or $n < i \leq n + m$ with $\bar{v}''_{i-n} = \tau$. Since $\mathcal{M}_\Pi$ and $\mathcal{M}_P$ are admissible, we must have $\alpha' = \tau$ or $\alpha'' = \tau$, respectively. However, the interface mapping does not allow τ as interface actions, therefore, the proof follows by contradiction.

  It follows that $\mathcal{M}$ does not allow synchronisation and renaming of τ's.
- *No cutting of τ's.* Let $(\Pi \parallel P)_i$ be a process with $\tau \in \mathcal{A}_{(\Pi\parallel P)_i}$ for some $i \in 1..(n + m)$. We distinguish the two cases $1 \leq i \leq n$ and $n < i < m$. It follows that $\tau \in \mathcal{A}_{\Pi_i}$ for the former case and $\tau \in \mathcal{A}_{P_{i-n}}$ for the latter case. Since both $\mathcal{M}_\Pi$ and $\mathcal{M}_P$ are admissible and no actions are removed in $(\mathcal{V} \backslash \mathcal{V}_\sigma)^\bullet$ and ${}^\bullet(\mathcal{W}\backslash\mathcal{W}_\sigma)$, in both cases there exists a $(\bar{v}, a) \in (\mathcal{V} \backslash \mathcal{V}_\sigma)^\bullet \cup {}^\bullet(\mathcal{W}\backslash\mathcal{W}_\sigma) \cup \sigma(\mathcal{V}, \mathcal{W})$ such that $\bar{v}_i = \tau$. Hence, the composite network $\mathcal{M}$ does not allow cutting of τ's.

Since the three admissibility properties hold, the composed network $\mathcal{M}$ satisfies Definition 4. □

DPBB is a congruence for LTS network composition. Proposition 2 shows that DPBB is a congruence for the composition of LTS networks according to Definition 7. It is worth noting that an interface mapping does not map τ's, i.e., synchronisation of τ-actions is not allowed. In particular, this means that interface actions must *not* be hidden when applying verification techniques on a component.

Note that Proposition 2 subsumes the composition of single LTSs, via composition of LTS networks of size one with trivial sets of intra-component synchronisation laws.

Proposition 2. *Consider LTS networks* $\mathcal{M}_\Pi = (\Pi, \mathcal{V})$, $\mathcal{M}_{\Pi'} = (\Pi', \mathcal{V}')$ *of size* n, *and* $\mathcal{M}_P = (P, \mathcal{W})$ *of size* m. *Let* σ *be an interface mapping describing the coupling between the interface actions in* $\mathcal{A}_\mathcal{V}$ *and* $\mathcal{A}_\mathcal{W}$. *The following holds*

$$\mathcal{M}_\Pi \underset{b}{\leftrightarrow}^\Delta \mathcal{M}_{\Pi'} \implies \mathcal{M}_\Pi \parallel_\sigma \mathcal{M}_P \underset{b}{\leftrightarrow}^\Delta \mathcal{M}_{\Pi'} \parallel_\sigma \mathcal{M}_P$$

Proof. Intuitively, we have $\mathcal{M}_\Pi \parallel_\sigma \mathcal{M}_P \underset{b}{\leftrightarrow}^\Delta \mathcal{M}_{\Pi'} \parallel_\sigma \mathcal{M}_P$ because $\mathcal{M}_\Pi \underset{b}{\leftrightarrow}^\Delta \mathcal{M}_{\Pi'}$ and the interface with $\mathcal{M}_P$ is respected. Since $\mathcal{M}_\Pi \underset{b}{\leftrightarrow}^\Delta \mathcal{M}_{\Pi'}$, whenever a transition labelled with an interface action α in $\mathcal{M}_\Pi$ is able to perform a transition together with $\mathcal{M}_P$, then $\mathcal{M}_{\Pi'}$ is able to simulate the interface α-transition and synchronise with $\mathcal{M}_P$. It follows that the branching structure and divergence is preserved. For the sake of brevity we define the following shorthand notations: $\mathcal{M} = \mathcal{M}_\Pi \parallel_\sigma \mathcal{M}_P$ and $\mathcal{M}' = \mathcal{M}_{\Pi'} \parallel_\sigma \mathcal{M}_P$. We show $\mathcal{M}_\Pi \underset{b}{\leftrightarrow}^\Delta \mathcal{M}_{\Pi'} \implies \mathcal{M} \underset{b}{\leftrightarrow}^\Delta \mathcal{M}'$.

Let B be a DPBB relation between $\mathcal{M}_\Pi$ and $\mathcal{M}_{\Pi'}$, i.e., $\mathcal{M}_\Pi \underset{b}{\leftrightarrow}^\Delta \mathcal{M}_{\Pi'}$. By definition, we have $\mathcal{M} \underset{b}{\leftrightarrow}^\Delta \mathcal{M}'$ iff there exists a DPBB relation C with $\mathcal{I}_\mathcal{M} \underset{b}{\leftrightarrow}^\Delta \mathcal{I}_{\mathcal{M}'}$. We define C as follows:

$$C = \{(\bar{s} \parallel \bar{r}, \bar{t} \parallel \bar{r}) \mid \bar{s} \, B \, \bar{t} \wedge \bar{r} \in \mathcal{S}_{\mathcal{M}_P}\}$$

The component that is subject to change is related via the relation B that relates the states in Π and Π'. The unchanged component of the network is related via the shared state $\bar{r}$, i.e., it relates the states of P to themselves.

To prove the proposition we have to show that C is a DPBB relation. This requires proving that C relates the initial states of $\mathcal{M}$ and $\mathcal{M}'$ and that C satisfies Definition 5.

- C *relates the initial states of* $\mathcal{M}$ *and* $\mathcal{M}'$, i.e., $\mathcal{I}_\mathcal{M} \, C \, \mathcal{I}_{\mathcal{M}'}$. We show that $\forall \bar{s} \in \mathcal{I}_\mathcal{M}. \exists \bar{t} \in \mathcal{I}_{\mathcal{M}'}. \bar{s} \, C \, \bar{t}$, the other case is symmetrical. Take an initial state $\bar{s} \parallel \bar{r} \in \mathcal{I}_\mathcal{M}$. Since $\mathcal{I}_{\mathcal{M}_\Pi} \, B \, \mathcal{I}_{\mathcal{M}_{\Pi'}}$ and $\bar{s} \in \mathcal{I}_{\mathcal{M}_\Pi}$, there exists a $\bar{t} \in \mathcal{I}_{\mathcal{M}_{\Pi'}}$ such that $\bar{s} \, B \, \bar{t}$. Therefore, we have $\bar{s} \parallel \bar{r} \, C \, \bar{t} \parallel \bar{r}$. Since $\bar{s} \parallel \bar{r}$ is an arbitrary state in $\mathcal{I}_\mathcal{M}$ the proof holds for all states in $\mathcal{I}_\mathcal{M}$. Furthermore, since the other case is symmetrical it follows that $\mathcal{I}_\mathcal{M} \, C \, \mathcal{I}_{\mathcal{M}'}$.

- If $\bar{s} \, C \, \bar{t}$ and $\bar{s} \xrightarrow{a}_\mathcal{M} \bar{s}'$ then either $a = \tau \wedge \bar{s}' \, C \, \bar{t}$, or $\bar{t} \xrightarrow{\tau}{}^*_{\mathcal{M}'} \hat{\bar{t}} \xrightarrow{a}_{\mathcal{M}'} \bar{t}' \wedge \bar{s} \, C \, \hat{\bar{t}} \wedge \bar{s}' \, C \, \bar{t}'$. To better distinguish between the two parts of the networks, we unfold C and reformulate the proof obligation as follows: If $\bar{s} \, B \, \bar{t}$ and $\bar{s} \parallel \bar{r} \xrightarrow{a}_\mathcal{M} \bar{s}' \parallel \bar{r}'$ then either $a = \tau \wedge \bar{s}' \, B \, \bar{t} \wedge \bar{r} = \bar{r}'$, or $\bar{t} \parallel \bar{r} \xrightarrow{\tau}{}^*_{\mathcal{M}'} \hat{\bar{t}} \parallel \bar{r} \xrightarrow{a}_{\mathcal{M}'} \bar{t}' \parallel \bar{r}' \wedge \bar{s} \, B \, \hat{\bar{t}} \wedge \bar{s}' \, B \, \bar{t}'$. Consider synchronisation law $(\bar{v} \parallel \bar{w}, a) \in (\mathcal{V} \backslash \mathcal{V}_\sigma)^\bullet \cup {}^\bullet(\mathcal{W} \backslash \mathcal{W}_\sigma) \cup \sigma(\mathcal{V}, \mathcal{W})$ enabling the transition $\bar{s} \parallel \bar{r} \xrightarrow{a}_\mathcal{M} \bar{s}' \parallel \bar{r}'$. We distinguish three cases:

1. $(\bar{v} \parallel \bar{u}, a) \in (\mathcal{V} \backslash \mathcal{V}_\sigma)^\bullet$. It follows that $\bar{w} = \bullet^m$, and thus, subsystem $\mathcal{M}_P$ does not participate. Hence, we have $\bar{r} = \bar{r}'$ and $(\bar{v}, a) \in \mathcal{V}$ enables a transition $\bar{s} \xrightarrow{a}_{\mathcal{M}_\Pi} \bar{s}'$. Since $\bar{s} \, B \, \bar{t}$, by Definition 5, we have:
   - $a = \tau$ with $\bar{s}' \, B \, \bar{t}$. Because $\bar{s}' \, B \, \bar{t}$ and $\bar{r} = \bar{r}'$, the proof trivially follows.
   - $\bar{t} \xrightarrow{\tau}{}^*_{\mathcal{M}_{\Pi'}} \hat{\bar{t}} \xrightarrow{a}_{\mathcal{M}_{\Pi'}} \bar{t}'$ with $\bar{s} \, B \, \hat{\bar{t}}$ and $\bar{s}' \, B \, \bar{t}'$. These transitions are enabled by laws in $\mathcal{V}' \backslash \mathcal{V}'_\sigma$. The set of derived laws are of the form $(\bar{v}' \parallel \bullet^m, \tau) \in (\mathcal{V}' \backslash \mathcal{V}'_\sigma)^\bullet$ enabling a τ-path from $\bar{t} \parallel \bar{r}$ to $\hat{\bar{t}} \parallel \bar{r}$, and there is a law $(\bar{v}' \parallel \bullet^m, a) \in (\mathcal{V}' \backslash \mathcal{V}'_\sigma)^\bullet$ enabling $\hat{\bar{t}} \parallel \bar{r} \xrightarrow{a}_{\mathcal{M}'} \bar{t}' \parallel \bar{r}$. Take $\bar{r}' := \bar{r}$ and the proof obligation is satisfied.

2. $(\bar{v} \parallel \bar{w}, a) \in {}^{\bullet}(\mathcal{W} \setminus \mathcal{W}_\sigma)$. It follows that $\bar{v} = \bullet^n$, and thus, subsystems $\mathcal{M}_\Pi$ and $\mathcal{M}_{\Pi'}$ do not participate; we have $\bar{s} = \bar{s}'$ and $\bar{r} \xrightarrow{a}_{\mathcal{M}_P} \bar{r}'$. We take $\bar{t}' := \bar{t}$. Hence, we can conclude $\bar{t} \parallel \bar{r} \xrightarrow{\tau}{}^*_{\mathcal{M}'} \bar{t} \parallel \bar{r} \xrightarrow{a}_{\mathcal{M}} \bar{t}' \parallel \bar{r}'$, $\bar{s} \; B \; \bar{t}$, and $\bar{s}' \; B \; \bar{t}'$.

3. $(\bar{v} \parallel \bar{w}, a) \in \sigma(\mathcal{V}, \mathcal{W})$. Both parts of the network participate in the transition $\bar{s} \parallel \bar{r} \xrightarrow{a}_{\mathcal{M}} \bar{s}' \parallel \bar{r}'$. By definition of $\sigma(\mathcal{V}, \mathcal{W})$, there are $(\bar{v}, \alpha) \in \mathcal{V}$, $(\bar{w}, \beta) \in \mathcal{W}$ and $(\alpha, \beta, a) \in \sigma$ such that $(\bar{v}, \alpha)$ enables a transition $\bar{s} \xrightarrow{\alpha}_{\mathcal{M}_\Pi} \bar{s}'$ and $(\bar{u}, \beta)$ enables a transition $\bar{r} \xrightarrow{\beta} \bar{r}'$. Since $\bar{s} \; B \; \bar{t}$, by Definition 5, we have:

   – $\alpha = \tau$ with $\bar{s}' \; B \; \bar{t}$. Since $\alpha \in \mathcal{A}_\mathcal{V} \setminus \{\tau\}$ we have a contradiction.
   – $\bar{t} \xrightarrow{\tau}{}^*_{\mathcal{M}'_{\Pi'}} \hat{t} \xrightarrow{\alpha}_{\mathcal{M}'_{\Pi'}} \bar{t}'$ with $\bar{s} \; B \; \hat{t}$ and $\bar{s}' \; B \; \bar{t}'$. Since τ actions are not mapped by the interface mapping we have a set of synchronisation laws of the form $(\bar{v}' \parallel \bullet^m, \tau) \in (\mathcal{V}' \setminus \mathcal{V}'_\sigma)^{\bullet}$ enabling a τ-path $\bar{t} \parallel \bar{r} \xrightarrow{\tau}{}^*_{\mathcal{M}'} \hat{t} \parallel \bar{r}$.
   Let $(\bar{v}', \alpha) \in \mathcal{V}'$ be the synchronisation law enabling the α-transition. Since $(\alpha, \beta, a) \in \sigma$, α is an interface action and does not occur in $\mathcal{V}' \setminus \mathcal{V}'_\sigma$. It follows that $(\bar{v}', \alpha) \in \mathcal{V}'_\sigma$, and consequently $(\bar{v}' \parallel \bar{w}, a) \in \sigma(\mathcal{V}', \mathcal{W})$. Law $(\bar{v}' \parallel \bar{w}, a)$ enables the transition $\hat{t} \parallel \bar{r} \xrightarrow{a}_{\mathcal{M}'} \bar{t}' \parallel \bar{r}'$, and the proof follows.

- If $\bar{s} \; C \; \bar{t}$ and $\bar{t} \xrightarrow{a}_{\mathcal{M}'} \bar{t}'$ then either $a = \tau \wedge \bar{s}' \; C \; \bar{t}$, or $\bar{s} \xrightarrow{\tau}{}^*_{\mathcal{M}} \hat{s} \xrightarrow{a}_{\mathcal{M}} \bar{s}' \wedge \bar{s} \; C \; \hat{t} \wedge \bar{s}' \; C \; \bar{t}'$. This case is symmetric to the previous case.

- If $\bar{s} \; C \; \bar{t}$ and there is an infinite sequence of states $(\bar{s}^k)_{k \in \omega}$ such that $\bar{s} = \bar{s}^0$, $\bar{s}^k \xrightarrow{\tau}_{\mathcal{M}} \bar{s}^{k+1}$ and $\bar{s}^k \; C \; \bar{t}$ for all $k \in \omega$, then there exists a state $\bar{t}'$ such that $\bar{t} \xrightarrow{\tau}{}^+_{\mathcal{M}'} \bar{t}'$ and $\bar{s}^k \; C \; \bar{t}'$ for some $k \in \omega$. Again we reformulate the proof obligation to better distinguish between the two components: if $\bar{s} \parallel \bar{r} \; C \; \bar{t} \parallel \bar{r}$ and there is an infinite sequence of states $(\bar{s}^k \parallel \bar{r}^k)_{k \in \omega}$ such that $\bar{s} \parallel \bar{r} = \bar{s}^0 \parallel \bar{r}^0$, $\bar{s}^k \parallel \bar{r}^k \xrightarrow{\tau}_{\mathcal{M}} \bar{s}^{k+1} \parallel \bar{r}^{k+1}$ and $\bar{s}^k \; B \; \bar{t}$ for all $k \in \omega$, then there exists a state $\bar{t}'$ such that $\bar{t} \parallel \bar{r} \xrightarrow{\tau}{}^+_{\mathcal{M}'} p' \parallel \bar{r}$ and $\bar{s}^k \; B \; \bar{t}'$ for some $k \in \omega$.
  We distinguish two cases:

1. All steps in the τ-sequence are enabled in $\mathcal{M}_\Pi$, i.e., $\forall k \in \omega. \; \bar{s}^k \xrightarrow{\tau}_{\mathcal{M}_\Pi} \bar{s}^{k+1}$. Since $\bar{s} \; B \; \bar{t}$, by condition 3 of Definition 5, it follows that there is a state $\bar{t}'$ with $\bar{t} \xrightarrow{\tau}{}^+\bar{t}'$ and $\bar{s}^k \; B \; \bar{t}'$ for some $k \in \omega$. Since τ is not an interface action, the synchronization laws enabling $\bar{t} \xrightarrow{\tau}{}^+\bar{t}'$ are also present in $\mathcal{M}'$. Hence, we have $\bar{t} \parallel \bar{r} \xrightarrow{\tau}{}^+\bar{t}' \parallel \bar{r}$ and $\bar{s}^k \; B \; \bar{t}'$ for $k \in \omega$.

2. There is a $k \in \omega$ with $\neg \bar{s}^k \xrightarrow{\tau}_{\mathcal{M}_\Pi} \bar{s}^{k+1}$. We do have $\bar{s}^k \parallel \bar{r}^k \xrightarrow{\tau}_{\mathcal{M}} \bar{s}^{k+1} \parallel \bar{r}^{k+1}$ with $\bar{s}^k \; B \; \bar{t}$ (see antecedent at the start of the 'divergence' case). Since the τ-transition is not enabled in $\mathcal{M}_\Pi$ the transition must be enabled by a synchronisation law $(\bar{v} \parallel \bar{w}, \tau) \in {}^{\bullet}(\mathcal{W} \setminus \mathcal{W}_\sigma) \cup \sigma(\mathcal{V}, \mathcal{W})$. We distinguish two cases:

   – $(\bar{v} \parallel \bar{w}, \tau) \in {}^{\bullet}(\mathcal{W} \setminus \mathcal{W}_\sigma)$. The transition $\bar{s}^k \parallel \bar{r}^k \xrightarrow{\tau}_{\mathcal{M}} \bar{s}^{k+1} \parallel \bar{r}^{k+1}$ is enabled by $(\bar{v} \parallel \bar{w}, \tau) \in {}^{\bullet}(\mathcal{W} \setminus \mathcal{W}_\sigma)$. Therefore, there is a transition $\bar{r}^k \xrightarrow{\tau}_{\mathcal{M}_P} \bar{r}^{k+1}$ enabled by $(\bar{w}, \tau) \in \mathcal{W} \setminus \mathcal{W}_\sigma$. Since this transition is part of an infinite τ-sequence, there is a path $\bar{s} \parallel \bar{r} \xrightarrow{\tau}{}^*_{\mathcal{M}} \bar{s}^k \parallel \bar{r}^k$. Furthermore, condition 1 of Definition 5 holds for C, hence, there is a state $\bar{t}' \in \mathcal{S}_{\mathcal{M}_{\Pi'}}$ and a transition $\bar{t} \parallel \bar{r} \xrightarrow{\tau}{}^*_{\mathcal{M}_P} \bar{t}' \parallel \bar{r}^k$ with $\bar{s}^k \parallel \bar{r}^k \; C \; \bar{t}' \parallel \bar{r}^k$. Therefore, we have $\bar{t} \parallel \bar{r} \xrightarrow{\tau}{}^+_{\mathcal{M}'} \bar{t}' \parallel \bar{r}^{k+1}$. Finally, since $\bar{s}^k \parallel \bar{r}^k \; C \; \bar{t}' \parallel \bar{r}^k$, it follows that $\bar{s}^k \; B \; \bar{t}'$.

- $(\bar{v} \parallel \bar{w}, \tau) \in \sigma(\mathcal{V}, \mathcal{W})$. By definition of $\sigma(\mathcal{V}, \mathcal{W})$, there are two laws $(\bar{v}, \alpha) \in \mathcal{V}$ and $(\bar{u}, \beta) \in \mathcal{W}$ with $(\alpha, \beta, \tau) \in \sigma$. The laws enable transitions $\bar{s}^k \xrightarrow{\alpha}_{\mathcal{M}_{\varPi}} \bar{s}^{k+1}$ and $\bar{r}^k \xrightarrow{\beta}_{\mathcal{M}_{\mathrm{P}}} \bar{r}^{k+1}$ respectively. Since $\bar{s}^k \; B \; \bar{t}$ and $\alpha \neq \tau$, by Definition 5, there are states $\hat{\bar{t}}, \bar{t}' \in \mathcal{S}_{\mathcal{M}_{\varPi'}}$ such that there is a sequence $\bar{t} \xrightarrow{\tau}{}^{*}_{\mathcal{M}_{\varPi'}} \hat{\bar{t}} \xrightarrow{\alpha}_{\mathcal{M}_{\varPi'}} \bar{t}'$ with $\bar{s} \; B \; \hat{\bar{t}}$ and $\bar{s}^{k+1} \; B \; \bar{t}'$. Let $(\bar{v}', \alpha) \in \mathcal{V}'$ be the law enabling the α-transition. Since $(\alpha, \beta, \tau) \in \sigma$, and consequently $(\bar{v}' \parallel \bar{w}, \tau) \in \sigma(\mathcal{X}', \mathcal{Y})$. Furthermore, the τ-path from $\bar{t}$ to $\hat{\bar{t}}$ is enabled by laws of the form $(\bar{v}'', \tau) \in \mathcal{V}' \setminus \mathcal{V}'_\sigma$. Hence, there is a series of transitions $\bar{t} \parallel \bar{r} \xrightarrow{\tau}{}^{*}_{\mathcal{M}'} \hat{\bar{t}} \parallel \bar{r}^k \xrightarrow{\tau}_{\mathcal{M}'} \bar{t}' \parallel \bar{r}^{k+1}$. Finally, recall that $\bar{s}^{k+1} \; B \; \bar{t}'$. Hence, also in this case the proof obligation is satisfied.

- If $\bar{s} C \bar{t}$ and there is an infinite sequence of states $(\bar{t}^k)_{k \in \omega}$ such that $\bar{t} = \bar{t}^0$, $\bar{t}^k \xrightarrow{\tau}_{\mathcal{G}_2} \bar{t}^{k+1}$ and $\bar{s} C \bar{t}^k$ for all $k \in \omega$, then there exists a state $\bar{s}'$ such that $\bar{s} \xrightarrow{\tau}{}^{+}_{\mathcal{G}_1} \bar{s}'$ and $\bar{s}' C \bar{t}^k$ for some $k \in \omega$. This case is symmetric to the previous case. $\square$

5   Decomposition of LTS Networks

In Sect. 4, we discuss the composition of LTS networks, in which a system is constructed by combining components. However, for compositional model checking approaches, it should also be possible to correctly decompose LTS networks. In this case the inter-component laws are already known. Therefore, we can derive a set of interface laws and an interface mapping specifying how the system is decomposed into components.

To be able to apply Proposition 2 for compositional state space construction, the composition of the decomposed networks must be equivalent to the original system. If this holds we say a decomposition is *consistent* with respect to $\mathcal{M}$.

Definition 8 (Consistent Decomposition). *Consider a network $\mathcal{M} = (\Sigma, \mathcal{X})$. Say network $\mathcal{M}$ is decomposed into components $\mathcal{N} = (\Pi, \mathcal{V})$ and $\mathcal{O} = (\mathrm{P}, \mathcal{W})$ with interface laws $\mathcal{V}_\sigma$ and $\mathcal{W}_\sigma$, where σ is the implied interface mapping. The decomposition of $\mathcal{M}$ in to components $\mathcal{N}$ and $\mathcal{O}$ is called consistent with respect to $\mathcal{M}$ iff $\mathcal{M} = \mathcal{N} \parallel_\sigma \mathcal{O}$, i.e., we must have $\Sigma = \Pi \parallel \mathrm{P}$ and $\mathcal{X} = (\mathcal{V} \setminus \mathcal{V}_\sigma)^\bullet \cup {}^\bullet(\mathcal{W} \setminus \mathcal{W}_\sigma) \cup \sigma(\mathcal{V}, \mathcal{W})$.*

To show that a decomposition is consistent with the original system it is sufficient to show that the set of inter-component laws of the original system is equivalent to the set of inter-component laws generated by the interface-mapping:

Lemma 1. *Consider a network $\mathcal{M} = (\Pi \parallel \mathrm{P}, \mathcal{V}^\bullet \cup {}^\bullet\mathcal{W} \cup \mathcal{X})$, with $\mathcal{X}$ the set of inter-component laws and disjoint sets $\mathcal{V}^\bullet$, ${}^\bullet\mathcal{W}$ and $\mathcal{X}$. A consistent decomposition of $\mathcal{M}$ into components $\mathcal{N} = (\Pi, \mathcal{V} \cup \mathcal{V}_\sigma)$ and $\mathcal{O} = (\mathrm{P}, \mathcal{W} \cup \mathcal{W}_\sigma)$, with interface laws $\mathcal{V}_\sigma$ and $\mathcal{W}_\sigma$ disjoint from $\mathcal{V}$ and $\mathcal{W}$, respectively, is guaranteed iff $\mathcal{X} = \sigma(\mathcal{V}_\sigma, \mathcal{W}_\sigma)$.*

Proof. The decomposition is consistent iff $\mathcal{V}^\bullet \cup {}^\bullet\mathcal{W} \cup \mathcal{X} = (\mathcal{V}\backslash\mathcal{V}_\sigma)^\bullet \cup {}^\bullet(\mathcal{W}\backslash\mathcal{W}_\sigma) \cup \sigma(\mathcal{V}\cup\mathcal{V}^\sigma, \mathcal{W}\cup\mathcal{W}^\sigma)$ and $\Pi \parallel P = \Pi \parallel P$. The latter is trivial. Furthermore, since $\mathcal{V}\cap\mathcal{V}_\sigma = \emptyset$ ($\mathcal{W}\cap\mathcal{W}_\sigma = \emptyset$) and by definition of $\mathcal{V}_\sigma$ ($\mathcal{W}_\sigma$), we have $\mathcal{V}^\bullet = (\mathcal{V}\backslash\mathcal{V}_\sigma)^\bullet$ (${}^\bullet\mathcal{W} = {}^\bullet(\mathcal{W}\backslash\mathcal{W}_\sigma)$). It follows from $\mathcal{V}\cap\mathcal{V}_\sigma = \emptyset$, $\mathcal{W}\cap\mathcal{W}_\sigma = \emptyset$, and Definition 7 that $\sigma(\mathcal{V}\cup\mathcal{V}^\sigma, \mathcal{W}\cup\mathcal{W}^\sigma) = \sigma(\mathcal{V}_\sigma, \mathcal{W}_\sigma)$. Hence, the decomposition is consistent iff $\mathcal{X} = \sigma(\mathcal{V}_\sigma, \mathcal{W}_\sigma)$. $\square$

Indeed, it is possible to derive an inconsistent decomposition as shown in Example 3.

Example 3 (Inconsistent Decomposition). Consider a set of inter-component laws $\mathcal{X} = \{(\langle a, b\rangle, c), (\langle b, a\rangle, c)\}$. Partitioning the laws results in the sets of interface laws $\mathcal{V}_\sigma = \{(\langle a\rangle, \gamma), (\langle b\rangle, \gamma)\}$ and $\mathcal{W}_\sigma = \{(\langle b\rangle, \gamma), (\langle a\rangle, \gamma)\}$ derived from some $\mathcal{V}$ and $\mathcal{W}$, respectively. This system implies the interface mapping $\sigma = \{(\gamma, \gamma, c)\}$. The derived set of inter-component laws is $\sigma(\mathcal{V}, \mathcal{W}) = \{(\langle a, a\rangle, c), (\langle a, b\rangle, c), (\langle b, a\rangle, c), (\langle b, b\rangle, c)\} \neq \mathcal{X}$. Hence, this decomposition is not consistent with the original system.

However, a consistent composition can *always* be derived. In Proposition 3 we show how to construct two sets of interface laws $\mathcal{V}_\sigma$ and $\mathcal{W}_\sigma$, and an interface mapping σ for component $\mathcal{M}_\Pi = (\Pi, \mathcal{V}\cup\mathcal{V}_\sigma)$ and $\mathcal{M}_P = (P, \mathcal{W}\cup\mathcal{W}_\sigma)$ such that the decomposition is consistent. Consider a synchronisation law $(\bar{v} \parallel \bar{w}, a)$, the idea is to encode this synchronisation law directly in the interface mapping, i.e., we create unique result actions $\alpha_{\bar{v}}$ and $\alpha_{\bar{w}}$ with $(\alpha_{\bar{v}}, \alpha_{\bar{w}}, a) \in \sigma$. This way it is explicit which interface law corresponds to which inter-component law.

Proposition 3. *Consider a network $\mathcal{M} = (\Pi \parallel P, \mathcal{V}^\bullet \cup {}^\bullet\mathcal{W} \cup \mathcal{X})$. We define the sets of interface laws as follows:*

$$\mathcal{V}_\sigma = \{(\bar{v}, \alpha_{\bar{v}}) \mid (\bar{v} \parallel \bar{w}, a) \in \mathcal{X}\}, \mathcal{W}_\sigma = \{(\bar{w}, \alpha_{\bar{w}}) \mid (\bar{v} \parallel \bar{w}, a) \in \mathcal{X}\}$$

where $\alpha_{\bar{v}}$ and $\alpha_{\bar{w}}$ are unique interface result actions identified by the corresponding interface law, that is, $\forall(\bar{v}', a) \in \mathcal{V} \cup \mathcal{V}_\sigma.\ a = \alpha_{\bar{v}} \implies \bar{v}' = \bar{v}$ and $\forall(\bar{w}', a) \in \mathcal{W} \cup \mathcal{W}_\sigma.\ a = \alpha_{\bar{w}} \implies \bar{w}' = \bar{w}$.

Finally, the interface mapping is defined as $\sigma = \{(\alpha_{\bar{v}}, \alpha_{\bar{w}}, a) \mid (\bar{v} \parallel \bar{w}, a) \in \mathcal{X}\}$. The decomposition into $\mathcal{M}_\Pi = (\Pi, \mathcal{V} \cup \mathcal{V}_\sigma)$ and $\mathcal{M}_P = (P, \mathcal{W} \cup \mathcal{W}_\sigma)$ is consistent.

Proof. By Lemma 1, we have to show $\mathcal{X} = \sigma(\mathcal{V}_\sigma, \mathcal{W}_\sigma)$.

$$\sigma(\mathcal{V}_\sigma, \mathcal{W}_\sigma) \stackrel{(1)}{=} \{(\bar{v} \parallel \bar{w}, a) \mid (\bar{v}, \alpha_{\bar{v}}) \in \mathcal{V}_\sigma \wedge (\bar{w}_{\bar{w}}, \beta) \in \mathcal{W}_\sigma \wedge (\alpha_{\bar{v}}, \alpha_{\bar{w}}, a) \in \sigma\}$$

$$\stackrel{(2)}{=} \{(\bar{v} \parallel \bar{w}, a) \mid (\bar{v} \parallel \bar{w}, a) \in \mathcal{X}\} = \mathcal{X}$$

where at (1) the definition of $\sigma(\mathcal{V}_\sigma, \mathcal{W}_\sigma)$ is unfolded, and (2) follows from construction of $\mathcal{V}_\sigma$, $\mathcal{W}_\sigma$, and σ. Hence, the decomposition is consistent with $\mathcal{M}$. $\square$

Proposition 4 shows that LTS networks resulting from the consistent decomposition of an admissible LTS network are also admissible. Hence, consistent decomposition is compatible with the compositional verification approaches presented in [12].

Proposition 4. *Consider an admissible LTS network* $\mathcal{M} = (\Pi \parallel \mathrm{P}, \mathcal{V}^\bullet \cup {}^\bullet \mathcal{W} \cup \mathcal{X})$ *of length* $n + m$. *If the decomposition is consistent, then the decomposed networks* $\mathcal{M}_\Pi = (\Pi, \mathcal{V} \cup \mathcal{V}_\sigma)$ *and* $\mathcal{M}_\mathrm{P} = (\mathrm{P}, \mathcal{W} \cup \mathcal{W}_\sigma)$ *are also admissible.*

Proof. We show that $\mathcal{M}_\Pi$ and $\mathcal{M}_\mathrm{P}$ satisfy Definition 4:

No synchronisation and renaming of τ's. Let $(\bar{v}, a) \in \mathcal{V} \cup \mathcal{V}_\sigma$ be a synchronisation law such that $\bar{v}_i = \tau$ for some $i \in 1..n$. We distinguish two cases:

- $(\bar{v}, a) \in \mathcal{V}_\sigma$. Since $(\bar{v}, a)$ is an interface law and the decomposition is consistent, its result action a may not be τ. However, since $\mathcal{M}$ is admissible, no renaming of τ's is allowed. By contradiction it follows that $(\bar{v}, a) \notin \mathcal{V}_\sigma$ completing this case.
- $(\bar{v}, a) \in \mathcal{V}^\bullet$. By construction, there exists a law $(\bar{v} \parallel \bullet^m, a) \in \mathcal{V}^\bullet$. Since $\mathcal{V}^\bullet \subseteq \mathcal{V}^\bullet \cup {}^\bullet \mathcal{W} \cup \mathcal{X}$, by admissibility of $\mathcal{M}$, we have $\forall j \in 1..n. \ \bar{v}_j \neq \bullet \implies i = j$ (no synchronisation of τ's) and $a = \tau$ (no renaming of τ's).

Hence, $\mathcal{M}_\Pi$ does not synchronize or rename τ's. The proof for $\mathcal{M}_\mathrm{P}$ is similar.

No cutting of τ's. Let Π_i be a process with $i \in 1..n$ such that $\tau \in \mathcal{A}_{\Pi_i}$. Since $\mathcal{M}$ is admissible there exists a law $(\bar{v} \parallel \bar{w}, a) \in \mathcal{V}^\bullet \cup {}^\bullet \mathcal{W} \cup \mathcal{X}$ such that $(\bar{v} \parallel \bar{u})_i = \tau$. We distinguish three cases:

- $(\bar{v} \parallel \bar{w}, a) \in \mathcal{V}^\bullet$. Since $(\bar{v} \parallel \bar{w})_i = \tau$ and $i \leq n$ it follows that $\bar{v}_i = \tau$. By construction of $\mathcal{V}^\bullet$, there is a $(\bar{v}, a) \in \mathcal{V}$ with $\bar{v}_i = \tau$.
- $(\bar{v} \parallel \bar{w}, a) \in {}^\bullet \mathcal{W}$. In this case we must have $i > n$ which contradicts our assumption: $i \in 1..n$. The proof follows by contradiction.
- $(\bar{v} \parallel \bar{w}, a) \in \mathcal{X}$. Then, $(\bar{v} \parallel \bar{w}, a)$ is an inter-component law with at least one participating process for each component. Hence, there exists a $j \in (n+1)..m$ such that $(\bar{v} \parallel \bar{w})_j \neq \bullet$. Moreover, since $\mathcal{M}$ is admissible, no synchronisation of τ's are allowed. Therefore, since $(\bar{v} \parallel \bar{w})_j \neq \bullet$, we must have $j = i$. However, this would mean $j \in 1..n$, contradicting $j \in (n+1)..m$. By contradiction the proof follows.

We conclude that $\mathcal{M}_\Pi$ does not cut τ's. The proof for $\mathcal{M}_\mathrm{P}$ is symmetrical.

All three admissibility properties hold for $\mathcal{M}_\Pi$ and $\mathcal{M}_\mathrm{P}$. Hence, the networks resulting from the decomposition satisfy Definition 4. $\square$

6   Application

In order to compare compositional approaches with the classical, non-compositional approach, we have employed CADP to minimise a set of models modulo DPBB.

Each model is minimised with respect to a given liveness property. To achieve the best minimisation we applied maximal hiding [25] in all approaches. Intuitively, maximal hiding hides all actions except for the interface actions and actions relevant for the given liveness-property.

As *composition strategy* we have used the *smart reduction* approach described in [11]. In CADP, the *classical approach*, where the full state space is constructed at once and no intermediate minimisations are applied, is the *root reduction* strategy. At the start, the individual components are minimised before they are combined in parallel composition, hence the name. We have measured the *running time* and *maximum number of states* generated by the two methods.

For compositional approaches, the running time and largest state space considered depends heavily on the composition order, i.e., the order in which the components are combined. The smart reduction approach uses a heuristic to determine the order in which to compose processes. In [11], it has been experimentally established that this heuristic frequently works very well. After each composition step the result is minimised.

Measurements. The results of our experiments are shown in Table 1. The *Model* column indicates the test case model corresponding to the measurements.

The *smart* and *root* sub-columns denote the measurement for the smart reduction and root reduction approaches, respectively.

In the *Running time (sec.)* column the running time until completion of the experiment is shown in seconds. Indicated in bold are the shortest running times comparing the *smart* and *root* sub-columns. The maximum running time of an experiment was set to 80 hours, after which the experiment was discontinued (indicated with −).

The columns *Max. #states* and *Max. #transitions* show the largest number of states and transitions, respectively, generated during the experiment. Of both methods the best result is indicated in bold.

Table 1. Experiments: smart reduction vs. root reduction

Model	Running time (sec.)		Max. #states		Max. #transitions		Reduced #states	Reduced #transitions
	Smart	Root	Smart	Root	Smart	Root		
1394	6.42	**4.20**	**102,983**	198,692	**187,714**	355,338	1	1
1394'	**34.92**	427.10	**2,832,074**	36,855,184	**5,578,078**	96,553,318	1	1
ACS	29.75	**5.36**	**1,854**	4,764	**4,760**	14,760	29	61
Cache	8.59	**3.25**	616	616	4631	4631	1	1
DES	**40.66**	941.82	**1,404**	64,498,297	**3,510**	518,438,860	1	1
HAVi-LE	**65.19**	484.52	**970,772**	15,688,570	**5,803,552**	80,686,289	131,873	644,695
HAVi-LE'	**47.46**	5,241.00	**453,124**	190,208,728	**2,534,371**	876,008,628	159,318	849,227
Le Lann	**42.36**	5,720.08	**12,083**	160,025,986	**701,916**	944,322,648	83,502	501,573
ODP	16.29	**5.20**	**10,397**	91,394	**87,936**	641,226	432	2,268
Peterson	**30.81**	−	**9**	−	**139**	−	9	22
Transit	**11.86**	56.26	**22,928**	3,763,192	**132,712**	39,925,524	636	3,188
Wafer stepper	**48.62**	52.90	**962,122**	3,772,753	**4,537,240**	16,977,692	905,955	4,095,389

The number of states and transitions after minimisation are shown in the *Reduced #states* and *Reduced #transitions* columns, respectively.

The experiments were run on the DAS-5 cluster [4] machines. They have an INTEL HASWELL E5-2630-v3 2.4 GHz CPU, 64 GB memory, and run CENTOS LINUX 7.2.

As test input we selected twelve case studies: four MCRL2 [10] models distributed with its toolset, seven CADP models, and one from the BEEM database [29].

Discussion. In terms of running time smart reduction performs best for eight of the models, whereas root reduction performs best in four of the models. In general, the smart reduction approach performs better for large models where the state space can be reduced significantly before composition. This is best seen in the *HAVi-LE'*, *Le Lann*, and *Peterson* use cases, where smart reduction is several hours faster.

In this set of models, root reduction performs best in relatively small models; *1394*, *ACS*, *Cache*, *Lamport*, and *ODP*. However, the difference in running times is negligible. Smart reduction starts performing better in the moderately sized models such as *Transit* and *Wafer stepper*. For smaller models the overhead of the smart reduction heuristic is too high to obtain any benefits from the nominated ordering.

In summary, compositional reduction is most efficient when it is expected that components reduce significantly and highly interleaving components are added last.

7   Conclusions

In this paper we have shown that DPBB is a congruence for parallel composition of LTS networks where there is synchronisation on given label combinations. Therefore, the DPBB equivalence may be used to reduce components in the compositional verification of LTS networks. It had already been shown that compositional verification of LTS networks is adequate for safety properties. As DPBB preserves both safety and liveness properties, compositional verification can be used to verify liveness properties as well.

Furthermore, we have discussed how to safely decompose an LTS network in the case where verification has to start from the system as a whole. Both the composition and consistent decomposition of LTS networks preserve the admissibility property of LTS networks. Hence, the composition operator remains compatible with the compositional verification approaches for LTS networks described by [12].

The proofs in this paper have been mechanically verified using the Coq proof assistant[3] and are available online (see footnote 2).

Although our work focuses on the composition of LTS networks, the results are also applicable on composition of individual LTSs. Our parallel composition

---

[3] https://coq.inria.fr.

operator subsumes the usual parallel composition operators of standard process algebra languages such as CCS [27], CSP [32], MCRL2 [10], and LOTOS [18].

Finally, we have run a set of experiments to compare compositional and traditional DPBB reduction. The compositional approach applies CADP's smart reduction employing a heuristic to determine an efficient compositional reduction order. The traditional reduction generates the complete state space before applying reduction. The compositional approach performed better in the medium to large models where the intermediate state space can be kept small.

Future work. An interesting direction for future work is the integration of the proof in a meta-theory for process algebra. This integration would give a straightforward extension of our results to parallel composition for process algebra formalisms.

This work has been inspired by an approach for the compositional verification of transformations of LTS networks [31, 36–39]. We would like to apply the results of this paper to the improved transformation verification algorithm [31], thus guaranteeing its correctness for the compositional verification of transformations of LTS networks.

In future experiments, we would like to involve recent advancements in the computation of branching bisimulation, and therefore also DPBB, both sequentially [16,17] and in parallel on graphics processors [41]. It will be interesting to measure the effect of applying these new algorithms to compositionally solve a model checking problem.

Finally, by encoding timing in the LTSs, it is possible to reason about timed system behaviour. Combining approaches such as [40,42] with our results would allow to compositionally reason about timed behaviour. We plan to investigate this further.

Acknowledgements. The authors would like to thank Frédéric Lang for his comments that helped to improve this paper.

References

1. Andersen, H.: Partial model checking. In: LICS, pp. 398–407. IEEE Computer Society Press (1995)
2. Andersen, H.: Partial model checking of modal equations: a survey. STTT **2**(3), 242–259 (1999)
3. Baier, C., Katoen, J.P.: Principles of Model Checking. MIT Press (2008)
4. Bal, H., Epema, D., de Laat, C., van Nieuwpoort, R., Romein, J., Seinstra, F., Snoek, C., Wijshoff, H.: A medium-scale distributed system for computer science research: infrastructure for the long term. IEEE Comput. **49**(5), 54–63 (2016)
5. Bertot, Y., Castéran, P.: Interactive Theorem Proving and Program Development, Coq' Art: The Calculus of Inductive Constructions. Texts in Theoretical Computer Science. Springer (2004)
6. Bloom, B.: Structural operational semantics for weak bisimulations. Theor. Comput. Sci. **146**(1), 25–68 (1995)

7. Clarke, E.M., Emerson, E.A., Jha, S., Sistla, A.P.: Symmetry reductions in model checking. In: Hu, A.J., Vardi, M.Y. (eds.) CAV 1998. LNCS, vol. 1427, pp. 147–158. Springer, Heidelberg (1998). doi:10.1007/BFb0028741
8. Clarke, E.M., Long, D.E., McMillan, K.L.: Compositional model checking. In: LICS, pp. 353–362. IEEE Computer Society Press, June 1989
9. Clarke, E., Grumberg, O., Peled, D.: Model Checking. The MIT Press, Cambridge (1999)
10. Cranen, S., Groote, J.F., Keiren, J.J.A., Stappers, F.P.M., de Vink, E.P., Wesselink, W., Willemse, T.A.C.: An overview of the mCRL2 toolset and its recent advances. In: Piterman, N., Smolka, S.A. (eds.) TACAS 2013. LNCS, vol. 7795, pp. 199–213. Springer, Heidelberg (2013). doi:10.1007/978-3-642-36742-7_15
11. Crouzen, P., Lang, F.: Smart reduction. In: Giannakopoulou, D., Orejas, F. (eds.) FASE 2011. LNCS, vol. 6603, pp. 111–126. Springer, Heidelberg (2011). doi:10.1007/978-3-642-19811-3_9
12. Garavel, H., Lang, F., Mateescu, R.: Compositional verification of asynchronous concurrent systems using CADP. Acta Informatica 52(4–5), 337–392 (2015)
13. van Glabbeek, R.J., Weijland, W.P.: Branching time and abstraction in bisimulation semantics. J. ACM 43(3), 555–600 (1996)
14. van Glabbeek, R., Luttik, S., Trčka, N.: Computation tree logic with deadlock detection. LMCS 5(4) (2009)
15. van Glabbeek, R., Luttik, S., Trčka, N.: Branching bisimilarity with explicit divergence. Fundam. Inf. 93(4), 371–392 (2009)
16. Groote, J.F., Wijs, A.: An $O(m \log n)$ algorithm for stuttering equivalence and branching bisimulation. In: Chechik, M., Raskin, J.-F. (eds.) TACAS 2016. LNCS, vol. 9636, pp. 607–624. Springer, Heidelberg (2016). doi:10.1007/978-3-662-49674-9_40
17. Groote, J., Jansen, D., Keiren, J., Wijs, A.: An $O(m \log n)$ algorithm for computing stuttering equivalence and branching bisimulation. ACM Trans. Comput. Logic 18(2), 13:1–13:34 (2017)
18. ISO/IEC: LOTOS – A Formal Description Technique Based on the Temporal Ordering of Observational Behaviour. International Standard 8807, International Organization for Standardization – Information Processing Systems – Open Systems Interconnection (1989)
19. Kozen, D.: Results on the propositional μ-calculus. Theor. Comput. Sci. 27, 333–354 (1983)
20. Krimm, J.-P., Mounier, L.: Compositional state space generation from Lotos programs. In: Brinksma, E. (ed.) TACAS 1997. LNCS, vol. 1217, pp. 239–258. Springer, Heidelberg (1997). doi:10.1007/BFb0035392
21. Lang, F.: Exp.Open 2.0: a flexible tool integrating partial order, compositional, and on-the-fly verification methods. In: Romijn, J., Smith, G., van de Pol, J. (eds.) IFM 2005. LNCS, vol. 3771, pp. 70–88. Springer, Heidelberg (2005). doi:10.1007/11589976_6
22. Lang, F.: Refined interfaces for compositional verification. In: Najm, E., Pradat-Peyre, J.-F., Donzeau-Gouge, V.V. (eds.) FORTE 2006. LNCS, vol. 4229, pp. 159–174. Springer, Heidelberg (2006). doi:10.1007/11888116_13
23. Lang, F.: Unpublished textual and PVS proof that branching bisimulation is a congruence for Networks of LTSs. This proof does not consider DPBB. Personal Communication (2016)
24. Maraninchi, F.: Operational and compositional semantics of synchronous automaton compositions. In: Cleaveland, W.R. (ed.) CONCUR 1992. LNCS, vol. 630, pp. 550–564. Springer, Heidelberg (1992). doi:10.1007/BFb0084815

25. Mateescu, R., Wijs, A.: Property-dependent reductions adequate with divergence-sensitive branching bisimilarity. Sci. Comput. Program. **96**(3), 354–376 (2014)

26. Mazzara, M., Lanese, I.: Towards a unifying theory for web services composition. In: Bravetti, M., Núñez, M., Zavattaro, G. (eds.) WS-FM 2006. LNCS, vol. 4184, pp. 257–272. Springer, Heidelberg (2006). doi:10.1007/11841197_17

27. Milner, R.: Communication and Concurrency. Prentice-Hall, New York (1989)

28. De Nicola, R., Vaandrager, F.: Action versus state based logics for transition systems. In: Guessarian, I. (ed.) LITP 1990. LNCS, vol. 469, pp. 407–419. Springer, Heidelberg (1990). doi:10.1007/3-540-53479-2_17

29. Pelánek, R.: BEEM: benchmarks for explicit model checkers. In: Bošnački, D., Edelkamp, S. (eds.) SPIN 2007. LNCS, vol. 4595, pp. 263–267. Springer, Heidelberg (2007). doi:10.1007/978-3-540-73370-6_17

30. Peled, D.: Ten years of partial order reduction. In: Hu, A.J., Vardi, M.Y. (eds.) CAV 1998. LNCS, vol. 1427, pp. 17–28. Springer, Heidelberg (1998). doi:10.1007/BFb0028727

31. de Putter, S., Wijs, A.: Verifying a verifier: on the formal correctness of an LTS transformation verification technique. In: Stevens, P., Wąsowski, A. (eds.) FASE 2016. LNCS, vol. 9633, pp. 383–400. Springer, Heidelberg (2016). doi:10.1007/978-3-662-49665-7_23

32. Roscoe, A.: The Theory and Practice of Concurrency. Prentice-Hall (1998)

33. Spaninks, L.: An Axiomatisation for Rooted Branching Bisimulation with Explicit Divergence. Master's thesis, Eindhoven University of Technology (2013)

34. Ulidowski, I., Phillips, I.: Ordered SOS process languages for branching and eager bisimulations. Inf. Comput. **178**(1), 180–213 (2002)

35. Verhoef, C.: A congruence theorem for structured operational semantics with predicates and negative premises. In: Jonsson, B., Parrow, J. (eds.) CONCUR 1994. LNCS, vol. 836, pp. 433–448. Springer, Heidelberg (1994). doi:10.1007/978-3-540-48654-1_32

36. Wijs, A.: Define, verify, refine: correct composition and transformation of concurrent system semantics. In: Fiadeiro, J.L., Liu, Z., Xue, J. (eds.) FACS 2013. LNCS, vol. 8348, pp. 348–368. Springer, Cham (2014). doi:10.1007/978-3-319-07602-7_21

37. Wijs, A.J.: Confluence detection for transformations of labelled transition systems. In: Proceedings of the 2nd Graphs as Models Workshop (GaM 2015). EPTCS, vol. 181, pp. 1–15. Open Publishing Association (2015)

38. Wijs, A., Engelen, L.: Efficient property preservation checking of model refinements. In: Piterman, N., Smolka, S.A. (eds.) TACAS 2013. LNCS, vol. 7795, pp. 565–579. Springer, Heidelberg (2013). doi:10.1007/978-3-642-36742-7_41

39. Wijs, A., Engelen, L.: REFINER: towards formal verification of model transformations. In: Badger, J.M., Rozier, K.Y. (eds.) NFM 2014. LNCS, vol. 8430, pp. 258–263. Springer, Cham (2014). doi:10.1007/978-3-319-06200-6_21

40. Wijs, A.: Achieving discrete relative timing with untimed process algebra. In: Proceedings of the 12th Conference on Engineering of Complex Computer Systems (ICECCS 2007), pp. 35–44. IEEE Computer Society Press (2007)

41. Wijs, A.: GPU accelerated strong and branching bisimilarity checking. In: Baier, C., Tinelli, C. (eds.) TACAS 2015. LNCS, vol. 9035, pp. 368–383. Springer, Heidelberg (2015). doi:10.1007/978-3-662-46681-0_29

42. Wijs, A., Fokkink, W.: From χ_t to μCRL: combining performance and functional analysis. In: Proceedings of the 10th Conference on Engineering of Complex Computer Systems (ICECCS 2005), pp. 184–193. IEEE Computer Society Press (2005)

Safety Analysis of Software Components of a Dialysis Machine Using Model Checking

M.D. Harrison[1,4]([✉]) [iD], M. Drinnan[2], J.C. Campos[3,4], P. Masci[3,4], L. Freitas[1],
C. di Maria[2], and M. Whitaker[2]

[1] School of Computing Science,
Newcastle University, Newcastle upon Tyne NE1 7RU, UK
`michael.harrison@ncl.ac.uk`
[2] Regional Medical Physics Department, Royal Victoria Infirmary,
Newcastle upon Tyne NE1 4LP, UK
[3] Dep. Informática, Universidade do Minho, Braga, Portugal
[4] HASLab, INESC TEC, Braga, Portugal

Abstract. The paper describes the practical use of a model checking technique to contribute to the risk analysis of a new paediatric dialysis machine. The formal analysis focuses on one component of the system, namely the table-driven software controller which drives the dialysis cycle and deals with error management. The analysis provided evidence of the verification of risk control measures relating to the software component. The paper describes the productive dialogue between the developers of the device, who had no experience or knowledge of formal methods, and an analyst who had experience of using the formal analysis tools. There were two aspects to this dialogue. The first concerned the translation of safety requirements so that they preserved the meaning of the requirement. The second involved understanding the relationship between the software component under analysis and the broader concern of the system as a whole. The paper focuses on the process, highlighting how the team recognised the advantages over a more traditional testing approach.

Keywords: Risk analysis · Formal methods · Model checking · Medical devices · Haemodialysis

1 Introduction

The risk analysis required to satisfy regulatory requirements (for example [4,16]) includes an assessment of the hazards associated with a medical device. These hazards include possible hardware and software failures. Examples of hardware failure include, for example, faulty connections or pump failure. Risk analysis, as part of a submission for certification by a regulator, is an onerous task typically requiring substantial amounts of test data. Developing such a submission is essential when dealing with life-critical medical systems. Medical device standards (see for example [4]) require that measures have been taken to ensure that risks associated with use of the device are as low as reasonably practical.

© Springer International Publishing AG 2017
J. Proença and M. Lumpe (Eds.): FACS 2017, LNCS 10487, pp. 137–154, 2017.
DOI: 10.1007/978-3-319-68034-7_8

The required measures include careful identification of hazards and demonstration that risks associated with these hazards have been mitigated. One part of demonstrating that hazards have been mitigated is to establish requirements of the system that demonstrate that there are barriers between a hazard and its consequence. Processes that are recommended to achieve such confidence include team based scrutiny of the use of documented processes as well as testing that requirements have been satisfied.

This paper describes part of a safety analysis process. It describes how model checking analyses were used to demonstrate that a particular software component within the system satisfied requirements described in a risk log. The focus of the paper is to look at the process and to discuss how the team used the model checking analysis to consider the broader safety requirements of the system. The formal analysis that was generated as a result of the process described in the paper was submitted as evidence to the regulator.

2   The NIDUS Device

Dialysis and ultrafiltration (removal of excess water) are extremely difficult procedures in small children with failing kidneys because the total volume of blood in the child's circulation is very small. The Newcastle experimental Infant Dialysis and Ultrafiltration System (NIDUS) has been used at Newcastle-upon-Tyne's Royal Victoria Infirmary (RVI) for some time. It does not use a traditional dialysis circuit, and the circuit volume of about 10 mL is suitable for treating infants with a total blood volume less than 100 mL. Before the device could be used more widely, it was necessary to identify and assess the risks of using it before the device could achieve regulatory approval.

The device is implemented using several software components. These include device drivers (for example, the motors that control the infusion pumps), components that enable the device to recognise and manage system failures (for example, the presence of bubbles in tubing) and components that provide the interface to allow the operator of the device to be aware of its status and to control the system. The component under consideration manages the drivers. Its logic of operation is organised as a control table. The table describes two aspects of the controller. It describes the attributes of the state of the device that control the dialysis process and it describes how the state of the device changes in response to events. Hence in Fig. 1, *RST_InitS1* (identified in the left hand column) is a state that has attributes *Power*, *Motor1*, *Motor2* etc. (top row) with values *ALLOW12V*, *M1FWDMAX*, *M2SAFE* etc. (as described in the row labelled *RST_InitS1*). At the same time the right hand side of the table describes transitions. Hence, for example an *M1Stall* event (as identified in the top row) causes a transition from the *RST_InitS1* state to the *RST_InitS2* state.

The controller involves 93 states and 30 events and the spreadsheet has been generated directly from the data structure that drives it. Each state attribute describes an attribute of the behaviour of the hardware system, for example:

*NAME	Power	Motor1	Motor2	Hep	Peri	Valve	Alarm	WashTimer	DialysisTimer	Flush	Mode	HardFault	Overpressure	Bubble	AgreeAir	12Voff	M1stall
iT PowerOn	TRIP12V	M1UNSTALL	M2UNSTALL	HEPUNSTALL	PERIUNSTALL	UNLATCH	INHIBIT	ZERO	ZERO	DISABLE	RESET	HardFault					
iT ColdStart	TRIP12V	M1SAFE	M2SAFE	HEPSAFE	PERISAFE	UNLATCH	INHIBIT	ZERO	HOLD	ENABLE	RESET	HardFault	ST ColdStart	ST ColdStart			
iT WarmStart	TRIP12V	M1SAFE	M2SAFE	HEPSAFE	PERISAFE	UNLATCH	INHIBIT	ZERO	HOLD	ENABLE	WASH	HardFault					
RESET stuff																	
tST Start	TRIP12V	M1SAFE	M2SAFE	HEPSAFE	PERISAFE	VALVESAFE	QUIET	ZERO	HOLD	ENABLE	RESET	HardFault	RST Errors	RST Errors		RST Ready	
tST Ready	ALLOW12V	M1SAFE	M2SAFE	HEPSAFE	PERISAFE	VALVESAFE	QUIET	ZERO	HOLD	ENABLE	RESET	HardFault	RST Errors	RST Errors		ST ColdStart	RST
tST Init1	ALLOW12V	M1FWD2MAX	M2SAFE	HEPSAFE	PERISAFE	PREP	ACTIVE	ZERO	HOLD	ENABLE	RESET	HardFault	RST Errors	RST Errors		ST ColdStart	RST Init52
tST Init2	ALLOW12V	M1STOP	M2FWD2MAX	HEPBCKMAX	PERISAFE	FLUSH	ACTIVE	ZERO	HOLD	ENABLE	RESET	HardFault	RST Errors	RST Errors		ST ColdStart	
tST InitReq	ALLOW12V	M1STOP	M2STOP	HEPSAFE	PERISAFE	FLUSH	ACTIVE	ZERO	HOLD	ENABLE	RESET	HardFault	RST Errors	RST Errors		ST ColdStart	
tST Relax	ALLOW12V	M1SAFE	M2SAFE	HEPSAFE	PERISAFE	VALVESAFE	ACTIVE	ZERO	HOLD	ENABLE	RESET	HardFault	RST Errors	RST Errors		ST ColdStart	
tST All	ALLOW12V	M1RESET	M2RESET	HEPRESET	PERISAFE	VALVESAFE	ACTIVE	ZERO	HOLD	ENABLE	RESET	HardFault	RST Errors	RST Errors			
RESET errors																	
tST Errors	TRIP12V	M1UNSTALL	M2UNSTALL	HEPUNSTALL	PERIUNSTALL	VALVESAFE	WARN	HOLD	HOLD	ENABLE	RESET	HardFault	RST Overpressure	RST Bubble			
tST Overpressure	TRIP12V	M1UNSTALL	M2UNSTALL	HEPUNSTALL	PERIUNSTALL	UNLATCH	WARN	HOLD	HOLD	VALVE	RESET	HardFault	RST Overpressure				
tST AckOverpressure	TRIP12V	M1UNSTALL	M2UNSTALL	HEPUNSTALL	PERIUNSTALL	UNLATCH	WARN	HOLD	HOLD	ENABLE	RESET	HardFault	RST Overpressure				
tST Bubble	TRIP12V	M1UNSTALL	M2UNSTALL	HEPUNSTALL	PERIUNSTALL	VALVESAFE	WARN	HOLD	HOLD	ENABLE	RESET	HardFault		RST Bubble			
tST AckBubble	TRIP12V	M1UNSTALL	M2UNSTALL	HEPUNSTALL	PERIUNSTALL	VALVESAFE	WARN	HOLD	HOLD	ENABLE	RESET	HardFault		RST Bubble			
Prime herauein																	
tEP Prime	TRIP12V	M1SAFE	M2SAFE	HEPSAFE	PERISAFE	FLUSH	NOTIFY	ZERO	HOLD	DISFWWARN	WASH	HardFault					
tEP Warn	TRIP12V	M1SAFE	M2SAFE	HEPSAFE	PERISAFE	UNLATCH	NOTIFY	ZERO	HOLD	ENABLE	WASH	HardFault					
WASH from fresh kit																	
VA Start	TRIP12V	M1SAFE	M2SAFE	HEPSAFE	PERISAFE	VALVESAFE	QUIET	ZERO	HOLD	ENABLE	WASHING	HardFault	WA Errors	WA Errors		WA Ready	WA
VA Ready	ALLOW12V	M1SAFE	M2SAFE	HEPSAFE	PERISAFE	VALVESAFE	QUIET	HOLD	HOLD	WASTOPEN	WASHING	HardFault	WA Errors	WA Errors			WA
WASH after any other activity																	
VA Restart	TRIP12V	M1SAFE	M2SAFE	HEPSAFE	PERISAFE	VALVESAFE	QUIET	HOLD	HOLD	ENABLE	WASHING	HardFault	WA Errors	WA Errors		WA Decision	WA
VA Decision	TRIP12V	M1SAFE	M2SAFE	HEPSAFE	PERISAFE	VALVESAFE	WARN	HOLD	HOLD	ENABLE	WASHING	HardFault	WA Errors	WA Errors			WA
VA Incomplete	ALLOW12V	M1SAFE	M2SAFE	HEPSAFE	PERISAFE	VALVESAFE	ACTIVE	HOLD	HOLD	WASTOPEN	WASHING	HardFault	WA Errors	WA Errors			WA
VA NotReady	ALLOW12V	M1SAFE	M2SAFE	HEPSAFE	PERISAFE	VALVESAFE	ACTIVE	HOLD	HOLD	ENABLE	WASHING	HardFault	WA Errors	WA Errors			WA
WASH start prime cycle																	
VA S1Prime	ALLOW12V	M1BCKMAX	M2STOP	HEPSAFE	PERIPERFUSE	PREP	ACTIVE	HOLD	HOLD	ENABLE	WASHING	HardFault	WA Errors	WA Errors		WA Stop	WA Errors
VA S1Flush	ALLOW12V	M1FWD2MAX	M2STOP	HEPSAFE	PERIPERFUSE	PREP	ACTIVE	HOLD	HOLD	ENABLE	WASHING	HardFault	WA Errors	WA Errors		WA Stop	WA Errors
WASH start washing cycles																	
VA S1Fill	ALLOW12V	M1BCKMAX	M2STOP	HEPSAFE	PERIPERFUSE	PREP	ACTIVE	HOLD	HOLD	ENABLE	WASHING	HardFault	WA Errors	WA Errors		WA Stop	WA Errors
VA FillRix	ALLOW12V	M1STOP	M2STOP	HEPSAFE	PERIPERFUSE	PREP	ACTIVE	HOLD	HOLD	ENABLE	WASHING	HardFault	WA Errors	WA Errors		WA Stop	WA Errors
VA S1S2	ALLOW12V	M1FWD2MAX	M2BCKMAX	HEPSAFE	PERIPERFUSE	DIAL	ACTIVE	TICK	HOLD	ENABLE	WASHING	HardFault	WA Errors	WA Errors		WA Stop	WA Errors
VA FlushRix	ALLOW12V	M1STOP	M2STOP	HEPSAFE	PERIPERFUSE	DIAL	ACTIVE	TICK	HOLD	ENABLE	WASHING	HardFault	WA Errors	WA Errors		WA Stop	WA Errors
VA S2Flush	ALLOW12V	M1STOP	M2FWD2MAX	HEPSAFE	PERIPERFUSE	FLUSH	ACTIVE	TICK	HOLD	ENABLE	WASHING	HardFault	WA Errors	WA Errors		WA Stop	WA Errors

Fig. 1. A fragment of the control table (Colour figure online)

- Attributes *Motor1*, *Motor2* and *Hep* describe the proximal, distal and heparin syringes respectively. Values of the attributes include whether the syringe pump is driving forward or backward, and whether "fast" or "slow".
- *Valve* and *Bubble* describe the valve assembly and the bubble detectors. The valve may, for example, be safe or open to the baby.
- *Flash* and *Alarm* describe features of the user interface. For example Flash shows, amongst other displays, that a clip is open or closed, and the Alarm can warn or notify or be quiet.

3   Verification Approach

The risk assessment for the device requires a multiplicity of evidence. These sources include clinical trials, software and hardware test results and documentation of the development process. The problem with trials and test results is that they do not guarantee the absence of problems. Our goal was to use formal analysis as one source of evidence that all risks have been assessed. This was made easier in the present case because the spreadsheet was an encoding of the data structure used to drive the controller. The analysis of the controller involved the following steps.

1. The developers created a risk log which described informal system safety requirements designed to mitigate hazards (Sect. 4). These covered the whole range of hardware and software hazards.
2. The state transition table was translated into a behavioural model that could be analysed using a model checker (Sect. 5).
3. Requirements, derived from the risk log, were then considered and those that related to the controller were expressed in a formal logic (Sect. 6).
4. These risk related properties were checked against the model that had been derived from the transition table. Where they failed, further discussion with the developers indicated either a flaw in the controller, or a situation which was considered either not to be hazardous, or to be a failure in the formulation of the property. The process of checking the properties, based on the requirements, often resulted in refinement of the properties or modifications to the control table or the controller mechanism. The results of this process were documented in the risk log (Sect. 7).

The process of property formulation and discussion was a significant element in the risk analysis of the controller.

4   Translating the Risk Log into Requirements

The risk log (see Fig. 2) formed the basis for the risk assessment. It described the requirements that were considered to mitigate risks and linked the requirements to the evidence that they were satisfied. It was this document that provided material relating to the software controller component that was the source of the dialogue between developers and the formal analyst. Regulatory authorities typically require that risk control measures are included as requirements (see BS EN 62304:2006 [4] for example). Each control measure should be verified and the verification documented. As already stated, verification is typically taken to mean that some form of systematic testing has taken place. The BS EN 62304 standard requires a risk analysis path: "from hazardous situation to the software item; from the software item to the software cause; from the software cause to the risk control measure; to the verification of the risk control measure". The process of proving regulatory requirements has been discussed in more detail in [14].

Some of the requirements in the risk log were either completely or partially relevant to the software controller and these provided the basis for the analysis. Converting a software controller requirement into a property of the model involved discussion between the developers and the analyst. When a formulated property failed, examples of the failure were presented to the development team. In Fig. 2 MAL.GENERROR is highlighted in red because the property that describes this requirement, at the particular stage of the risk assessment process at which the log was current, was false. As will be illustrated, this property was further refined and the red highlighting removed. Note that the spreadsheet in Fig. 1 shows similar highlighting indicating changes to the control table that arose and thus required an iteration of the analysis.

Ref	Requirement	
MAL.GENINHIBIT	The alarm is only inhibited during the RESET phase.	It is always the case that wh
MAL.GENBABY	The BABY valve can only be open while the system is in DIALYSIS mode.	It is always the case that wh
MAL.GENS1MOVE	During access to the baby, the BABY valve is open.	It is always the case that wh M1 IN { M1Withdraw, M1R(
MAL.GENS2STOP	During access to the baby, the distal syringe is never running.	It is always the case that wh M1 IN { M1Withdraw, M1R(
MAL.GENERROR	For all error conditions and all system states, the next state will be an ERROR state.	For all error conditions and Note this condition logically all errors have been cleared IF ErrorCondition THEN Nex
MAL.GENS2S1	During DIALYSIS, when the distal syringe is moving forwards then the proximal syringe is necessarily moving backwards.	It is always the case that wh IF M2 IN { M2Fwd } -> M1 I|
MAL.GENS1S2	During DIALYSIS, when the distal syringe is moving backwards then the proximal syringe is necessarily moving forwards.	It is always the case that wh IF M2 IN { M2Bck } -> M1 IN

Fig. 2. Risk Log in development (Colour figure online)

In this way requirements were refined iteratively, involving the whole team. Our aim was to formulate a requirement of the controller as a property of the model and if the property failed explain why it failed. Failure of a property could mean that: (i) the model did not capture the functionality of the device; (ii) the property was not correctly formulated; (iii) there was an issue in the design that could either be dealt with in another way, for example hardware or through some mitigating process. An additional mitigating factor might be, for example, a requirement on the clinician to strictly adhere to an operating procedure. This analysis process was documented to provide evidence that all reasonable measures had been taken to ensure the safety of the device. This encouraged the developers to be confident that the device was safe as well as indicating small design changes to improve safety. When treating premature and sick infants, proper *in vivo* testing is almost impossible and the consequences of failure can be very serious. This formal process has proved invaluable. An example of a requirement in the risk log described in Fig. 2, and used as illustration in Sect. 6, is:

> "During DIALYSIS, when the digital syringe is moving forwards then the proximal syringe is necessarily moving backwards."

The developer produced a partial translation of this in discussion with the analyst. The formulation indicates the logic without noting the temporal dimension of the property or the precise nature of the sets {*M2Fwd*} and {*M1Bck*}.

If M2 in {M2Fwd} → M1 in {M1Bck}

5   Translating the State Transition Table into a Formal Model

5.1   The Specification Language

The simple state transition table used to drive the controller readily lends itself to a mechanical process. We used the IVY tool [5] because it was readily available to us. It provides a front end to the NuSMV model checker [6]. IVY supports an action orientated logic language MAL (Modal Action Logic) that provides a textual structure similar to the diagrammatic structure of tools such as SRC [10]. A reason for using this particular toolset was that we were interested in the possibility of producing a tool that would be more easily understandable to an interdisciplinary team. Our goal is that IVY be used eventually without formal methods expertise. The intention was that the tool should provide a key element in communication within the team while at the same time providing the evidence that a requirement under analysis was satisfied.

MAL enables the easy description of state machines such as the table that drives the dialysis machine. Attributes are used to capture the information present in the state of the device and actions transform these states. MAL describes a logic of actions and is used to write production rules that describe the effect of actions on the state of the device. This style of specification was found easy to use by software engineers [15]. For this reason MAL was preferred to the notation which is used by the NuSMV model checker. The language also enables the expression of deontic operations, in particular permissions were used in our analysis. Non-determinism is possible when more than one action is allowed in the same state of the described model. MAL rules are a convenient way to describe the behaviour of the state table that drives the dialyser. The logic provides:

- a modal operator [_]_ : [ac]expr is the value of expr after the occurrence of action ac — the modal operator is used to define the effect of actions;
- a special reference event []: []expr is the value of expr in the initial state(s) — the reference event is used to define the initial state(s);
- a deontic operator per: per(ac) meaning action ac is permitted to happen next — to control when actions might happen;
- a deontic operator obl: obl(ac) meaning action ac is obliged to happen some time in the future. Note that obl was not used in this analysis.

The notation also supports the usual propositional operators. As an illustration, the following example declares two boolean attributes that describe whether the device is on (poweredon), whether it is dialysing (dialysingstate) and two actions (start and pause). It describes the effect of the action pause as setting the attribute dialysingstate to false and leaving the attribute poweredon unchanged. Priming is used to identify the value of the attribute after the action takes place. A permission predicate restricts the pause action to only happen when the system is dialysing and powered on. The keep function preserves the value of the attribute poweredon in the next state. If an attribute is not modified explicitly or is not in the keep list, then its value in the next state is left unconstrained.

interactor *dialyser*
  attributes
    poweredon, dialysingstate : *boolean*
  actions
    start pause
  axioms
    [*pause*] !*dialysingstate'* & keep(*poweredon*)
    per(*pause*) → *dialysingstate* & *poweredon*

5.2 The Translation

The spreadsheet was translated systematically into MAL. During the analysis an automatic translator was developed based on translation patterns (explained further below) identified during the manual process. The automatic translator takes the CSV file representing the state transition model and produces its corresponding MAL representation following a translation strategy described in [8]. This ensures that the MAL model represents the finite state model, as described by the spreadsheet, accurately.

As an illustration of the translation consider the situation when an event occurs and the controller software changes the state. We consider the transition involving *M1Stall* in state *RST_InitS1* highlighted in Fig. 1. Events are described in MAL as actions. These actions transition to different states depending on the current state. The controller software assumes that a pipeline of events exists, each tick of the system process causes the next event to be taken from the pipeline. If the pipeline is empty then a specified default transition is taken. The model includes no specification of a pipeline of events, rather it assumes that at any stage of the process the pipeline may become empty and as a consequence the "default" event / action is taken. When several actions are possible because the guard for each of them is satisfied then one of the actions is taken non-deterministically. There are some circumstances where it is necessary to prove properties that assume that the pipeline is never empty. For these situations we added an additional meta-attribute that becomes false if a default action occurs in a path ($dfltchk$).

The MAL description of the effect of $M1Stall$, when the event occurs in state RST_InitS1, is as follows:

$$statedist = sdRSTInitS1 \rightarrow [acM1Stall] \; trRSTInitS2$$

This MAL rule describes a transformation. When the state is $RSTInitS1$ the action $acM1Stall$ leads to the state $RSTInitS2$. The attribute $statedist$ indicates the current state. If $RSTInitS1$ is the current state then $statedist$ takes the value $sdRSTInitS1$. The model defines a set of transformations that change current state to specified new states. Hence $trRSTInitS2$ specifies a transformation to the state $RSTInitS2$ as is described below.

$$
\begin{aligned}
trRSTInitS2 = \; & Power' = ALLOW12V \; \& \; Motor1' = M1STOP \; \& \\
& Motor2' = M2FWDMAX \; \& \; Hep' = HEPSAFE \; \& \\
& Peri' = PERISAFE \; \& \; Valve' = FLUSH \& \\
& Alarm' = ACTIVE \; \& \; WashTimer' = ZERO \; \& \\
& DialysisTimer' = HOLD \; \& \; Flash' = ENABLE \; \& \\
& Mode' = RESET \; \& \; statedist' = sdRSTInitS2
\end{aligned}
$$

This transformation specifies new values for each of the attributes, for example the value of the attribute $Motor1$ becomes $M1STOP$ etc. This state transition is further augmented in the model to include attributes that do not appear explicitly in the state transition table as follows:

$$
\begin{aligned}
seclr' = \; & GREEN \; \& \; !audiblealert' \; \& \; fkey1' = F1BLANK \; \& \\
& fkey2' = F2BLANK \; \& \; fstop' = F3STOP
\end{aligned}
$$

These additional attributes deal with features of the controller that are only listed as comments in the spreadsheet, and have the following meaning, and are not currently supported by the translator.

statedist marks the current state, designed to ease the model's identification of the current state.

seclr describes the colour of the state pane on the display.

audiblealert whether the alert if any is audible.

fkey1 the function display for $key1$.

fkey2 the function display for $key2$.

fstop the function display for $stop$.

6 Requirements Expressed in Formal Logic

6.1 Refining a Sketch Requirement as a CTL Property

As discussed in Sect. 4, the risk log contains a list of requirements developed in response to known hazards. The example to be considered in more detail was initially sketched by developers as:

If M2 in {M2Fwd} → M1 in {M1Bck}

This semi-formal representation indicates that it should always be the case that if the state of the motor $M2$ is "moving forward" then the motor $M1$ should be "moving backward". Further discussion with the developers produced refinement of this sketch requirement. The two sets *M2FWD* and *M1BCK* were described as "enumerations" in MAL using the following syntax:

M2FWD = { M2FWDMAX, M2FWDUNUF }
M1BCK = { M1BCKMAX, M1BCKUF, M1WITHDRAW }

All these states involved forward and backward motion in the two motors. Having defined the relevant state attributes as specified in the spreadsheet model, the next step was to formulate a precise version of the property as a basis for the analysis. The notation used was that supported by the NuSMV model checking tool.

The property notation CTL [7] is widely used and provides two kinds of temporal operator: operators over paths and operators over states. Paths represent the possible future behaviours of the system. When p is a property expressed over paths, $A(p)$ expresses the property that p holds for all paths and $E(p)$ that p holds for at least one path. Operators are also provided over states. When q and s are properties over states, $G(q)$ expresses the property that q holds for all the states of the examined path; $F(q)$ that q holds for some states over the examined path; $X(q)$ expresses the property that q holds for the next state of the examined path; while $[qUs]$ means that q holds until s holds in the path.

CTL contains a subset of the possible formulae that arise from the combination of these operators. $AG(q)$ means that q holds for all the states of all the paths; $AF(q)$ means that q holds for at least one state in all the paths; $EF(q)$ means that q holds in at least one state in at least one path; $EG(q)$ means that q holds for all states in at least one path; $AX(q)$ means that q holds in the next state of all paths; $EX(q)$ means that there is at least one path for which q holds in the next state; $A[qUs]$ means that q holds until some other property s holds in all paths; $E[qUs]$ means there exists at least one path in which q holds until some property s.

6.2 Categories of Requirements

The discussion of all the elements of the risk log led to a consideration of requirements that fall into the following categories:

P1: specified states are inaccessible in dangerous circumstances. The property described in Sect. 6.1 is an example of such a property. Another example is that: "it should not be possible to dialyse an infant with heparin in the blood circuit".

P2: when the dialysis machine is error free it always generates a correct dialysis sequence. This sequence includes wash and dialysis stages.

P3: when an error event occurs then the device is taken to an appropriate error state.

P4: states can only be reached if combinations of states have happened in the past. An example of such a property is that relevant reminders are always displayed to "close a clamp before the next phase of the cycle can commence".

7 Risk Related Properties Checked of the Model

The particular requirements that fall into these categories will be considered in detail in this section. An important part of the description is the discussion within the team that triggered the refinement of initial versions of properties.

P1: Unsafe Combinations of states cannot occur

The requirement (of Sect. 6.1) was formulated in CTL (using the MAL notation "*in*" for membership of an enumerated set) as:

$$AG(Motor2 \ in \ M2FWD \rightarrow Motor1 \ in \ M1BCK) \tag{1}$$

This property specifies that it is always the case, for all states, that when *Motor2* is in a forward state then *Motor1* is in a backward state. This property is not true of the model (as was revealed during an analysis meeting) producing a counter-example that indicates one set of circumstances in which the property fails. Figure 3 describes the sequence starting from the initial state (column 1), ending at a state where the property fails to be true (column 6). Columns indicate values held by attributes. These are named in the left hand column (i.e., column 0). For example, the attribute *Power* has value *ALLOW12V* in column 4. The colour yellow is used to indicate that a state attribute has changed value between successive states. The path indicates (as shown in the row marked *main.action*) that from the initial state the device defaults (that is it takes the action *acDefault*) because there are no events in the queue. This action is followed by *Key2*, followed by *12voff*, *12von* and *M1stall* which leads to the state where the property fails. Discussion during the risk meeting explored the implications of the sequence and came to the conclusion that this exception was acceptably safe and could therefore be excluded. A process then continued of excluding states before formulating a property that excluded all discovered exceptions:

$$AG(Motor2 \ in \ M2FWD \rightarrow (Motor1 \ in \ M1BCK \ |$$
$$statedist \ in \ \{sdRSTInitS2, sdWAS2Empty,$$
$$sdWAFlushRlx, sdWAS2Flush\})$$

The risk analysis team considered each of these exceptions and noted that the common property of these counter-examples was that they occurred when the device was not in dialysis mode, hence the following property was constructed:

$$AG((Motor2\ in\ M2FWD\ \&$$
$$Mode\ in\ \{DIALYSE, DIALYSING\})$$
$$\rightarrow Motor1\ in\ M1BCK)$$

The property formulated as a result of this observation is true for the model. It could be argued that visual inspection of the spreadsheet would have been sufficient to indicate the problem in this particular case. However this systematic approach to finding paths to potentially hazardous states provides an exhaustive approach.

main.action	1	2	3	4	5	6
		acDefault	acKey2	ac12Voff	ac12Von	acM1stall
Alarm	INHIBIT	INHIBIT	QUIET	QUIET	ACTIVE	ACTIVE
DialysisTimer	ZERO	HOLD	HOLD	HOLD	HOLD	HOLD
Flash	DISABLE	ENABLE	ENABLE	ENABLE	ENABLE	ENABLE
Hep	HEPUNSTAL	HEPSAFE	HEPUNSTAL	HEPSAFE	HEPSAFE	HEPSAFE
Mode	RESET	RESET	RESET	RESET	RESET	RESET
Motor1	M1UNSTALL	M1SAFE	M1UNSTALL	M1SAFE	M1FWDMAX	M1STOP
Motor2	M2UNSTALL	M2SAFE	M2UNSTALL	M2SAFE	M2SAFE	M2FWDMAX
Peri	PERIUNSTAL	PERISAFE	PERISAFE	PERISAFE	PERISAFE	PERISAFE
Power	TRIP12V	TRIP12V	TRIP12V	ALLOW12V	ALLOW12V	ALLOW12V
Valve	UNLATCH	UNLATCH	VALVESAFE	VALVESAFE	PREP	FLUSH
WashTimer	ZERO	ZERO	ZERO	ZERO	ZERO	ZERO

Fig. 3. Counter-example to Property 1

P2: Staying in the dialysis cycle

The requirement described in the risk log is expressed as follows:

MAL.DIALCYCLE: Unless there are errors or user actions, the system stays in the 'dialysis cycle'

The requirement aims to ensure that, barring error events or user interventions, the transition table will always cause the device to complete the same haemodialysis process. To check the requirement it is first assumed that no such cycle exists. This property should fail and give, as an example of failure, one cycle that is of the appropriate form. Once the cycle is discovered, and it is the correct 'dialysis cycle', the next stage is to show that it is the only possible cycle that can be generated using the relevant actions.

The first step in demonstrating this requirement is to find a cycle, show it is the only cycle and check that is the required cycle. The cycle must begin with the action *M1out* in the state *DIA_Wdraw*. The approach therefore is to show that, once reached, this state is reached again. However it is necessary to be more precise than this. The cycle must be achieved with a subset of actions, excluding for example error actions or user interventions. Only specific actions are recognised are valid "drivers" of the cycle. A "meta"-attribute *motorsandwaits* is therefore introduced that is set true by the first action and preserved by operations : *M1in*, *M2in* and *Wait1second*. All other actions set the *motorsandwaits* attribute to false. A counter-example to the CTL property:

$$AG(statedist = sdDIAWdraw \rightarrow$$
$$AX(AG(!(motorsandwaits \,\& \qquad\qquad (2)$$
$$statedist = sdDIAWdraw))))$$

should then generate the cycle. This is illustrated in the trace fragment in Fig. 4. The sequence fragment starts with the state *DIAWdraw* (bottom row, column 23) when *motorsandwaits* is false and ends with the state *DIAWdrawRlx* (column 29). The sequence of actions that make up the cycle are shown in a row at the top of the table (*acM1out* etc.). This sequence is indeed the "dialysis cycle" as acknowledged by the domain experts during a meeting. The other rows show the values of the state attributes relating to each state as represented by a column of the table. The value of *motorsandwaits* is shown in the penultimate row and remains true throughout. This, however, is only part of the analysis because it identifies *one* cycle only. It does not exclude the possibility that there are others. It is further necessary to check that no other sequences can be produced using this subset of actions, i.e., the discovered cycle is unique. This can be achieved by using properties that require that at each step of the cycle any valid action will result in the next step of the cycle as discovered in the counter-example.

So for each state a property, demonstrating uniqueness is proved, for example:

$$AG(statedist = sdDIAWdraw \rightarrow$$
$$AX(motorsandwaits \rightarrow statedist = sdDIAWdrawRlx))$$

	23	24	25	26	27	28	29
main.action	ac12Von	acM1out	acWait1sec	acM1in	acM2in	acWait1sec	acM1in
Alarm	ACTIVE	ACTIVE	ACTIVE	ACTIVE	ACTIVE	ACTIVE	ACTIVE
DialysisTimer	TICK	TICK	TICK	TICK	TICK	TICK	TICK
Flash	NOSAMPLE	NOSAMPLE	DOSAMPLE	ENDSAMPLE	NOSAMPLE	NOSAMPLE	NOSAMPLE
Hep	HEPINFUSE	HEPINFUSE	HEPINFUSE	HEPINFUSE	HEPINFUSE	HEPINFUSE	HEPINFUSE
Mode	DIALYSING	DIALYSING	DIALYSING	DIALYSING	DIALYSING	DIALYSING	DIALYSING
Motor1	M1WITHDR	M1STOP	M1FWDUNU	M1BCKUF	M1STOP	M1RETURN	M1WITHDR
Motor2	M2STOP	M2STOP	M2BCKUF	M2FWDUNU	M2STOP	M2STOP	M2STOP
Peri	PERIPERFUS	PERIPERFUS	PERIPERFUS	PERIPERFUS	PERIPERFUS	PERIPERFUS	PERIPERFUS
Power	ALLOW12V	ALLOW12V	ALLOW12V	ALLOW12V	ALLOW12V	ALLOW12V	ALLOW12V
Valve	BABY	BABY	DIAL	DIAL	DIAL	BABY	BABY
WashTimer	ZERO	ZERO	ZERO	ZERO	ZERO	ZERO	ZERO
motorsandwaits	FALSE	TRUE	TRUE	TRUE	TRUE	TRUE	TRUE
statedist	sdDIAWdra	sdDIAWdra	sdDIAS1S2	sdDIAS2S1	sdDIARetur	sdDIARetur	sdDIAWdra

Fig. 4. Proving the 'dialysis cycle'

Each state in the discovered cycle is considered and it is demonstrated that the only successor in each state, using the subset of events, is the next state found in the original cycle.

P3: Errors lead to error states

An important issue in the risk log was to ensure that error events would always lead to error states. This was expressed in the risk log as:

> MAL-GENERROR: For all error conditions and all system states, the next state will be an error state.

It was also required that the device would remain in an error state if further error events occur. To formulate the property a set of actions that represent the error events is first defined using MAL notation.

$$ErrorEventSet = acHardFault \mid acOverpressure \mid$$
$$acBubble \mid acPeriStall$$

The set *ErrorStateSet* is defined in the model as an enumerated set that includes all the states that are determined to be error states. The required property was then agreed to be:

$$AG(AX(ErrorEventSet \rightarrow statedist\ in\ ErrorStateSet))$$

During the meeting this property was checked and found to be false. The reason for this failure, as determined by the counter-example, was that the Alarm can be inhibited and when this happens the property fails to be true. The property was therefore refined to include *Alarm* ! = *INHIBIT*.

$$AG(Alarm\ ! =\ INHIBIT \rightarrow$$
$$AX(ErrorEventSet \rightarrow statedist\ in\ ErrorStateSet))$$

This property is also false. The state that offends in this case had not been counted as an error state and should have been. The set *ErrorStateSet* was therefore further augmented. The final refinement of the property further restricts to those states for which *Mode* is not *RESET*.

$$AG(Alarm\ ! =\ INHIBIT\ \&\ Mode\ ! =\ RESET \rightarrow \tag{3}$$
$$AX(ErrorEventSet \rightarrow statedist\ in\ ErrorStateSet))$$

Finally *STWarmStart* must also be excluded. This state is not considered to be problematic. Its occurrence is clear and will not cause confusion. These successive refinements have weakened the property and therefore a justification is required at each stage that the refined property is adequate mitigation for the possibility of an unrealised error. Discussion with the developers confirmed that this weakened formulation of the property was sufficient mitigation for possible risks and an explanation is provided in the risk log.

P4: States can only be reached if combinations of states have happened in the past

As was noted in the case of property P2, additional "meta-attributes" were introduced to the model so that it was possible to enrich the properties that could be proved using the model checker. In the case of P2, *motorsandwaits* was introduced to enable consideration of sequences of a subset of non error actions. Other requirements in the risk log could not be formalised as CTL properties using the original attributes of the model. In particular those properties that related to combinations of states that had happened in the past required such formulation. An example of a requirement of this kind is concerned with whether information is provided by the user interface to indicate to the user of the machine that a specific action should be carried out. *Flash* is a state attribute in the model that specifies the content of an information display. For example:

> "MAL.HEPCLIP: The user is instructed to close clip before changing syringe, and re-open afterwards."

Several Flash messages, specified by the attribute *Flash*, indicate dialyser warning displays. For example, *Flash = HEPCLOSE* indicates that "close the heparin clip" has been transmitted. The attribute *hepclipopen* was included in the model specification and is set to true and continues to be true after a flash message that indicates that the heparin clip is open: *Flash = HEPOPEN*. It is made false by *Flash* taking values *HEPCLOSE* or *HEPSYRINGE*. The following fragment involving the *Hepin* specifies a transition to the state *HEPClip*. This state includes a change to the *Flash* attribute *Flash' = HEPCLOSE* and therefore *hepclipopen* is set to false.

> $statedist\ in\ \{sdDIAReady\} \rightarrow [acHepin]$
> $\quad trHEPClip\ \&\ !motorsandwaits'\ \&\ keep(\ldots)\ \&\ !hepclipopen'$

We then check the property:

> $AG(Mode = DIALYSING \rightarrow hepclipopen)$

The property asserts that you can only reach a dialysing state if a message to open the clip was the most recent flash relating to the clip and that the message had previously occurred. This property checked to be false. The state *HEPPrime* is also a clear indication to open the clip but does not involve the relevant flash. The model was changed therefore so that the meta-attribute was also set to true when visiting *HEPPrime*. The property then becomes true.

8   Discussion and Related Work

The contribution of this paper is a practical demonstration of the use of formal techniques to analyse a component of a safety critical system. The approach was not novel. Similar techniques were being described and applied in the 1990s.

For example, a mature set of tools have been developed by Heitmeyer's team using SRC [10]. Their approach uses a tabular notation to describe requirements which makes the technique relatively acceptable to developers. Atlee and Gannon described a similar approach in [2]. In some domains, other than medical domains, formal mathematically based methods have been effective in analysing and assessing risks systematically (see for example, [3,13]). Despite the success of these techniques there is a continuing perception that formal methods are not easy to use and that they cannot be scaled to substantial systems. These barriers to their use have limited their uptake in medical domains. Recent research with the cooperation of the US Food and Drugs Administration (FDA) have led to increased possibilities for their potential use [12,14]. The novelty here has been to apply this technique in a medical team where typically small teams with limited resources are involved.

The translation of the table into MAL, including meta-attributes, involved 682 lines, including 119 lines of state definitions and 152 lines of type and constant definitions. The development of the first model, by hand, took about seven hours. It was possible to make most changes to the model and show the results interactively during meetings with the development team without disturbing the flow of the meeting. Hence the refinement of requirements and the careful analysis of the hazards were facilitated by the process. The analysis involved 23 properties. On the rare occasions when it was not possible to refine a property during the meeting, for example when meta-attributes were required, this could be achieved within an hour outside the meeting. Verifying all the properties together on a MacBook Pro with Intel Core i5 clocked at 2.9 GHz, with 8 GB RAM and SSD memory, took 1.7 s. The exercise shows that, with appropriate expertise and using available artefacts (the table, safety requirements), the use of formal methods required little additional effort and supported effective discussion of the risks between the developers.

There are several ways in which it can be demonstrated that a device satisfies safety requirements using formal techniques. One way of doing this is to develop the device formally by refining the model as supported by tools such as Event B [1]. An initial model is first developed that specifies the device characteristics and incorporates the safety requirements. This initial model is gradually refined using details about how specific functionalities are implemented. This was not a realistic approach in the present case because, when the analysis was to be done, the device had already been developed. Indeed such techniques are not feasible given the typical resources available to medical device developers. Alternatively a model could be generated from the program code of an existing device, using a set of transformation rules that guarantee correctness, as discussed in [11]. This approach could have been used for other software aspects of the device, however it is unclear how well such techniques scale. Proving that the model of this component of the software is correct with respect to the device was not a problem for the particular example because the software was driven by a table and the table was translated directly into the model. The analysis does not attempt to prove that the software drivers themselves were implemented correctly.

9   Conclusion

The risk analysis process described in the paper succeeded because the controller is table driven and it was relatively easy to generate a model from the table. It also succeeded because a mixed disciplinary team was involved. This team included one person who was able to use the formal tools and provide an explanation of the requirements and model formulations. It is standard practice to use a table to drive software that controls a multi-step process as in this case. However there are cases where this does not happen and moreover, as in this case, the software covered by the controller is only part of the software. The dialysis machine also includes user interface features, for example capacity to enter new values for thresholds relevant to the dialysis process. These are involved in the initial set-up of the machine. Other analyses, involving several of the authors, have focussed on existing IV infusion pumps [9]. In these cases such a table driven process, with the capacity to be automated, has not been possible. The analysis described in this paper therefore raises questions about the potential for extending this approach to a broader class of medical systems. The challenges raised by this analysis in the context of small-scale developments, such as this one, are:

Systematic Modelling: While formal approaches to the development of software that refine safety requirements exist (see [17]), these are not yet feasible to use given the available tools and skills of existing small development teams. In this case the formal methods expertise was recruited short-term for the purpose.

Mixed Disciplinary Teams: There was substantial benefit in recognising and using expertise from sources outside the development team. A mixed discipline approach is already in practice in the case of small companies or innovative pre-commercial developments. It would make sense therefore to add these analytical skills to the toolkit available to the device developers.

Mixed Styles of Analysis: As in this case a well defined and yet important software component may be analysed formally. The formal analysis of the controller table can also improve the testing coverage of the device drivers themselves although this was not done in this case. It is also good practice to have multiple independent arguments to demonstrate the safety of the system. Hence it makes sound sense to use formal techniques to improve confidence in the risk analysis.

This paper illustrates how formal techniques may be used successfully as part of the risk analysis process associated with the development of a medical device. This is part of the submission that has gone forward for regulation. The safety requirements that were formulated and proved, and improvements in the light of requirements failure, illustrate how the analysis led to improvement in the safety of the design while providing a concise basis for evidence that part of the system is safe. The technique is readily repeatable. Tools that have been developed allow the automated development of models from control tables. The analysis approach complements testing techniques and provides a systematic solution to the safety assessment of critical devices.

Acknowledgements. This work has been funded by: EPSRC research grant EP/G059063/1: CHI+MED (Computer–Human Interaction for Medical Devices). It has also been financed by the ERDF – European Regional Development Fund through the Operational Programme for Competitiveness and Internationalisation - COMPETE 2020 Programme, and by National Funds through the FCT – Fundação para a Ciência e a Tecnologia (Portuguese Foundation for Science and Technology) within project POCI-01-0145-FEDER-006961.

References

1. Abrial, J.-R.: Modeling in Event-B: System and Software Engineering. Cambridge University Press, New York (2010)
2. Atlee, J.M., Gannon, J.: State-based model checking of event-driven system requirements. IEEE Trans. Softw. Eng. **19**(1), 24–40 (1993)
3. Barnes, J., Chapman, R., Johnson, R., Everett, B., Cooper, D.: Engineering the tokeneer enclave protection software. In: IEEE International Symposium on Secure Software Engineering. IEEE (2006)
4. BSI: Medical device software - software life cycle processes. Technical report BS EN 62304:2006, British Standards Institution, CENELEC, Avenue Marnix 17, B-1000 Brussels (2008)
5. Campos, J.C., Harrison, M.D.: Systematic analysis of control panel interfaces using formal tools. In: Graham, T.C.N., Palanque, P. (eds.) DSV-IS 2008. LNCS, vol. 5136, pp. 72–85. Springer, Heidelberg (2008). doi:10.1007/978-3-540-70569-7_6
6. Cimatti, A., Clarke, E., Giunchiglia, E., Giunchiglia, F., Pistore, M., Roveri, M., Sebastiani, R., Tacchella, A.: NuSMV 2: an opensource tool for symbolic model checking. In: Brinksma, E., Larsen, K.G. (eds.) CAV 2002. LNCS, vol. 2404, pp. 359–364. Springer, Heidelberg (2002). doi:10.1007/3-540-45657-0_29
7. Clarke, E.M., Grumberg, O., Peled, D.A.: Model Checking. MIT Press, Cambridge (1999)
8. Freitas, L., Stabler, A.: Translation strategies for medical device control software. Technical report, Newcastle University, August 2015
9. Harrison, M.D., Masci, P., Campos, J.C., Curzon, P.: Demonstrating that medical devices satisfy user related safety requirements. In: Huhn, M., Williams, L. (eds.) FHIES 2014. LNCS, vol. 9062, pp. 113–128. Springer International Publishing, Cham (2017)
10. Heitmeyer, C., Kirby, J., Labaw, B., Bharadwaj, R.: SCR: a toolset for specifying and analyzing software requirements. In: Hu, A.J., Vardi, M.Y. (eds.) CAV 1998. LNCS, vol. 1427, pp. 526–531. Springer, Heidelberg (1998). doi:10.1007/BFb0028775
11. Holzmann, G.J.: Trends in software verification. In: Araki, K., Gnesi, S., Mandrioli, D. (eds.) FME 2003. LNCS, vol. 2805, pp. 40–50. Springer, Heidelberg (2003). doi:10.1007/978-3-540-45236-2_4
12. Kim, B., Ayoub, A., Sokolsky, O., Lee, I., Jones, P., Zhang, Y., Jetley, R.: Safety-assured development of the GPCA infusion pump software. In: Proceedings of the Ninth ACM International Conference on Embedded software, EMSOFT 2011, pp. 155–164. ACM, New York (2011)
13. Klein, G., Andronick, J., Elphinstone, K., Murray, T.C., Sewell, T., Kolanski, R., Heiser, G.: Comprehensive formal verification of an OS microkernel. ACM Trans. Comput. Syst. **32**(1), 2 (2014)

14. Masci, P., Ayoub, A., Curzon, P., Harrison, M.D., Lee, I., Sokolsky, O., Thimbleby, H.: Verification of interactive software for medical devices: PCA infusion pumps and FDA regulation as an example. In: Proceedings ACM Symposium Engineering Interactive Systems (EICS 2013), pp. 81–90. ACM Press (2013)

15. Monk, A.F., Curry, M., Wright, P.C.: Why industry doesn't use the wonderful notations we researchers have given them to reason about their designs. In: Gilmore, D.J., Winder, R.L., Detienne, F. (eds.) User-Centred Requirements For Software Engineering, pp. 185–189. Springer, Berlin, Heidelberg (1991)

16. US Food and Drug Administration: General principles of software validation: final guidance for industry and FDA staff. Technical report, Center for Devices and Radiological Health, January 2002. http://www.fda.gov/medicaldevices/deviceregulationandguidance

17. Yeganefard, S., Butler, M.: Structuring functional requirements of control systems to facilitate refinement-based formalisation. In: Proceedings of the 11th International Workshop on Automated Verification of Critical Systems (AVoCS 2011), vol. 46. Electronic Communications of the EASST (2011)

TOM: A Model-Based GUI Testing Framework

Miguel Pinto[1,2], Marcelo Gonçalves[1,2], Paolo Masci[1,2],
and José Creissac Campos[1,2(⊠)]

[1] HASLab, INESC TEC, Braga, Portugal
[2] Dep. Informática, Universidade do Minho, Braga, Portugal
`jose.campos@di.uminho.pt`

Abstract. Applying model-based testing to interactive systems enables the systematic testing of the system by automatically simulating user actions on the user interface. It reduces the cost of (expensive) user testing by identifying implementations errors without the involvement of human users, but raises a number of specific challenges, such as how to achieve good coverage of the actual use of the system during the testing process. This paper describes TOM, a model-based testing framework that uses a combination of tools and mutation testing techniques to maximize testing of user interface behaviors.

Keywords: Model-based testing · User interfaces · Tool support

1 Introduction

User interface testing is an important aspect of interactive computing systems development, and a range of techniques can be useful in this context. Analysis techniques based on user experiments are mostly concerned with assessing the quality from the users' perspective (e.g. satisfaction, reliability, learnability, efficiency – cf. the notion of usability [7]). They can be used to explore a limited number of scenarios, and do not allow developers to identify all potential user interface problems. Model-based verification tools provide an alternative perspective, and enable the exhaustive analysis of core usability aspects such as mode visibility and consistency of response to user actions (cf. [4]). However, usability properties proved over the models are "inherited" by the final system implementation only if the final system faithfully implements the models.

Model-based Testing (MBT) [18] is a technology that can help bridge this gap between model-based verification and a system's implementation. It is a black-box testing technique that compares the behavior of an implemented system (called SUT, System Under Test) with that prescribed by a model of the same system (the Oracle). One advantage of MBT is that it facilitates full automation of the testing process, from test case generation to test execution.

Several authors have explored a range of approaches for using MBT on user interfaces: based on reverse engineered models [1,6] or purpose built models [15] representing the UI behavior; using Oracles that capture the control dialogues

© Springer International Publishing AG 2017
J. Proença and M. Lumpe (Eds.): FACS 2017, LNCS 10487, pp. 155–161, 2017.
DOI: 10.1007/978-3-319-68034-7_9

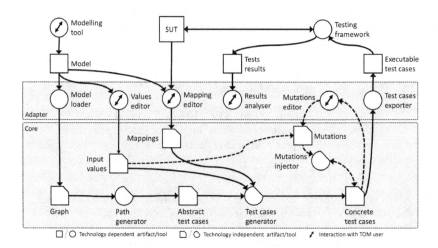

Fig. 1. TOM framework: conceptual architecture

implemented in the UI (e.g., to capture normative interactions between users and system [3,17]); or using predefined patterns to generate test cases based on given Oracles [12,13]. Different alternatives have also been explored for executing test cases: using code instrumentation, UI automation frameworks, or higher-level co-execution tools.

Memon was among the first to apply MBT to graphical user interfaces [11]. He developed the GUITAR [14] testing framework, which supports a variety of model-based testing techniques. The framework uses a reverse engineering process to generate a model of the SUT. One limitation of GUITAR and other similar tools (see [9] for a recent survey of similar tools) is that oracles focus on the SUT, making it harder to select test cases that are relevant from the user's perspective. In this work, we introduce TOM, a model-based testing framework that aims to address this gap by enabling automatic generation of user relevant test cases.

Contribution. The specific contributions of this paper are: (i) a presentation of the architecture and prototype implementation of the TOM framework; (ii) an example application of the framework to an existing Web application.

2   The TOM Framework

The framework adopts a modular approach to better support the exploration of different model-based testing techniques. It is divided into two layers (see Fig. 1): the Adapter Layer, and the Core Layer.

The Adapter Layer is the interface between the core of the framework, and the oracles and test automation frameworks. It includes a set of Model Loaders responsible for importing a UI model, and a set of Test Cases Exporters necessary for generating test cases. A number of other components support the user during the configuration process and while running the test cases: a Values Editor is provided to support editing of values to be used as inputs; a Mapping Editor links a state machine model of the UI to the graphical UI of the SUT; a Mutations Editor allows users to define the type of mutations to be introduced in the test cases; and a Results Analyzer presents test results.

The Core Layer uses a graph representation of the SUT to perform the generation of test cases. The generation process uses a directed graph produced by the Adapter Layer. Each node in the graph represents a dialogue unit in the interface (e.g. a modal window, or a page in a Web application), and contains information about the actual content of the dialogue unit and the validations checks to be performed over it. Edges represent changes to the interface in response to user actions (e.g. button clicks). A Path Generator component in the Core Layer generates Abstract test cases as paths over the directed graph. These paths represent normative usage scenarios of the system. These usages are specified in a way that is independent of any specific implementation, as they are expressed over the graph. They are converted into concrete test cases by a Test Cases Generator component in the Core Layer. This component uses two additional sources of information (provided by the Adapter Layer): a mapping between the state machine and the graphical UI of the SUT, and input values for specific UI widgets. Finally, a Mutations component generates additional test cases with the aim of achieving fault coverage. The considered fault classes are based on Reason's use error types [16] (slips, lapses and mistakes). Mutations are introduced in the normative usage scenarios, either randomly or according to user defined criteria, to check the impact of these use errors.

Prototype Implementation. We have implemented an Adapter Layer for Web applications[1] as a Google Chrome extension (see Fig. 2, left). The Adapter captures the user interaction with a Web page to create a first version of the model. It then supports editing the model (to add new states and transition not covered in the capture phase, define the values to be used and the validations to check), as well as the mapping between the final model and the graphical user interface. A companion component exports test cases to Selenium WebDriver, a tool to automate testing of web pages.

The directed graph representing the UI model is expressed in SCXML [19]. The main tags are: `<state>`, used to represent dialogue units; and `<transition>`, used to represent events. `<state>` tags have a type that defines the characteristics of the dialogue unit. An example state type is 'Form', which represents a modal window where a number of input fields must be input before the interaction can proceed. Validation checks are declared in the state using `<onentry>` and `<onexit>` tags, which are assessed when entering or leaving a state, respectively. Example validation checks include: `displayed?` (checks whether a given element is visible); `is_selected` (checks whether an element in a drop-down list or check-box is selected); `enabled?` (checks whether an element is enabled); `attribute` (checks the value of an attribute of an HTML element); and `regex` (checks whether an element contains a value that matches a regular expression). Transition tags can use a

---

[1] Available at http://gitlab.inesctec.pt/jccampos/ise-public-builds.

`<step>` attribute to decompose a logically atomic action into its constituent physical actions. Example transitions are `<select>` (the action of selecting an option in a drop-down menu); `<submit>` (the action of ending a dialogue unit) and `<error>` (events triggered in the case of errors).

The Path Generator module converts the SCXML file into a graph using the JGraphT Java library. JGraphT provides a number of traversal algorithms (from calculating the shortest path between two nodes using Dijkstra's algorithm to calculating all paths), which can be used on the graph to yield abstract test cases. Test case generation is controlled by defining a start and an end state, and upper bounds on the number of visits/traversals to nodes/edges on the graph.

The Mutation component simulates use errors as follows: Slip errors are a change of the order of execution of normative user actions; Lapses are an elimination of an action; and Mistakes are a change of a value in a form. While these formulations are rather simple, they are sufficient for assessing the utility of the mutation approach used in the TOM framework.

3   Demonstrative Example

This section presents an example use of TOM to test OntoWorks, a Web application supporting online editing and querying of ontologies (see Fig. 2, right). Features include: visualization and execution of queries; loading, removing, editing and visualization of ontologies; association of queries to ontologies.

Building the Model. The TOM Editor was used to aid build the system model. The final model consisted of 15 states and 24 transitions. A screen-shot of the editor while building the model is in Fig. 2: it shows the "home" state, which includes two transitions and a login form. Transitions for the home state lead to states "About us" and "Sign up". Modeling the OntoWorks system in

Fig. 2. TOM Web editor (left) and OntoWorks (right)

the TOM Editor took about 5 h, a significant reduction compared to a previous manual modeling effort which took 27 h. The bottleneck of the manual modeling effort was the cost of mapping each element of the state machine to the web page. In the current model of the system there are 102 such mappings, mostly obtained automatically. After constructing the model, validation checks were added to the states. This was manually done with support from the tool (e.g., to identify elements in the page). In total, 61 validation checks were defined, 57 when entering the web page and 4 when leaving. The "displayed?" validation was the most used (27 times). Three user-defined mutations were configured, which are specifically targeted at Web applications: pressing the back button; refreshing the page; double-clicking a user interface element.

Generation of Test Cases. The predefined *AllDirectedPaths* algorithm from JGraphT was used to traverse the graph. To ensure that the algorithm traverses all nodes and edges at least once, the following constraints were defined: the number of visits to nodes is at most 1, and the number of visits to edges is at most 2. A total of 273 paths were generated, which are automatically converted into concrete test cases for OntoWorks using the exporter for Selenium WebDriver. Starting from these paths, TOM generated 2,730 additional test cases based on the identified mutation strategies. The test cases were run in Google Chrome. In case of error, a screen-shot of the web page was saved.

Results. A total of 935 step failures were obtained during the execution of the tests. The tests highlighted a latent implementation problem in the OntoWorks application (a same identifier was used twice in the same page, when it should have been unique), and gave us important insights on how to improve the generation and execution of test cases. These aspects are now discussed.

Positive and Negative Tests. Careful analysis of the test results revealed that several test failures were actually desired behavior of the system. For example, swapping the order of input in the user name and password fields prevents the login process. This indicates that we need to introduce the notions of "positive" and "negative" tests (i.e., tests that should be considered as passed if the interaction succeeds vs. tests that should be considered as passed if the interaction fails). Whether it will be possible to automatically categorize mutated tests into positive/negative tests needs to be explored.

Cascading Errors. While our main goal was to detect as many errors as possible in a single test, we observed that a failed step in a test case tends to propagate to the remainder steps of the test case, causing the subsequent steps to fail too. The three steps that failed in the non-mutated tests category are an example of this. The problem happens in the login form: the user name input field is being reported as not visible. This error occurs because Selenium is attempting to populate a form field that is hidden at runtime. Manual inspection of the form, however, showed the field visible on the form. After inspection of the code it was realized that there were two elements with the same identifier in the same page, when they should have been unique. Therefore the failure in the test highlighted a latent implementation error. Subsequent failures in the test where due to the fact that the login process had failed, and not because of problems with the SUT. A redesign of the test case generation module is currently under way, that flags a test as failed as soon as a step in the sequence fails.

4 Conclusion

This paper described the TOM framework, which aims at supporting the model-based testing of interactive computing system. The architecture and main functionalities of the framework were introduced, including all steps necessary for the creation of the user interface model and the generation and execution of test cases. A layer supporting MBT of Web application was also developed and an example illustrating its application was described. The example makes use of TOM Editor, a model editor for web applications. The example application allowed us to identify a number of lines for future work: from the need to better consider the role of mutations in the test case generation process, to fine-tuning the executable test cases generation process. The definition of coverage criteria is also a topic for future work. The framework was developed in a modular and structured way, allowing the addition of new features. We plan to explore further the integration with task modeling tool-sets such as HAMSTERS [2], taking advantage of information task models might have about use error to improve the test cases generation and mutation processes (see [5]). Other extensions under development include interface modules for Alloy [8] and the PVSio-web [10] prototyping tool.

Acknowledgements. Work financed by the ERDF (European Regional Development Fund) through the COMPETE 2020 Programme, and by National Funds through the Portuguese funding agency, FCT - Fundação para a Ciência e a Tecnologia, within project POCI-01-0145-FEDER-016826.

References

1. Amalfitano, D., Fasolino, A.R., Tramontana, P., Ta, B.D., Memon, A.M.: MobiGUITAR: automated model-based testing of mobile apps. IEEE Softw. **32**(5), 53–59 (2015)
2. Barboni, E., Ladry, J.-F., Navarre, D., Palanque, P., Winckler, M.: Beyond modelling: an integrated environment supporting co-execution of tasks and systems models. In: Proceedings of EICS 2010, pp. 165–174. ACM (2010)
3. Barbosa, A., Paiva, A.C., Campos, J.C.: Test case generation from mutated task models. In: Proceedings of EICS 2011, pp. 175–184. ACM (2011)
4. Campos, J.C., Harrison, M.D.: Interaction engineering using the IVY tool. In: Proceedings of EICS 2009, pp. 35–44. ACM, New York (2009)
5. Campos, J.C., Fayollas, C., Martinie, C., Navarre, D., Palanque, P., Pinto, M.: Systematic automation of scenario-based testing of user interfaces. In: Proceedings of EICS 2016, pp. 138–148. ACM (2016)
6. Gimblett, A., Thimbleby, H.: User interface model discovery: towards a generic approach. In: Proceedings of EICS 2010, pp. 145–154. ACM (2010)

7. International Organization for Standardization: ISO 9241–11: ergonomic require-ments for office work with visual display terminals (VDTs) - part 11: guidance on usability. International Organization for Standardization **1998**(2), 28 (1998)

8. Jackson, D., Abstractions, S.: Logic, Language, and Analysis. The MIT Press, Cambridge (2006)

9. Lelli, V., Blouin, A., Baudry, B., Coulon, F.: On model-based testing advanced GUIs. In: Proceedings of 2015 IEEE 8th International Conference on Software Test-ing, Verification and Validation Workshops (ICSTW), 11th Workshop on Advances in Model Based Testing (A-MOST). IEEE (2015)

10. Masci, P., Oladimeji, P., Zhang, Y., Jones, P., Curzon, P., Thimbleby, H.: PVSio-web 2.0: joining PVS to HCI. In: Kroening, D., Păsăreanu, C.S. (eds.) CAV 2015. LNCS, vol. 9206, pp. 470–478. Springer, Cham (2015). doi:10.1007/978-3-319-21690-4_30

11. Memon, A.M.: A comprehensive framework for testing graphical user interfaces. Ph.D. thesis, University of Pittsburgh (2001)

12. Moreira, R., Paiva, A.C.: PBGT Tool: an integrated modeling and testing envi-ronment for pattern-based GUI testing. In: Proceedings of ASE 2014, pp. 863–866. ACM (2014)

13. Morgado, I.C., Paiva, A.C.: The iMPAcT tool: testing ui patterns on mobile appli-cations. In: Proceedings of ASE 2015, pp. 876–881 (2015)

14. Nguyen, B., Robbins, B., Banerjee, I., Memon, A.: GUITAR: an innovative tool for automated testing of GUI-driven software. Autom. Softw. Eng. **21**(1), 65–105 (2014)

15. Paiva, A.C.: Automated specification-based testing of graphical user interfaces. Ph.D. thesis, Engineering Faculty of Porto University, Department of Electrical and Computer Engineering (2007)

16. Reason, J.: Human Error. Cambridge University Press, New York (1990)

17. Silva, J.L., Campos, J.C., Paiva, A.C.: Model-based user interface testing with Spec Explorer and ConcurTaskTrees. Electron. Notes Theoret. Comput. Sci. **208**, 77–93 (2008)

18. Utting, M., Legeard, B., Testing, P.M.-B.: A Tools Approach. Morgan Kaufmann Publishers Inc., Burlington (2007)

19. W3C: State Chart XML (SCXML): State Machine Notation for Control Abstrac-tion. W3C Recommendation, September 2015

Correctness-by-Learning of Infinite-State Component-Based Systems

Haitham Bou-Ammar, Mohamad Jaber[(✉)], and Mohamad Nassar

American University of Beirut, Beirut, Lebanon
{hb71,mj54,mn115}@aub.edu.lb

Abstract. We introduce a novel framework for runtime enforcement of safe executions in component-based systems with multi-party interactions modeled using BIP. Our technique frames runtime enforcement as a sequential decision making problem and presents two alternatives for learning optimal strategies that ensure fairness between correct traces. We target both finite and infinite state-spaces. In the finite case, we guarantee that the system avoids bad-states by casting the learning process as a one of determining a fixed point solution that converges to the optimal strategy. Though successful, this technique fails to generalize to the infinite case due to need for building a dictionary, which quantifies the performance of each state-interaction pair. As such, we further contribute by generalizing our framework to support the infinite setting. Here, we adapt ideas from function approximators and machine learning to encode each state-interaction pairs' performance. In essence, we autonomously learn to abstract similar performing states in a relevant continuous space through the usage of deep learning. We assess our method empirically by presenting a fully implemented tool, so called RERL. Particularly, we use RERL to: (1) enforce deadlock freedom on a dining philosophers benchmark, and (2) allow for pair-wise synchronized robots to autonomously achieve consensus within a cooperative multi-agent setting.

1 Introduction

Building correct and efficient software systems in a timely manner is still a very challenging task despite the existence of a plethora of techniques and methods. For instance, correctness can be ensured using static analysis such as model checking [5,6,19] or dynamic analysis such as runtime verification [8]. Static analysis mainly suffers from state-space explosion whereas dynamic analysis suffers from its accuracy (reachability cover) and efficiency. To overcome the problem of state-space explosion, abstraction techniques [9] can be used, however, it has the effect of false negatives. Moreover, software synthesis, correct-by-design, was introduced to automatically generate implementation from high-level designs. However, correct-by-design was proven to be NP-hard [17] in some cases and undecidabile [18] in some main classical automatic synthesis problems. On the other hand, developing implementations that are compliant with their specifications require a careful attention from designers and developers.

© Springer International Publishing AG 2017
J. Proença and M. Lumpe (Eds.): FACS 2017, LNCS 10487, pp. 162–178, 2017.
DOI: 10.1007/978-3-319-68034-7_10

Can we relax the development process by giving the option to over-approximate the behaviors of the implementations, i.e., introduce additional behaviors w.r.t. the given specification? This relaxation would drastically simplify the development process, though it may introduce errors.

In this paper, we introduce a new runtime enforcement technique that takes a software system with extra behaviors (w.r.t. a specification) and uses static and dynamic techniques with the help of machine learning to synthesize more accurate and precise behavior, i.e., remove the extra ones w.r.t. the given specification. We apply our method to component-based systems with multi-party interactions modeled using BIP [1]. BIP (Behavior, Interaction and Priority) allows to build complex systems by coordinating the behavior of atomic components. BIP has a rigorous operational semantics: the behavior of a composite component is formally described as the composition of the behaviors of its atomic components. From a given state of the components, the operational semantics define the next allowed interactions and their corresponding next states. D-Finder [2] is used to verify the correctness of BIP systems. While D-Finder uses compositional and abstraction techniques, it suffers from state-space explosion and producing false negatives. Dynamic analysis techniques [4,7] are also proposed for BIP systems. However, they only support a limited level of recovery. A detailed comparison is discussed in the related work.

Our technique frames runtime enforcement as a sequential decision making problem and presents two alternatives for learning optimal strategies that ensure fairness between correct traces. That is, the policy should not avoid correct traces from execution. We target both finite and infinite state-spaces. In the finite case, we guarantee that the system avoids bad-states by casting the learning process as a one of determining a fixed point solution that converges to the optimal strategy. Though successful, this technique fails to generalize to the infinite case due to need for building a dictionary, which quantifies the performance of each state-interaction pair, i.e., reduce the non-determinism by only allowing interactions leading to states that conform with the specifications. As such, we further contribute by generalizing our framework to support the infinite setting. Here, we adapt ideas from function approximators and machine learning to encode each state-interaction pairs' performance. In essence, we autonomously learn to abstract similar performing states in a relevant continuous space through the usage of deep learning. We assess our method empirically by presenting a fully implemented version called RERL. Particularly, we use RERL to: (1) enforce deadlock freedom on a dining philosophers benchmark, and (2) allow for pair-wise synchronized robots to autonomously achieve a consensus within a cooperative multi-agent setting.

The remainder of this paper is structured as follows. Section 2 discusses related work. Section 3 recall the necessary concepts of the BIP framework. Section 4 presents our main contribution, a runtime enforcement framework for component-based systems (finite and infinite state-space) using machine learning. Section 5 describes RERL, a full implementation of our framework and its evaluation using two benchmarks. Section 6 draws some conclusions and perspectives.

2   Related Work

Runtime enforcement of component-based systems has been introduced in [4] to ensure the correct runtime behavior (w.r.t. a formal specification) of a system. The authors define series of transformations to instrument a component-based system described in the BIP framework. The instrumented system allows to observe and avoid any error in the behavior of the system. The proposed method was fully implemented in RE-BIP. Although, contrarily to our method, the proposed method is sound (i.e., it always avoids bad states), it mainly suffers from two limitations. First, it only considers a 1-step recovery. That is, if the system enters a correct state from which all the reachable states are bad states, the method fails. Second, the instrumented system introduces a huge overhead w.r.t. original behavior. This overhead would be drastically increased to support more than 1-step recovery.

In [15,16], the authors introduced a predictive runtime enforcement framework that allows to build an enforcement monitor with or without a-priori knowledge of the system. The enforcement monitor ensures that the system complies with a certain property, by delaying or modifying events. The proposed method is theoretical and cannot be applied to real software systems as delaying or modifying events would require an infinite memory and also is not practical in software systems.

In [10], the authors proposed a game-theoretic method for synthesizing control strategies to maximize the resilience of software systems. The method allows the system to not take transition leading to bad states using game-theoretic method. Consequently, similar to RE-BIP, the proposed approach only allows a 1-step recovery. In other words, they need to do a back propagation from the bad states to re-label all good states as bad states when all their corresponding traces would lead to bad states, which is not feasible in case of infinite-state system.

Recent work [11,13,14] establishes techniques to synthesize code using genetic programming. In particular, the method randomly generates an initial population of programs based on a given configuration and then they apply mutation functions to optimize a given fitness function (w.r.t. specification). Nonetheless, the method was applied to communication protocols without reporting success rates. Moreover, deep learning is much more expressive than genetic programming, which failed to learn complex structures. Moreover, it is not clear how to automatically derive a fitness function from a given specification.

3   Behavior, Interaction and Priority (BIP)

We recall the necessary concepts of the BIP framework [1]. BIP allows to construct systems by superposing three layers of design: Behavior, Interaction, and Priority. The *behavior* layer consists of a set of atomic components represented by transition systems. The *interaction* layer provides the collaboration between components. Interactions are described using sets of ports. The *priority* layer is used to specify scheduling policies applied to the interaction layer, given by a strict partial order on interactions.

3.1 Atomic Components

We define *atomic components* as transition systems with a set of ports labeling individual transitions. These ports are used for communication between different components.

Definition 1 (Atomic Component). *An* atomic component B *is a labeled transition system represented by a triple* $(Q, P, \rightarrow)$ *where Q is a set of states, P is a set of communication ports, $\rightarrow \subseteq Q \times P \times Q$ is a set of possible transitions, each labeled by some port.*

For any pair of states $q, q' \in Q$ and a port $p \in P$, we write $q \xrightarrow{p} q'$, iff $(q, p, q') \in \rightarrow$. When the communication port is irrelevant, we simply write $q \rightarrow q'$. Similarly, $q \xrightarrow{p}$ means that there exists $q' \in Q$ such that $q \xrightarrow{p} q'$. In this case, we say that p is *enabled* in state q.

In practice, atomic components are extended with variables. Each variable may be bound to a port and modified through interactions involving this port. We also associate a guard and an update function (i.e., action) to each transition. A guard is a predicate on variables that must be true to allow the execution of the transition. An update function is a local computation triggered by the transition that modifies the variables.

Figure 1(a) shows an atomic component P that corresponds to the behavior of a philosopher in the dining-philosopher problem, where $Q = \{e, h\}$ denotes eating and hungry, $P = \{rel, get\}$ denotes releasing and getting of forks, and $\rightarrow = \{e \xrightarrow{rel} h, h \xrightarrow{get} e\}$.

3.2 Composition Component

For a given system built from a set of n atomic components $\{B_i = (Q_i, P_i, \rightarrow_i)\}_{i=1}^{n}$, we assume that their respective sets of ports are pairwise disjoint, i.e., for any two $i \neq j$ from $\{1..n\}$, we have $P_i \cap P_j = \emptyset$. We can therefore define the set $P = \bigcup_{i=1}^{n} P_i$ of all ports in the system. An *interaction* is a set $a \subseteq P$ of ports. When we write $a = \{p_i\}_{i \in I}$, we suppose that for $i \in I$, $p_i \in P_i$, where $I \subseteq \{1..n\}$.

Similar to atomic components, BIP extends interactions by associating a guard and a transfer function to each of them. Both the guard and the function are defined over the variables that are bound to the ports of the interaction. The guard must be true to allow the interaction. When the interaction takes place, the associated transfer function is called and modifies the variables.

Definition 2 (Composite Component). *A* composite component *(or simply* component*) is defined by a composition operator parameterized by a set of interactions* $\Gamma \subseteq 2^P$. $B \stackrel{def}{=} \Gamma(B_1, \ldots, B_n)$, *is a transition system* $(Q, \Gamma, \rightarrow)$, *where* $Q = \bigotimes_{i=1}^{n} Q_i$ *and $\rightarrow$ is the least set of transitions satisfying the following rule:*

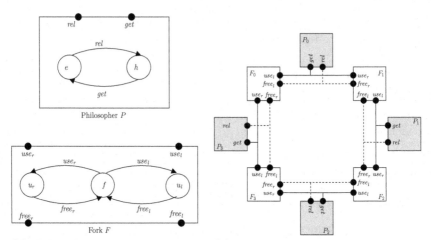

(a) Philosopher P and fork F atomic components.

(b) Dining philosophers composite component with four philosophers.

Fig. 1. Dining philosophers.

$$\frac{a = \{p_i\}_{i \in I} \in \Gamma \qquad \forall i \in I : q_i \xrightarrow{p_i}_i q'_i \qquad \forall i \notin I : q_i = q'_i}{q = (q_1, \ldots, q_n) \xrightarrow{a} q' = (q'_1, \ldots, q'_n)}$$

The inference rule says that a composite component $B = \Gamma(B_1, \ldots, B_n)$ can execute an interaction $a \in \Gamma$, iff for each port $p_i \in a$, the corresponding atomic component B_i can execute a transition labeled with p_i; the states of components that do not participate in the interaction stay unchanged.

Figure 1(b) illustrates a composite component $\Gamma(P_0, P_1, P_2, P_3, F_0, F_1, F_2, F_3)$, where each P_i (resp. F_i) is identical to component P (resp. F) in Fig. 1(a) and $\Gamma = \Gamma_{get} \cup \Gamma_{rel}$, where $\Gamma_{get} = \bigcup_{i=0}^{3} \{P_i.get, F_i.use_l, F_{(i+1)\%4}.use_r\}$ and $\Gamma_{rel} = \bigcup_{i=0}^{3} \{P_i.rel, F_i.free_l, F_{(i+1)\%4}.free_r\}$.

Notice that several distinct interactions can be enabled at the same time, thus introducing non-determinism in the product behavior. One can add priorities to reduce non-determinism. In this case, one of the interactions with the highest priority is chosen non-deterministically.

Definition 3 (Priority). *Let $C = (Q, \Gamma, \rightarrow)$ be the behavior of the composite component $\Gamma(\{B_1, \ldots, B_n\})$. A priority model $\prec$ is a strict partial order on the set of interactions Γ. Given a priority model $\prec$, we abbreviate $(a, a') \in \prec$ by $a \prec a'$. Adding the priority model $\prec$ over $\Gamma(\{B_1, \ldots, B_n\})$ defines a new composite component $B = \prec(\Gamma(\{B_1, \ldots, B_n\}))$ noted $\mathtt{prio}(C)$ and whose behavior is defined by $(Q, \Gamma, \rightarrow_\prec)$, where $\rightarrow_\prec$ is the least set of transitions satisfying the following rule:*

$$\frac{q \xrightarrow{a} q' \qquad \neg(\exists a' \in \Gamma, \exists q'' \in Q : a \prec a' \wedge q \xrightarrow{a'} q'')}{q \xrightarrow{a}_\prec q'}$$

An interaction a is enabled in $\mathtt{prio}(C)$ whenever a is enabled in C and a is maximal according to $\mathtt{prio}$ among the active interactions in C.

BIP provides both centralized and distributed implementations. In the centralized implementation, a centralized engine guarantees to execute only one interaction at a time, and thus conforms to the operational semantics of the BIP. The main loop of the BIP engine consists of the following steps: (1) Each atomic component sends to the engine its current location; (2) The engine enumerates the list of interactions in the system, selects the enabled ones based on the current location of the atomic components and eliminates the ones with low priority; (3) The engine non-deterministically selects an interaction out of the enabled interactions; (4) Finally, the engine notifies the corresponding components and schedules their transitions for execution.

Alternatively, BIP allows the generation of distributed implementations [3] where non-conflicting interactions can be simultaneously executed.

Definition 4 (BIP system). *A BIP system is a tuple* $(B, \boldsymbol{q_0})$, *where* $\boldsymbol{q_0}$ *is the initial state with* $\boldsymbol{q_0} \in \bigotimes_{i=1}^{n} Q_i$ *being the tuple of initial states of atomic components.*

For the rest of the paper, we fix an arbitrary BIP-system $(B, \boldsymbol{q_0})$, where $B = \prec(\Gamma(\{B_1, \ldots, B_n\}))$ with semantics $C = (Q, \Gamma, \rightarrow)$.

We abstract the execution of a BIP system as a trace.

Definition 5 (BIP trace). *A BIP trace* $\rho = (\boldsymbol{q_0} \cdot a_0 \cdot \boldsymbol{q_1} \cdot a_1 \cdots \boldsymbol{q_{i-1}} \cdot a_{i-1} \cdot \boldsymbol{q_i})$ *is an alternating sequence of states of* Q *and interactions in* Γ; *where* $\boldsymbol{q_k} \xrightarrow{a_k} \boldsymbol{q_{k+1}} \in \rightarrow$, *for* $k \in [0, i-1]$.

Given a trace $\rho = (\boldsymbol{q_0} \cdot a_0 \cdot \boldsymbol{q_1} \cdot a_1 \cdots \boldsymbol{q_{i-1}} \cdot a_{i-1} \cdot \boldsymbol{q_i})$, ρ^{q_i} (resp. ρ_i^a) denotes the ith state (resp. interaction) of the trace, i.e., $\boldsymbol{q_i}$ (resp. a_i). Also, $\boldsymbol{\rho}(C)$ denotes the set of all the traces of an LTS C.

4 Problem Definition and Methodology

We frame the problem of run time enforcement as a sequential decision making (SDM) one, by which the BIP engine has to be guided to select the set of interactions over extended execution traces that maximize a cumulative return. We formalize SDMs as the following five-tuple $\left\langle Q, \tilde{Q}, \Gamma, \rightarrow, R_+, R_-, \gamma \right\rangle$. Here, Q represents the set of all possible states, $\tilde{Q} \subseteq Q$ the set of "bad" states that need to be avoided, Γ the set of allowed interactions, and $\rightarrow$ represents the transition model. R_+ and R_- are two positive and negative scalar parameters, which allow us to define the reward function quantifying the selection of the engine. Clearly, the engine gets rewarded when in a state $\boldsymbol{q} \notin \tilde{Q}$, while penalized if $\boldsymbol{q} \in \tilde{Q}$. Using this intuition, one can define a reward function of the states written as:

$$\mathcal{R}(\boldsymbol{q}) = \begin{cases} R_+ & : \boldsymbol{q} \notin \tilde{Q} \\ R_- & : \boldsymbol{q} \in \tilde{Q}. \end{cases}$$

Given the above reward definition, we finally introduce $\gamma \in [0,1)$ to denote the discount factor specifying the degree to which rewards are discounted over time as the engine interacts with each of the components.

At each time step t, the engine observes a state $q_t \in Q$ and must choose an interaction $a_t \in \mathcal{A}_{q_t} \subseteq \Gamma$, transitioning it to a new state $q_t \xrightarrow{a_t} q_{t+1}$ as given by $\rightarrow$ and yielding a reward $\mathcal{R}(q_{t+1})$, where $\mathcal{A}_{q_t}$ denotes all enabled interactions from state q_t, i.e., $\mathcal{A}_{q_t} = \{a \mid \exists q' : q_t \xrightarrow{a} q' \in \rightarrow\}$. We filter the choice of the allowed interactions, i.e., $\mathcal{A}_{q_t}$, at each time-step by an interaction-selection rule, which we refer to as the policy π. We extend the sequential decision making literature by defining policies that map between the set of states, Q, and any combination of the allowed interactions, i.e., $\pi : Q \rightarrow 2^{\Gamma}$, where for all $q \in Q : \pi(q) \subseteq \mathcal{A}_q$. Consequently, the new behavior of the composite component, guided by the policy π, is defined by $C_\pi = (Q, \Gamma, \rightarrow_\pi)$, where $\rightarrow_\pi$ is the least set of transitions satisfying the following rule:

$$\frac{q \xrightarrow{a} q' \qquad a \in \pi(q)}{q \xrightarrow{a}_\pi q'}$$

The goal now is to find an optimal policy $\pi^\star$ that maximizes the *expected* total sum of the rewards it receives in the long run, while starting from an initial state $q_0 \in Q$. We will evaluate the performance of a policy π by: $\texttt{eval}(\pi|q_0) = \mathbb{E}_{\rho(C_\pi)}\left[\sum_{t=0}^{T} \gamma^t \mathcal{R}(q_{t+1})\right]$, where $\mathbb{E}_{\rho(C_\pi)}$ denotes the expectation under all the sets of all the allowed (by the policy π) possible traces, and T is the length of the trace. Notice that we index the value of the state by the policy π to explicitly reflect the dependency of the value on the policy being followed from a state q_t. Interestingly, the definition of the evaluator asserts that the value of a state q_t is the expected instantaneous reward plus the expected discounted value of the next state. Clearly, we are interested in determining the optimal policy $\pi^\star$, which upon its usage yields maximized values for any $q_t \in Q$. As such our goal is to determine a policy π that solves: $\pi^\star \equiv \max_\pi \texttt{eval}(\pi|q_0)$.

Finally, being in a state q, we quantify the performance of the state-interaction pairs using the function $\mathbb{P} : Q \times \Gamma \rightarrow \mathbb{R}$. Given such a performance measure $\mathbb{P}$, the engine can follow the policy π, defined as follows:

$$\pi(q) = \arg\max_a\{\mathbb{P}(q,a) \mid a \in \mathcal{A}(q)\}. \tag{1}$$

In other words, given a state q, policy π selects the enabled interaction that has maximum evaluation from that state. Clearly, an interaction must have a maximum evaluation when it is guaranteed that its execution will not lead to a bad state.

In what comes next, we define two methods capable of computing such performance measures, i.e., $\mathbb{P}$, (consequently policies) in finite as well as infinite state-space.

4.1   Finite State-Space - Value Iteration

Due to the number of possible policies at each time step, it is a challenge to compute the value for all possible options. Instead, we propose the application of a dynamic programming algorithm known as value iteration, summarized in Algorithm 1 to find the optimal policy efficiently.

In essence, Algorithm 1 is iteratively updating the performance measures of all the state-interaction pairs (until either (1) we reach a predefined bound, i.e., bound; or (2) the values are within a predefined ϵ), by choosing these interactions that maximize the instantaneous rewards, as well as the future information encoded through $V(q')$. Contrary to state-space-exploration algorithms, our method remedies the need to construct the full labeled transition system as we only require the knowledge of the successor state from a given state-interaction pair with no regard to its reachability properties. Notice also that though line 4 in Algorithm 1 requires a loop over all states computational time can be highly reduced by following a sampling-based procedure, where fractions of the state-space are considered. Notice, however, the successfulness of the attained policy comes hand-in-hand with the fraction of the state space sampled. In other words, the higher the fraction, the closer to optimality is the policy and vice versa.

Algorithm 1. Value Iteration Finite State Space

1: **Input:** Initialization of $V(q)$ for all $q \in Q$, precision parameter ϵ
2: **error** $= \epsilon + 1$
3: **while** k $<$ bound $\wedge$ **error** $\geq \epsilon$ **do**
4:     **for each** $q \in Q$ **do**
5:         **for each** $a \in \mathcal{A}_q$ **do**
6:             tmp $= \mathcal{R}(q') + \gamma V(q')$, where $q \xrightarrow{a} q'$
7:             **error** $= \max(\text{error}, |\text{tmp} - \mathbb{P}(q, a)|)$
8:             $\mathbb{P}(q, a) = $ tmp
9:         **end for**
10:         $V(q) = \max_{a \in \mathcal{A}_q} \mathbb{P}(q, a)$
11:     **end for**
12:     k $=$ k $+ 1$
13: **end while**

4.2   Infinite State-Space - Deep Value Iteration

The methodology detailed so-far suffers when considering infinite state-spaces as it requires exact representation of performance measures and policies. In general, an exact representation can only be achieved by storing distinct estimates of the return for every state-interaction pair. When states are continuous (i.e., components with variables or large state-space), such exact representations are no longer possible and performance measures need to be represented approximately.

Approximation in the continuous setting is not only a problem of representation. Two additional types of approximation are needed. Firstly, sample-based approximation is necessary in any of these frameworks. Secondly, the algorithm must repeatedly solve a difficult minimization problem. To clarify, consider Algorithm 1, where every iteration necessitates a loop over *every state-interaction pair*. When state space contains an infinite number of elements, it is impossible to loop over all pairs in finite time. Instead, a sample-based update that only considers a finite number of such pairs has to be used.

In this section, our goal is to develop an algorithm capable of avoiding the problems above. This ultimately leads us to a method for run-time enforcement operating in continuous state spaces. To commence, we introduce a function approximator, encoded through a neural network (NN), to represent a good approximation of performance measures of all state-interaction pairs. The goal of this approximator is to *autonomously generalize* over the state-space, such that similarly behaving states cluster together. Before commencing with our algorithm, we next introduce a concise introduction to NNs, accompanied with its generalization to the deep setting.

4.3   Neural Networks (NNs)

In an artificial NN, a neuron is a logistic unit, which is fed inputs through input wires. This unit can perform computations resulting in outputs that are transmitted through the output wires.

An artificial NN is simply a set of these logistic units strung together as shown in Fig. 2. Each two layers are connected together using weight parameters. As such, the NN in Fig. 2 possesses two weighting matrices, $\boldsymbol{\Theta}^{(1)}$ and $\boldsymbol{\Theta}^{(2)}$. Here, we used $\boldsymbol{\Theta}^{(l)}$ to denote the weights connecting layers l and $l+1$.

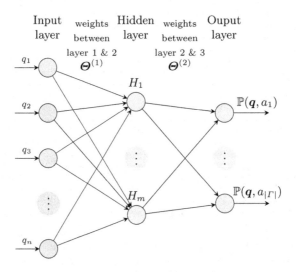

Fig. 2. A high-level depiction of an artificial NN.

Definitely, the dimensionality of $\boldsymbol{\Theta}^{(l)}$ depends on the number of units in each of the two layers[1].

For example, in our case, the dimension of the input layer is equal to the number of components (each input receives the current state of a component), and the dimension of the output layer is equal to the number of interactions. The number of hidden layers and the number of neurons per hidden layer can be configured depending on the functions to be learnt.

Feed Forward. Given the notation introduced above, we are now ready to discuss the computations that are performed by a NN. Intuitively, between every two layers the inputs from the previous layer are, first, linearly (through the weight matrices) propagated forward and then nonlinearly transformed (through the sigmoids) to produce an output on the successor layer. Recursing this process, which we refer to as forward propagation, over the total layers of the network will produce an output on the final layer L.

Training & Backward Propagation. Having described feed forward propagation, the next step is to detail the strategy by which NNs determine the model parameters (i.e., the $\boldsymbol{\Theta}^{(l)}$ matrices – denoted by $\boldsymbol{\Theta}$, i.e., $\boldsymbol{\Theta} = \{\boldsymbol{\Theta}^{(1)}, \ldots, \boldsymbol{\Theta}^{(L)}\}$). In standard regression or classification problems, back-propagation is the algorithm adopted. Given an input data point, back-propagation commences as follows. First, forward propagation is executed and the network is made to output a value. This value is then compared to the real output from the data set producing an error. This error is then propagated backwards to every other layer and used to update connecting weights. Such updates typically involve gradient-based methods (e.g., stochastic gradients).

Unfortunately, the direct application of NNs in our context is challenging since the performance measures $\mathbb{P}$ has to build, through sampling, a *labeled* data set (with states being inputs and state-interaction values as outputs) to train on. The goal now is to determine at compile-time a good approximation of $\mathbb{P}$ through exploring an infinite state-space.

4.4 Deep Value Iteration – Infinite State Space

In Algorithm 2, we present a solution for approximating the performance measures $\mathbb{P}_{\boldsymbol{\Theta}}$[2] of all the state-interaction pairs in case of infinite state-space.

In particular, we use an NN that takes a BIP state as input, encoded as a vector of size n, where n is the number of atomic components (i.e., the ith input encodes the local state of atomic component B_i). The output of the NN encodes the performance measures $\mathbb{P}$ for each interaction. As such, the ith output of the NN encodes the safety of executing interaction a_i.

On a high-level, the algorithm operates in two loops. The first is episode-based, while the second runs for a horizon T. At each episode, the goal is to collect relevant labeled data, encoding a trace of the system, to improve the

---

[1] In practice, a bias term is added to increase the expressiveness of the functions learnt by the NN.

[2] Note that $\mathbb{P}$ is indexed by $\boldsymbol{\Theta}$ as its output depends on $\boldsymbol{\Theta}$.

Algorithm 2. Deep-Value Iteration Infinite State Space

1: Initialize replay memory $\mathcal{D}$ to capacity N, and the NN weights randomly, K
2: **for** episode $= 1$ to M **do**
3:    Set initial state to $\boldsymbol{q_0}$
4:    **for** $t = 1$ to T **do**
5:       With some probability ϵ select a random interaction a_t
6:       With a probability $1 - \epsilon$ select interaction $a_t = \arg\max_{a \in \mathcal{A}_{q_t}} \mathbb{P}_{\Theta}(\boldsymbol{q_t}, a)$
7:       Execute interaction a_t and observe reward, r_{t+1}, and successor state $\boldsymbol{q_{t+1}}$
8:       Store transition $(\boldsymbol{q_t}, a_t, r_{t+1}, \boldsymbol{q_{t+1}})$ on replay memory $\mathcal{D}$
9:       Sample random minibatch of transitions $(\boldsymbol{q_j}, a_j, r_{j+1}, \boldsymbol{q_{j+1}})$ of size N_2 from $\mathcal{D}$ and create output label by

$$y_j = \begin{cases} r_{j+1} & \text{if } \boldsymbol{q_{j+1}} \text{ is a bad state} \\ r_{j+1} + \gamma \max_{a \in \mathcal{A}_{q_{j+1}}} \mathbb{P}_{\Theta^-}(\boldsymbol{q_{j+1}}, a) & \text{if } \boldsymbol{q_{j+1}} \text{ is a correct state} \end{cases}$$

10:   **end for**
11:   Retrain network on the N_2 data points with y_j being the labels.
12:   Update $\boldsymbol{\Theta^-}$ to $\boldsymbol{\Theta}$ every K episodes.
13: **end for**

---

approximation – encoded through the NN – of the performance measure, as summarized in lines 5–10 in the algorithm.

A trace is selected as follows. First, the algorithm selects an allowed inter-action either randomly (line 5) with a probability ϵ (i.e., exploration) or by exploiting (line 6) the current estimate of the performance measure. In other words, given the current state $\boldsymbol{q}$, forward propagation is first executed to pro-duce $\mathbb{P}_{\Theta}(\boldsymbol{q}, a_i)$. As such, the enabled interaction that has a maximum perfor-mance measure is selected, i.e., $\arg\max_{a \in \mathcal{A}_q} \mathbb{P}_{\Theta}(\boldsymbol{q}, a)$. Next, the engine exe-cutes the interaction and stores both the dynamical transition and its usefulness (i.e., reward) in a replay memory data set, $\mathcal{D}$. We use a technique known as experience replay [12] where we store the transitions executed at each step, $(\boldsymbol{q_t}, a_t, r_{t+1}, \boldsymbol{q_{t+1}})$ in a replay memory $\mathcal{D}$. By using memory replay the behavior distribution is averaged over many of its previous transitions, smoothing out learning and avoiding oscillations or divergence in the parameters.

To ensure that the learning algorithm takes learning memory into account, we sample a set of size N_2, with the help of alternative NN (with weight matrices $\boldsymbol{\Theta^-}$). This is due to the fact that the backward propagation (used for train-ing) discussed previously operates successfully for relatively "shallow" networks, i.e., networks with low number of hidden layers. As the number of these layers increases (i.e., deep NN), propagating gradients backward becomes increasingly challenging leading to convergence to local minima. To circumvent the above problems, we adapt a solution by which gradient updates are not performed at each iteration of the training algorithm. In particular, we assume additional knowledge modelled via an alternative NN that encodes previously experienced traces. This NN is used as a reference that we update after a preset number of iterations. As such, old knowledge encountered by the agent is not hindered by novel observations.

Consequently, we form a data set $\mathcal{D}$ (line 8) in preparation to retrain the original NN, while taking the history of traces into account. The process by which we generate these labels is in essence similar to finite value iterator. The main difference, however, is the usage of sample-based transitions to train a NN.

4.5 Fairness

Deep value iteration allows to compute Θ, and hence $\mathbb{P}_{\Theta}$ for all state-interaction pairs. As defined in Eq. 1, the policy then can be defined using $\mathbb{P}$. For this, as we are dealing with real numbers, the same trace would be selected all the time by engine, which is running that policy. As such, other correct traces will not be reachable in the obtained system. For instance, given a global state, a policy would select the interaction leading to a state with maximum performance measure value, even though there exist other interactions leading to other correct traces. To remedy this, we define a fair policy that is allowed to deviate from the optimal policy with a degree of fairness. The fair policy is defined as follows.

$$\pi(q) = \{a \mid a \in \mathcal{A}_q \wedge \mathbb{P}_{\Theta}(q, a) \geq \texttt{max}_q - \texttt{fair}\}, \tag{2}$$

where, $\texttt{max}_q = \max_{a \in \mathcal{A}_q} \mathbb{P}_{\Theta}(q, a)$. $\texttt{fair}$ is the tolerance against the optimal policy. The value of $\texttt{fair}$ depends on (1) the value of good and bad rewards, and (2) the horizon used in deep value iteration algorithm. Clearly, the more fairness the more deviation from the optimal policy we get.

5 Experimental Results

In this section, we present RERL an implementation of our proposed approach and its evaluation in terms of (1) accuracy of avoiding bad states and, (2) compilation and runtime efficiency.

5.1 Implementation

RERL is an implementation (developed in Java) of our method with several modules. The implementation is available at http://staff.aub.edu.lb/~mj54/rerl. RERL is equipped with a command line interface that accepts a set of configuration options. It takes the name of the input BIP file, a file containing the bad states (explicitly or symbolically) to be avoided, and optional flags (e.g., discount factor, number of episodes, horizon length), and it automatically generates a C++ implementation of the input BIP system embedded with a policy to avoid bad states.

```
> java -jar RERL.jar [options] input.bip output.cpp badStates.txt
```

5.2   Evaluation

Dining philosophers. Figure 3 shows an example of dining philosophers modeled in BIP that may deadlock. A deadlock will arise when philosopher P_0 allocates its right fork F_0, then philosopher P_1 allocates its right fork F_1. That is, a deadlock state is defined as the concatenation when all the philosophers allocate their right forks. We used RERL to enforce deadlock freedom on this example. We vary the number of philosophers from 2 to 47 increasing by 5. The total number of states is equal to 6^n, where n is the number of philosophers. Clearly, value iteration method would explode when the number of philosophers is greater than 12. As for the deep value iteration, we ran it with 50 epochs[3], 50 hidden neuron[4] units and 5 as degree of fairness. The degree of fairness was chosen to be consistent with the good $(+1)$ and bad reward (-1). Then, we run the system until it executes 10^5 iterations. The normal implementation always enters the deadlock state whereas when we apply deep value iteration the obtained implementation always avoid the deadlock state. We also evaluated the runtime overhead induced by the policy, which at every computation step needs to do a forward propagation on the trained neural network to select the best next interactions. Moreover, we compare this overhead against RE-BIP, a tool-set to enforce properties in BIP systems, but which is limited to only a one-step recovery. In this example, one-step recovery is sufficient to avoid deadlock, however, as we will see later it fails in the second benchmark as a k step recovery is needed. Table 1 summarizes the runtime execution times in case of infinite (while varying number of hidden neuron units), i.e., deep value iteration, finite, i.e., value iteration, and RE-BIP. Clearly, the infinite-based implementation drastically outperforms RE-BIP, when the number of hidden neuron units is less than 100. Although the finite-based outperforms RE-BIP and guarantees to enforce correct execution, it fails when the size of the system becomes large.

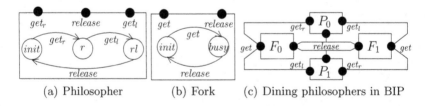

(a) Philosopher   (b) Fork   (c) Dining philosophers in BIP

Fig. 3. Dining philosophers with possible deadlock.

Pair-wise synchronized robots. In this benchmark, we model a set of robots placed on a map of size $n \times n$. Initially, all robots are placed at position $(0,0)$. We consider that robots can only move up or to the right, that is, cannot go back after taking a move. Moreover, robot i must synchronize with either robot $i-1$

---

[3] One epoch consists of one full training cycle on the training set.

[4] We use fine-tuning technique to select these parameters.

Table 1. Execution times (in seconds).

No. of Philo.	Infinite					Finite	RE-BIP
	10	50	100	500	1000		
2	0.7	2.8	5.5	27	55	1.2	29
7	1.4	6	11.3	58	130	12.2	72
12	2.3	9	17.5	90	186	43	122
17	3	11.8	23.2	121	251	NA	173
22	3.9	15.6	29.3	154	322	NA	269
27	5.5	18.7	35	190	405	NA	301
32	5.9	22.5	41.8	229	491	NA	407
37	7.1	25	48.5	279	567	NA	450
42	7.7	28.2	54.9	325	648	NA	566
47	9.7	32.6	60.5	396	764	NA	652

or $i + 1$ (modulo the number of robots) in order to move and both must move with the same direction. Clearly, this would require to create controllers to allow robots to follow that specification. The state of each robot can be modeled by two integers denoting the current position of the robot. We also assume the grid has mines (i.e., bad states) at the top row and the top half most left of the map (i.e., red places in Fig. 4). Bottom half most left places are considered safe. Also, we assume that the green location has an exit, which allows the robot to safely exit the map.

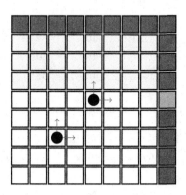

Fig. 4. Map of pair-wise synchronizing robots (Color figure online)

We have modeled robots and their pair-wise synchronization using BIP by allowing them to move to any border locations. Then, we define bad states (i.e., red location) and the goal is to generate a policy that allows robots not go to a bad state. Notice that RE-BIP cannot be used to avoid states as if a robot enters a location on the top half of the map, then 1-step recovery would try all the possible next actions and then fail. For instance, the robot (black circle) on the top has two choices, either moves right or up. The two choices lead the robot to go to a correct state. However, if the robot would take the move up action, it will enter a region where 1-step recovery will fail. We have tested RERL using value iteration and deep value iteration by varying the size of the map and the number of robots. Tables 2, 3 and 4 depict (1) the success rate when using deep value iteration, value iteration and standard implementation, (2) the time needed to converge in case of deep value iteration, and (3) the number of iterations needed to converge in case of finite value iteration. We ran each configuration 10000 times to compute the success rate. We notice that the value iteration provides a success rate of 100%, however, it fails when the size of the system increases. As for the deep value iteration, the system is learning to avoid bad states or states that could lead to bad states and it achieves a high success rate. For instance, if we take a map with 29×29 grid size and 8 robots (i.e., 841^8 possible states), the standard implementation has 15.1% success rate whereas when using deep value iteration we reach 95.6% success rate. As the state space in this example has a well-defined structure, we only needed 10 hidden neuron

Table 2. Evaluation of two robots with different grid sizes.

Grid size	Infinite		Finite		Standard
	Succ. %	Conv. (s)	Succ. %	Conv. (it.)	Succ. %
5	96.8	0.85	100	7	61.7
9	98.6	0.98	100	9	63.3
13	98.5	1.09	100	26	61.6
17	99.4	1.13	100	34	58.4
21	99.3	1.29	100	42	63.2
25	99.9	1.4	100	50	59.2
29	99.6	1.5	100	58	61.8

Table 3. Evaluation of four robots with different grid sizes.

Grid size	Infinite		Finite		Standard
	Succ. %	Conv. (s)	Succ. %	Conv. (it.)	Succ. %
5	95.5	0.9	100	7	30.5
9	93.9	1.08	NA	NA	30.7
13	94.7	1.23	NA	NA	30.6
17	97.8	1.52	NA	NA	28.6
21	97.9	1.82	NA	NA	29.8
25	98.1	2.2	NA	NA	30.1
29	97.8	2.5	NA	NA	30.1

Table 4. Evaluation of eight robots with different grid sizes.

Grid size	Infinite		Finite		Standard
	Succ. %	Conv. (s)	Succ. %	Conv. (it.)	Succ. %
5	92.9	1.1	NA	NA	12.2
9	93.9	1.5	NA	NA	13.8
13	97.4	1.6	NA	NA	15.1
17	95.3	2.2	NA	NA	13.8
21	94.9	3.0	NA	NA	17.1
25	94.8	3.3	NA	NA	14.2
29	95.6	3.6	NA	NA	15.1

units to train our network by using deep value iteration algorithm. For this, we notice the efficiency of the compile time, e.g., only 3.6 s are needed to train a system consisting of 841^8 states and to reach a 95.6% success rate.

6   Conclusions and Perspectives

In this paper, we introduced a new technique that combines static analysis and dynamic analysis with the help of machine learning techniques, in order to optimally ensure the correct execution of software systems. Experimental results show that it is possible to learn reachability of bad behaviors by only exploring part of the system. For future work, we consider several directions. First, we plan to study more expressive properties (e.g., liveness). Second, we consider to generate a partial state semantics, and hence, allow to automatically generate multi-threaded implementations. Third, we consider to generate decentralized policies to facilitate the generation of efficient distributed implementations.

References

1. Basu, A., Bensalem, S., Bozga, M., Combaz, J., Jaber, M., Nguyen, T., Sifakis, J.: Rigorous component-based system design using the BIP framework. IEEE Softw. **28**(3), 41–48 (2011)
2. Bensalem, S., Bozga, M., Nguyen, T.-H., Sifakis, J.: D-Finder: a tool for compositional deadlock detection and verification. In: Bouajjani, A., Maler, O. (eds.) CAV 2009. LNCS, vol. 5643, pp. 614–619. Springer, Heidelberg (2009). doi:10.1007/978-3-642-02658-4_45
3. Bonakdarpour, B., Bozga, M., Jaber, M., Quilbeuf, J., Sifakis, J.: A framework for automated distributed implementation of component-based models. Distrib. Comput. **25**(5), 383–409 (2012)
4. Charafeddine, H., El-Harake, K., Falcone, Y., Jaber, M.: Runtime enforcement for component-based systems. In: Proceedings of the 30th Annual ACM Symposium on Applied Computing, Salamanca, Spain, pp. 1789–1796, 13–17 April 2015

5. Clarke, E.M.: My 27-year quest to overcome the state explosion problem. In: Proceedings of the 24th Annual IEEE Symposium on Logic in Computer Science, LICS 2009, Los Angeles, CA, USA, p. 3, 11–14 August 2009
6. Clarke, E.M., Klieber, W., Novácek, M., Zuliani, P.: Model checking and the state explosion problem. In: Tools for Practical Software Verification, LASER, International Summer School, Elba Island, Italy, Revised Tutorial, pp. 1–30 (2011)
7. Falcone, Y., Jaber, M., Nguyen, T., Bozga, M., Bensalem, S.: Runtime verification of component-based systems in the BIP framework with formally-proved sound and complete instrumentation. Softw. Syst. Model. **14**(1), 173–199 (2015)
8. Falcone, Y., Zuck, L.D.: Runtime verification: the application perspective. STTT **17**(2), 121–123 (2015)
9. Flanagan, C., Qadeer, S.: Predicate abstraction for software verification. In: Conference Record of POPL 2002: The 29th Symposium on Principles of Programming Languages, Portland, OR, USA, pp. 191–202, 16–18 January 2002
10. Huang, C., Peled, D.A., Schewe, S., Wang, F.: A game-theoretic foundation for the maximum software resilience against dense errors. IEEE Trans. Softw. Eng. **42**(7), 605–622 (2016)
11. Katz, G., Peled, D.A.: Synthesizing, correcting and improving code, using model checking-based genetic programming. In: Hardware and Software: Verification and Testing - Proceedings of the 9th International Haifa Verification Conference, HVC 2013, Haifa, Israel, pp. 246–261, 5–7 November 2013
12. Lin, L.J.: Reinforcement Learning for Robots Using Neural Networks. Ph.D. thesis, Pittsburgh, PA, USA (1992). uMI Order No. GAX93-22750
13. Peled, D.: Automatic synthesis of code using genetic programming. In: Margaria, T., Steffen, B. (eds.) ISoLA 2016, Part I. LNCS, vol. 9952, pp. 182–187. Springer, Cham (2016). doi:10.1007/978-3-319-47166-2_12
14. Peled, D.: Using genetic programming for software reliability. In: Falcone, Y., Sánchez, C. (eds.) RV 2016. LNCS, vol. 10012, pp. 116–131. Springer, Cham (2016). doi:10.1007/978-3-319-46982-9_8
15. Pinisetty, S., Preoteasa, V., Tripakis, S., Jéron, T., Falcone, Y., Marchand, H.: Predictive runtime enforcement. In: Proceedings of the 31st Annual ACM Symposium on Applied Computing, Pisa, Italy, pp. 1628–1633, 4–8 April 2016
16. Pinisetty, S., Tripakis, S.: Compositional runtime enforcement. In: Rayadurgam, S., Tkachuk, O. (eds.) NFM 2016. LNCS, vol. 9690, pp. 82–99. Springer, Cham (2016). doi:10.1007/978-3-319-40648-0_7
17. Pnueli, A., Rosner, R.: On the synthesis of a reactive module. In: Conference Record of the Sixteenth Annual ACM Symposium on Principles of Programming Languages, Austin, Texas, USA, pp. 179–190, 11–13 January 1989
18. Pnueli, A., Rosner, R.: Distributed reactive systems are hard to synthesize. In: 31st Annual Symposium on Foundations of Computer Science, St. Louis, Missouri, USA, vol. II, pp. 746–757, 22–24 October 1990
19. Queille, J.P., Sifakis, J.: Specification and verification of concurrent systems in CESAR. In: Dezani-Ciancaglini, M., Montanari, U. (eds.) Programming 1982. LNCS, vol. 137, pp. 337–351. Springer, Heidelberg (1982). doi:10.1007/3-540-11494-7_22

The Implementation of Object Propositions: The Oprop Verification Tool

Ligia Nistor$^{(\boxtimes)}$ and Jonathan Aldrich

School of Computer Science, Carnegie Mellon University, Pittsburgh, PA, USA
{lnistor,aldrich}@cs.cmu.edu

Abstract. In this paper we present Oprop, a tool that implements the theory of object propositions. We have recently introduced object propositions as a modular verification technique that combines abstract predicates and fractional permissions. The Oprop tool, found as a web application at lowcost-env.ynzf2j4byc.us-west-2.elasticbeanstalk.com, verifies programs written in a simplified version of Java augmented with the object propositions specifications. Our tool parses the input files and automatically translates them into the intermediate verification language Boogie, which is verified by the Boogie verifier that we use as a back end. We present the details of our implementation, the rules of our translation and how they are applied on an example. We describe an instance of the challenging Composite design pattern, that we have automatically verified using the Oprop tool, and prove the equivalence between formulas in Oprop and their translation into Boogie.

Keywords: Formal · Verification · Oprop · Object · Propositions · Linear · Logic · Java · Boogie · Translation · Equivalence · Proof · Tool · Web · Service

1 Motivation

In this paper we present a practical verification tool, Oprop, for object-oriented programs in single-threaded settings. In 2014 we published a method for modular verification [23] of object-oriented code in the presence of aliasing. Our approach, *object propositions*, builds on separation logic and inherits its modularity advantages, but provides additional modularity by allowing developers to hide shared mutable data that two objects have in common. The implementations of the two objects have a shared fractional permission [5] to access the common data (for example each of the two objects has a field pointing to the same object and thus each object has a half fraction to that object), but this need not be exposed in their external interface.

Our work is modular to a class: in each class we define predicates that objects of other classes can rely on. We get the modularity advantages while also supporting a high degree of expressiveness by allowing the modification of multiple objects. Like separation logic and permissions, but unlike conventional object

© Springer International Publishing AG 2017
J. Proença and M. Lumpe (Eds.): FACS 2017, LNCS 10487, pp. 179–197, 2017.
DOI: 10.1007/978-3-319-68034-7_11

invariant and ownership-based work (including [20,21]), our system allows "ownership transfer" by passing unique permissions around (permissions with a fraction of 1). Unlike separation logic and permission systems, but like object invariant work and its extensions (for example, the work of Summers and Drossopoulou [27]), we can modify objects without owning them. More broadly, unlike either ownership or separation logic systems, in our system object A can depend on an invariant property of object B even when B is not owned by A, and when A is not "visible" from B. This has information-hiding and system-structuring benefits. Part of the innovation is combining the two mechanisms above so that we can choose between one or the other for each object, and even switch between them for a given object. By being able to formally verify different classes and methods of those classes independently of each other and automatically using our Oprop tool, our work can be used to formally verify component-based software.

The contributions of this paper are a description of how we implemented our methodology in the Oprop tool, a proof of soundness of our core translation technique, and experience verifying the Composite pattern and a few smaller examples with the tool. In Sect. 2 we give a background presentation of object propositions, together with an example class written in the Oprop language. Section 3 presents the tool and how it can be accessed as a web application. Sections 4 and 5 present an intuitive description of the formal translation rules from Oprop into Boogie and the formal proof of equivalence between formulas written in Oprop and their Boogie translation. We conclude by showing the examples that we automatically verified using Oprop and compare our work to existing approaches, showing how our work contributes to the state of the art in the area of tool based approaches that facilitate the application of formal methods for component based software.

2   The Theory of Object Propositions

The object proposition methodology [23] uses abstract predicates [24] to characterise the state of an object, embeds those predicates in a logical framework and specifies sharing using fractional permissions [5]. When an object a has a fractional permission to object b it means that one of the fields of a is a reference to b. Object propositions are associated with object references in the code. Programmers can use them in writing method pre- and post-conditions and in the packing/unpacking annotations that they can insert in the code as part of verification.

To verify a method, the *abstract* predicate in the object proposition for the receiver object is interpreted as a *concrete* formula over the current values of the receiver object's fields (including for fields of primitive type *int*). Following Fähndrich and DeLine [9], our verification system maintains a *key* for each field of the receiver object, which is used to track the current values of those fields through the method. A key $o.f \rightarrow x$ represents read/write access to field f of object o holding a value represented by the concrete value x.

To gain read or write access to the fields of an object, we have to *unpack* it [8]. After a method finishes working with the fields of a shared object (an object for which we have a fractional permission, with a fraction less than 1) our proof rules ensure that the same predicate as before the unpacking holds of that shared object. If the same predicate holds, we are allowed to pack back the shared object to that predicate. Since for an object with a fractional permission of 1 there is no risk of interferences, we don't require packing to the same predicate for this kind of objects.

Object propositions are unique in providing a separation logic with fractions, in which developers can unpack an object that is shared with a fractional permission, modify its fields, and pack it again as long as the new field values validate the original abstract predicate. The programming language that we are using is inspired by Featherweight Java [13], extended to include object propositions. We retained only Java concepts relevant to the core technical contribution of this paper, omitting features such as inheritance, casting or dynamic dispatch that are important but are handled by orthogonal techniques. Since they contain fractional permissions which represent resources that have to be consumed upon usage, object propositions are consumed upon usage and their duplication is forbidden. Therefore, we use linear logic [11] to write the specifications. Pre- and post-conditions are separated with a linear implication $\multimap$ and use multiplicative conjunction ($\otimes$), additive disjunction ($\oplus$) and existential/universal quantifiers (where there is a need to quantify over the parameters of the predicates).

$$
\begin{aligned}
\text{Prog} &::= \overline{\text{ClDecl}}\ e \\
\text{ClDecl} &::= \texttt{class}\ C\ \{\ \overline{\text{FldDecl}}\ \overline{\text{PredDecl}}\ \overline{\text{MthDecl}}\ \} \\
\text{FldDecl} &::= \mathsf{T}\ f \\
\text{PredDecl} &::= \texttt{predicate}\ Q\,(\overline{\mathsf{T}}\ \mathsf{x})\ \equiv \mathsf{R} \\
\text{MthDecl} &::= \mathsf{T}\ m\,(\overline{\mathsf{T}}\ \mathsf{x})\ \text{MthSpec}\ \{\ \overline{e};\ \texttt{return}\ e\ \} \\
\text{MthSpec} &::= \mathsf{R} \multimap \mathsf{R} \\
\mathsf{R} &::= \mathsf{P}\ |\ \mathsf{R} \otimes \mathsf{R}\ |\ \mathsf{R} \oplus \mathsf{R}\ | \\
&\quad \exists \mathsf{x}{:}\mathsf{T}.\mathsf{R}\ |\ \exists \mathsf{z}{:}\texttt{double}.\mathsf{R}\ |\ \exists \mathsf{z}{:}\texttt{double}.\mathsf{z}\ \text{binop}\ \mathsf{t} \Rightarrow \mathsf{R}\ | \\
&\quad \forall \mathsf{x}{:}\mathsf{T}.\mathsf{R}\ |\ \forall \mathsf{z}{:}\texttt{double}.\mathsf{R}\ |\ \forall \mathsf{z}{:}\texttt{double}.\mathsf{z}\ \text{binop}\ \mathsf{t} \Rightarrow \mathsf{R}\ | \\
&\quad \mathsf{t}\ \text{binop}\ \mathsf{t} \Rightarrow \mathsf{R} \\
\mathsf{P} &::= r\#\mathsf{k}\ Q\,(\overline{\mathsf{t}})\ |\ \texttt{unpacked}(r\#\mathsf{k}\ Q\,(\overline{\mathsf{t}}))\ | \\
&\quad r.f \to \mathsf{x}\ |\ \mathsf{t}\ \text{binop}\ \mathsf{t} \\
\mathsf{k} &::= \tfrac{n_1}{n_2}\ (\text{where}\ n_1, n_2 \in \mathbb{N}\ \text{and}\ 0 < n_1 \leq n_2)\ |\ \mathsf{z} \\
\mathsf{e} &::= \mathsf{t}\ |\ r.f\ |\ r.f = \mathsf{t}\ |\ r.m\,(\overline{\mathsf{t}})\ | \\
&\quad \texttt{new}\ C\,(Q\,(\overline{\mathsf{t}})\,[\overline{\mathsf{t}}])\,(\overline{\mathsf{t}})\ | \\
&\quad \texttt{if}\ (\mathsf{t})\ \{\ \mathsf{e}\ \}\ \texttt{else}\ \{\ \mathsf{e}\ \}\ |\ \texttt{let}\ \mathsf{x} = \mathsf{e}\ \texttt{in}\ \mathsf{e}\ | \\
&\quad \mathsf{t}\ \text{binop}\ \mathsf{t}\ |\ \mathsf{t}\ \&\&\ \mathsf{t}\ |\ \mathsf{t}\ \|\ \mathsf{t}\ |\ !\ \mathsf{t}\ | \\
&\quad \texttt{pack}\ r\#\mathsf{k}\ Q\,(\overline{\mathsf{t}})\,[\overline{\mathsf{t}}]\,\texttt{in}\ \mathsf{e}\ |\ \texttt{unpack}\ r\#\mathsf{k}\ Q\,(\overline{\mathsf{t}})\,[\overline{\mathsf{t}}]\,\texttt{in}\ \mathsf{e} \\
\mathsf{t} &::= \mathsf{x}\ |\ n\ |\ \texttt{null}\ |\ \texttt{true}\ |\ \texttt{false} \\
\mathsf{x} &::= r\ |\ i \\
\text{binop} &::= +\ |\ -\ |\ \%\ |\ =\ |\ !=\ |\ \leq\ |\ <\ |\ \geq\ |\ > \\
\mathsf{T} &::= C\ |\ \texttt{int}\ |\ \texttt{boolean}\ |\ \texttt{double}
\end{aligned}
$$

Fig. 1. Grammar of object propositions

We show the syntax of our simple class-based object-oriented language, that we call the Oprop language, in Fig. 1. In rule ClDecl each class can define one or more abstract predicates Q in terms of concrete formulas R. Each method in the rule MthDecl comes with pre- and post-condition formulas. Formulas R include object propositions P, terms t, primitive binary predicates, conjunction, disjunction, keys $r.f \rightarrow x$, and quantification. We distinguish effectful expressions from simple terms, and assume the program is in let-normal form. The pack and unpack expression forms are markers for when packing and unpacking occurs in the proof system. In the grammar, r represents a reference to an object and i represents an integer. The variable z represents a metavariable for fractions and it has type *double*. In a program, a fraction can be a constant of type double or it can be represented by a metavariable. The horizontal bar above a symbol means that there could be one or more occurrences of that symbol.

The example SimpleCell.java in Fig. 2 shows an Oprop class. We created the SimpleCell example to illustrate how we can modify an object even if we do not have a full permission to it. Also, we can rely only on the specifications of methods in order to reason about them, which strengthens our modularity claim.

Note that even though the class is written in the Oprop language, the extension of the file remains *.java*. This example differs from our grammar in a couple of ways: every Oprop input file has to have the declaration of the enclosing package as first statement, and the linear conjunction and disjunction that we use in our formal grammar in Fig. 2 are replaced by && and || in the Oprop code.

Figure 2 shows the declaration of the SimpleCell class, the declaration of the predicates, the changeVal method and its specification, and the main() method. When the object c is created in the main() method, line 17, we have to specify the predicate that holds for it in case the object becomes shared in the future. Since the predicate PredVal defined on line 5 has one existentially quantified variable and the Boogie tool cannot successfully instantiate existential variables, we give the witness 2 for the variable int v existentially quantified in the body of the predicate PredVal. In general, whenever there is an existential Oprop statement in the code, we pass the witnesses for that statement explicitly. The tilde sign in the specification of the changeVal method on line 9 is there to differentiate between variables k used for fractions and other variables that are used as parameters to predicates.

When we unpack a predicate, as we do on line 12, we check that the provided witness is the right one; we do not assume that the programmer provided the right witness. We implemented the translation strategy in this way because the programmer might make a mistake and provide the wrong witness.

3   The Oprop Tool

The Oprop tool, found at lowcost-env.ynzf2j4byc.us-west-2.elasticbeanstalk.com as a web application, takes as input any number of files written in Java and annotated with object propositions specifications. The tool produces for each input file the corresponding Boogie translation file. We have written in Java the

```
1   package x;
2   class SimpleCell {
3     int val;
4     SimpleCell next;
5     predicate PredVal() = exists int v : this.val -> v && v<15
6     predicate PredNext() = exists SimpleCell obj :
7       this.next -> obj && (obj#0.34 PredVal())
8     void changeVal(int r)
9     ~double k : requires (this#k PredVal()) && (r<15)
10    ensures this#k PredVal()
11    {
12      unpack(this#k PredVal())[this.val];
13      this.val = r;
14      pack(this#k PredVal())[r];
15    }
16    void main() {
17      SimpleCell c = new SimpleCell(PredVal()[2])(2, null);
18      SimpleCell a = new SimpleCell(PredNext()[c])(2, c);
19      SimpleCell b = new SimpleCell(PredNext()[c])(3, c);
20      unpack(a#1 PredNext())[c];
21      unpack(b#1 PredNext())[c];
22      c.changeVal(4);
23    }
24  }
```

Fig. 2. SimpleCell.java

translation rules from Oprop into the Boogie language and we are deploying them in the form of a jar file on the Oprop web application. If the user has provided multiple files as input, there will be multiple files produced as output. In the background, the tool concatenates the multiple files into a single one. The concatenation of the translated input files will be accessible to the user on the last page of the web application, under the link *inputBoogie.bpl*. The final result of the verification - the Boogie tool run on the*inputBoogie.bpl* file - is accessible by clicking on the link *result.txt*. The user will be able to see if the original Java file augmented with the object propositions annotations was verified or not. If an error message is displayed, the user has the option of going back to the original Java file and adding more annotations that might help the formal verification and then uploading the new file to restart the process.

The translation part of the Oprop tool is composed of two parts: JExpr [2] and the Boogie translation. JExpr is a parser for a very small subset of Java. We took this off-the-shelf parser and added support for the parsing of object propositions annotations. The JExpr system consists of the following components: a JavaCC parser, a set of Abstract Syntax Tree classes, a Contextual Semantic Analysis visitor and a type resolution class used by the Contextual Visitor. We implemented the Boogie translation in a file called *BoogieVisitor.java*. In this file we implement the translation rules presented in Sect. 4. By implementing the visitor design pattern, we visit all the nodes of the Abstract Syntax Tree and perform the translation for each one. We have nodes such as *FieldDeclaration, PredicateDeclaration, MethodDeclaration, ObjectProposition, FieldSelection, MethodSelection, BinaryExpression, FormalParameter, AllocationExpression,* etc.

The resulting Boogie translation is fed into the Boogie verifier, in the background of our web application. The Boogie verifier uses the Z3 high-performance theorem prover [7] to answer whether the program was verified successfully or not. The Z3 theorem prover works very well for our methodology, since our abstract predicates use integers to express the properties of fields. Reasoning about integers in an automated way can be difficult, but Z3 is one of the most prominent satisfiability modulo theories (SMT) solvers and it is used in related tools such as Boogie [3], Dafny [17], Chalice [16] and VCC [6].

4   Translating Object Propositions into Boogie

In order for us to be able to use Z3 for the verification of the generated conditions, we need to encode our extended fragment of linear logic into Boogie, which is based on first order logic and uses maps as first class citizens of the language. A detailed description of the syntax and semantics of the Boogie language can be found in [18] available at http://research.microsoft.com/~leino/papers.html. By 'extended fragment of linear logic' we mean the fragment of linear logic containing the operators $\otimes$ and $\oplus$, that we extend with the specifics of our object propositions methodology. Specifically, we need to encode R described in the grammar in Sect. 2. The crux of the encoding is in how we treat the fractions of the object propositions, how we keep track of them and how we assert statements about them. For object propositions, we encode whether they are packed or unpacked, the amount of the fraction that they have and the values of their parameters. Fractions are intrinsically related to keeping track of resources, the principal idea of linear logic. The challenge was to capture all the properties of the Oprop language and soundly translate them into first order logic statements. We were able to use the *map* data structure that the Boogie language provides to model the heap and the fields of each class. The maps were also helpful for keeping track of the fractions associated with each object, as well as for knowing which object propositions were packed and which were unpacked at all points in the code.

Our translation of linear logic (LL) into first order logic (FOL) is given in the following paragraphs of this subsection, where we present the most interesting rules of translation of our Oprop language into the Boogie intermediate verification language. The translation of SimpleCell.java from Fig. 2 into the Boogie language is given in Figs. 3 and 4, and we point to the lines in these two figures for each translation rule that we describe. We give the intuition for each translation rule, in the order that it appears in Figs. 3 and 4.

At the start of each Boogie program we declare the type `Ref` that represents object references, as can be seen on line 1 in the `SimpleCell` example.

A class declaration is made of the field, predicate, constructor and method declarations. The function trans represents the formal translation function.

```
1   type Ref;
2   const null: Ref;
3   var val: [Ref]int;
4   var next: [Ref]Ref;
5   var packedPredNext: [Ref] bool;
6   var fracPredNext: [Ref] real;
7   var packedPredVal: [Ref] bool;
8   var fracPredVal: [Ref] real;
9
10  procedure PackPredNext(obj: Ref, this:Ref);
11    requires (packedPredNext[this]==false) &&
12      (((fracPredVal[next[this]] >= 0.34))) && (next[this]==obj)
        ;
13  procedure UnpackPredNext(obj: Ref, this:Ref);
14    requires packedPredNext[this] &&
15      (fracPredNext[this] > 0.0);
16    requires (next[this]==obj);
17    ensures (((fracPredVal[next[this]] >= 0.34))) && (next[this
        ]==obj);
18
19  procedure PackPredVal(v:int, this:Ref);
20    requires (packedPredVal[this]==false) &&
21      ((v<15)) && (val[this]==v);
22  procedure UnpackPredVal(v:int, this:Ref);
23    requires packedPredVal[this] &&
24      (fracPredVal[this] > 0.0);
25    requires (val[this]==v);
26    ensures ((v<15)) && (val[this]==v);
27
28  procedure SimpleCell(v:int, n:Ref, this:Ref)
29    modifies next,val;
30    ensures ((val[this]==v)&&(next[this]==n));
31    ensures (forall x: Ref::((x!=this)==>(next[x]==old(next[x]))
        ));
32    ensures (forall x: Ref::((x!=this)==>(val[x]==old(val[x]))))
        ;
33  { val[this]:=v;
34    next[this]:=n; }
35
36  procedure changeVal(r:int, this:Ref)
37    modifies packedPredVal,val;
38    requires (this != null) && (((packedPredVal[this] ) &&
39      (fracPredVal[this] > 0.0))&&(r<15));
40    ensures ((packedPredVal[this] ) &&
41      (fracPredVal[this] > 0.0));
42    requires (forall x:Ref :: packedPredVal[x]);
43    ensures (forall x:Ref :: packedPredVal[x]);
44    ensures (forall x:Ref :: (fracPredVal[x]==old(fracPredVal[x
        ])));
```

Fig. 3. simplecell.bpl

```
50  {
51    assume ( forall  y : Ref  ::  ( fracPredVal [ y ]  >=  0.0 )  );
52    call  UnpackPredVal ( val [ this ] ,  this );
53    packedPredVal [ this ]  :=  false ;
54    val [ this ]:= r ;
55    call  PackPredVal ( r ,  this );
56    packedPredVal [ this ]  :=  true ;
57  }
58
59  procedure  main ( this : Ref )
60    modifies  fracPredNext , fracPredVal , next ,
61      packedPredNext , packedPredVal , val ;
62    requires  ( forall  x : Ref  ::  packedPredNext [ x ]);
63    requires  ( forall  x : Ref  ::  packedPredVal [ x ]);
64  {
65    var  c : Ref ;
66    var  a : Ref ;
67    var  b : Ref ;
68    assume  ( c != a )  &&  ( c != b )  &&  ( a != b )  ;
69    assume  ( forall  y : Ref  ::  ( fracPredNext [ y ]  >=  0.0 )  );
70    call  SimpleCell ( 2 , null , c );
71    packedPredVal [ c ]  :=  false ;
72    call  PackPredVal ( 2 , c );
73    packedPredVal [ c ]  :=  true ;
74    fracPredVal [ c ]  :=  1.0 ;
75    call  SimpleCell ( 2 , c , a );
76    packedPredNext [ a ]  :=  false ;
77    call  PackPredNext ( c , a );
78    fracPredVal [ c ]  :=  fracPredVal [ c ]  −  0.34 ;
79    packedPredNext [ a ]  :=  true ;
80    fracPredNext [ a ]  :=  1.0 ;
81    call  SimpleCell ( 3 , c , b );
82    packedPredNext [ b ]  :=  false ;
83    call  PackPredNext ( c , b );
84    fracPredVal [ c ]  :=  fracPredVal [ c ]  −  0.34 ;
85    packedPredNext [ b ]  :=  true ;
86    fracPredNext [ b ]  :=  1.0 ;
87    call  UnpackPredNext ( c ,  a );
88    fracPredVal [ c ]  :=  fracPredVal [ c ]  +  0.34 ;
89    packedPredNext [ a ]  :=  false ;
90    call  UnpackPredNext ( c ,  b );
91    fracPredVal [ c ]  :=  fracPredVal [ c ]  +  0.34 ;
92    packedPredNext [ b ]  :=  false ;
93    call  changeVal ( 4 , c );
94  }
```

Fig. 4. simplecell.bpl - cont

For a complete list of translation rules and their explanations, please refer to Sect. 4.3.1 in [22].

$$\text{trans(ClDecl)} \quad ::= \quad \dfrac{\overline{\text{trans(FldDecl)}} \; \overline{\text{trans(PredDecl)}}}{\text{trans(ConstructorDecl)} \; \overline{\text{trans(MthDecl)}}}$$

Each field is represented by a map from object references to values, representing the value of that field. You can see the maps declared for the fields `val` and `next` on lines 3 and 4.

$$\text{trans(FldDecl)} \quad ::= \quad \texttt{var f: [Ref]} \, \text{trans}(T);$$

We declare a map from a reference `r` to a real representing the fraction `k` for each object proposition `r#k` $Q(\bar{t})$. We declare a second map from a reference `r` to a boolean, keeping track of which objects are packed. Each key points to `true` if and only if the corresponding object proposition is packed for that object. For each predicate `Q`, we have a map keeping track of fractions and a map keeping track of the packed objects. The result of these translation rules is shown on lines 5 to 8 in the `SimpleCell` example.

For each predicate `Pred` we have a map `fracPred` declared as follows

`var fracPred : [Ref] real`. You can see two such maps on lines 6 and 8 of Fig. 3 representing the fraction maps for the predicates `PredNext` and `PredVal`. For each object `obj`, this map points to the value of type real of the fraction `k` that is in the object proposition `obj#k` $\text{Pred}(\bar{t})$. The map `fracPred` represents all the permissions on the stack. Since `fracPred` is a global variable it always contains the values of the fractions for all objects. An important distinctions is that in a method we only reason about the values stored in `fracPred` for locally accessible objects (objects that are mentioned in the precondition of that method). As we go through the body of that method, the value of `fracPred` for the objects that are touched in any way changes.

The declaration of an abstract predicate `Q` has two steps: we write a procedure *PackQ* that is used for packing the predicate `Q`, and a procedure *UnpackQ* that is used for unpacking it.

The procedure `PackQ` is called in the code whenever we have to pack an object proposition, according to the *pack(...)* annotations that the programmer inserted in the code. Right after calling the *PackQ* procedure, we write `packedQ[this] := true;` in the Boogie code. After calling the *PackQ* procedure, we also write the statements that manipulate the fractions that appear in the body of the predicate that we are packing. When packing a predicate, we subtract from the current value of fractions.

Whenever there is a packed object proposition in the body of a predicate, for example assume that in the body of the predicate `P` we have the packed object proposition `r1#k` `Q()`, we model it in the following way: in the procedures `UnpackP` and `PackP` we have `requires (fracQ[r1] > 0.0)` and `ensures (fracQ[r1] > 0.0)` respectively. Note that we do not have `requires packedQ[r1]` and `ensures packedQ[r1]` respectively, in the body of a predicate. The intuition here is that we do not know whether an object proposition appearing in the definition of a predicate is unpacked. For the pre- and post-conditions of procedures our methodology guarantees that if an object proposition is unpacked, it will appear in the specifications as unpacked. All unpacked object propositions will be stated in the specifications of methods. For all procedures where we might have unpacked object propositions in the pre-conditions of that procedure, we add a statement of the form **requires** (forall y:Ref :: (y!=obj1) ==> packedQ[y]). This statement states that all the object propositions that are not explicitly mentioned to be unpacked will be considered packed. For the **requires forall** statement just mentioned, assume that the object **obj1** has been explicitly mentioned in an unpacked object proposition. The upside is that we can rely on such **ensures forall** statements but we also need to prove them as post-conditions of procedures. You can see the procedures **PackPredNext** and **PackPredVal** for predicates **PredNext** and **PredVal** on lines 10 to 12 and 19 to 21 respectively.

Note that the predicate **PredVal** has an existential statement in its definition, for the variable v for which we instead use the global variable of the field **val** in the Boogie translation. The implementation of this idea can be seen in the **SimpleCell** example on line 21, where the **val** field is existentially quantified and the Boogie global variable **val[this]** is used instead in the definition of the predicate. We side-effect the predicate **PredVal** to add the existential parameter v, as can be seen in the formal translation rule from Fig. 5. This parameter is added to the list of parameters of the enclosing predicate, as can be seen on line 19.

```
function  addExistential(trans(R),  t:trans(T))
{
    MethodOrPredDeclaration  result;
    let  methodOrPred(params)  be  the  method
    or  predicate  in  the  body  of  which  R  is  found;
    update  methodOrPred(params)  to  be  methodOrPred(params,  t:
        trans(T));
    result  :=  methodOrPred(params,  t:trans(T));
    return  result;
}
```

Fig. 5. addExistential() translation helper function

Similarly, the procedure **UnpackQ** is called in the code whenever we need to unpack an object proposition, whenever we need to access the field of an object or we need to add together fractions in order to get the right permission (usually when we need a permission of 1 in order to modify a predicate). The procedure **UnpackQ** is inserted in the code whenever the programmer inserted the *unpack(...)* annotation in the Java code. Right after calling the procedure **UnpackQ**, we write packedQ[this] := false; in the code. We also write the statements that add to the fractions that appear in the body of the predicate that we are packing. You can see the procedures **UnpackPredVal** and **UnpackPredNext** for predicates **PredVal** and **PredNext** on lines 22 to 26 and

13 to 17. Note that in the **ensures** statement of the predicate **PredNext** we did not write **fracPredNext[this]** $>= 0.34$. This not needed because we are going to add this fraction in the caller, right after calling **UnpackPredNext**.

For each class we write a constructor. For the class **SimpleCell** the translation of the constructor is on lines 28 to 34.

A method is translated into a **procedure** in Boogie.

$$\text{trans(MthDecl)} ::= \textbf{procedure } \texttt{m(} \overline{\text{trans(T)}} \texttt{ x)} \textbf{ returns } \texttt{(r:trans(T))}$$
$$\text{trans(MthSpec)}$$
$$\texttt{\{ } \underline{\textbf{assume } (\text{forall } y\text{:Ref} :: (\text{fracQ}[y] >= 0.0));}$$
$$\overline{\text{trans}(e_1)} \texttt{ ; var r := } \text{trans}(e_2)\texttt{; return r; \}}$$

When specifying a method, we have to specify the variables that it modifies, its precondition and its postcondition. We define the method **changeVal** in the **SimpleCell** class on lines 36 to 57. For each method we have added two kinds of statements that we call **requires forall** and **ensures forall**.

The **requires forall** statement explicitly states the object propositions that are packed at the beginning of a method, which are almost all object propositions in most cases. Since there are no unpacked object propositions in the preconditions of the method **changeVal**, the **requires forall** states that all the object propositions for the **PredVal** predicate are packed. Each **requires forall** or **ensures forall** statement refers to a single predicate and thus each method might have multiple such statements.

The **modifies** clause of a procedure in Boogie has to state all the global variables that this procedure modifies, through assignment, and all the variables that are being modified by other procedures that are called inside this procedure. The **modifies** clause that Boogie needs for each procedure states that all the values of a certain field have been modified, for all references. This leads to us not being able to rely on many properties that were true before entering a procedure. We counteract the effect of the **modifies** by adding statements of the form **ensures (forall y: Ref :: (fracP[y] == old(fracP[y])))** and **ensures (forall y:Ref :: (packedP[y] == old(packedP[y])))**, for all **fracP**, **packedP** or global fields maps that were mentioned in the **modifies** clause of the current procedure. Of course, if the value of the maps **fracP**, **packedP**, etc. does change in the method we do not add these **ensures forall** statements.

If we have multiple declarations of the form **var c: Ref, var d: Ref**, we also add the assumption statement **assume (c!=d)** as on line 68 because the Boogie tool does not assume that these two variables are different, while the Java semantics does assume this. We explicitly assume in the beginning of the body of each method that all fractions that are mentioned in the pre- or postconditions of that method are larger than 0, as on line 69. We need to explicitly add these assumptions because the Boogie tool does not have any pre-existing assumptions about our global maps representing fractions.

An object proposition $r\#k$ $Q(\bar{t})$ is generally translated by stating that the value of the **packedQ** map for the parameters t and reference r is true and the value of **fracQ** for the same parameters and reference is $>= k$ if k is a constant or is >0 if k is a metavariable. You can see the translation of the packed object proposition `obj#0.34 PredVal()` both inside the `PackPredNext` and `UnpackPredNext` procedures corresponding to the predicate `PredNext`.

When the programmer wants to pack an object to a predicate `Q`, he needs to write the statement `call PackQ(..., this)` in the program. When translating this call to `Pack`, the Oprop tool writes `packedQ[this] := true`. You can see an example of such a call to `Pack` on lines 71 to 74, together with the statements that assign `true` to the global `packed` map for this object and the statement that subtracts the fraction that is used for the predicate `PredVal` and the object c when the packing occurs. The user specifies to our tool which predicate they intend to pack to by adding the name of that predicate and the parameters to that predicate, if there are any, in the call to the constructor. This can be seen on lines 17–19 in Fig. 2 right after the name of the constructor `SimpleCell`. For our `SimpleCell` example the constructor is called multiple times in our `main` function and you can see one such call and the statements that are written right after the call on lines 70 to 74 in the `.bpl` translation. The user specifies to our Oprop tool which predicate they intend to pack to by writing the name of the predicate, together with any parameters that the predicate needs, in the call to the constructor.

Similarly, when we unpack an object from an object proposition that refers to predicate `Q`, we write the statement `call UnpackQ(..., this)`. Right after this statement we write `packedQ[this] := false`. You can see an example of such a call on lines 87 to 89. As opposed to packing, where we usually consume a fraction of an object proposition, when we unpack an object proposition we obtain a fraction and so we have a fraction manipulation statement that adds to the current value of a fraction, as seen on line 88.

5   Equivalence of Translation

In this section, we present soundness and completeness theorems stating that a formula in the Oprop language is translated into an equivalent formula in the first-order logic supported by Boogie. We focus on the equivalence of formulas because that is the heart of our translation approach; modeling the detailed constructs of Java has been done in other settings and is of less interest. Furthermore, the semantics of Boogie are given as trace sets, a formalism somewhat distant from the standard dynamic semantics we used in our prior work. Regardless, an informal argument for the equivalence of the rest of the translation is available in the first author's thesis [22] for the interested reader.

We present semantics for our subset of linear logic in Figs. 6 and 7. In these figures Γ contains typings for term variables, Π_0 contains the persistent truths and Π_1 contains the resources. We have adapted these rules from a particularly elegant formalization of linear logic from Prof. Frank Pfenning's 2012 Carnegie Mellon course notes [25]. Note that we have divided the Π that we used in Sect. 2 into Π_0 and Π_1, to separate the persistent truths and the ephemeral resources. In fact the context Π contains the preconditions of the particular method inside

$$\frac{\Gamma; \Pi_0; \Pi_1 \vdash \ r\#\text{k}/2 \ Q(\bar{\text{t}}) \otimes r\#\text{k}/2 \ Q(\bar{\text{t}})}{\Gamma; \Pi_0; \Pi_1 \vdash \ r\#\text{k} \ Q(\bar{\text{t}})} \ (OPack_1)$$

$$\frac{\Gamma; \Pi_0; \Pi_1 \vdash \ r\#\text{k*2} \ Q(\bar{\text{t}})}{\Gamma; \Pi_0; \Pi_1 \vdash \ r\#\text{k} \ Q(\bar{\text{t}}) \otimes r\#\text{k} \ Q(\bar{\text{t}})} \ (OPack_2)$$

$$\frac{\Gamma; \Pi_0; \Pi_1 \vdash \ r\#\text{k}/2 \ Q(\bar{\text{t}}) \otimes \texttt{unpacked}(r\#\text{k}/2 \ Q(\bar{\text{t}}))}{\Gamma; \Pi_0; \Pi_1 \vdash \ \texttt{unpacked}(r\#\text{k} \ Q(\bar{\text{t}}))} \ (OUnpack_1)$$

$$\frac{\Gamma; \Pi_0; \Pi_1 \vdash \ \texttt{unpacked}(r\#\text{k}/2 \ Q(\bar{\text{t}})) \otimes \texttt{unpacked}(r\#\text{k}/2 \ Q(\bar{\text{t}}))}{\Gamma; \Pi_0; \Pi_1 \vdash \ \texttt{unpacked}(r\#\text{k} \ Q(\bar{\text{t}}))} \ (OUnpack_2)$$

$$\frac{\Gamma; \Pi_0; \Pi_1 \vdash \ \texttt{unpacked}(r\#\text{k*2} \ Q(\bar{\text{t}}))}{\Gamma; \Pi_0; \Pi_1 \vdash \ \texttt{unpacked}(r\#\text{k} \ Q(\bar{\text{t}})) \otimes \texttt{unpacked}(r\#\text{k} \ Q(\bar{\text{t}}))} \ (OUnpack_3)$$

$$\frac{\Gamma; \Pi_0; \Pi_1, r.f \to x \vdash \ true}{\Gamma; \Pi_0; \Pi_1 \vdash \ r.f \to \text{x}} \ (OField)$$

$$\frac{\Gamma \vdash \text{t1} : T \quad \Gamma \vdash \text{t2} : T \quad \Gamma \vdash \ \text{binop} : (T, T) \to T_2 \quad \Gamma; \Pi_0, \text{t1 binop t2}; \Pi_1 \vdash \ true}{\Gamma; \Pi_0; \Pi_1 \vdash \ \text{t1 binop t2}} \ (OBin)$$

Fig. 6. Semantics for Linear Logic Formulas

which we have to prove a formula R and we have the equality $\Pi = \Pi_0; \Pi_1$. We are presenting the entailment relation in this section to both define precisely what it means in our system and allow us to prove properties about it.

In our restricted setting, the main difference between linear and classical logic is that object propositions are treated as resources, with the amount of resource represented by the fraction. A threat to sound translation is that a partial fraction of a proposition in the context could be used twice in the classical setting, but must only be used once in the linear setting. To prevent this, our translation converts the formula to disjunctive normal form and coalesces all fractions within each disjunction, thus ensuring that the entire fraction required is present in the context even in the classical setting.

Theorem 1 (Completeness Theorem). *For a formula R that is written in linear logic and parses according to the grammar in Sect. 2, if* $\Gamma; \Pi_0; \Pi_1 \vdash^{LL}$ R *then* $trans(\Gamma; \Pi_0; \Pi_1) \vdash^{FOL} trans(R)$.

Proof. The proof is by induction on the rules in Figs. 6 and 7. For each formula R we have to prove that if R is true in linear logic then trans(R) is true in first order logic. Due to space constraints, we show a representative case and leave the rest to [22], Sect. 4.5.

– **Case** $OPack_1$
  To prove: If $\Gamma; \Pi_0; \Pi_1 \vdash^{LL}$ P then $trans(\Gamma; \Pi_0; \Pi_1) \vdash^{FOL} trans(P)$ where:
  1. P = $r\#\text{k} \ Q(\bar{\text{t}})$

$$\frac{\Gamma; \Pi_0; \Pi_1 \vdash \ \mathsf{R1} \quad \Gamma; \Pi_0; \Pi_1' \vdash \ \mathsf{R2}}{\Gamma; \Pi_0; \Pi_1, \Pi_1' \vdash \ \mathsf{R1} \otimes \mathsf{R2}} \ (\otimes)$$

$$\frac{\Gamma; \Pi_0; \Pi_1 \vdash \ \mathsf{R1}}{\Gamma; \Pi_0; \Pi_1 \vdash \ \mathsf{R1} \oplus \mathsf{R2}} \ (\oplus_L)$$

$$\frac{\Gamma; \Pi_0; \Pi_1 \vdash \ \mathsf{R2}}{\Gamma; \Pi_0; \Pi_1 \vdash \ \mathsf{R1} \oplus \mathsf{R2}} \ (\oplus_R)$$

$$\frac{\Gamma \vdash \ \mathsf{M}{:}\mathsf{T} \quad \Gamma; \Pi_0; \Pi_1 \vdash \ \mathsf{R}\{\mathsf{M}/\mathsf{x}\}}{\Gamma; \Pi_0; \Pi_1 \vdash \ \exists \mathsf{x}{:}\mathsf{T}.\mathsf{R}} \ (\exists_1)$$

$$\frac{\Gamma \vdash \ \mathsf{F}{:}\mathsf{double} \quad \Pi_0 \vdash \ \mathsf{F} > 0 \quad \Gamma; \Pi_0; \Pi_1 \vdash \ \mathsf{R}\{\mathsf{F}/\mathsf{z}\}}{\Gamma; \Pi_0; \Pi_1 \vdash \ \exists \mathsf{z}{:}\mathsf{double}.\mathsf{R}} \ (\exists_2)$$

$$\frac{\Gamma \vdash \ \mathsf{F}{:}\mathsf{double} \quad \Pi_0 \vdash \ \mathsf{F} \ \mathsf{binop} \ \mathsf{t} \quad \Gamma; \Pi_0; \Pi_1 \vdash \ \mathsf{R}\{\mathsf{F}/\mathsf{z}\}}{\Gamma; \Pi_0; \Pi_1 \vdash \ \exists \mathsf{z}{:}\mathsf{double}.\mathsf{z} \ \mathsf{binop} \ \mathsf{t} \Rightarrow \mathsf{R}} \ (\exists_3)$$

$$\frac{\Gamma, m : T; \Pi_0; \Pi_1 \vdash \ \mathsf{R}\{m/\mathsf{x}\}}{\Gamma; \Pi_0; \Pi_1 \vdash \ \forall \mathsf{x}{:}\mathsf{T}.\mathsf{R}} \ (\forall_1)$$

$$\frac{\Gamma, \mathsf{f}{:}\mathsf{double}; \Pi_0, \mathsf{f} > 0; \Pi_1 \vdash \ \mathsf{R}\{\mathsf{f}/\mathsf{z}\}}{\Gamma; \Pi_0; \Pi_1 \vdash \ \forall \mathsf{z}{:}\mathsf{double}.\mathsf{R}} \ (\forall_2)$$

$$\frac{\Gamma, f : double; \Pi_0, \mathsf{f} \ \mathsf{binop} \ \mathsf{t}; \Pi_1 \vdash \ \mathsf{R}\{\mathsf{f}/\mathsf{z}\}}{\Gamma; \Pi_0; \Pi_1 \vdash \ \forall \mathsf{z}{:}\mathsf{double}.\mathsf{z} \ \mathsf{binop} \ \mathsf{t} \Rightarrow R} \ (\forall_3)$$

$$\frac{\Gamma; \Pi_0; \Pi_1 \vdash \ \mathsf{t1} \ \mathsf{binop} \ \mathsf{t2} \Rightarrow \mathsf{R}}{\Gamma; \Pi_0, \mathsf{t1} \ \mathsf{binop} \ \mathsf{t2}; \Pi_1 \vdash \ \mathsf{R}} \ (tbint)$$

$$\frac{}{\Gamma; \Pi_0; \Pi_1, \mathsf{R} \vdash \ \mathsf{R}} \ (id)$$

Fig. 7. Semantics for Linear Logic Formulas - cont

2. $\mathrm{trans}(P) = \mathtt{packedQ[r]} \ \&\& \ \mathrm{translateObjectProposition}(r\#k \ Q(\bar{t}))$
   (defined in Fig. 8) and

3. $$\frac{\Gamma; \Pi_0; \Pi_1 \vdash \ r\#k/2 \ Q(\bar{t}) \otimes r\#k/2 \ Q(\bar{t})}{\Gamma; \Pi_0; \Pi_1 \vdash \ r\#k \ Q(\bar{t})} \ (OPack_1)$$

Proof:

From the $OPack_1$ rule we know that
if $\Gamma; \Pi_0; \Pi_1 \vdash^{LL} r\#k \ Q(\bar{t})$ then $\Gamma; \Pi_0; \Pi_1 \vdash^{LL} r\#k/2 \ Q(\bar{t}) \otimes r\#k/2 \ Q(\bar{t})$.
Using the induction hypothesis, we know that $\mathrm{trans}(\Gamma; \Pi_0; \Pi_1) \vdash^{FOL}$
$\mathrm{trans}(r\#k/2 \ Q(\bar{t}) \otimes r\#k/2 \ Q(\bar{t}))$. Using the definition of the translateAnd()
function from Fig. 9, we obtains that $\mathrm{trans}(\Gamma; \Pi_0; \Pi_1) \vdash^{FOL} \mathrm{trans}(r\#(k/2 +$

```
function translateObjectProposition(r#k Q(t))
returns String {
    String result = "";
    if (k is a constant) {
        result += "(fracQ[r] >= k) &&";
    } else {
        result += "(fracQ[r] > 0.0) &&"; }
    if parameter t corresponds to a field of r {
        say that field is field1;
        result += "(field1[r]==t)"; }
    result += body of predicate Q with the formal parameters
            replaced by the actual ones;
    return result;
}
```

Fig. 8. translateObjectProposition() translation helper function

k/2) $Q(\bar{t})$), i.e., trans($\Gamma; \Pi_0; \Pi_1$) $\vdash^{FOL}$ trans($r\#(k)$ $Q(\bar{t})$). This means that if P holds in LL then trans(P) holds in FOL. Q.E.D.

Theorem 2 (Soundness Theorem). *For a formula R that is written in linear logic and parses according to the grammar in Sect. 2, if trans($\Gamma; \Pi_0; \Pi_1$) $\vdash^{FOL}$ trans(R) then $\Gamma; \Pi_0; \Pi_1 \vdash^{LL}$ R.*

Proof. The proof will follow the cases of R in the grammar in Sect. 2, but it will be done by induction on the complexity of formula R. For each formula R we have to prove that if trans(R) is true in first order logic then R is true in linear logic.

– **Case** $P3$
  To prove: If trans($\Gamma; \Pi_0; \Pi_1$) $\vdash^{FOL}$ trans(P) then $\Gamma; \Pi_0; \Pi_1 \vdash^{LL}$ P, where:

```
function translateAnd(R1, R2) returns FOLFormula {
    let R = DNF(R1 cross R2)
    let R' = FOL(coalesce(R))
    return transAtoms(R') }
where
    DNF(R) converts linear formula R to disjuctive normal form
    coalesce(R) merges atoms in the same conjunction by adding
            fractions
    FOL(R) replaces linear connectives with first−order logic
            connectives
    transAtoms(R) translates the atoms of R, leaving connectives
            unchanged
}
```

Fig. 9. translateAnd() translation helper function

1. $R = P = r.f \to x$
2. $\text{trans}(P) = (f[r] == x)$

Proof:
If $(f[r] == x)$ holds in FOL, by the identity rule from FOL we know that $(f[r] == x)$ is in $\text{trans}(\Pi_1)$. Knowing that we devised f to be a map that for the key r holds the current value of field $r.f$, it means that the value of field f of reference r is equal to x in LL.

The other cases of the formal proof can be found in [22], Sect. 4.5. In Sect. 4.6 of [22] we also present an informal soundness argument.

6   Evaluation

The Composite design pattern [10] expresses the fact that clients treat individual objects and compositions of objects uniformly. Verifying implementations of the Composite pattern is challenging, especially when the invariants of objects in the tree depend on each other [15], and when interior nodes of the tree can be modified by external clients, without going through the root. As a result, verifying the Composite pattern is a well-known challenge problem proposed by Leavens *et al.* [15], with some attempted solutions presented at SAVCBS 2008 (e.g. [4,14]). We have already presented our formalization and manual proof of the Composite pattern using fractions and object propositions in our published paper [23]. One of the biggest accomplishments that we present in this paper is that we were able to automatically verify the Composite pattern using the Oprop tool. The fact that our tool can automatically verify the challenging Composite pattern is proof of its maturity.

The annotated Composite.java file be seen in the example.zip folder that can be downloaded from the first page of the Oprop web application at lowcost-env.ynzf2j4byc.us-west-2.elasticbeanstalk.com. The Composite.java file presents the predicates `left`, `right`, `count` and `parent`, together with the annotated methods `updateCountRec`, `updateCount` and `setLeft` that we are able to modularly verify independently of each other, just by looking at their pre- and post-conditions. We implement a popular version of the Composite design pattern, as an acyclic binary tree, where each Composite has a reference to its left and right children and to its parent. Each Composite caches the size of its subtrees in a count field, so that a parent's count depends on its children's count. Clients can add a new subtree at any time, to any free position. This operation changes the count of all ancestors, which is done through a notification protocol. The pattern of circular dependencies and the notification mechanism are hard to capture with verification approaches based on ownership or uniqueness.

This folder also contains the SimpleCell.java file, together with the files DoubleCount.java and Link.java that we formally verified using Oprop. The class DoubleCount.java represents objects which have a field *val* and a field *dbl*, such that *dbl==2*val*. This property represents the invariant of objects of type Doublecount. We want to verify that this invariant is maintained by the method *increment*. The example Link.java illustrates how we deal with predicates that have parameters. As we verify more programs, we are adding examples to this folder. Note that when an example cannot be verified, the user will see a list of errors produced by the Boogie backend, detailing which specifications could not be proved. In that case the user should go back to the original example and modify the pre- and post-conditions of methods, or the pack/unpack annotations in the body of methods so that the verification can be successfully performed.

7 Related Work

Other researchers have encoded linear logic or fragments of it into first order logic. In his Ph.D. thesis [26] Jason Reed presents an encoding of the entirety of linear logic into first order logic. The major technical difference between Reed's encoding and ours is that he encodes uninterpreted symbols while our encoding is done inside the theory of object propositions - the smaller fragment of linear logic on top of which we have added the object propositions. His encoding is suited to any formula written in linear logic, irrespective of its meaning, while ours is targeted towards formulas written in our extended fragment of linear logic, that have a specific semantics.

Heule *et al.* [12] present an encoding of abstract predicates and abstraction functions in the verification condition generator Boogie. Their encoding is sound and handles recursion in a way that is suitable for automatic verification using SMT solvers. It is implemented in the automatic verifier Chalice. Since our system differs from theirs in the way we handle fractions (they need a full permission in order to be able to modify a field, while we are able to modify fields even if we have a fractional permission to the object enclosing the field), we came up with an encoding that is specific to our needs in our Oprop tool.

Müller *et al.* [19] created the Viper toolchain, that also uses Boogie and Z3 as a backend, and can reason about persistent mutable state, about method permissions or ownership, but they also need a full permission to modify shared data. There are other formal verification tools for object oriented programs, such as KeY [1], VCC [6] or Dafny [17], that implement other methodologies.

8 Conclusion

We have presented the Oprop tool that implements the object proposition methodology, a modular approach that can be used successfully in the verification of component-based software. We described the translation rules on which the tool is based, by referring to one example class and we proved the equivalence between formulas in Oprop and their translation into Boogie. We gave insight into the automatic verification of an instance of the Composite pattern and other examples and described the mode of usage of our web application where the tool can be accessed.

References

1. Ahrendt, W., Beckert, B., Bubel, R., Hähnle, R., Schmitt, P.H., Ulbrich, M. (eds.): Deductive Software Verification - The KeY Book - From Theory to Practice. Programming and Software Engineering, vol. 10001. Springer, Heidelberg (2016)
2. Appel, A.W., Palsberg, J.: Modern Compiler Implementation in Java, 2nd edn. Cambridge University Press, New York (2003)
3. Barnett, M., Chang, B.-Y.E., DeLine, R., Jacobs, B., Leino, K.R.M.: Boogie: a modular reusable verifier for object-oriented programs. In: de Boer, F.S., Bonsangue, M.M., Graf, S., de Roever, W.-P. (eds.) FMCO 2005. LNCS, vol. 4111, pp. 364–387. Springer, Heidelberg (2006). doi:10.1007/11804192_17
4. Bierhoff, K., Aldrich, J.: Permissions to specify the composite design pattern. In: Proceedings of SAVCBS 2008 (2008)
5. Boyland, J.: Checking interference with fractional permissions. In: Cousot, R. (ed.) SAS 2003. LNCS, vol. 2694, pp. 55–72. Springer, Heidelberg (2003). doi:10.1007/3-540-44898-5_4
6. Cohen, E., Moskal, M., Schulte, W., Tobies, S.: Local verification of global invariants in concurrent programs. In: Touili, T., Cook, B., Jackson, P. (eds.) CAV 2010. LNCS, vol. 6174, pp. 480–494. Springer, Heidelberg (2010). doi:10.1007/978-3-642-14295-6_42
7. de Moura, L., Bjørner, N.: Z3: an efficient SMT solver. In: Ramakrishnan, C.R., Rehof, J. (eds.) TACAS 2008. LNCS, vol. 4963, pp. 337–340. Springer, Heidelberg (2008). doi:10.1007/978-3-540-78800-3_24
8. DeLine, R., Fähndrich, M.: Typestates for objects. In: Odersky, M. (ed.) ECOOP 2004. LNCS, vol. 3086, pp. 465–490. Springer, Heidelberg (2004). doi:10.1007/978-3-540-24851-4_21
9. Fähndrich, M., DeLine, R.: Adoption and focus: practical linear types for imperative programming. In: PLDI, pp. 13–24 (2002)
10. Gamma, E., Helm, R., Johnson, R., Vlissides, J.: Design Patterns: Elements of Reusable Object-Oriented Software. Addison-Wesley, Boston (1994)
11. Girard, J.-Y.: Linear logic. Theor. Comput. Sci. **50**(1), 1–102 (1987)
12. Heule, S., Kassios, I.T., Müller, P., Summers, A.J.: Verification condition generation for permission logics with abstract predicates and abstraction functions. In: Castagna, G. (ed.) ECOOP 2013. LNCS, vol. 7920, pp. 451–476. Springer, Heidelberg (2013). doi:10.1007/978-3-642-39038-8_19
13. Igarashi, A., Pierce, B.C., Wadler, P.: Featherweight Java: a minimal core calculus for Java and GJ, pp. 132–146 (2001)
14. Jacobs, B., Smans, J., Piessens, F.: Verifying the composite pattern using separation logic. In: Proceedings of SAVCBS 2008 (2008)
15. Leavens, G.T., Rustan, K., Leino, M., Müller, P.: Specification and verification challenges for sequential object-oriented programs. Form. Asp. Comput. **19**(2), 159–189 (2007)
16. Leino, K.R.M., Müller, P.: A basis for verifying multi-threaded programs. In: Castagna, G. (ed.) ESOP 2009. LNCS, vol. 5502, pp. 378–393. Springer, Heidelberg (2009). doi:10.1007/978-3-642-00590-9_27
17. Leino, K.R.M.: Dafny: an automatic program verifier for functional correctness. In: Clarke, E.M., Voronkov, A. (eds.) LPAR 2010. LNCS, vol. 6355, pp. 348–370. Springer, Heidelberg (2010). doi:10.1007/978-3-642-17511-4_20
18. Leino, K.R.M.: This is boogie 2. Manuscript KRML 178 (2008)

19. Müller, P., Schwerhoff, M., Summers, A.J.: Viper: a verification infrastructure for permission-based reasoning. In: Jobstmann, B., Leino, K.R.M. (eds.) VMCAI 2016. LNCS, vol. 9583, pp. 41–62. Springer, Heidelberg (2016). doi:10.1007/978-3-662-49122-5_2

20. Müller, P. (ed.): Modular Specification and Verification of Object-Oriented Programs. LNCS, vol. 2262. Springer, Heidelberg (2002). doi:10.1007/3-540-45651-1

21. Müller, P., Poetzsch-Heffter, A., Leavens, G.T.: Modular invariants for layered object structures. Sci. Comput. Program. **62**(3), 253–286 (2006)

22. Nistor, L.: CMU Ph.D. thesis (in preparation). http://www.cs.cmu.edu/~lnistor/thesis.pdf

23. Nistor, L., Aldrich, J., Balzer, S., Mehnert, H.: Object propositions. In: Jones, C., Pihlajasaari, P., Sun, J. (eds.) FM 2014. LNCS, vol. 8442, pp. 497–513. Springer, Cham (2014). doi:10.1007/978-3-319-06410-9_34

24. Parkinson, M., Bierman, G.: Separation logic and abstraction. In: POPL, pp. 247–258 (2005)

25. Pfenning, F.: (2012). http://www.cs.cmu.edu/~fp/courses/15816-s12/

26. Reed, J.: A hybrid logical framework. Ph.D. thesis. Technical report CMU-CS-09-155 (2009)

27. Summers, A.J., Drossopoulou, S.: Considerate reasoning and the composite design pattern. In: Barthe, G., Hermenegildo, M. (eds.) VMCAI 2010. LNCS, vol. 5944, pp. 328–344. Springer, Heidelberg (2010). doi:10.1007/978-3-642-11319-2_24

Certification of Workflows
in a Component-Based Cloud of High
Performance Computing Services

Allberson B. de Oliveira Dantas[1]([✉]), F. Heron de Carvalho Junior[1],
and Luis S. Barbosa[2,3]

[1] MDCC, Universidade Federal do Ceará, Campus do Pici, Fortaleza, Brazil
{allberson,heron}@lia.ufc.br
[2] HASLab INESC TEC, Universidade do Minho,
Campus de Gualtar, Braga, Portugal
[3] UNU-EGOV, United Nations University, Guimarães, Portugal
lsb@di.uminho.pt

Abstract. The orchestration of high performance computing (HPC)
services to build scientific applications is based on complex workflows.
A challenging task consists of improving the reliability of such workflows,
avoiding faulty behaviors that can lead to bad consequences in practice.
This paper introduces a certifier component for certifying scientific workflows in a certification framework proposed for HPC Shelf, a cloud-based
platform for HPC in which different kinds of users can design, deploy
and execute scientific applications. This component is able to inspect
the workflow description of a parallel computing system of HPC Shelf
and check its consistency with respect to a number of safety and liveness
properties specified by application designers and component developers.

1 Introduction

Contrariwise to other engineering disciplines, reliability is often disregarded in
current software development. Actually, testing and *a posteriori* empirical error
detection dominate the practice of software industry, compared to formal verification and correct-by-construction techniques.

The problem is that software and computational systems are inherently complex. Each line of code is a potential source of errors, and programs often exhibit
a huge number of potential states, making it difficult to predict their behavior
and verify their properties in a rigorous way. This difficulty is more evident in
emerging heterogeneous computing environments in High Performance Computing (HPC), where concurrent programs are omnipresent.

Scientific Workflow Management Systems (SWfMS) have been largely applied
by scientists and engineers for the design, execution and monitoring of reusable
data processing task pipelines in scientific discovery and data analysis [24].
In these systems, workflows are commonly represented by components that
absorb all the orchestration logic required to solve a specific problem. Applications emerge by composition of workflows and different sorts of computational

J. Proença and M. Lumpe (Eds.): FACS 2017, LNCS 10487, pp. 198–215, 2017.
DOI: 10.1007/978-3-319-68034-7_12

components, usually provided in generic or tailored libraries. Increasing the reliability of the available workflows is considered a challenging task in the sense that deadlocks must be avoided, crucial operations must be effectively executed, and no faulty behaviors should be induced as a result of badly designed workflows.

HPC Shelf is a proposal of a component-oriented platform to provide cloud-based HPC services. It offers an environment to develop applications matching the needs of specialists (i.e. experts on the relevant scientific or engineering domain) who are supposed to deal with domain-specific, heavy computational problems by orchestrating a set of parallel components tuned to classes of parallel computing platforms. Orchestrations in HPC Shelf are driven by a SWfMS called SAFe (*Shelf Application Framework*) [9]. Parallel computing systems implement applications in HPC Shelf by composing components that address functional and non-functional concerns, representing both hardware and software elements.

In such a scenario, this paper approaches the problem of *certifying* scientific workflows through the verification of typical behavioral properties (e.g. safety and liveness) they are expected to exhibit, therefore increasing their confidence levels. We are interested not only in discovering design errors on workflows, but also on improving their specifications based on the verification results. This work is based on a certification framework [10] previously proposed by the authors for HPC Shelf. Such a framework is basically a VaaS (Verification-as-a-Service) platform, where *certifier* components can be created and connected to other (certifiable) components within a parallel computing system under design. Certifier components orchestrate a set of *tactical* components in certification tasks. The latter, on the other hand, encapsulate the functionalities of one or more existing verification infrastructures, commonly composed of provers, model checkers and other elements, and run on parallel computing platforms of HPC Shelf, for accelerating the certification process.

This paper proposes a new kind of certifier components, designated by SWC2 (Scientific Workflow Component Certifier), for statically certifying workflows of parallel computing systems over the parallel computing infrastructure of HPC Shelf. Some of the main patterns found in this class of workflows and their verification are discussed. The proposed approach is further illustrated by resorting to a specific SWC2 component and a related tactical component, which encapsulates the mCRL2 verification toolset.

Related work. Several studies on the formalization and verification of business workflows have been proposed in literature. These include Event-Condition-Action rules (triggers) [6,14,18], logic-based methods [3,5,23], Petri Nets [1,2,25] and State Charts [27]. The approach proposed here, however, is innovative in the sense that no initiatives were found regarding the formalization and verification of scientific workflow patterns.

Paper structure. HPC Shelf is succinctly presented in Sect. 2. Section 3 presents an overview of the certification framework. Section 4 introduces workflow certifiers. Section 5, in turn, discusses the way workflows in HPC Shelf are translated to behavioral models in mCRL2. The approach is illustrated with a case study in Sect. 6. Finally, Sect. 7 concludes the paper.

2   HPC Shelf

HPC Shelf is a cloud computing platform for cloud-based HPC applications. It receives problem specifications from *specialist users* and build computational solutions for them. For that, the platform offers, to *application providers*, tools for building parallel computing systems by orchestrating components that comply to Hash, a model of intrinsically parallel components [7], representing both computations (software) developed by *component developers*, and parallel computing platforms (hardware) offered by *platform maintainers*. Specialists, providers, developers and maintainers are the stakeholders of HPC Shelf.

2.1   Component Kinds in HPC Shelf

HPC Shelf defines different kinds of components: virtual ***platforms***, representing distributed-memory parallel computing platforms; ***computations***, implementing parallel algorithms by exploiting the features of a class of virtual platforms; ***data sources***, storing data that may interest to computations; ***connectors***, which couple a set of computations and data sources placed in distinct virtual platforms; and ***bindings***, for connecting *service* and *action* ports exported by components for communication and synchronization of tasks, respectively.

A *service binding* connects a *user* to a *provider* port, allowing a component to consume a service offered by another component. In turn, *action bindings* connect a set of action ports that export the same set of action names. Two actions of the same name whose action ports are connected in two components execute when both components make them active at the same time (*rendezvous*). Figure 1 depicts a scenario illustrating components and their bindings.

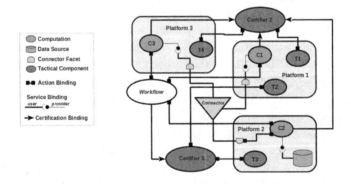

Fig. 1. Components in a hypothetical parallel computing system.

Components have a predefined action port, called *LifeCycle* which respond to a number of actions for life-cycle control. Action **resolve** selects a component implementation and a virtual platform for it, according to a system of *contextual* *contracts* (see below). Action **deploy** deploys a selected component in a parallel computing platform. Action **instantiate** instantiates a deployed component, which becomes ready for communication with other components through service and action ports. Finally, action **release** releases a component from the platform on which it is instantiated, when it is no longer useful.

2.2 Architecture

The architecture of HPC Shelf is structured around three main elements, Front-End, Core and Back-End, as described below.

The Front-End is SAFe (*Shelf Application Framework*) [9], a collection of Java or C# classes and design patterns that *providers* use for deriving applications. They use SAFe *Scientific Workflow Language* (SAFeSWL) for specifying parallel computing systems, divided into an *architectural* and an *orchestration* subsets. The former is used to specify solution components and their bindings. The later orchestrates them. The workflow component of a parallel computing system is a special connector that runs in SAFe for performing the SAFeSWL orchestration.

The Core manages the life-cycle of components, offering services for *developers* and *maintainers* register components and their contracts. For that, the Core implements an underlying component resolution mechanism based on *contextual contracts*. Applications access the services of the Core for resolving contracts and deploying the components of their parallel computing systems.

The Back-End is a service offered by a *maintainer* to the Core for the deployment of virtual platforms. Once deployed, virtual platforms may communicate directly with the Core for instantiating components, which become ready for direct communication with applications through service and action bindings.

2.3 Contextual Contracts

HPC Shelf employs a system of *contextual contracts* [8] that separates interface and implementation of components (abstract and concrete components, respectively), so that one or more concrete components may exist in the Core's catalog for a given abstract component. Different components will meet different assumptions on the requirements of the host application and the features of the parallel computing platforms where they can be instantiated (*execution context*). For that, an abstract component has a *contextual signature*, composed of a set of *context parameters*. In turn, a concrete component must be associated with a type, i.e. a *contextual contract*, defined by an abstract component and a set of *context arguments* that valuate its context parameters. During orchestration, when the action **resolve** of a component is activated, a resolution procedure is triggered to choose a concrete component matching the corresponding contract.

3 The Certification Framework

We have proposed a certification framework for components in HPC Shelf [10], which introduced the kind of **certifier** components. The connection between a certifier and a certifiable component is called *certification binding*. It also introduced the auxiliary kind of **tactical** components, for encapsulating proof infrastructures orchestrated by certifiers in verification tasks.

3.1   Parallel Certification Systems

A parallel certification system is like a parallel computing system for performing the certification procedure of a certifier component. It comprises a set of tactical components, deployed in virtual platforms where the required verification infrastructures are deployed; a certifier component, which orchestrates the tactical components through a workflow written in TCOL (Tactical Component Orchestration Language); a set of certifiable components, linked to the certifier through certification bindings. The certifier runs on SAFe, like the workflow component.

For a certifiable component to be certified, one or more certifier components whose certification ports are compatible to the certification port of the certifiable component must be chosen from the catalog and connected to it through certification bindings. When the workflow activates the new action **certify** in the life-cycle port of the certifiable component, the parallel certification system of each certifier performs its certification procedure to certify it.

The certification of a component with respect to a certifier component is idempotent, that is, it is executed once, even though **certify** is activated multiple times in one or more applications. Each certifier distinguish which properties it may verify are either mandatory or optional. At the end of the certification process, the component is considered to be certified with respect to the certifier component if all mandatory properties have been proven. If so, the component receives a *certificate* with respect to the certifier, which is registered in the catalog of components in an unforgeable format. Finally, the certification of a certifiable component is a pre-requisite for running it in an application.

By supporting the association of multiple certifiable components to the same certifier, SAFe makes application providers able to optimize resources, by instantiating a single parallel certification system for all of them, instead of one for each one of them. This is an important feature in a cloud computing environment.

3.2   Tactical Components

A tactical component represents a proof infrastructure, integrating a set of verification tools. It can perform a flow of execution that includes receiving a code written in the language it understands, execute validations, conversions and, finally, verify properties on such a code. Tactical components are able to exploit the parallelism features of their virtual platforms for accelerating verifications.

Besides the *LifeCycle* port, a tactical component has two other ports. Firstly, it has a user service port, with the following operations: receiving the code of the certifiable component from the certifier component, possibly previously translated by the certifier component into the language that the tactical component understands; receiving from the certifier component formal properties to be verified on that code; allowing the certifier component to monitor the progress of the verification of properties; and returning to the certifier the result of the verification process. Secondly, it has an action port called *Verify*, containing the actions **verify_perform**, **verify_conclusive** and **verify_inconclusive**.

When **verify_perform** is activated, the tactical component starts the verification process of the formal properties assigned to it. When this process finishes, it activates **verify_conclusive**, if the verification result was conclusive for all properties (true or false), or **verify_inconclusive**, meaning that the verification of one or more properties was inconclusive (null). The verification of a property is inconclusive when the tactical component is prevented in some way from applying its verification technique to prove or refute the property. Such a situation may occur when there is some infrastructure failure on the virtual platform that places the tactical component, when the property is written in a format that is not understood by the tactical component, or when the verification timeout of the verification tool is reached. In such a case, the certifier may restart the verification process for the failed tactical component.

4   The SWC2 Certifier

If HPC Shelf can accommodate different types of component certifiers, it makes sense to consider a specific type of certifier addressing the verification of properties of the application workflow itself, rather than the functional properties of its individual components. This section introduces such a certifier — designated by SWC2 (from *Scientific Workflow Certifier Component*). Its purpose is to certify SAFeSWL workflows through the verification of a set of behavioural properties, currently resorting to a single proof infrastructure — the mCRL2 tool.

But what are the relevant properties a scientific workflow is expected to comply? The question is addressed below, based on our own experience with SAFe specifications and a recent state-of-the-art survey [9]. Other SWfMS, such as Askalon [21], BPEL Sedna [26], Kepler [20], Pegasus [12], Taverna [28] and Triana [17], were also investigated.

Firstly, scientific workflows are typically coarse-grained, due to the sort of specialized algorithms they perform. Such algorithms demand for intensive calculations, possibly taking advantage of HPC techniques and infrastructures. Coarse-grained components encapsulate most of the computational complexity of scientific workflows. Thus, orchestration languages aimed at the creation of these workflows generally offer few constructors, often limited to plain versions of sequencing, branching, iteration, parallelism and asynchronism.

On the other hand, scientific workflows are usually represented by components and execution dependencies among them, abstracting away from the computing platforms on which they run. However, during the execution of a component in a workflow, *resolution* procedures may be applied to find out which computing platform best fits its requirements. Thus, it may be interesting to verify statically if the computational actions of components are always activated after the computing platforms where they are placed have been resolved.

Scientific workflows usually adopt abstract descriptions of components, i.e. they fix only interfaces exposing available operations, without associating the component to a specific implementation. At an appropriate time of the workflow execution, a *resolution* procedure may be triggered for discovering an appropriate component implementation. Thus, it is relevant to ensure that the activation of computational actions of components is made after their effective resolution.

In order to minimize the waste of computational resources, the computing platform where a component is placed may be instantiated only when the component is strictly necessary and released when it is no longer needed. This pattern introduces three operations in the life-cycle of components: *deployment*, which installs the component implementation and possibly required libraries in the target computing platform; *instantiation*, comprising the allocation of necessary resources and configuration of the runtime environment; and, finally, *releasing*, when resources assigned to the components are deallocated. The consistency of the activation order of these operations may be statically verified. Finally, note that consistency checking of the life-cycle of components is supported by the concrete workflow certifier SWC2Impl described in Sect. 4.1.

But other types of workflows are also to be considered. Actually, in addition to the workflow component, which exogenously activates actions of the relevant components, each of those has an internal workflow that synchronizes with the workflow component for activating its computational operations. The *composition* of the application workflow with the internal workflows extracted from the components' code may refine the verification process, making possible to check more specialized, useful properties.

Component internal workflows recognized by HPC Shelf are those which enable/disable its actions. Each *component workflow* of a component C consists of a set of rules of the form:

$$C ::= act_1 \rightarrow act_2 \downarrow \mid \top \rightarrow act_2 \downarrow \mid act_1 \rightarrow act_2 \nmid \qquad \text{(component rule)}$$

Let Act_C be the set of all action names of any action port of a component C, and let $act_1, act_2 \in Act_C$. Rule $act_1 \rightarrow act_2 \downarrow$ says that when act_1 completes, act_1 is disabled and act_2 enabled. In turn, the rule $\top \rightarrow act_2 \downarrow$ means that act_2 is always enabled. Finally, rule $act_1 \rightarrow act_2 \nmid$ indicates that, on completion of act_1, act_1 and act_2 become disabled. Examples of component workflows are presented in the case study.

The orchestration of fine-grained components is considered too expensive in scientific workflows. In general, the time required to make the component ready (component resolution, deployment and instantiation) may exceed its effective computation time. Thus, fine-grained components with similar characteristics may be grouped into a coarse-grained component, called a *cluster* component. The activation of an action of a cluster component translates to the activation of a workflow responsible for activating each of the fine-grained components. This behavior may be incorporated into the workflow verification model for generating a more accurate specification of the computational system.

Note that cluster components in HPC Shelf are parallel ones, i.e. an activation of an action of a cluster component is in fact a parallel activation of all corresponding actions in the related fine-grained components. An example of cluster component in the case study below.

4.1   Formal Properties and Contextual Contracts

In general, properties can be divided in three classes: *default, application* and *ad hoc*. Default properties are common to any workflow. Typically, they include absence of deadlocks and infinite loops, and life-cycle consistency. Their verification is enabled through the following contextual signature:

$$\text{SWC2 } [\textit{deadlock\_absence} = D : \text{DATYPE}, \textit{infinite\_loop\_absence} = I : \text{ILATYPE},$$
$$\textit{life\_cycle\_verification} = L : \text{LCVTYPE}, \textit{ad\_hoc\_properties} = A : \text{AHTYPE}]$$

Context parameters ***deadlock_absence***, ***infinite_loop_absence*** and ***life_cycle_verification*** determines which sort of property is to be verified. Note that *ad hoc* properties are specified by the user resorting to the formal language supported by the certifier and stored in the workflow. The parameter ***ad_hoc_properties*** determines whether these properties are accepted.

From the contextual signature of SWC2, a contextual contract can be derived for concrete certifiers. An example is the following contract of the concrete certifier SWC2Impl:

$$\text{SWC2Impl : SWC2 } [\textit{deadlock\_absence} = \text{DEADLOCKABSENCE},$$
$$\textit{infinite\_loop\_absence} = \text{INFINITELOOPABSENCE},$$
$$\textit{life\_cycle\_verification} = \text{LIFECYCLEVERIFICATION},$$
$$\textit{ad\_hoc\_properties} = \text{ADHOCPROPERTIES}]$$

This means that SWC2Impl verifies deadlock absence, infinite loop absence and life-cycle consistency, and accepts *ad hoc* properties. To accomplish this it currently orchestrates a single tactical component, MCRL2, which extends the contextual signature TACTICAL with a parameter ***version*** specifying a version of the mCRL2 toolset:

$$\text{TACTICAL } [\textit{message\_passing\_interface} = M : \text{MPITYPE},$$
$$\textit{number\_of\_nodes} = N : \text{INTEGER}, \textit{number\_of\_cores} = C : \text{INTEGER}]$$

$$\text{MCRL2 } [\textit{version} = V : \text{VERSIONTYPE}, \textit{message\_passing\_interface} = M : \text{MPITYPE},$$
$$\textit{number\_of\_nodes} = N : \text{INTEGER}, \textit{number\_of\_cores} = C : \text{INTEGER}]$$
$$\text{extends TACTICAL } [\textit{message\_passing\_interface} = M,$$
$$\textit{number\_of\_nodes} = N, \textit{number\_of\_cores} = C]$$

The parameter ***message_passing_interface*** configures the message passing library used by the tactical component (e.g. MPI [13]). In turn, ***number_of_nodes*** and ***number_of_cores*** specifies the (minimum) number of processing nodes and cores per node that will be required for execution of the tactical component. The orchestration performed by SWC2Impl is governed by the TCOL fragment depicted in Fig. 2.

Finally, mCRL2Impl is declared as a concrete tactical component encapsulating version 201409.1 of the mCRL2 toolset, implemented through the MPICH2 library[1] and resorting to at least four cores per processing node:

---

[1] http://www.mpich.org/.

```
0  <sequence>
1      <perform action="resolve"          id_port="mCRL2-life-cycle"/>
2      <perform action="deploy"           id_port="mCRL2-life-cycle"/>
3      <perform action="instantiate"      id_port="mCRL2-life-cycle"/>
4      <perform action="verify_perform"   id_port="mCRL2-verify"/>
5      <perform action="release"          id_port="mCRL2-life-cycle"/>
6  </sequence>
```

Fig. 2. The orchestration code of the certifier SWC2Impl in TCOL.

$$\text{mCRL2Impl : MCRL2 } [\textit{version } = 201409.1,$$
$$\textit{message\_passing\_interface } = \text{MPICH2, } \textit{number\_of\_cores } = 4]$$

In SWC2Impl, the contextual contract of the inner MCRL2 tactical component makes mCRL2Impl a possible candidate, since it only requires MPI:

$$\text{MCRL2 } [\textit{message\_passing\_interface } = \text{MPI}]$$

For certifying a workflow, the provider must create, using the architectural subset of SAFeSWL, a certification binding between the workflow component and a SWC2 component, represented by a contract like

$$\text{SWC2 } [\textit{deadlock\_absence } = \text{DEADLOCKABSENCE, } \textit{ad\_hoc\_properties } = \text{ADHOCPROPERTIES}]$$

This contract declares that the provider looks for a certifier that verifies deadlock absence and accepts *ad hoc* properties. Clearly, SWC2Impl is a candidate.

The certifier component determines which default and application properties are either optional or mandatory, and providers determine this for *ad hoc* ones.

5   Translating SAFeSWL to mCRL2

The verification of a SAFeSWL workflow requires its translation to the specific notation of the tactical component which will take care of it. As explained above, mCRL2 [15,16] was chosen here to support workflow verification. System behaviors in mCRL2 are specified in a process algebra reminiscent of ACP [4]. Processes are built from a set of user-declared actions and a small number of combinators including *multi-action* synchronization, *sequential*, *alternative* and *parallel* composition, and abstraction operators (namely, action *relabeling*, *hiding* and *restriction*). Actions can be parameterized by data and conditional constructs, giving support to conditional, or data-dependent, systems' behaviors. Data is defined in terms of abstract, equational data types [22]; behaviors, on the other hand, are given operationally resorting to labeled transition systems.

mCRL2 provides a modal logic with fixed points, extending Kozen's propositional modal μ-calculus [19] with data variables and quantification over data domains. The flexibility attained by nesting least and greatest fixpoint operators with modal combinators allows for the specification of complex properties. For simplifying formulas, mCRL2 allows the use of regular expressions over the set of actions as possible labels of both necessity and eventuality modalities. The use of regular expressions provides a set of macros for property specification which are enough in practical situations.

5.1 The Translation Process

The translation process follows directly the operational rules (Fig. 4) defined for a formal version of the orchestration subset of SAFeSWL (Fig. 3).

Let W be the workflow component of a parallel computing system. In such a grammar, c ranges over component identifiers, h ranges over naturals and $act \in Act_W$. For each component, we assume a minimal set of workflow actions, including life cycle ones ($\{\mathtt{resolve}_c, \mathtt{deploy}_c, \mathtt{instantiate}_c, \mathtt{release}_c\} \subseteq Act_W$).

The semantics of W consists of a task T_W, given by the rules in Fig. 4, and initial state $\langle T_W, \mathtt{stop}, \emptyset, \emptyset, \emptyset, \emptyset \rangle$. The symbol stop denotes task completion. Each execution state consists of a tuple $\langle T_1, T_2, E, L, S, F \rangle$, where T_1 is the next task to be evolved; T_2 is the following task to be evolved; E are the actions enabled in

$$T ::= L \mid G \mid T_1; T_2 \mid T_1 || T_2 \mid \mathtt{repeat}\ T \qquad \text{(task)}$$

$$L ::= act \mid \mathtt{break} \mid \mathtt{continue} \mid \mathtt{start}(h, act) \mid \mathtt{wait}(h) \mid \mathtt{cancel}(h) \qquad \text{(literal)}$$

$$G ::= act{\downarrow}T \mid act{\downarrow}T + G \qquad \text{(guarded tasks)}$$

Fig. 3. Formal Grammar of the Orchestration Subset of SAFeSWL.

$$\text{(big-step)}\quad \frac{state \xrightarrow{x} state'' \quad state'' \stackrel{xs}{\Longrightarrow} state'}{state \stackrel{x \cdot xs}{\Longrightarrow} state'}$$

$$\text{(action)}\quad \frac{a \in E}{\langle a, T, E, L, S, F \rangle \xrightarrow{a} \langle T, \mathtt{stop}, E, L, S, F \rangle}$$

$$\text{(parallel-left)}\quad \frac{\langle T_1, \mathtt{stop}, E, L, S, F \rangle \stackrel{xs}{\Longrightarrow} \langle T_1', R_1, E', L', S', F' \rangle}{\langle T_1 || T_2, T, E, L, S, F \rangle \stackrel{xs}{\Longrightarrow} \langle (T_1'; R_1 || T_2, T, E', L', S', F' \rangle}$$

$$\text{(stop-par-left)}\quad \frac{}{\langle \mathtt{stop} || T_2, T, E, L, S, F \rangle \to \langle T_2, T, E, L, S, F \rangle}$$

$$\text{(select-left)}\quad \frac{a \in E}{\langle a{\downarrow}T_1 + G, T_2, E, L, S, F \rangle \to \langle T_1, T_2, E, L, S, F \rangle}$$

$$\text{(select-right)}\quad \frac{a \notin E \quad \langle G, T_2, E, L, S, F \rangle \to \langle T_3, T_2, E, L, S, F \rangle}{\langle a{\downarrow}T_1 + G, T_2, E, L, S, F \rangle \to \langle T_3, T_2, E, L, S, F \rangle}$$

$$\text{(sequence)}\quad \frac{}{\langle (T_1; T_2), T, E, L, S, F \rangle \to \langle T_1, (T_2; T), E, L, S, F \rangle}$$

$$\text{(repeat)}\quad \frac{}{\langle \mathtt{repeat}\ T_1, T_2, E, L, S, F \rangle \to \langle T_1, \mathtt{stop}, E, (T_1, T_2) \cdot L, S, F \rangle}$$

$$\text{(continue)}\quad \frac{}{\langle \mathtt{continue}, T, E, (T_i, T_f) \cdot L, S, F \rangle \to \langle T_i, T, E, (T_i, T_f) \cdot L, S, F \rangle}$$

$$\text{(break)}\quad \frac{}{\langle \mathtt{break}, T, E, (T_i, T_f) \cdot L, S, F \rangle \to \langle T_f, \mathtt{stop}, E, L, S, F \rangle}$$

$$\text{(start)}\quad \frac{a \in E \quad fresh(h)}{\langle \mathtt{start}(a, h), T, E, L, S, F \rangle \xrightarrow{start(a,h)} \langle T, \mathtt{stop}, E, L, S \cup \{(a, h)\}, F \rangle}$$

$$\text{(wait)}\quad \frac{h \in F}{\langle \mathtt{wait}(h), T, E, L, S, F \rangle \to \langle T, \mathtt{stop}, E, L, S, F \rangle}$$

$$\text{(finish)}\quad \frac{(a, h) \in S}{\langle T_1, T_2, E, L, S, F \rangle \xrightarrow{(a,h)} \langle T_1, T_2, E, L, S - \{(a, h)\}, F \cup \{h\} \rangle}$$

$$\text{(cancel)}\quad \frac{(a, h) \in S}{\langle \mathtt{cancel}(h), T, E, L, S, F \rangle \to \langle T, \mathtt{stop}, E, L, S - \{(a, h)\}, F \rangle}$$

Note: rules (parallel-right) and (stop-par-right) are omitted in this figure, since they are symmetric to (parallel-left) and (stop-par-left), respectively.

Fig. 4. Operational semantics of the orchestration subset of SAFeSWL.

the components; L is a stack of pairs with the beginning and the end of the repeat blocks scoping the current task; S is a set of pairs with actions asynchronously activated that have not yet been finished and their handles; and F is a set of handles associated to finished asynchronous actions.

For simplicity, the behavior imposed by the internal workflows of components is omitted, which enable/disable their actions and directly manipulate E.

Rule `big-step` denotes a big-step transition relation between execution states. Rule `action` states that a state containing the activation of an enabled action causes the system to observe the action and go to the state in which the next task is evaluated. Rule `sequence` indicates sequential evaluation of tasks. Rule (`parallel-left`) states that if a state X with a task T_1 leads to any state Y in any number of steps, the parallelization of T_1 with a task T_2, starting from X, leads to Y, however propagating the parallelism to the next task. Rule `stop-par-left` denotes parallel termination (join). Rule `select-left` indicates that the activated action must be enabled. Rule `select-right` states that a disabled action may not be activated. Rule `repeat` performs a task T_1 and stores in L the iteration beginning and end tasks, which are performed, respectively, through rules `continue` and `break`. Rule `start` says that an enabled action and a handle not yet used can be associated and added to S, emitting an action to the system $(start(A, h))$. Rule `finish` indicates that an action asynchronously activated can actually occur, having its handle registered in F and emitting an action to the system $((a,h))$. Rule `wait` states that waiting for a finished asynchronous action has no effect. Finally, rule `cancel` cancels an asynchronous action.

We may now briefly present an informal description of the translation process. Rule (`action`) states that every SAFeSWL action is an observable mCRL2 action. Rule (`sequence`) states that a sequence of two tasks in SAFeSWL is translated by the sequential composition of the corresponding translations. Rules (`parallel-left`) and (`parallel-right`) mean that the translation of a set of parallel tasks takes place by the creation of mCRL2 processes in a fork-join paradigm. Rules (`select-left`) and (`select-right`) indicate the need for the creation of mCRL2 processes that control the state (enabled/disabled) of actions. Rules (`repeat`), (`continue`) and (`break`) indicate, respectively, the need for the creation of a mCRL2 process that manages a repetition task in order to detect the need for a new iteration, the return back to the beginning of the iteration, or the end of the iteration. Rule (`start`) states the need for the creation of an asynchronous mCRL2 process that will eventually perform the action. Moreover, it is also needed to create a manager process that stores the state of all actions started asynchronously (pending or finished). Finally, rules (`wait`) and (`cancel`) indicate the need for the communication with such a manager to, depending on the state of the asynchronous action, block the calling process or cancel the asynchronous process launched for the action.

5.2 Default Properties in mCRL2

The first default property is deadlock absence, specified as DA : [true*]⟨true⟩true, i.e. there is always a possible next action at every point in the workflow.

A workflow that contains a **repeat** task may perform an infinite loop when a **break** is not reachable within its scope. We may check infinite loop absence (ILA) by verifying if all mCRL2 $break(i)$ actions can occur from a certain point on, where i is the index of the related **repeat** task, using the following formula:

$$\text{ILA} : \; \forall i : Nat.[\text{true}*]\langle \text{true} * .break(i)\rangle\text{true}$$

The remaining properties express life-cycle restrictions in terms of precedence relations specified by formulas like

$$\text{LC1} : \; \forall c : Nat.[!resolve(c) * .deploy(c)]\text{false}$$
$$\&\& \; \langle \text{true} * .resolve(c).!release(c) * .deploy(c)\rangle\text{true}$$

This formula is applied to each component c, restricted to orchestrated components in order to reduce the model checking search space. The first part of the conjunction states that a **deploy** may not be performed before a **resolve**. Note that ! stands for set complement, thus the expression $[!a]$ false states that all evolutions by an action different from a are forbidden. The second part states that a **deploy** may be performed, since a **resolve** has been performed before and there is not a **release** between **resolve** and **deploy**. Similar restrictions may be specified for different pairs of life-cycle actions using a similar pattern, such as:

$$\text{LC2} : \; \forall c : Nat.[!deploy(c) * .instantiate(c)]\text{false}$$
$$\&\& \; \langle \text{true} * .deploy(c).!release(c) * .instantiate(c)\rangle\text{true}$$
$$\text{LC3} : \; \forall c, a : Nat.[!instantiate(c) * .compute(c, a)]\text{false}$$
$$\&\& \; \langle \text{true} * .instantiate(c).!release(c) * .compute(c, a)\rangle\text{true}$$
$$\text{LC4} : \; \forall c : Nat.[!instantiate(c) * .release(c)]\text{false}$$
$$\&\& \; \langle \text{true} * .instantiate(c).!release(c) * .release(c)\rangle\text{true}$$

Here, **compute**(c, a) represents the computational action a of a component c, declared in the architectural description of the workflow.

6 A Case Study

MapReduce is a programming model implemented by a number of large-scale data parallel processing frameworks, firstly proposed by *Google Inc.* [11]. A user must specify: a *map function*, which is applied by a set of parallel *mapper* processes to each element of an input list of *key/value* pairs (KV-pairs), returning a set of elements in an intermediary list of KV-pairs; and a *reduce function*, which is applied by a set of parallel *reducer* processes to all intermediate values associated with the same *key* across all mappers, yielding a list of output pairs.

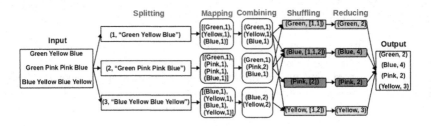

Fig. 5. A classic example of word counting with MapReduce.

Figure 5 depicts a simple example of MapReduce for processing a text containing lines of words *green, yellow, blue* and *pink*. At the end of the processing, the expected output is the number of occurrences of each color in the text.

We have designed a framework of components for MapReduce computations in HPC Shelf, comprising the following components: DATASOURCE, a *data source* that stores the input data structure; MAPPER, a *computation* that implements a set of parallel mapping agents; REDUCER, a *computation* that implements a set of parallel reducing agents; DATASINK, a *data source* that stores the output data structure, generated from the output pairs produced by the reducing agents; SPLITTER, a *connector* that takes the list of input pairs from the data source (first iteration) and outputs pairs generated by the reducing agents (produced in the previous iteration) and either distributes them to the mapping agents (to start a new iteration) or sends them to the data sink (to end the process); and SHUFFLER is a *connector* that groups intermediate keys produced by the mapping agents and redistributes them among the reducing agents.

Figure 6 depicts the architecture of a simple iterative MapReduce parallel computing system. Each computation/connector has three ports: a user and provider service port, from which they input KV-pairs and output KV-pairs, respectively; and a single *action* port, called *TaskChunk*, for orchestrating tasks.

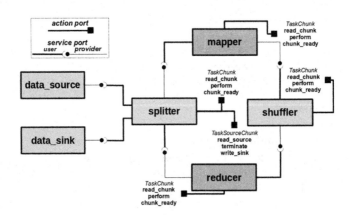

Fig. 6. The MapReduce architecture.

KV-pairs are transmitted (between splitter and shuffler) and processed (by mapper and reducer) incrementally for optimizing communication granularity and overlapping mapping and reducing phases in the same iteration.

TaskChunk has the three action names: **chunk_ready**, for signaling that a new chunk of KV-pairs is available; **read_chunk**, for inputing KV-pairs from the next chunk; **perform**, for processing the KV-pairs read from a chunk.

For our purposes, the contextual signatures of the abstract components and the contextual contracts of the concrete components, whose instances were presented, can be omitted. The SAFeSWL workflow script will be not shown here, but it is available from http://www.lia.ufc.br/~allberson/swc2.

6.1 Internal Workflows of MapReduce Components

The following simplified version of the internal workflows of MapReduce components is enough for proving all properties relevant to this case study:

$$shuffler = mapper = reducer = combiner =$$
$$\{\top \to resolve\downarrow, \top \to deploy\downarrow, \top \to instantiate\downarrow,$$
$$\top \to read\_chunk\downarrow, \top \to perform\downarrow, perform \to chunk\_ready\downarrow\}$$
$$splitter = shuffler \ \cup \ \{\top \to read\_source\downarrow, \top \to write\_sink\downarrow,$$
$$perform \to terminate\downarrow\}$$

6.2 Certification of the MapReduce Workflow

Consider the certification architecture depicted in Fig. 7. It contains a certification binding linking the MapReduce workflow to SWC2, containing the valuation described in Sect. 4.1, which aims to choose SWC2Impl. When the application is started by SAFe, a parallel certification system is automatically instantiated and executed. During the certification process, SWC2Impl was chosen, with mCRL2Impl, also described in Sect. 4.1, as its tactical component, over a virtual platform containing 4 processing nodes. The result of the translation of the MapReduce workflow into mCRL2 is available at www.lia.ufc.br/~allberson/swc2.

6.3 MapReduce *Ad Hoc* Properties

The MapReduce *ad hoc* properties include a *safety* and a *liveness* group. The former describes precedences of execution between two distinct components or component actions. Two examples, among a list of 11, are shown for illustrative purposes. Note that the numbers in the formulas correspond to specific component and action identifiers, as they appear in the original SAFeSWL code.

$$\text{SbM} : \ [!compute(3, 352) * .compute(5, 551)]false$$
$$\text{MbC} : \ [true * .compute(5, 551).!compute(3, 352) * .$$
$$compute(5, 551)]false$$

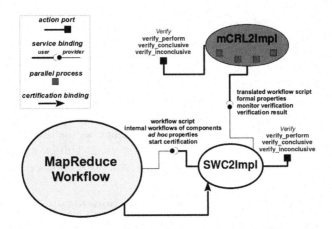

Fig. 7. Certification architecture for the MapReduce workflow.

Property SbM states that the action **read_chunk** (551), of mapper (5), must be preceded by the action **perform** (352), of splitter (3). On its turn, the second property expresses that the action **perform** (352), of splitter (3), must occur between two executions of the action **read_chunk** (551), of mapper (5).

The liveness group includes a broader ontology of properties. For example,

LIV1 : $\langle true * .guard(3, 342) \rangle$ true

LIV2 : $\forall c : Nat, a : Nat. \nu X.\mu Y.[compute(c, a)]Y \&\& [!compute(c, a)]X$

LIV3 : $[true*](\forall c : Nat, a : Nat => \mu Y.([!compute(c, a)]Y \&\& < true > true))$

Property LIV1 ensures the existence of workflow traces including the execution of a particular action (**terminate** (342), of splitter (3)). The second property expresses the fact that an action can only be executed along non consecutive periods. Finally, LIV3 is a non starvation condition, that is, for every reachable state it is possible to execute **compute**(c, a), for any possible value of c and a. Note the quantification over the workflow components and actions.

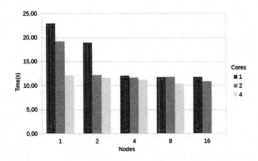

Fig. 8. MapReduce workflow certification times.

The 20 formal properties (both default and *ad hoc*) verified were distributed among the 4 units of the tactical component, and proven. Figure 8 depicts the average times for the certification of the MapReduce workflow, by varying the number of processing nodes and processing cores per node. As expected a judicious use of parallelism can cut the execution time in half in most cases.

7 Conclusions and Future Work

In the previous sections, we have made a case for the introduction, within a platform for orchestrating parallel components, of a specific component whose purpose is to verify behavioral properties of workflow that link different components which make up an application. This has a *reflexive* character: a component that contributes to certify the emergent orchestrated behavior in an application.

This idea was made concrete in the context of the HPC Shelf platform, in which we characterized SWC2 – a scientific workflow certifier. The role of SWC2 within an application is clear: it increases the confidence on the underlying workflow specification and may avoid anomalous or erroneous behaviours introduced by design errors. Moreover, a relevant characteristic of the architecture proposed for the certification process resides in the fact that new tactical components and workflow certifiers can be smoothly added, to deal with the verification of different classes of properties. For example, the development of new tactical components for SWC2, encapsulating other verification tools, such as Uppaal or Interactive Markov Chains, to deal with time constraints or probabilistic behavior, respectively, is part of our current work.

The workflow certifier in HPC Shelf, as well as the underlying certification framework, is still an ongoing project. However, an initial prototype was developed in C#/MPI and validated through a number of benchmark examples in the development of scientific computing applications. The example discussed in this paper — MapReduce, available from github.com/UFC-MDCC-HPC/ HPC-Shelf-Certification — provides an interesting illustration.

In any case, the relevant message is conceptual, going beyond its concrete implementation in the HPC Shelf platform. Actually, we believe that the notions of workflow certifier, tactical component and parallel certification system can be successfully employed in the certification of workflows in widespread SWfMS, such as Pegasus or Taverna.

References

1. Aalst, W.M.P.: Verification of workflow nets. In: Azéma, P., Balbo, G. (eds.) ICATPN 1997. LNCS, vol. 1248, pp. 407–426. Springer, Heidelberg (1997). doi:10. 1007/3-540-63139-9_48
2. Adam, N.R., Atluri, V., Huang, W.-K.: Modeling and analysis of workflows using petri nets. J. Intell. Inf. Syst. 10(2), 131–158 (1998)
3. Attie, P., Singh, M., Sheth, A.P., Rusinkiewicz, M.: Specifying and enforcing inter-task dependencies. In: 19th International Conference on Very Large Data Bases, Dublin, Ireland, 24–27 August 1993, Proceedings, pp. 134–145 (1993)

4. Baeten, J.C.M., Basten, T., Reniers, M.A., Algebra, P.: Equational theories of communicating processes. Cambridge Tracts in Theoretical Computer Science (50). Cambridge University Press, Cambridge (2010)
5. Davulcu, H., Kifer, M., Ramakrishnan, C.R., Ramakrishnan, I.V.: Logic based modeling and analysis of workflows. In: Proceedings of the Seventeenth ACM SIGACT-SIGMOD-SIGART Symposium on Principles of Database Systems, pp. 25–33. ACM (1998)
6. Dayal, U., Hsu, M., Ladin, R.: Organizing long-running activities with triggers and transactions. In: ACM SIGMOD Record, vol. 19, pp. 204–214. ACM (1990)
7. de Carvalho Junior, F.H., Lins, R.D., Correa, R.C., Araújo, G.A.: Towards an architecture for component-oriented parallel programming. Concurr. Comput.: Pract. Exp. **19**(5), 697–719 (2007)
8. de Carvalho Junior, F.H., Rezende, C.A., Silva, J.C., Al Alam, W.G.: Contextual abstraction in a type system for component-based high performance computing platforms. Sci. Comput. Program. **132**, 96–128 (2016)
9. de Carvalho Silva, J., de Carvalho Junior, F.H.: A platform of scientific workflows for orchestration of parallel components in a cloud of high performance computing applications. In: Castor, F., Liu, Y.D. (eds.) SBLP 2016. LNCS, vol. 9889, pp. 156–170. Springer, Cham (2016). doi:10.1007/978-3-319-45279-1_11
10. de Oliveira Dantas, A.B., de Carvalho Junior, F.H., Soares Barbosa, L.: A framework for certification of large-scale component-based parallel computing systems in a cloud computing platform for HPC services. In: Proceedings of the 7th International Conference on Cloud Computing and Services Science. CLOSER, vol. 1, pp. 229–240. ScitePress (2017)
11. Dean, J., Ghemawat, S.: Mapreduce: simplified data processing on large clusters. Commun. ACM **51**(1), 107–113 (2008)
12. Deelman, E., Singh, G., Su, M.-H., Blythe, J., Gil, Y., Kesselman, C., Mehta, G., Vahi, K., Berriman, G.B., Good, J., et al.: Pegasus: a framework for mapping complex scientific workflows onto distributed systems. Sci. Program. **13**(3), 219–237 (2005)
13. Dongarra, J., Otto, S.W., Snir, M., Walker, D.: An Introduction to the MPI Standard. Technical report CS-95-274, University of Tennessee, January 1995
14. Fu, X., Bultan, T., Hull, R., Su, J.: Verification of vortex workflows. In: Margaria, T., Yi, W. (eds.) TACAS 2001. LNCS, vol. 2031, pp. 143–157. Springer, Heidelberg (2001). doi:10.1007/3-540-45319-9_11
15. Groote, J.F., Mathijssen, A., Reniers, M., Usenko, Y., van Weerdenburg, M.: The formal specification language mCRL2. In: Methods for Modelling Software Systems: Dagstuhl Seminar 06351 (2007)
16. Groote, J.F., Mousavi, M.R.: Modeling and Analysis of Communicating Systems. MIT Press, Cambridge (2014)
17. Harrison, A., Taylor, I., Wang, I., Shields, M.: WS-Rf workflow in triana. Int. J. High Perform. Comput. Appl. **22**(3), 268–283 (2008)
18. Hull, R., Llirbat, F., Siman, E., Su, J., Dong, G., Kumar, B., Zhou, G.: Declarative workflows that support easy modification and dynamic browsing. ACM SIGSOFT Softw. Eng. Notes **24**(2), 69–78 (1999)
19. Kozen, D.: Results on the propositional μ-calculus. Theoret. Comput. Sci. **27**, 333–354 (1983)
20. Ludäscher, B., Altintas, I., Berkley, C., Higgins, D., Jaeger, E., Jones, M., Lee, E.A., Tao, J., Zhao, Y.: Scientific workflow management and the kepler system. Concurr. Comput.: Pract. Exp. **18**(10), 1039–1065 (2006)

21. Qin, J., Fahringer, T., Pllana, S.: UML based grid workflow modeling under ASKALON. In: Kacsuk, P., Fahringer, T., Németh, Z. (eds.) Distributed and Parallel Systems: From Cluster to Grid Computing (DAPSYS 2006), pp. 191–200. Springer, Boston (2006). doi:10.1007/978-0-387-69858-8_19

22. Sannella, D., Tarlecki, A.: Foundations of Algebraic Specifications and Formal Program Development. Cambridge University Press, Cambridge (2011)

23. Senkul, P., Kifer, M., Toroslu, I.H.: A logical framework for scheduling workflows under resource allocation constraints. In: Proceedings of the 28th International Conference on Very Large Data Bases, pp. 694–705. VLDB Endowment (2002)

24. Taylor, I.J., Deelman, E., Gannon, D.B., Shields, M.: Workflows for e-Science: Scientific Workflows for Grids. Springer, New York (2006)

25. Van der Aalst, W.M.P.: The application of petri nets to workflow management. J. Circ. Syst. Comput. **8**(01), 21–66 (1998)

26. Wassermann, B., Emmerich, W., Butchart, B., Cameron, N., Chen, L., Patel, J.: Sedna: a BPEL-based environment for visual scientific workflow modeling. In: Taylor, I.J., Deelman, E., Gannon, D.B., Shields, M. (eds.) Workflows for e-Science, pp. 428–449. Springer, London (2007). doi:10.1007/978-1-84628-757-2_26

27. Wodtke, D., Weikum, G.: A formal foundation for distributed workflow execution based on state charts. In: Afrati, F., Kolaitis, P. (eds.) ICDT 1997. LNCS, vol. 1186, pp. 230–246. Springer, Heidelberg (1997). doi:10.1007/3-540-62222-5_48

28. Wolstencroft, K., Haines, R., Fellows, D., Williams, A., Withers, D., Owen, S., Reyes, S.S., Dunlop, I., Nenadic, A., Fisher, P., et al.: The Taverna workflow suite: designing and executing workflows of web services on the desktop, web or in the cloud. Nucleic Acids Res. **41**(W1), W557 (2013)

Fault Localization in Service Compositions

Heike Wehrheim[(✉)]

Department of Computer Science, Paderborn University, Paderborn, Germany
wehrheim@upb.de

Abstract. Service-oriented architectures aim at the assemblance of service compositions out of independent, small services. In a model-based design, such service compositions first of all exist as formal models, describing the employed services with their interfaces plus their assemblance. Such formal models allow for an early analysis with respect to user requirements. While a large number of such analysis methods exist today, this is less so for techniques localizing *faults* in erroneous service compositions.

In this paper, we extend an existing technique for fault localization in software to the model-based domain. The approach employs *maximum satisfiability solving* (MAX-SAT) of trace formulae encoding faulty program runs. Contrary to software, we can, however, not use testing as a way of determining such faulty runs, but instead employ SMT solving. Moreover, due to the usage of undefined function symbols encoding concepts of domain ontologies, the trace formula also needs an encoding of the logical structure producing the fault. We furthermore show how to use *weights* on soft constraints in the MAX-SAT instance to steer the solver to particular types of faults.

1 Introduction

Service-oriented architectures (SOA) aim at the configuration of service compositions out of existing, independently deployable services. With micro services, this fundamental principle has recently found new impetus. In a formal model-based design, the employed services are equipped with well-defined interface descriptions, and the composition can hence be checked with respect to user requirements before assemblance. Many such analysis methods for service compositions exist today (e.g. [5,9,10,17,20,21]), using a variety of formalisms for modelling.

While formal analysis techniques are numerous, this is less so for techniques localizing the *cause* of faults in erroneous compositions. Analysis techniques building on model checking return counter examples, but they do not give hints on whether to change the way of composition or to change services, and in case of the latter which service to change. For software, this is a more frequently studied

This work was partially supported by the German Research Foundation (DFG) within the Collaborative Research Centre "On-The-Fly Computing" (SFB 901).

J. Proença and M. Lumpe (Eds.): FACS 2017, LNCS 10487, pp. 216–232, 2017.
DOI: 10.1007/978-3-319-68034-7_13

question. Techniques like delta debugging [7,25], slicing [1,24] or statistical methods [16] all aim at localizing the cause of faults in programs. Performance blame analysis [6] targets the identification of software components causing long runtimes.

In [15], Krämer and Wehrheim studied the applicability of software error localization techniques to service compositions. It turned out that it is in general difficult to transfer such techniques to a model-based setting: Software fault localization typically requires the executability of the entity under examination, i.e., requires code or requires entities with some accompanied interpretation, compilation or simulation tool as to execute them. Programs are being run on one or – in case of statistical methods – even a large number of test cases, and the outcome of these tests is used to determine potential error locations. Models of service compositions, however, typically cannot be executed as no concrete service implementations might exist yet, and modelling languages often do not come with interpreters providing some form of execution.

A notable exception to the requirement of executability in fault localization is the work of Jose et al. [13]. While they also study programs and make use of testing, they in addition employ bounded model checking for test input generation. This is similar to the SMT-based verification technique which we already employ for service compositions [23]. The basic principle of Jose et al. is the encoding of faulty program runs as trace formulae, and the localization of likely fault causes (in the faulty program trace) via maximum satisfiability solving (MAX-SAT).

In this paper, we transfer this concept to the model-based setting. The main challenge for this is directly the fact that we work on the level of models: instead of (only) using the typical programming language types, service interfaces are formulated via the concepts of *domain ontologies*, and service assemblance uses predicates and rules of these ontologies. Semantically, such concepts and predicates have no fixed interpretation; only ontology rules sometimes slightly restrict their meaning. A faulty test input (as required by Jose et al.) can thus not simply be an input variable of the program with its value. A trace formula encoding a faulty run cannot simply accumulate the concrete statements in the run, but needs to incorporate service calls of which just the interfaces are known. Technically, concepts and predicates of ontologies will in our approach be encoded as undefined function symbols, and a test input is then a complete logical structure fixing an interpretation of these symbols together with a valuation of variables in this logical structure. On this basis, we construct (1) logical formulae encoding the query for correctness of the whole service composition based on a given domain ontology and (2) trace formulae encoding faulty runs in case of errors based on the logical structure used for the fault. Satisfiability of these formulae are solved using the SMT solver Z3 [18]. Out of the trace formula, we can derive *fault sets* via maximum satisfiability solving, i.e., locations in the service composition which – when changed – correct errors. We furthermore allow to *prioritize* fault types, e.g., when we prefer to see faults in service calls over faults in the structure of the service composition. To this end, we impose weights on constraints in the MAX-SAT instance. Finally, we suggest a technique for finding more likely faults by identifying service composition entities which are the cause of faults in several cases.

The technique we propose here identifies single entities in service compositions as faults. It thus complements the techniques introduced by Krämer and Wehrheim [14] which aim at a repair of faulty service compositions via the replacement of large parts of the composition.

The paper is structured as follows. In the next section, we introduce some necessary background in logic and introduce the model of service compositions we employ in this paper. Section 3 describes correctness checking for service composition which is the basis for identifying faulty service compositions. The following section then introduces our technique for fault localization, for prioritization of fault types and the computation of likely faults. The last section concludes. Our description of the employed techniques is almost always given in terms of Z3 syntax, i.e., we give logical formulae in the SMT-Lib format [4].

2   Background

We start with describing the necessary background in logics, services and service composition. For the latter, we follow the definitions of Walther and Wehrheim [23].

A service composition describes the assemblance of services from a specific domain (e.g., tourism or health domain). The concepts occurring in such a domain and their interrelations are typically fixed in an ontology. Ontologies can be given in standardized languages, like for instance OWL [2]. Here, we simply fix the ingredients of ontologies[1].

Definition 1. *A rule-enhanced ontology $K = (\mathcal{T}, \mathcal{P}, \mathcal{F}, R)$ consists of a finite set of type (or concept) symbols $\mathcal{T}$ together with constants of these types, a finite set of predicate symbols $\mathcal{P}$, where every $p \in \mathcal{P}$ denotes an n-ary relation on types, a finite set of function symbols $\mathcal{F}$ and a set R of rules which are predicate logic formulae over some variables Var and the constants using $\mathcal{P}$ and $\mathcal{F}$. We use $\Phi_K(Var)$ to describe the set of such formulae.*

Here, we implicitly assume the types to contain integers and booleans with the usual constants. Rules, which are not part of every ontology language, are used to describe relationships between concepts or properties of predicates (e.g., commutativity). An example of a rule language for ontologies can for instance be found in [12].

The running example of our paper operates in the tourism domain, containing types like *Restaurant*, *Rating* and *Location* and a constant $R0$ of type *Restaurant*. On these, the ontology contains two predicates and two functions:

$$isHigh : \quad Rating \;\rightarrow\; \textbf{bool}$$
$$isVegan : Restaurant \rightarrow \textbf{bool}$$
$$ratOf : Restaurant \rightarrow Rating$$
$$locOf : Restaurant \rightarrow Location$$

---

[1] For simplicity, subconcept relations of ontologies are not considered here.

For simplicity, the knowledge base contains just two rules specifying properties of the constant $R0$: $isHigh(ratOf(R0))$ and $isVegan(R0)$.

With its types, an ontology defines – in a logical sense – a large number of *undefined function symbols*. It remains undefined what a *Restaurant* really is; it is just a name. The interpretation of these symbols and the universes of the types are not defined. A logical structure (or *logical model*) fixes this interpretation.

Definition 2. *Let* $K = (\mathcal{T}, \mathcal{P}, \mathcal{F}, R)$ *be an ontology. A logical structure over* K, $\mathcal{S}_K = (\mathcal{U}, \mathcal{I})$, *consists of*

- $\mathcal{U} = \bigcup_{T \in \mathcal{T}} \mathcal{U}_T$ *the universe of values,*
- $\mathcal{I}$ *an* interpretation *of the predicate and function symbols, i.e., for every* $p \in \mathcal{P}$ *of type* $T_1 \times \ldots \times T_n \to$ ***bool*** *and every* $f \in \mathcal{F}$ *of type* $T_1 \times \ldots \times T_n \to T$ *we have a predicate*

$$\mathcal{I}(p) : \mathcal{U}_{T_1} \times \ldots \times \mathcal{U}_{T_n} \to \mathcal{U}_{\textbf{bool}}$$

and a function

$$\mathcal{I}(f) : \mathcal{U}_{T_1} \times \ldots \times \mathcal{U}_{T_n} \to \mathcal{U}_T,$$

respectively, and
- *we require the logical structure to satisfy all rules of the ontology.*

Ontologies provide the concepts which can be used to describe the functionality of services. A *service signature* $(Svc, \mathcal{T}_{in}, \mathcal{T}_{out})$ over an ontology K first of all specifies the *name* Svc of the service as well as the type of its input $\mathcal{T}_{in} \in \mathcal{T}$ and the type of its output $\mathcal{T}_{out} \in \mathcal{T}$. We restrict ourselves to services with single inputs and outputs. A service description in addition adds semantical information to this interface.

Definition 3. *A* service description $(sig, I, O, pre_{Svc}, post_{Svc})$ *of a service named Svc over an ontology* K *consists of a service signature* $sig = (Svc, \mathcal{T}_{in}, \mathcal{T}_{out})$, *input variable* i *and output variable* o, *a precondition* pre_{Svc} *over the input variable and a postcondition* $post_{Svc}$ *over input and output variable, both elements of* $\Phi_K(\{i, o\})$.

The interface of a service thus states what the service requires to hold true upon calling it (preconditions) and what it guarantees when it has finished (postcondition). Services can be assembled by means of a workflow language. While there are different languages in use (e.g. WS-BPEL [19]), we simply employ a programming language like notation here.

Definition 4. *Let* $K = (\mathcal{T}, \mathcal{P}, \mathcal{F}, R)$ *be an ontology and Var a set of variables typed over* $\mathcal{T}$. *The syntax of a* workflow W *over* K *is given by the following rules:*

$$W ::= Skip \mid u := t \mid W_1; W_2 \mid u := Svc(v)$$
$$\mid \textbf{if } B \textbf{ then } W_1 \textbf{ else } W_2 \textbf{ fi} \mid \textbf{while } B \textbf{ do } W \textbf{ od}$$

with variables $u, v \in Var$, *expression* t *of type* $type(u)$, $B \in \Phi_K(Var)$, *and Svc a service name.*

Name	: RESTAURANTCHECKER
Inputs	: *in* with *type*(*in*) = *Restaurant*
Outputs	: *out* with *type*(*out*) = *Restaurant*,
	loc with *type*(*loc*) = *Location*
Services	: *GetRating* : *Restaurant* → *Rating*,
	GetLocation : *Restaurant* → *Location*

Precondition : true
Postcondition: $isHigh(ratOf(out)) \land isVegan(out)$

```
 1  if isVegan(in) then
 2  |   r := GetRating(in);
 3  |   if ¬isHigh(r) then
 4  |   |   out := in;
 5  |   else
 6  |   |   out := R0;
 7  |   fi
 8  else
 9  |   out := R0;
10  fi
11  loc := GetLocation(out);
```

Fig. 1. Service composition RESTAURANTCHECKER

Herein, we allow for standard expressions on integers and booleans. A complete service composition then consists of such a workflow together with a name, its inputs and outputs, a list of the employed services and their pre- and postcondition.

Figure 1 shows our running example of a service composition. In this, we use two services: *GetRating* with precondition *true* and postcondition $r = ratOf(in)$ and *GetLocation* with precondition *true* and postcondition $loc = locOf(out)$ (already instantiated to the variables used in the workflow).

A service composition is furthermore equipped with an overall pre- and postcondition. These pre- and postconditions constitute requirements on the service composition: whenever the whole composition is started with an input satisfying the precondition, it should terminate and at the end satisfy the postcondition. Our example service composition is not correct in that sense: whenever the input to the composition is a vegan restaurant (satisfying *isVegan*(*in*)) with a low rating (satisfying ¬*isHigh*(*r*) for *r* being the rating of *in*), the service composition will output the value of *in* which does not satisfy the (first clause of the) postcondition.

For defining this in a more formal way, we furthermore need the definition of a state: given a logical structure $\mathcal{S}$, a *state in* $\mathcal{S}$ is a mapping from variables to values of the universe, $\sigma : Var \to \mathcal{U}$. In [23], a semantics for workflows is given which is parameterised in a logical structure: for a workflow W, $[\![W]\!]_{\mathcal{S}}$ is a mapping from a set of states in $\mathcal{S}$ to sets of states. We will not repeat the definition here, instead we concentrate on verification and fault localization. The semantics of service calls of Walther and Wehrheim [23] fixes (a) a service to be executable only when the precondition holds in the current state, otherwise it blocks, and (b) the after-state to satisfy the postcondition. As the postcondition is just a logical expression, there may be more than one after-state satisfying the postcondition. A service call thus introduces nondeterminism. The property (a) will play no role in the following; for a technique for computing precondition violations on service calls see [14].

Definition 5. *A service composition with workflow W is* correct *with respect to pre- and postconditions pre and post if the following holds for all logical structures S for K:*

$$[\![W]\!]_S([\![pre]\!]_S) \subseteq [\![post]\!]_S,$$

where for a formula $p \in \Phi_K$ without free variables, we let $[\![p]\!]_S$ denote the set of states in S satisfying p.

This is a standard partial correctness[2] definition: whenever we start the service composition in a state satisfying the precondition, the state reached when the service composition is completed should satisfy the postcondition. The task of fault localization now requires finding the locations in the workflow which are the cause of incorrectness.

3   Correctness Checking

In our setting, fault localization directly builds on the results of correctness checking. Therefore, we next present our technique for checking correctness of service compositions. In its basic approach, we follow Walther and Wehrheim [22] here, however, with some adaptation to fit the approach to the later fault localization. The main adaptation concerns *naming*: while Walther and Wehrheim [22] build one formula for the whole service composition, we build separate formulae for the parts of the composition (i.e. one formula for a condition in an if statement, one for a service call and so on). The formulae are assigned different names, and we can later use these names for the hard and soft constraints in the MAX-SAT instance.

3.1   Brief Introduction to Z3 Syntax

We start with a very brief description of the Z3 syntax which we employ.

Declarations. We use three types of declarations: (1) Declaring new sorts (types), written as (declare-sort <name>), (2) declaring function symbols, written as (declare-fun <name> <signature>), and (3) declaring constants, written as (declare-const <name> <sort>). The declared sorts, functions and constants can from then on be used. Note that we do not fix the interpretation of these new concepts.

---

[2] Total correctness would involve defining termination functions for loops.

```
1  if isVegan(in) then
2  |     r := GetRating(in);
3  |     if ¬isHigh(r) then
4  |     |     out1 := in;
5  |     else
6  |     |     out2 := R0;
7  |     end
8  |     out3 := φ(out1, out2)
9  else
10 |     out4 := R0;
11 end
12 out := φ(out3, out4);
13 loc := GetLocation(out);
```

Fig. 2. Service composition RESTAURANTCHECKER in SSA-form

Definitions. Definitions, written as (define-fun <name> <sig> <def>), allow to give an interpretation to functions.

Assertions. Assertions fix the facts that we would like to hold true. When asked for satisfiability, Z3 checks whether all assertions jointly can be made true. This involves trying to find an interpretation for the unknown (but declared and used) concepts.

Logic. Z3 uses standard predicate logic for writing logical expressions (e.g., quantifiers, boolean connectives). The connective ite stands for a conditional expression (if-then-else).

3.2 Encoding the Service Composition

Checking the correctness of a service composition proceeds in two steps: in a first step, we bring the service composition into static-single-assignment (SSA) form. Second, we translate the workflow, its precondition, the ontology and the negation of the postcondition into a logical formula which is then checked for satisfiability. We thereby check whether it is possible to start in a state satisfying the precondition but end in a state not satisfying the postcondition.

SSA forms require a variable to be assigned to at most once in the program text (for a technique for computing SSA forms see [8]). Our service composition is not yet in SSA form, as it for instance has three assignments to *out*. Figure 2 shows its SSA form. At merges of control flow (if, while) so called φ-nodes (assignments) are inserted in order to unite variables assigned to in different branches.

Given such an SSA-form, the translation next proceeds as follows. Table 1 shows the translation of the workflow (directly given in Z3 syntax, the solver we use). Every statement of the workflow is translated to a function declaration and this declaration is asserted to hold true. The thereby introduced names for statements will later prove helpful for fault localization. For assignments, we assert the variable to be equal to the assigned expression. For service calls, we assert the postcondition of the service to be true (as said before, precondition

Table 1. Translation of workflow statements

Statement	Z3 code
k: *Skip*	–
k: $u := t$	`(define-fun ak () Bool (= u t))`
	`(assert ak)`
k: $u := Svc(v)$	`(define-fun ak () Bool post`$_{Svc}$`(u,v))`
	`(assert ak)`
k: **if** B **then** W_1 **else** W_2 **fi**; $u := \phi(v_1, v_2)$	`(declare-const condk Bool)`
	`(define-fun ck () Bool (= condk B))`
	`(define-fun branchk () Bool (= u (ite condk v1 v2)))`
	`(assert ck)`
	`(assert branchk)`
k: inv : **while** B **do** W **od**; $u := \phi(v_1, v_2)$	`(declare-const condk Bool)`
	`(define-fun ck () Bool (= condk B))`
	`(define-fun loopk () Bool (= u (ite condk v1 v2)))`
	`(assert ck)`
	`(assert loopk)`
	`(define-fun invk () Bool (and inv(u) (not B(u))))`
	`(assert invk)`

violations are not checked here). In the definition, the term $\mathtt{post}_{Svc}(\mathtt{u},\mathtt{v})$ refers to the logical formula as specified for the postcondition in the service description.

For if statements, we get two function declarations: one giving a name to the condition and the other setting variables to the correct version according to the condition and the ϕ-nodes. In the table, we assume every if and while statement to be followed by just one ϕ-node. The translation can, however, easily be generalized to more than one such node. The ϕ-nodes are translated to assertions equating the assigned variable to one of the parameters, based on the condition in the if and while statement, respectively. For loops, we assume a *loop invariant* to be given (see [23]). The invariant together with the negation of the loop condition acts like a postcondition of the whole loop block. The invariant is checked to actually be an invariant in a separate step. The assertion for a loop thus states that the invariant and the negation of the loop condition holds after the loop, where the variables in both formulae have to be instantiated to the *current variable version* as given by the ϕ-node after the loop.

In addition, we need a translation of the ontology. This requires declaring all types, constants, predicates and functions and asserting the rules to hold true. Table 2 gives this translation.

In summary, this translation gives us a formula φ_{SC} for the workflow, a formula φ_K for the ontology and two formulae *pre* and *post* for the translation of the service composition's pre- and postcondition. The translation for service composition RESTAURANTCHECKER is given in the appendix. The solver is now

Table 2. Translation of ontology $K = (\mathcal{T}, \mathcal{P}, \mathcal{F}, R)$

Entity	Z3 code
type $T \in \mathcal{T}$	`(declare-sort T)`
constant $c : T$	`(declare-const c T)`
predicate $p : T_1 \times \ldots \times T_n \to \mathbf{bool} \in \mathcal{P}$	`(declare-fun p (T1 ... Tn) Bool)`
function $f : T_1 \times \ldots \times T_n \to T \in \mathcal{F}$	`(declare-fun f (T1 ... Tn) T)`
rule $r \in R$	`(assert r)`

queried about the satisfiability of

$$pre \wedge \varphi_{SC} \wedge \varphi_K \wedge \neg post \tag{1}$$

(plus about the satisfiability of $inv \wedge \varphi_W \wedge \neg inv'$ for all loops with invariant inv, loop body W and SSA form tagging variables after the loop with primes). In case of our example service composition, the answer to (1) is "sat", i.e., it is possible that the composition's postcondition is not fulfilled at the end. Together with this answer, the solver returns a logical structure (which we call *fault structure*), i.e., universes for all sorts (types) and interpretations of the undefined predicate and function symbols, plus a state σ mapping all variables in the service composition to values of the universe. This state can be seen as the final state of the service composition, i.e., the state in which the negation of the postcondition is satisfied. Since the service composition is in SSA-form, the state of a variable is, however, never changed anyway (loops are summarized in the loop invariant). For our running example, Fig. 3 shows this information; the appendix contains it in the form returned by Z3. The fault structure constitutes our input to fault localization.

4 Fault Localization

Fault localization now proceeds by taking the "faulty" input to the service composition, i.e., the universe, interpretation and the state of the input to the service composition, together with the service composition and ontology, and solving a *partial maximum satisfiability* problem. Essentially, we are determining which parts of the service composition plus *non-negated* postcondition can simultaneously be satisfied on the faulty input. The complementary part contains the potential faults.

4.1 Computing Fault Sets

A partial maximum satifiability problem pMAX-SAT takes as input a predicate logic formula in conjunctive normal form. In this, some clauses are marked *hard* (definitely need to be satisfied) and others are marked as *soft* (need not

$$\mathcal{U}_{Restaurant} = \{Res!val!0, Res!val!1\}$$
$$\mathcal{U}_{Rating} = \{Rat!val!0, Rat!val!1\}$$
$$\mathcal{U}_{Location} = \{Loc!val!0\}$$
$$isVegan(Res!val!0) = true$$
$$isVegan(Res!val!1) = true$$
$$isHigh(Rat!val!0) = true$$
$$isHigh(Rat!val!1) = false$$
$$ratOf(Res!val!0) = Rat!val!0$$
$$ratOf(Res!val!1) = Rat!val!1$$
$$\sigma(in) = Res!val!1$$

Fig. 3. "Fault structure" for example service composition

necessarily be satisfied). The pMAX-SAT solver determines a maximum number of clauses which satisfies these constraints. In addition, Z3 – when used as pMAX-SAT solver [11] – allows to give *weights* to soft clauses. A weight sets a penalty for not making a clause satisfied, and Z3 determines solutions with minimal penalties. We will make use of this for prioritizing certain faults over others.

For fault localization, we build a *trace formula* encoding the faulty "run" of the service composition. In our model-based setting, the trace formula needs to contain the whole (logical) fault structure $\mathcal{S}$ and the state σ of the fault. Table 3 shows the translation of this to Z3 input. For the universe, we declare all values of a type and state all variables of that type to just take values of the universe. For predicates and functions, we enumerate all cases of argument and result values. Out of the state, we just fix the value of the input to the service composition. This translation gives us two more formulae: $\varphi_{\mathcal{S}}$ and φ_{σ}. These two formulae describe a structure and state on which the postcondition cannot be satisfied.

Proposition 1. *Let SC be a service composition with pre- and postcondition pre and post, respectively, and K an ontology. Let $pre \wedge \varphi_{SC} \wedge \varphi_K \wedge \neg post$ be satisfiable and $(\mathcal{S}, \sigma)$ be the logical structure and state making the formula true. Then*

$$pre \wedge \varphi_{SC} \wedge \varphi_K \wedge post \wedge \varphi_{\mathcal{S}} \wedge \varphi_{\sigma}$$

is unsatisfiable.

For fault localization, we next ask for partial maximum satisfiability, making all assertions hard except for those of the service composition (the fault is in the service composition). The query thus is (underlining all hard constraints)

$$\underline{pre} \wedge \varphi_{SC} \wedge \underline{\varphi_K} \wedge \underline{post} \wedge \varphi_{\mathcal{S}} \wedge \varphi_{\sigma}$$

For every clause in this formula, the solver can tell us whether the clause has or has not been made true. Let $F = \{c_1, \ldots, c_n\}$ be the set of (soft) clauses not

Table 3. Translation of logical structure $\mathcal{S}$ and state σ

Entity	Z3 code
universe	`(declare-fun v1 T) ... (declare-fun vn T)`
$\mathcal{U}_T = \{v_1, \ldots, v_n\}$	`(assert (forall ((x T)) (or (= x v1) ... (= x vn))))`
predicate	
$\mathcal{I}(p)(v_1, \ldots, v_n) = true$	`(assert (p v1 ... vn))`
$\mathcal{I}(p)(v_1, \ldots, v_n) = false$	`(assert (not (p v1 ... vn)))`
function	
$\mathcal{I}(f)(v_1, \ldots, v_n) = v$	`(assert (= v (f v1 ... vn)))`
input i, $\sigma(i) = v$	`(assert (= i v))`

made true. F constitutes (one) *fault set*. By changing all assertions (and hence statements) in F, the service composition can be corrected. Similarly to Jose et al. [13], we can also find different fault sets (for the same fault) by adding a new hard constraint $c_1 \vee \ldots \vee c_n$ to our formula.

In case of our example service composition, the solver is always returning a singleton fault set. The fault sets we get by repeatedly starting the solver and adding new hard clauses are $F_1 = \{branch3\}$ (the if statement in line 3 itself), $F_2 = \{cond3\}$ (condition of if statement in line 3), $F_3 = \{cond1\}$ (condition of if statement in line 1), $F_4 = \{a4\}$ (assignment in line 4) and $F_5 = \{a2\}$ (assignment in line 2). A correction of any one of these can make the service composition correct. The easiest way for correction is to change the condition in line 3 to $isHigh(r)$.

4.2 Prioritizing Fault Types

The MAX-SAT solver typically returns the fault sets in any order, not giving preferences to any soft clause. If we are interested in certain types of faults and prefer to see these first, we need to assign *weights* to soft clauses. Z3 then solves an optimization problem: it tries to find a maximum satisfiability solution which minimizes penalties. A weight therein incurs a penalty on not making the clause true (with penalty 1 being standard).

If our interest is thus in localizing faults in conditions or service calls first and delaying more difficult faults in if- or while-statements to later phases, we could tag the corresponding clauses with higher penalties. For our translation we could replace the assertions for if-statements and loops by

```
(assert-soft branchk :weight 2)
(assert-soft invk :weight 3)
```

This gives high penalities to if- and even higher to while-statements. The solver would then first return fault sets with assignments, service calls and conditions. In our case, the fault set F_1 would then be returned as the last set.

Name   : RESTAURANTCHECKER2
Inputs   : *in* with *type(in) = Restaurant*
Outputs   : *out* with *type(out) = Restaurant*
Precondition : true
Postcondition: *isVegan(out)* ∧ (*isCheap(out)* ∨ *isHAcc(out)*)

```
 1  if ¬(isVegan(in)) then
 2  |   if isCheap(in) then
 3  |   |   out := in;
 4  |   fi
 5  |   if isHAcc(in) then
 6  |   |   out := in;
 7  |   fi
 8  else
 9  |   out := R0;
10  fi
```

Fig. 4. Service composition RESTAURANTCHECKER2

4.3 Finding Faults Occurring Multiple Times

The previous technique helps to prioritize certain fault types over others. For narrowing down the number of faults to look at, we can also determine the statements occurring as faults in more than one "faulty run", i.e., in our case in more than one logical structure $\mathcal{S}$ making formula (1) true. For this, consider the example service composition in Fig. 4.

The service composition RESTAURANTCHECKER2 is supposed to check whether the restaurant of input parameter *in* is vegan plus either cheap (*isCheap*) or accessible to handicapped persons (*isHAcc*). We assume the knowledge base to specify *isCheap(R0)*. Again, the service composition is not correct. Fault localization gives us – now phrased in terms of the service composition, not its translation to SMT code – the two fault sets $F_1^1 = \{\neg(isVegan(in))\}$ and $F_2^1 = \{isHAcc(in)\}$, both based on the same logical structure and state invalidating the postcondition. The state σ with its valuation of the input *in* describes a "test run" of the service composition passing through lines 1, 2 and 3. We call $\mathcal{F}^1 = F_1^1 \cup F_2^1$ a *test-specific fault set*. The idea is now to generate different "test inputs" and compute their fault sets.

To this end, we add an assertion forcing the current value of the input to take a different interpretation via predicate complementation. Let $\mathcal{I}$ be the interpretation and σ the state returned by query (1). Let i be the input to the service composition and T its type. We now choose a unary predicate $p : T \rightarrow Bool$ from our ontology. If $\mathcal{I}(p)(\sigma(i))$ is true, we add an assertion $\neg(p(i)$, otherwise $p(i)$. For our example, we add

```
(assert (not (isHAcc in)))
```

If formula (1) together with this assertion is still satisfiable, we repeat the fault localization procedure thereby getting new fault sets. If the formula is not satisfiable, we choose a different predicate to be complemented and retry. This way, we get several test-specific fault sets $\mathcal{F}^1, \mathcal{F}^2, \ldots$. The intersection of these test-specific fault sets gives us faults which – when corrected – can correct more than one faulty test input at the same time.

In our case, we get a second test-specific fault set

$$\mathcal{F}^2 = \{\neg(isVegan(in)), isCheap(in)\} \ .$$

Intersection with $\mathcal{F}^1$ gives us $\neg(isVegan(in))$, which is where the correction should be applied.

In general, predicates to be complemented should not be arbitrarily chosen. Predicates occurring in boolean conditions of the service composition are to be preferred over others (as they steer the execution to different branches). If none of the unary predicates bring us new fault sets, arbitrary n-ary predicates can be considered as well.

5   Conclusion

In this paper, we have introduced a fault localization technique for service compositions. It builds on an existing method for *software* fault localization via maximum satisfiability solving. Due to our setting of model-based development, our approach needs to account for several additional aspects: (1) In contrast to software, models are not executable and hence faulty test inputs cannot be derived via testing but only via SMT solving; (2) concepts of ontologies are undefined function symbols in a logical sense and hence have no fixed interpretation; (3) faulty inputs alone are not sufficient for fault localization when no interpretation is known. In addition to plain fault localization, we furthermore provide a method for prioritizing fault types and for finding faults occurring in multiple runs.

This fault localization technique is currently implemented within the modelling and verification tool SeSAME [3]. First experiments show that fault localization can be done within seconds and often just proposes singleton faults which can easily be corrected. However, more experiments are needed to see whether this observation can be generalized to more cases.

A   Z3 Code

Encoding of the correctness check for RESTAURANTCHECKER:

```
; types of the ontology
(declare-sort Res)
(declare-sort Loc)
(declare-sort Rat)
; constants and functions of the ontology
(declare-const R0 Res)
```

```
(declare-fun ratOf (Res) Rat)
(declare-fun isHigh (Rat) Bool)
(declare-fun isVegan (Res) Bool)
(declare-fun locOf (Res) Loc)
; variables used in SSA form of service composition
(declare-const r Rat)
(declare-const in Res)
(declare-const out Res)
(declare-const out1 Res)
(declare-const out2 Res)
(declare-const out3 Res)
(declare-const out4 Res)
(declare-const loc Loc)
; variables used for conditions in if's
(declare-const cond1 Bool)
(declare-const cond2 Bool)
; two rules of the knowledge base: restaurant R0 has a high rating
and is vegan
(assert (isHigh (ratOf R0)))
(assert (isVegan R0))
; the service composition
(define-fun c1 () Bool (= cond1 (isVegan in)))
(define-fun c2 () Bool (= cond2 (not (isHigh r))))
(assert c1)
(assert c2)
(define-fun a1 () Bool (= r (ratOf in)))
(define-fun a2 () Bool (= out1 in))
(define-fun a3 () Bool (= out2 R0))
(define-fun a4 () Bool) (= out4 R0))
(define-fun a5 () Bool (= loc (locOf out)))
(assert a1) (assert a2) (assert a3) (assert a4) (assert a5)
(define-fun branch2 () Bool (= out3 (ite cond2 out1 out2)))
(define-fun branch1 () Bool (= out (ite cond1 out3 out4)))
(assert branch1) (assert branch2)
; the negated postcondition
(assert (or (not (isHigh (ratOf out))) (not (isVegan out))))
; checking for satisfiability of all asserts
(check-sat)
; getting an interpretation if it exists
(get-model)
```

Fault structure returned as model of above query:

```
;; universe for Res:
;; Res!val!1 Res!val!0
;; -----------
;; definitions for universe elements:
```

```
(declare-fun Res!val!1 () Res)
(declare-fun Res!val!0 () Res)
;; cardinality constraint:
(forall ((x Res)) (or (= x Res!val!1) (= x Res!val!0)))
;; -----------
;; universe for Rat:
;; Rat!val!1 Rat!val!0
;; -----------
;; definitions for universe elements:
(declare-fun Rat!val!1 () Rat)
(declare-fun Rat!val!0 () Rat)
;; cardinality constraint:
(forall ((x Rat)) (or (= x Rat!val!1) (= x Rat!val!0)))
;; -----------
;; universe for Loc:
;; Loc!val!0
;; -----------
;; definitions for universe elements:
(declare-fun Loc!val!0 () Loc)
;; cardinality constraint:
(forall ((x Loc)) (= x Loc!val!0))
;; -----------
(define-fun R0 () Res Res!val!0)
(define-fun out1 () Res Res!val!1)
(define-fun out2 () Res Res!val!0)
(define-fun out () Res Res!val!1)
(define-fun out4 () Res Res!val!0)
(define-fun in () Res Res!val!1)
(define-fun cond2 () Bool true)
(define-fun cond1 () Bool true)
(define-fun out3 () Res Res!val!1)
(define-fun loc () Loc Loc!val!0)
(define-fun r () Rat Rat!val!1)
(define-fun isHigh ((x!0 Rat)) Bool
      (ite (= x!0 Rat!val!0) true (ite (= x!0 Rat!val!1) false
      true)))
(define-fun ratOf ((x!0 Res)) Rat
      (ite (= x!0 Res!val!0) Rat!val!0
            (ite (= x!0 Res!val!1) Rat!val!1 Rat!val!0)))
(define-fun isVegan ((x!0 Res)) Bool
      (ite (= x!0 Res!val!0) true (ite (= x!0 Res!val!1) true
      true)))
(define-fun locOf ((x!0 Res)) Loc
      (ite (= x!0 Res!val!1) Loc!val!0 Loc!val!0)))
```

References

1. Agrawal, H., Demillo, R., Spafford, E.: Debugging with dynamic slicing and back-tracking. Softw. Pract. Exp. **23**, 589–616 (1993)
2. Antoniou, G., Harmelen, F.: Web ontology language: OWL. In: Staab, S., Studer, R. (eds.) Handbook on Ontologies. IHIS, pp. 91–110. Springer, Heidelberg (2009). doi:10.1007/978-3-540-92673-3_4
3. Arifulina, S., Walther, S., Becker, M., Platenius, M.C.: SeSAME: modeling and analyzing high-quality service compositions. In: ACM/IEEE International Conference on Automated Software Engineering, ASE 2014, Vasteras, Sweden, 15–19 September 2014, pp. 839–842 (2014). http://doi.acm.org/10.1145/2642937.2648621
4. Barrett, C., Stump, A., Tinelli, C.: The SMT-LIB standard: version 2.0. In: Gupta, A., Kroening, D. (eds.) Proceedings of the 8th International Workshop on Satisfiability Modulo Theories (Edinburgh, UK) (2010). http://homepage.cs.uiowa.edu/~/papers/BarST-SMT-10.pdf
5. Becker, S., Koziolek, H., Reussner, R.: The Palladio component model for model-driven performance prediction. J. Syst. Softw. **82**(1), 3–22 (2009). specialIssue: SoftwarePerformance-ModelingandAnalysis. http://www.sciencedirect.com/science/article/pii/S0164121208001015
6. Brüseke, F., Wachsmuth, H., Engels, G., Becker, S.: PBlaman: performance blame analysis based on Palladio contracts. Concurr. Comput.: Pract. Exp. **26**(12), 1975–2004 (2014). http://dx.doi.org/10.1002/cpe.3226
7. Cleve, H., Zeller, A.: Locating causes of program failures. In: Proceedings of 27th International Conference on Software Engineering, ICSE 2005, pp. 342–351. ACM (2005). http://doi.acm.org/10.1145/1062455.1062522
8. Cytron, R., Ferrante, J., Rosen, B.K., Wegman, M.N., Zadeck, F.K.: Efficiently computing static single assignment form and the control dependence graph. ACM Trans. Program. Lang. Syst. **13**(4), 451–490 (1991)
9. Engels, G., Güldali, B., Soltenborn, C., Wehrheim, H.: Assuring consistency of business process models and web services using visual contracts. In: Schürr, A., Nagl, M., Zündorf, A. (eds.) AGTIVE 2007. LNCS, vol. 5088, pp. 17–31. Springer, Heidelberg (2008). doi:10.1007/978-3-540-89020-1_2
10. Güdemann, M., Poizat, P., Salaün, G., Ye, L.: VerChor: a framework for the design and verification of choreographies. IEEE Trans. Serv. Comput. **9**(4), 647–660 (2016). http://dx.doi.org/10.1109/TSC.2015.2413401
11. Hoder, K., Bjørner, N., de Moura, L.: μZ– an efficient engine for fixed points with constraints. In: Gopalakrishnan, G., Qadeer, S. (eds.) CAV 2011. LNCS, vol. 6806, pp. 457–462. Springer, Heidelberg (2011). doi:10.1007/978-3-642-22110-1_36
12. Horrocks, I., Patel-Schneider, P.F., Boley, H., Tabet, S., Grosof, B., Dean, M.: SWRL: a semantic web rule language combining OWL and RuleML (2004). http://www.w3.org/Submission/2004/SUBM-SWRL-20040521/
13. Jose, M., Majumdar, R.: Cause clue clauses: error localization using maximum satisfiability. In: Hall, M.W., Padua, D.A. (eds.) Proceedings of the 32nd ACM SIGPLAN Conference on Programming Language Design and Implementation, PLDI 2011, San Jose, CA, USA, 4–8 June 2011, pp. 437–446. ACM (2011). http://doi.acm.org/10.1145/1993498.1993550
14. Krämer, J., Wehrheim, H.: A formal approach to error localization and correction in service compositions. In: Milazzo, P., Varró, D., Wimmer, M. (eds.) STAF 2016. LNCS, vol. 9946, pp. 445–457. Springer, Cham (2016). doi:10.1007/978-3-319-50230-4_35

15. Krämer, J., Wehrheim, H.: A short survey on using software error localization for service compositions. In: Aiello, M., Johnsen, E.B., Dustdar, S., Georgievski, I. (eds.) ESOCC 2016. LNCS, vol. 9846, pp. 248–262. Springer, Cham (2016). doi:10. 1007/978-3-319-44482-6_16

16. Liblit, B., Aiken, A., Zheng, A.X., Jordan, M.I.: Bug isolation via remote program sampling. In: Cytron, R., Gupta, R. (eds.) Proceedings of the ACM SIGPLAN 2003 Conference on Programming Language Design and Implementation 2003, San Diego, California, USA, 9–11 June 2003, pp. 141–154. ACM (2003). http:// doi.acm.org/10.1145/781131.781148

17. Mirandola, R., Potena, P., Riccobene, E., Scandurra, P.: A reliability model for service component architectures. J. Syst. Softw. **89**, 109–127 (2014)

18. de Moura, L., Bjørner, N.: Z3: an efficient SMT solver. In: Ramakrishnan, C.R., Rehof, J. (eds.) TACAS 2008. LNCS, vol. 4963, pp. 337–340. Springer, Heidelberg (2008). doi:10.1007/978-3-540-78800-3_24

19. Ouyang, C., Verbeek, E., van der Aalst, W.M.P., Breutel, S., Dumas, M., ter Hofstede, A.H.M.: Formal semantics and analysis of control flow in WS-BPEL. Sci. Comput. Program. **67**(2–3), 162–198 (2007)

20. Reynisson, A.H., Sirjani, M., Aceto, L., Cimini, M., Jafari, A., Ingólfsdóttir, A., Sigurdarson, S.H.: Modelling and simulation of asynchronous real-time systems using Timed Rebeca. Sci. Comput. Program. **89**, 41–68 (2014). http://dx.doi.org/10.1016/j.scico.2014.01.008

21. Schäfer, W., Wehrheim, H.: Model-driven development with MECHATRONIC UML. In: Engels, G., Lewerentz, C., Schäfer, W., Schürr, A., Westfechtel, B. (eds.) Graph Transformations and Model-Driven Engineering. LNCS, vol. 5765, pp. 533–554. Springer, Heidelberg (2010). doi:10.1007/978-3-642-17322-6_23

22. Walther, S., Wehrheim, H.: Knowledge-based verification of service compositions - an SMT approach. In: 18th International Conference on Engineering of Complex Computer Systems, ICECCS 2013, pp. 24–32. IEEE Computer Society (2013)

23. Walther, S., Wehrheim, H.: On-the-fly construction of provably correct service compositions - templates and proofs. Sci. Comput. Program. **127**, 2–23 (2016). http://dx.doi.org/10.1016/j.scico.2016.04.002

24. Weiser, M.: Program slicing. In: Proceedings of 5th International Conference on Software Engineering, ICSE 1981, pp. 439–449. IEEE Press (1981). http://dl.acm. org/citation.cfm?id=800078.802557

25. Zeller, A.: Yesterday, my program worked. Today, it does not. Why? In: Nierstrasz, O., Lemoine, M. (eds.) ESEC/SIGSOFT FSE -1999. LNCS, vol. 1687, pp. 253–267. Springer, Heidelberg (1999). doi:10.1007/3-540-48166-4_16

Correct Composition of Dephased Behavioural Models

Juliana Bowles and Marco B. Caminati[✉]

School of Computer Science, University of St Andrews,
KY16 9SX St Andrews, St Andrews, UK
{jkfb,mbc8}@st-andrews.ac.uk

Abstract. Scenarios of execution are commonly used to specify partial behaviour and interactions between different objects and components in a system. To avoid overall inconsistency in specifications, various automated methods have emerged in the literature to compose (behavioural) models. In recent work, we have shown how the theorem prover Isabelle can be combined with the constraint solver Z3 to efficiently detect inconsistencies in two or more behavioural models and, in their absence, generate the composition. Here, we extend our approach further and show how to generate the correct composition (as a set of valid traces) of dephased models. This work has been inspired by a problem from a medical domain where different care pathways (for chronic conditions) may be applied to the same patient with different starting points.

1 Introduction

To cope with the complexity of modern systems, design approaches combine a variety of languages and notation to capture different aspects of a system, and separate structural from behavioural models. In itself behavioural modelling is also difficult, and rather than attempt to model the complete behaviour of a (sub)system [22], it is easier to focus on several possible scenarios of execution separately. Scenarios give a partial understanding of a component and include interactions with other system components. In industry, individual scenarios are often captured using UML's sequence diagrams [19]. Given a set of scenarios, we then need to check whether these are correct and consistent, and to do so we first need to obtain the combined overall behaviour. The same ideas apply if we model (partial) business processes within an organisation, for instance using BPMN [18]. In either case, we need a means to compose models (scenarios or processes), and when this cannot be done, detect and resolve inconsistencies.

Composing systems manually can only be done for small systems. As a result, in recent years, various methods for automated model composition have been introduced [1,3,4,6,7,12,15,20,21,23,24,26]. Most of these methods involve introducing algorithms to produce a composite model from simpler models originating from partial specifications and assume a formal underlying semantics [12].

This research is supported by EPSRC grant EP/M014290/1.

J. Proença and M. Lumpe (Eds.): FACS 2017, LNCS 10487, pp. 233–250, 2017.
DOI: 10.1007/978-3-319-68034-7_14

In our recent work [3, 4, 7], we have used constraint solvers for automatically constructing the composed model. This involves generating all constraints associated to the models, and using an automated solver to find a solution (the composed model) for the conjunction of all constraints. We used Alloy [11] in [3, 4] and Z3 [16] in [7]. We conducted several experiments in [7], showing that Z3 performs much better than Alloy for large systems. Using Alloy for model composition, mostly in the context of structural models, is an active area of research [21, 26], but the use of Z3 is a novelty of [7]. Even though we used Z3 in [7], we did not explore Z3's arithmetic capabilities, nor did we deal with incompatible constraints. We have addressed both points more recently in [8].

As in our earlier work, our approach in [8] used event structures [25] as an underlying semantics for sequence diagrams in accordance to [5, 14], and explored how the theorem prover Isabelle [17] and constraint solver Z3 [16] could be combined to detect and solve partial specifications and inconsistencies over event structures. In this paper, we go one step further in improving the process of automatically generating correct composition models (through a set of valid traces) for behavioural models that may contain inconsistencies. We introduce a notion of *dephased* models prior to composition, to make it possible to combine models which do not start execution simultaneously, and where the *pace* of execution or a notion of *priority* in each model may be different as well. The effect is a reduction of detected inconsistencies (if any), and the automated generation of what are valid context-specific traces of execution. This work has been inspired by a problem from a medical domain where different care pathways (for chronic conditions) may be applied to the same patient with different starting points (diagnosis). As an additional contribution, we present in Sect. 4 an original, general method to provide formal correctness proof for SMT code.

This paper is structured as follows. The motivation and contribution of the work presented here are discussed in Sect. 2, while in Sect. 3 we recall our formal model (labelled event structures). Section 4 describes how Isabelle and Z3 are combined to compute valid traces of execution in specific settings. We describe the role that Isabelle plays in our work in Sect. 5. We conclude the paper with a description of related work in Sect. 6, and a discussion of future work in Sect. 7.

2   Context and Contribution

Continuing the work started in [8], we exploit the interface between Isabelle and Z3 to obtain a versatile tool for the specification, analysis and computation of the behaviour of complex distributed concurrent systems. By specifying our partial behavioural models in Isabelle we can check automatically their correctness, obtain their composition (if it exists) and fill any gaps, while being able to prove at any point that the models are valid [8]. If our model contains inconsistent behaviours, we are able to locate the conflicting events. However, we argue in this paper, that we may be overlooking valid behaviour in some cases, and we explore an approach to fine-tune the detection of inconsistent behaviour further. In order to do so we allow models to be *dephased*, that is, different scenarios (or similarly for processes) may start execution at different times and continue execution at a different pace. We also consider a notion of priority of (locations in) a model. We develop a technique to find valid traces by defining exactly how the different scenarios come together (i.e., how they are dephased) and which traces are closer to satisfying assumed model priorities.

The problem we are addressing has been inspired by a problem from a medical domain where different care pathways (essentially processes or behavioural models) for chronic conditions are being applied to the same patient, such that:

- different pathway steps are executed at a different *pace*. For instance, for one condition we may need observations to be carried out every month, whereas for others every three months is sufficient.
- one of the conditions may be prevalent, in other words, has higher *priority*.
- some of the possible medications prescribed at a given *step* in the pathway may have higher *priority* due to better treatment effectiveness. For instance, the use of metformin in the treatment of type2 diabetes.
- the diagnosis of different conditions for a patient are likely to have occurred at different times. For instance, the diagnosis of chronic kidney disease often follows (and may be a consequence of) an earlier diagnosis of type 2 diabetes. This leads to the corresponding care pathways starting execution at different times, in other words, their execution is *dephased*.

In particular, having an automated technique that allows us to find valid combined traces taking into account priorities is useful as it gives us a flexible mechanism to identify *different solutions* in similar but different cases. For instance, patients with the same conditions overall but with different orders of diagnosis or prevalent condition. To keep the presentation of this paper more focused, we omit the medical details and instead show how the approach works for an abstract example. Consider the following example using UML sequence diagrams [19].

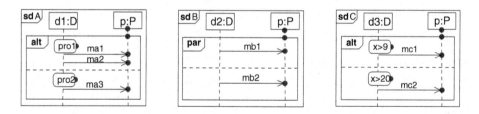

Fig. 1. Three scenarios involving the same object instances.

Figure 1 shows three scenarios involving the same instance p and different instances of the same class D, that is, d1, d2, d3. The scenarios use interaction fragments for alternative behaviour (indicated by an `alt` on the top-left corner) and parallel behaviour (indicated by a `par` on the top-left corner). Other fragment operators exist but are not used in this paper (cf. [19] for details).

Interaction fragments contain one or more operands, which in the case of an alternative may be preceded by a constraint or guard. The alternative fragment in sdA uses two constraints for the operands, namely pro1 and pro2, and we note that they are not necessarily mutually exclusive. We may want to associate a priority to pro1, to indicate for instance that if it holds we will want the corresponding operand to execute (instead of the second operand and regardless of whether pro2 holds or not). UML does not have direct notation to indicate this, but we can assume the existence of a priority tag (not shown) and we will add a priority notion to our formal model. For the messages shown (for instance, ma1, mb1, mc1, and so on), we assume that when they are received, they imply an occurrence for instance p. The marked points along the lifelines and next to the conditions are what we call *locations*, borrowing terminology from Live Sequence Charts (LSCs) [10]. They do not serve a purpose at the design level but make it easier to understand the formal semantics (cf. [14] for details).

Assume that we know that the occurrence of ma1 conflicts with mc1, and ma2 conflicts with mb2. This is not encoded directly in the scenarios above, but is domain knowledge contained elsewhere. For instance, in a medical context it is known that certain combinations of drugs when given together cause adverse reactions and should hence not be given to a patient at the same time.

We now want to obtain the composition of these three diagrams in such a way that the known underlying conflicts are taken into account. To the best of our knowledge the only automated approach that can detect the conflicts in the scenarios above given such additional constraints is our work in [8]. We now extend our approach to find valid paths in a composed model that avoids these conflicts.

Clearly, to avoid the conflicts the easiest thing to do is to take the second alternative in sdA assuming that pro2 holds. No conflict is present in that case. However, it may be the case that pro1 holds as well and it has an associated higher priority (preference) leading to the execution of ma1 followed by ma2. The question is whether we can still obtain a valid trace that includes this preference and avoids the known message conflicts. Our approach developed here gives an answer to this question under the assumption that simultaneous occurrence of conflicting messages is avoided. Notions of current state, pace and occurrence priority are used as parameters to find valid traces in a composed model. We describe how these are treated formally in the next sections. In this paper, we focus on the formal semantics, the composition and valid traces defined at that level, and the formal methods used to detect them. We do not come back to a design level, but we assume the underlying formal models used here have been generated from scenarios or process descriptions. See our earlier work for an idea of the transformation defined at the metamodel level [3,4,7]. See [13] for a description of the medical problem of treating patients with multimorbidities.

3   Formal Model

The model we use to capture the semantics of a sequence diagram is a labelled (prime) event structure [25], or event structure for short. The advantages of an event structure are the underlying simplicity of the model and how it naturally describes fundamental notions present in behavioural models including sequential, parallel and iterative behaviour (or the unfoldings thereof) as well as nondeterminism (cf. [5,14]).

In an event structure, we have a set of event occurrences together with binary relations for expressing causal dependency (called *causality*) and nondeterminism (called *conflict*). The causality relation implies a (partial) order among event occurrences, while the conflict relation expresses how the occurrence of certain events excludes the occurrence of others (e.g., an event occurring in one operand of an alternative fragment excludes events in another operand). From the two relations defined on the set of events, a further relation is derived, namely the *concurrency* relation *co*. Two events are concurrent if and only if they are completely unrelated, i.e., neither related by causality nor by conflict. As a derived notion we thus obtain a way to model events associated to locations from different operands in a parallel fragment. The formal definition, as provided for instance in [14], is as follows.

Definition 1. *An* event structure *is a triple* $E = (Ev, \rightarrow^*, \#)$ *where* Ev *is a set of events and* $\rightarrow^*, \# \subseteq Ev \times Ev$ *are binary relations called* causality *and* conflict, *respectively. Causality* $\rightarrow^*$ *is a partial order. Conflict* $\#$ *is symmetric and irreflexive, and propagates over causality, i.e.,* $e \# e' \wedge e' \rightarrow^* e'' \Rightarrow e \# e''$ *for all* $e, e', e'' \in Ev$. *Two events* $e, e' \in Ev$ *are concurrent,* e *co* e' *iff* $\neg(e \rightarrow^* e' \vee e' \rightarrow^* e \vee e \# e')$. $C \subseteq Ev$ *is a* configuration *iff (1)* C *is conflict-free:* $\forall e, e' \in C \neg(e \# e')$ *and (2)* downward-closed: $e \in C$ *and* $e' \rightarrow^* e$ *implies* $e' \in C$.

We assume *discrete* event structures. Discreteness imposes a finiteness constraint on the model, i.e., there are always only a finite number of causally related predecessors to an event, known as the *local configuration* of the event (written $\downarrow e$). A further motivation for this constraint is given by the fact that every execution has a starting point or configuration. A *trace of execution* in an event structure is a maximal configuration. An event e may have an immediate successor e' according to the order $\rightarrow^*$: in this case, we will usually write $e \rightarrow e'$. The relation given by $\rightarrow$ is called *immediate causality*.

Event structures are enriched with a labelling function $\mu : Ev \rightarrow 2^L$ that maps each event onto a subset of elements of L. This labelling function is necessary to establish a connection between the semantic model (event structure) and the syntactic model it is describing. The set L of labels in our case either denote formulas (constraints over integer variables, e.g., $x > 9$ or $y = 5$), logical propositions (e.g., pro1) or actions (e.g., ma1). If for an event $e \in Ev$, $\mu(e)$ contains an action α, then e denotes the occurrence of that action α. If $\mu(e)$ contains a formula or logical proposition φ then φ must hold when e occurs.

We consider an additional labelling function $\nu : Ev \rightarrow \mathbb{N} \times \mathbb{N}$ to associate to each event its *priority* and *duration*. For an event e with $\nu(e) = (p, \_)$, the highest the value of p the higher the priority associated to the event. The second component of $\nu(e) = (\_, d)$ gives d, the time units spent at event e. The labelling function ν is used later when fine-tuning the composition with respect to label conflicts.

A labelled event structure over a set of labels L is a triple $M = (Ev, \mu, \nu)$. Let $M_1, \ldots, M_n$ with $M_i = (E_i, \mu_i, \nu_i)$ a finite set of labelled event structures over sets of labels L_i with $1 \le i \le n$. Let $\mathcal{L} = \bigcup_{i=1}^{n} L_i$. A finite set of *label constraints* defined over $\mathcal{L}$ is given by $\Gamma \subseteq L_i \times L_j$ where $i \ne j$ characterising label conflicts.

We do not show how to generate an event structure from a sequence diagram, just the general idea. The locations along the lifelines of sequence diagrams are associated to one or more events. Locations within different operands of an alternative fragment correspond to events in conflict, whereas locations within operands of a parallel fragment correspond to concurrent events. The events associated to the locations along a lifeline are related by causality (partial order). For more details see for instance [14].

Recall the example of Fig. 1 introduced in the previous section. The locations along the lifeline of instance p have been marked in Fig. 1. The locations associated to the conditions/guards of the alternative fragments belong to the instances of class D, but that distinction is irrelevant for our purposes. The label conflicts are given by $\Gamma = \{(ma1, mc1), (ma2, mb2)\}$. The behaviour of p in the individual diagrams of Fig. 1 is shown in the three event structures M_A, M_B and M_C of Fig. 2, where the events are associated to the marked locations of the corresponding sequence diagram as expected. The defined labels are as follows: $\mu_A(e_2) = \{pro1, ma1\}$, $\mu_A(e_3) = \{pro2, ma3\}$, and $\mu_A(e_4) = \{ma2\}$ for the event structure associated to sdA; $\mu_B(g_2) = \{mb1\}$ and $\mu_B(g_3) = \{mb2\}$ associated to sdB; and $\mu_C(f_2) = \{x > 9, mc1\}$ and $\mu_C(f_3) = \{x > 20, mc3\}$ associated to sdC.

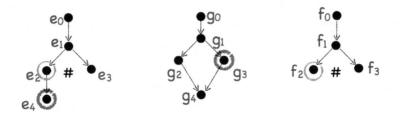

Fig. 2. Corresponding event structures for instance p.

The labels of some of the events above are inconsistent/conflicting according to Γ, namely events e_2 and f_2, and events e_4 and g_3. When obtaining the composition of the models above we need to make sure the label inconsistencies are detected and avoided. A composed model that avoids the labels could reduce the composition to the trace of execution $\tau_1 = \{e_0, e_1, e_3, g_0, g_1, g_2, g_3, g_4, f_0, f_1, f_3\}$ or τ_2 (identical to τ_1 except that it contains f_2 instead of f_3). However, these traces may not be the best traces of execution. The labels on events are only inconsistent if they occur simultaneously, and if we know where instance p is within each of the scenarios we may be able to avoid it. The labelling function ν gives us that information.

Assume the following ν labels for some of the events in our example: $\nu(e_0) = \nu(g_0) = \nu(f_0) = (1,1)$, $\nu(e_1) = \nu(g_1) = \nu(f_1) = (1,1)$, $\nu(e_2) = (5,3)$, $\nu(e_3) = (1,3)$, $\nu(e_4) = (5,2)$, $\nu(g_2) = (1,2)$, $\nu(g_3) = (1,1)$, $\nu(f_1) = (1,1)$, $\nu(f_2) = (3,3)$ and $\nu(f_3) = (1,2)$. Consider the possible traces of execution shown in Fig. 3 with time evolving from the left to the right, and considering the events in sdA with highest priority (here assumed to have value 5).

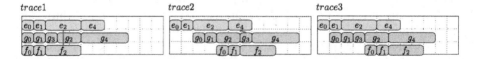

Fig. 3. Possible traces of execution with and without inconsistencies.

The traces illustrate how the event duration and the (dephased) order in which execution is done for the different scenarios may or may not contain inconsistencies. The first two example traces contain inconsistencies, because events with label conflicts occur at the same time. A resolution for $trace1$ could replace the occurrence of f_2 with f_3 (compromising on the effectiveness of f_2 but guaranteeing the higher priority of e_2), and for $trace2$ could change the order of occurrence of g_2 and g_3. Note that when having a conflict between two events with an assigned priority we always try to satisfy the event with the highest priority first. Here e_2 has priority 5 and f_2 has priority 3, so we favour e_2. If both events had the same priority the resolution would pick one of the events at random. In $trace3$ no inconsistencies are present and all events have the highest priority. In the next section we show how we can generate automatically the valid traces for a set of labelled event structures given a set of label conflicts and the degree that each structure is being dephased.

4   Isabelle and Z3 Combined

We combine two formal techniques to *calculate automatically the outcome* of the composition of two or more behavioural models as a set of allowed traces and to determine that the *result is correct*: the theorem prover Isabelle [17] and the SMT solver Z3 [16].

Isabelle is a theorem prover or proof assistant which provides a framework to accommodate logical systems (deductive rules, axioms), and compute the validity of logical deductions according to a given system. In this paper, we use Isabelle's library based on *higher-order logic* (HOL). In HOL, the basic notions are type specification, function application, lambda abstraction, and equality. In addition to be able to check logical inference over logical systems, theorem provers such as Isabelle also contain automated deduction tools, and interfaces to external tools such as SMT solvers and automated theorem provers. We use the theorem prover to guarantee the correctness of our models, the composition result and traces.

A satisfiability modulo theories (SMT) solver is a computer program designed to check the satisfiability of a set of formulas (known as *assertions*) expressed in first-order logic, where for instance arithmetic operations and comparison are understood, and additional relations and functions can be given a semantic meaning in order to make the problem satisfiable. Within proof assistants, SMT solvers are used to find proofs by adding already proved theorems to the list of assertions, and by negating the statement to be proved to reach a contradiction. If a SMT solver returns unsat, then a proof can be reconstructed from the given assertions. The integration between Isabelle and SMT solvers such as Z3 provides users an additional powerful combination to be able to produce more proofs automatically. We use the SMT solver to identify label inconsistencies, which may require the use of arithmetic operations and comparison, and to find a solution which avoids the inconsistencies and considers the additional labelling information given by ν.

Let $M_1, \ldots, M_n$, with $M_i = ((Ev_i, \rightarrow_i^*, \#_i), \mu_i, \nu_i)$ and $1 \leq i \leq n$ over a set of labels L_i, be a list of finite event structures. Let $\Gamma \subseteq L_i \times L_j$ with $i \neq j$ denote the set of label conflicts. We assume that the corresponding sets of events are pairwise disjoint. In what follows we denote the immediate causality $\rightarrow_i$ by G_i, and set

$$G := \bigcup_{i=1,\ldots,n} G_i,$$

$$\# := \bigcup_{i=1,\ldots,n} \#_i.$$

Given a relation R over a set Y and a set $X \subseteq Y$, we introduce the notation $R^\rightarrow(X)$ to denote the image of X through R.

We will now proceed in steps: first, we show how to compute traces, then we show how to use ν to obtain the preferred one, depending on the duration and priority assigned to single events. In doing so, we will write formulas close to the first-order logic language used by SMT solvers; for the sake of readability, however, we will employ some simplifications. In particular, we adopt infix notation instead of prefix notation, we use set-theoretical styling instead of predicates (e.g., writing $(j, k) \in G_i$ in lieu of $G_i\ j\ k$), and we omit type specifications.

4.1   Trace Calculation

To represent an execution trace, we need to express which events are part of it, and in which order. The first piece of information will be given by a boolean function over all the events, namely isSelected.

We can compute isSelected using an SMT solver as follows. Let us illustrate the procedure for a fixed event structure Ev_i. The conditions of isSelected being conflict-free and downward-closed (see Definition 1) are straightforward to express:

$$\forall j, k \in Ev_i.\ \text{isSelected}(j) \wedge \text{isSelected}(k) \rightarrow \neg(j\#k)$$

$$\forall j \in \text{Range}\,(G_i)\,.\ \text{isSelected}\,(j) \to \bigwedge_{k \in \left(G_i^{-1}\right)^{\to}\{j\}} \text{isSelected}\,(k)$$

The two formulas above capture the notion of configuration (see Definition 1) in a way amenable to SMT solvers. To compute traces of execution (Sect. 3), we have to capture the notion of a *maximal* configuration. This notion implies quantifying over configurations, which is not allowed in the first-order logic universe of SMT solvers: sets in general are not first-class objects. However, the notion of maximality can be reformulated in the case of configurations of finite event structures as follows:

$$\forall z \in Ev_i.\ \exists y \in Ev_i. \qquad \begin{array}{c} ((y \# z \wedge \text{isSelected}\,(y)) \vee \\ ((y, z) \in G_i \wedge \neg\, \text{isSelected}\,(y))). \end{array} \tag{1}$$

The formulas above can be used to compute traces via an SMT solver; more precisely, the events for which isSelected is true represent the event set of a trace, and the event set of any legal trace satisfies the assertions above. We will formally prove the correctness of this statement in Sect. 5.

To add an order to this set, we proceed as follows. First, taken a single G_i, we need to obtain the corresponding partial order P_i (effectively obtaining the original causality relation $\to_i^*$), which can be derived from the following assertions:

$$\forall j,\ k.\,(j, k) \in G_i \to (j, k) \in P_i,$$
$$\forall j,\ k,\ l.\,(j, k) \in P_i \wedge (k, l) \in P_i \to (j, l) \in P_i,$$
$$\forall j \in Ev_i.\,(j, j) \in P_i,$$
$$\forall j,\ k.\,(j, k) \in P_i \wedge (k, j) \in P_i \to j = k.$$

We now use P_i to obtain a sorting of all the selected events of Ev_i. This can be done by introducing an injective function $s_i : Ev_i \to \mathbb{N}$, and then imposing that it is order-preserving (between the partial order P_i and the canonical order relation for natural numbers), surjective over the integer interval $[1, \ldots, |Ev_i|]$, and such that $s_i\,(j) < s_i\,(k)$ whenever j is selected and k is not:

$$\forall j,\ k.\,(j, k) \in P_i \to s_i\,(j) \le s_j\,(k),$$
$$\forall j,\ k \in Ev_i.j \ne k \to s_i\,(j) \ne s_i\,(k),$$
$$\forall j \in Ev_i.s_i\,(j) \ge 1$$
$$\forall j \in Ev_i.s_i\,(j) \le |Ev_i|$$
$$\forall j,\ k \in Ev_i.\,\text{isSelected}\,(j) \wedge \neg\, \text{isSelected}\,(k) \to s_i\,(j) < s_i\,(k)\,.$$

4.2   Using ν for Trace Selection

As done in the example of Fig. 3, we want to be able to determine whether events from distinct event structures overlap, in order to decide whether the conflict they might have is triggered or not. We associate a clock function to each event, expressing the time when the event starts. To calculate it, we use the sorting functions s_i obtained in the previous section, together with the duration of each event provided by ν. This can be done by requiring that an event following another (according to s_i) starts exactly when the latter ends:

$$\forall j,\ k \in Ev_i.$$
$$(\text{isSelected}\ j \wedge \text{isSelected}\ k \wedge s_i(j) \leq |Ev_i| \wedge s_i(k) \leq |Ev_i| \wedge s_i(k) - s_i(j) = 1)$$
$$\rightarrow \text{clock}(k) = \text{clock}(j) + \nu_2(j),$$

where ν_2 is the second component of ν, yielding the duration.

The formula above leaves the clocks of the roots undetermined, hence we need to set them separately. This allows us to introduce dephasing between different models, by specifying different clocks for the roots of different models, which means starting each model at dephased times. Finally, the concept of clock allows us to avoid inconsistencies due to events mutually in conflict, but whose occurrence is not simultaneous.

To attain this goal, we assign a priority (which we also refer to as score) to each event and to each pair of events from distinct models, through the function priority and Score, respectively, both yielding integer values. Score (j, k) will take into account both the absolute conflict between events j and k, and their clock, in order to decide whether they are in conflict given a trace (recall, from the definition above and the definition of s_i in previous section, that each trace determines clock values for each event). Formally, this is obtained by the following requirement, repeated for all $m \neq n$, $m, n \in \{1, \ldots, n\}$:

$$\forall j \in Ev_m,\ k \in Ev_n.\, \text{isSelected}(j) \wedge \text{isSelected}(k) \rightarrow \text{Score}(j, k) =$$
$$f(\text{clock}(j), \text{clock}(k), \nu_2(j), D(\mu(j), \mu(k))),$$

where D calculates the absolute conflict (a negative number) between events based on their label, and is passed to f. Further, f combines that with the distance of the event occurrences to obtain the effective result, as follows:

$$f(x_1, x_2, y, z) := \begin{cases} z, & \text{if } x_2 - x_1 \in [0, y] \\ 0, & \text{otherwise.} \end{cases}$$

Besides conflicts between events in distinct models, the other criterion when picking a trace is the absolute priority of each event. Therefore, we also require

$$\forall j.\, \text{isSelected}(j) \rightarrow \text{priority}(j) = \nu_1(j)$$
$$\forall j.\, \neg\, \text{isSelected}(j) \rightarrow \text{priority}(j) = 0,$$

where ν_1 is the first component of ν, yielding the priority.

To obtain the final trace, we sum over all the Score (j, k) and over all the values priority (j), and pick the trace maximising such sum. To do so, we need to exploit the optimizing part of the SMT solver Z3, νZ [2].

4.3 Example

We test the output of our approach with respect to the simple example of Fig. 3. In the first case (*trace*1 of Fig. 3), all the models start executing together, and the SMT solver yields the optimal trace on the left of Table 1. The incompatibility between g_3 and e_4 does not pose problems, since those two events cannot overlap. However, the solver has been forced to choose between the branch starting at e_2 and f_2. Given that the e_2 branch has the highest priority overall, it has been picked. But event f_2 also has a high priority, which leads to his choice over f_3, as soon as dephasing allows that. We now test that this is indeed the case. The right-hand side of Table 1 displays the output resulting from running the same experiment, but with f_0 happening at time 4 and g_0 happening at time 1 (corresponding to *trace*3 in Fig. 3):

Table 1. Outputs corresponding to *trace*1 (left) and *trace*3 (right)

clock	event	order	priority	duration
0	e0	1	1	1
0	f0	1	1	1
0	g0	1	1	1
1	e1	2	1	1
1	f1	2	1	1
1	g1	2	1	1
2	e2	3	5	3
2	f3	3	1	2
2	g2	3	1	2
4	g3	4	1	1
5	e4	4	5	2
5	g4	5	1	4

clock	event	order	priority	duration
0	e0	1	1	1
1	e1	2	1	1
1	g0	1	1	1
2	e2	3	5	3
2	g1	2	1	1
3	g3	3	1	1
4	f0	1	1	1
4	g2	4	1	2
5	e4	4	5	2
5	f1	2	1	1
6	f2	3	3	3
6	g4	5	1	4

Now, the incompatibility between e_2 and f_2 can be avoided by dephasing, and indeed both events are part of the new trace. We also note that the incompatibility between e_4 and g_3 has also been avoided by swapping the execution of g_2 and g_3, as expected.

5 Verification

The first-order language used in SMT solvers often requires laborious and error-prone translation from higher-level mathematical abstractions. Let us take the notion of event structure as an example: the concepts of partial order, and relation in general are expressed typically through sets of ordered pairs. However, the notion of set is not directly available in SMT-LIB, and one is forced to choose a lower-level representation of it. For example, by representing relations

J. Bowles and M.B. Caminati

as boolean predicates taking two arguments; this, in turn, typically makes higher-level operations (such as composition, image, taking the domain, injectivity, etc.) more complicated.

A way of tackling the complexity arising from this translation, and to make sure that it correctly represents the involved objects, is to write the wanted original definitions in a higher-order language (for example higher-order logic, HOL) which allows to express them easily. In the same language, we can of course also write definitions closer to the ones required for SMT solvers. The crucial point is that Isabelle provides an SMT-LIB generator which can generate, from the latter definitions, SMT assertion directly executable by SMT solvers. And, at the same time, we can prove, inside Isabelle, the equivalence between the standard definitions and those closer to the SMT language. Since the latter directly generate the SMT code used for our computations, the formal equivalence proof is also a proof of correctness for our generated SMT code.

Hence, we write in Isabelle a definition of event structure which is close to Definition 1:

```
abbreviation "isLes causality conflict =
propagation conflict causality & sym conflict &
irrefl conflict & trans causality &
antisym causality & reflex causality".
```

Above `isLes causality conflict` returns `true` exactly when `causality` and `conflict` constitute a valid event structure. In the definition above, causality and conflicts are sets of pairs, which permits to use the standard property of symmetry (`sym`), transitivity (`trans`) already present in the Isabelle libraries. We only needed to introduce `propagation` as a direct translation of the propagation condition occurring in Definition 1, which we omit here.

On the other hand, an equivalent definition is also introduced in Isabelle:

```
abbreviation "IsLes Causality Conflict =
Propagation Conflict Causality & Sym Conflict &
Irrefl Conflict & Trans Causality &
Antisym Causality & Reflex Causality",
```

which is similar to the previous one, but where `Causality` and `Conflict` are no longer sets, but predicates.

This allows us to use the definition of `IsLes` for producing SMT code directly through Isabelle's SMT generator. Since this generator is originally provided for theorem proving, and not for direct SMT computations as we are interested here, we have to trick Isabelle into proving a lemma:

```
lemma assumes "IsLes Causality Conflict" shows False
sledgehammer run [provers=z3, minimize=false,
          overlord=true, timeout=1] (assms)
```

The lemma above makes some assumptions (hypotheses) written after the keyword `assumes`. The assumptions include that the two relations described constitute a valid event structure. The keyword `shows` introduces the thesis (here `False`) and `sledgehammer` is Isabelle's command for referencing outside

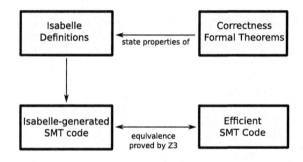

Fig. 4. Overview of the formal verification of the SMT code.

tools (ATPs, SMT solvers), used here to run Z3. We note that the argument `assms` is used to instruct `sledgehammer` to ignore any other theorems in the Isabelle library and consider only the stated assumptions.

In the lines above, Isabelle will pass to Z3 a file which contains one declaration for each of the relations `Causality` and `Conflict`, and assertions for each of the stated hypotheses. In the present case, we only have one hypothesis, which will result in an SMT definition of event structure, directly usable for our computations.

The last step to certify the correctness of this SMT generated code is to prove the equivalence of `isLes` and `IsLes`, which is attained through the following theorem:

```
theorem "IsLes causality conflict ↔
   (isLes (pred2set Causality) (pred2set Conflict))",
```

where `pred2set` converts from relations represented as predicates into relations represented as sets.

The idea of using Isabelle as an interface to SMT code becomes even more fruitful in cases where the SMT code used for computing a given object departs substantially from the original or standard mathematical definition of that object. This usually happens, e.g., because the original definition is not directly expressible as a finite number of formula in first-order logic (the language of SMT solvers), or because, even if it is, it is inefficient. In such cases, we can express both the original definition and the definition used for SMT computing in Isabelle, which we can then use both to generate the SMT code for the latter and to formally prove the equivalence of the two definitions, as from the diagram in Fig. 4. As an example, let us take the trace computation seen at the beginning of Sect. 4.1: there we had to resort to an alternative, less intelligible definition of maximality of configuration (1), because the original definition implied quantifying over all configurations.

In Isabelle, we can easily render the pen-and-paper definitions of event structure (which we have seen earlier), of configuration and of trace. We start by writing the condition specifying that our candidate configuration C is conflict-free:

```
definition "isConflictFree Cf C = ((C × C) ∩ Cf = {})",
```

and the condition about C being downward closed:

```
definition "isDownwardClosed Ca C =
    (C ⊆ events Ca &
    (∀ e f. e ∈ C & (f, e) ∈ Ca → f ∈ C))".
```

This allows the immediate definition of configuration:

```
definition "isConfiguration Ca Cf C =
    isConflictFree Cf C & isDownwardClosed Ca C",
```

and that of being a trace:

```
definition "isTrace Ca Cf C =
    isConfiguration Ca Cf C &
    (∀ Y. Y ⊃ C → ¬ (isConfiguration Ca Cf Y))",
```

where the last line expresses the maximality of the configuration C. We write the same line (i.e., maximality) in the way seen in Sect. 4.1:

```
abbreviation "isMaximalConfSmt Ca Cf C ==
    (∀ z ∈ events Ca − C.
      z ∈ Cf''C ∨ (immediatePredecessors Ca {z})−C ≠ {})",
```

where $\texttt{immediatePredecessors Ca } \{z\}$ returns all the events e satisfying $e \to z$ (we recall that $\to$ is the immediate causality obtained from $\to^*$). Finally, the following Isabelle theorem states that (1) is equivalent, for a configuration of a finite event structure, to the original trace definition:

```
theorem correctness: assumes "finite Ca" "isLes Ca Cf"
    "isConfiguration Ca Cf C" shows
    "(isTrace Ca Cf C) ↔ isMaximalConfSmt Ca Cf C"
```

We note that the theorem assumes that C is a configuration: this is not a problem because, as seen in Sect. 4.1, the notion of configuration admits a straightforward formulation in SMT, while the problematic one is that of *maximality* for a configuration. We also note that $\texttt{isMaximalConfSmt}$ builds on $\texttt{immediatePredecessors Ca}$, rather than directly on $\texttt{Ca}$. This is also not a problem, since the SMT computations we introduced in Sect. 4.1 take as input the immediate causality relations $G_i, i = 1, \ldots, n$, and use them to calculate via SMT the causalities $\to_i^*$.

The Isabelle definition $\texttt{isMaximalConfSmt}$ can be used to automatically generate SMT code through $\texttt{sledgehammer}$, as we did with $\texttt{IsLes}$. This corresponds to the vertical arrow on the left in Diagram 4. In this case, however, the obtained SMT code is not as efficient as the one we manually wrote in Sect. 4.1: it is a general fact that the efficiency of SMT code can depend dramatically on formal details, such as eliminating quantifiers by explicit enumeration, rewriting the assertions in normal forms, etc. . . We want to keep both the efficiency of the manually-written SMT code and the correctness of the Isabelle-generated SMT code. Our solution is to take both, and prove their equivalence using the SMT solver itself. This corresponds to the horizontal arrow at the bottom of Diagram 4, and can be implemented as follows. We introduce an SMT boolean function $\texttt{maximality}$

which is true exactly when (1), repeated for each $i = 1, \ldots, n$, is true. We also introduce another boolean function maximalityIsabelle, defined by using the SMT code generated by Isabelle using isMaximalConfSmt. If maximality and maximalityIsabelle were not equivalent, there would be some isSelected satisfying one but not the other. Therefore, we challenged the SMT solver as follows:

```
(assert (or (and maximality (not maximalityIsabelle))
            (and (not maximality) maximalityIsabelle))),
```

obtaining the answer (unsat), which guarantees that the SMT code we use for trace maximality calculation is correct. Correctness, as usually, means that if we trust the SMT solver, Isabelle, and the environment in which they run, then we can trust that the result of our computation is indeed a trace. Not only: we can rest assured that any trace will satisfy the SMT formula (i.e., Formula 1) passed to the solver for the computation. To increase our confidence in the results, we could also prove the correctness of the remaining computations, i.e., the trace selection (Sect. 4.1). The general mechanism represented in Fig. 4 could again be applied: we would need to write an Isabelle formal specification of the desired property guiding the trace selection, write an Isabelle definition to generate SMT code, and an Isabelle theorem proving that the latter obeys the former. Finally, we would use the SMT solver to prove that the Isabelle-generated SMT code and the manually written SMT code are equivalent. Again, this would imply correctness as soon as we trust the solver and Isabelle; additionally, in this case we would also need to trust νZ (see end of Sect. 4.2), which is not used in trace computation but only in trace selection.

6   Related Work

Systems are usually designed through a combination of several models, some to capture structural aspects and some to describe more complex aspects of behaviour. As argued in [10], modelling the complete behaviour of a component or subsystem is difficult and error prone. Instead, it is easier to formulate partial behaviour as scenarios in Live Sequence Charts (LSCs), UML sequence diagrams or similar. One of the problems that arises from partial modelling is potentially inconsistent or incomplete behaviour.

When looking at the integration of several model views or diagrams, Widl et al. [24] deal with composing concurrently evolved sequence diagrams in accordance to the overall behaviour given in state machines. They make direct use of SAT-solvers for the composition. Liang et al. [15] present a method of integrating sequence diagrams based on the formalisation of sequence diagrams as typed graphs. Both these papers focus on less complex structures. For example, they do not deal with combined fragments, which can potentially cause substantial complexity. Bowles and Bordbar [6] present a method of mapping a design consisting of class diagrams, OCL constraints and sequence diagrams into a mathematical model for detecting and analysing inconsistencies. It uses the same underlying categorical construction as done in [5] but it has not been automated.

On the other hand, Zhang et al. [26] and Rubin et al. [21] use Alloy for the composition of class diagrams. They transform UML class diagrams into Alloy and compose them automatically. They focus on composing static models and the composition code is produced manually.

We used Alloy to automatically compose sequence diagrams in [3,4]. Our experience with Alloy has shown that it has limitations which have a direct impact on the scalability of the approach [7]. There is an exponential growth in time when trying to compose diagrams with an increasing number of elements, which becomes unusable in practice. The Alloy analyzer is SAT solver-based and SAT- solving time may increase enormously, depending on factors such as the number of variables and the average length of the clause [9]. Z3 [16] performs much better and we have used it in more recent work [7,8,13]. We do not know of other approaches using Z3 for model composition.

We are addressing inconsistent combination of behavioural models in this paper. A SAT-based approach, such as Alloy, would allow us to detect inconsistencies and highlight them, as a result of not being able to generate a solution for the composition. When two or more scenarios combined have inconsistencies, a designer benefits not only from knowing which inconsistencies there are, but what traces of execution can bypass the inconsistencies. In practice, it is unlikely that inconsistencies can be removed altogether, and instead we want to find the traces that are valid, avoid the inconsistencies, and may satisfy additional criteria such as priorities. SAT solvers cannot be used in this case whereas we have shown that SMT solvers can in another context [13]. The present paper makes a novel contribution by showing how SMT solvers such as Z3 can be used to find the best solution to a generally unsolvable problem of composing models with known inconsistencies. Finally, the typical combination of SMT solvers and proof assistants is done to help finding proofs, and we bring this combination into a completely different setting for detecting and resolving problems in complex behaviour.

7   Conclusions

Inspired by a problem from the medical domain, we have explored a novel approach to compose scenarios and their underlying, possibly dephased, traces of execution. Our approach allows us to detect and avoid inconsistencies (if possible) to generate a valid set of traces of execution for a composed model. The traces can be fine-tuned to take into account additional requirements on the degree of priority that one model or certain steps in a process (events in our approach) have over other models or alternatives. Moreover, our approach is able to find the best trace of execution with respect to these constraints. Key to our approach is the use of SMT solvers to search for the best solution. Our approach uses a novel combination of the theorem prover Isabelle and the constraint solver Z3, where the theorem prover is fundamental to guarantee the correctness of the approach and to facilitate the interaction with Z3 through the provided SMT-LIB generator. This is important because, on one hand, writing SMT code directly is time-consuming and error-prone while, on the other hand, the existing interfaces of SMT solvers with higher-level languages (e.g., APIs) are not currently, to the best of our knowledge, formally verified.

This paper focused on the semantics of the underlying behavioural models. Separately we are developing mechanisms to visualise the solutions obtained back to the designer. We have used Graphviz in our earlier work in [3,4] to show the composition solution obtained with Alloy. In future work we want to explore visualisations that work directly on the modelling approaches used by designers, and in particular in the case of inconsistencies, can show them more effectively; thus we also aim at achieving an increased adoption of our approach by designers, which in turn is needed to test and validate our techniques on realistic application problems. Work is in progress to generalize the time representation to allow the duration of an event to be a range, rather than a specific amount of time units. A further direction for future work is to make the scheme presented here to deal with incompatibilities and priorities even more flexible by using soft constraints: currently, the trace selection is performed by expressing a maximisation problem with hard constraints only; however, soft constraints can be implemented, e.g., via the SMT-LIB command `check-sat-assuming`. Finally, future work will also tackle the issue of finding a way to accommodate indefinite loops and non-terminating behaviours, possibly present in given models, in our approach.

References

1. Araújo, J., Whittle, J., Kim, D.: Modeling and composing scenario-based requirements with aspects. In: RE 2004, pp. 58–67. IEEE Computer Society Press (2004)
2. Bjørner, N., Phan, A.-D., Fleckenstein, L.: νz - An Optimizing SMT Solver. In: Baier, C., Tinelli, C. (eds.) TACAS 2015. LNCS, vol. 9035, pp. 194–199. Springer, Heidelberg (2015). doi:10.1007/978-3-662-46681-0_14
3. Bowles, J., Alwanain, M., Bordbar, B., Chen, Y.: Matching and Merging Scenarios Automatically with Alloy. In: Hammoudi, S., Pires, L.F., Filipe, J., das Neves, R.C. (eds.) MODELSWARD 2014. CCIS, vol. 506, pp. 100–116. Springer, Cham (2015). doi:10.1007/978-3-319-25156-1_7
4. Bowles, J.K.F., Bordbar, B., Alwanain, M.: A Logical Approach for Behavioural Composition of Scenario-Based Models. In: Butler, M., Conchon, S., Zaïdi, F. (eds.) ICFEM 2015. LNCS, vol. 9407, pp. 252–269. Springer, Cham (2015). doi:10.1007/978-3-319-25423-4_16
5. Bowles, J.K.F.: Decomposing Interactions. In: Johnson, M., Vene, V. (eds.) AMAST 2006. LNCS, vol. 4019, pp. 189–203. Springer, Heidelberg (2006). doi:10.1007/11784180_16
6. Bowles, J., Bordbar, B.: A formal model for integrating multiple views. In: ACSD 2007, pp. 71–79. IEEE Computer Society Press (2007)
7. Bowles, J., Bordbar, B., Alwanain, M.: Weaving true-concurrent aspects using constraint solvers. In: Application of Concurrency to System Design (ACSD 2016). IEEE Computer Society Press, June 2016
8. Bowles, J.K.F., Caminati, M.B.: Mind the gap: addressing behavioural inconsistencies with formal methods. In: 23rd Asia-Pacific Software Engineering Conference (APSEC). IEEE Computer Society (2016)

9. D'Ippolito, N., Frias, M.F., Galeotti, J.P., Lanzarotti, E., Mera, S.: Alloy+HotCore: A Fast Approximation to Unsat Core. In: Frappier, M., Glässer, U., Khurshid, S., Laleau, R., Reeves, S. (eds.) ABZ 2010. LNCS, vol. 5977, pp. 160–173. Springer, Heidelberg (2010). doi:10.1007/978-3-642-11811-1_13

10. Harel, D., Marelly, R.: Come, Let's Play. Scenario-based Programming Using LSCs and the Play-Engine. Springer, Heidelberg (2003)

11. Jackson, D.: Software Abstractions: Logic, Language and Analysis. MIT Press, Cambridge (2006)

12. Klein, J., Hélouët, L., Jézéquel, J.: Semantic-based weaving of scenarios. In: AOSD 2006, pp. 27–38. ACM (2006)

13. Kovalov, A., Bowles, J.K.F.: Avoiding Medication Conflicts for Patients with Multimorbidities. In: Ábrahám, E., Huisman, M. (eds.) IFM 2016. LNCS, vol. 9681, pp. 376–390. Springer, Cham (2016). doi:10.1007/978-3-319-33693-0_24

14. Küster-Filipe, J.: Modelling concurrent interactions. Theoret. Comput. Sci. **351**, 203–220 (2006)

15. Liang, H., Diskin, Z., Dingel, J., Posse, E.: A General Approach for Scenario Integration. In: Czarnecki, K., Ober, I., Bruel, J.-M., Uhl, A., Völter, M. (eds.) MODELS 2008. LNCS, vol. 5301, pp. 204–218. Springer, Heidelberg (2008). doi:10.1007/978-3-540-87875-9_15

16. de Moura, L., Bjørner, N.: Z3: An Efficient SMT Solver. In: Ramakrishnan, C.R., Rehof, J. (eds.) TACAS 2008. LNCS, vol. 4963, pp. 337–340. Springer, Heidelberg (2008). doi:10.1007/978-3-540-78800-3_24

17. Nipkow, T., Wenzel, M., Paulson, L.C. (eds.): Isabelle/HOL–A Proof Assistant for Higher-Order Logic. LNCS, vol. 2283. Springer, Heidelberg (2002)

18. OMG: Business Process Model and Notation. Version 2.0. OMG, documentid: formal/2011-01-03 (2011). http://www.omg.org

19. OMG: UML: Superstructure. Version 2.4.1. OMG, documentid: formal/2011-08-06 (2011). http://www.omg.org

20. Reddy, R., Solberg, A., France, R., Ghosh, S.: Composing sequence models using tags. In: Proceedings of MoDELS Workshop on Aspect Oriented Modeling (2006)

21. Rubin, J., Chechik, M., Easterbrook, S.: Declarative approach for model composition. In: MiSE 2008, pp. 7–14. ACM (2008)

22. Uchitel, S., Brunet, G., Chechik, M.: Synthesis of partial behavior models from properties and scenarios. IEEE Trans. Software Eng. **35**(3), 384–406 (2009)

23. Whittle, J., Araújo, J., Moreira, A.: Composing aspect models with graph transformations. In: Proceedings of the 2006 International Workshop on Early Aspects at ICSE, pp. 59–65. ACM (2006)

24. Widl, M., Biere, A., Brosch, P., Egly, U., Heule, M., Kappel, G., Seidl, M., Tompits, H.: Guided Merging of Sequence Diagrams. In: Czarnecki, K., Hedin, G. (eds.) SLE 2012. LNCS, vol. 7745, pp. 164–183. Springer, Heidelberg (2013). doi:10.1007/978-3-642-36089-3_10

25. Winskel, G., Nielsen, M.: Models for Concurrency. In: Abramsky, S., Gabbay, D., Maibaum, T. (eds.) Handbook of Logic in Computer Science: Semantic Modelling, vol. 4, pp. 1–148. Oxford Science Publications, Oxford (1995)

26. Zhang, D., Li, S., Liu, X.: An approach for model composition and verification. In: NCM 2009, pp. 1102–1107. IEEE Computer Society Press (2009)

Author Index

Printed in the United States
By Bookmasters